Industry in Developing Countries

Third World industrialisation is one of the most important phenomena in the global economy, and has been interpreted in a wide range of different ways. This book surveys the empirical evidence on industrialisation in developing countries and relates it to the relevant economic theory as well as discussing alternative strategies of industrialisation and the range of policy instruments available to implement these strategies. In particular, the book focuses on the three theories of Third World industrialisation that have predominated – the structuralist, the Marxist, and the neo-classical.

Importantly, industrialisation in developing countries is not a uniform process, and this book emphasises the discrepancies between the newly industrialising countries of South East Asia and the poorest countries of Africa. Given such heterogeneity, establishing appropriate criteria for assessing industrial performance in different countries is a problem, and the author pays close attention to establishing such criteria. He concludes by offering an analysis of the conditions under which certain policy instruments appear to have operated successfully in a survey of industrial performance across a wide range of countries.

This book is essential reading for all advanced students of development economics.

Dr John Weiss is Senior Lecturer at the Development and Project Planning Centre, University of Bradford, UK.

INDUSTRY IN DEVELOPING COUNTRIES
Theory, Policy and Evidence

John Weiss

R

ROUTLEDGE
London and New York

First published 1988 by Croom Helm Ltd
First published in paperback by Routledge 1990
11 New Fetter Lane, London EC4P 4EE

Simultaneously published in the USA and Canada
by Routledge
a division of Routledge, Chapman and Hall, Inc.
29 West 35th Street, New York, NY 10001

Printed and bound in Great Britain
by Mackays of Chatham Ltd, Kent

British Library Cataloguing in Publication Data

Weiss, John
    Industry in developing countries: theory,
    policy and evidence.
    1. Developing countries – Industries
    I. Title
    338.09172′4   HC59.7

    ISBN 0-7099-3654-0
        0-415-04935-0 (Pbk)

Library of Congress Cataloging in Publication Data

Weiss, John.
        Industry in developing countries: theory, policy, and evidence/
    John Weiss.
            p.   cm.
        Bibliography p.
        Includes index:
        ISBN 0-7099-3654-0
        1. Developing countries — Industries. 2. Developing countries —
    Economic policy. 3. Industry and state — Developing countries.
    I. Title.
    HC59.7.W454   1988
    338.09172′4 — dc 19   87-31031
    0-415-04935-0 (Pbk)

To Francis

Contents

Tables

Acknowledgements

All authors owe debts of gratitude to many people. I would like to acknowledge first my enormous debt to my family. My mother and aunts supported me in many ways through all stages of my education, and helped me to attain my current relatively privileged position as an academic observer of events in the Third World. In addition, my aunt Miss Teresa Burns helped me in preparing much of the manuscript of this book, with the same patience and accuracy that she has applied when preparing many earlier studies.

My wife Francisca has both provided constant encouragement and borne the costs in terms of disruption to family life with much understanding. Through her I have gained many insights into one developing country, Mexico, and she ensures that my involvement in development studies is a personal as well as a professional commitment.

I am grateful to my colleagues at Bradford — Steve Curry, Michael Tribe and Michael Yaffey — who commented on sections of the book. Steve Curry, in particular, read much of the manuscript and gave many helpful comments. I am, of course, responsible for any errors that remain.

John Cody of UNIDO gave me the opportunity to work on the question of industrial policy reform and some of the findings of an earlier study for UNIDO by myself and my colleague Richard Kitchen are drawn on in this book.

Elizabeth Dada, Shirley Hanley and Jean Hill typed parts of the manuscript and I am very appreciative of all their efforts.

Preface

Two activities forced me to consider the issues covered in this book. One is a series of lectures I give on Development Theory at the Project Planning Centre, University of Bradford, as part of the M.Sc. degree in National Development and Project Planning. The other is work undertaken for the United Nations Industrial Development Organisation (UNIDO) on approaches to industrial reform for developing countries. This book examines alternative theoretical approaches to and evidence on industrial development in developing countries since about 1960. Given its origins it is a survey of the field rather than a presentation of original data or results. However, the final chapter reflects my own ideas on industrial policy.

It is hoped that this book will be of interest both to postgraduate students working on development issues, and to industrial planners wishing to familiarise themselves with the more recent literature regarding industrial development in developing countries. There are several well-known text-books on economic development and this book should be seen as a complement to rather than substitute for these. There are also several specialist texts on industrialisation that address issues similar to those covered here: these include the very comprehensive, but now somewhat dated Sutcliffe (1971), and more recently Cody *et al.* (1980) and Kirkpatrick *et al.* (1984). It is hoped that the present work has a sufficiently different perspective from these to warrant separate attention.

The book is in eight chapters, but covers three broad areas: data on industrial and general economic performance in developing countries post-1960; alternative theoretical approaches to industrialisation; and industrial policy reform in developing countries.

Attempting a survey of a very wide field such as this in a relatively short book means that to some extent the coverage must be selective. Nonetheless it is hoped that the main issues in the recent literature on industrialisation are covered adequately, although inevitably the coverage of countries is wide and individual countries do not receive detailed attention.

ALTERNATIVE SCHOOLS OF THOUGHT

There are widely differing positions on the policy alternatives open to developing countries and the book considers the competing positions on industrialisation by reference to alternative schools of thought. The schools identified are Structuralist, Radical and Neoclassical, which is a categorisation now used fairly frequently in text-books on economic development.[1] Subsequent chapters define these perspectives and here it is necessary to note only that Structuralists, who argue that the structure of an economy, particularly the size of its industrial sector, is a key determinant of long-run growth can be seen as representing the conventional wisdom on developing countries in the 1950s and 1960s. Radicals are those who approach industrialisation from a wider political-economy perspective; Neoclassicals, on the other hand, can be seen as representing the application of conventional economic theory to development issues. The views of the latter have become increasingly influential in policy discussions in recent years.

It has become common to draw parallels with the natural sciences and suggest that the study of economics can also be explained by the concept of a scientific paradigm. A broad definition of a paradigm can be taken as a world view shared by scientists or researchers working on a topic, such as the problem of economic development and industrialisation. This shared world view determines the problems posed for study, the intellectual framework and methods employed to examine these problems, and the criteria judged appropriate for their resolution. The difficulty with the application of the paradigm concept to the social sciences is that unlike the natural or physical sciences, the former are characterised by a variety of world views, and a lack of shared assumptions. This has led some to reject the use of the scientific paradigm in discussions of the evolution of knowledge in the social sciences. Because of the controversial nature of the paradigm concept in relation to social sciences, this study prefers to talk of alternative theoretical approaches or schools of thought, rather than of competing pardigms. It should be noted that the three broad approaches to the study of industrialisation distinguished here, have been described elsewhere as competing paradigms.[2] However what these alternatives are labelled is much less important than the fact that they represent competing perspectives, and that authors working within one perspective often fail to confront directly the analyses and policy prescriptions of authors working within another. This study is an attempt to allow explicit comparison between these alternative approaches in relation to industrialisation. The implication is that each contains important insights, that should not be neglected by those whose basic sympathy may lie with another school.

It is felt that reference to alternative schools or theoretical approaches is a helpful way of discussing views on industrialisation. However, use of the concept of a school of thought can imply that there are universally agreed views held by all members of each school, and that all major writers on the subject can be placed neatly in one school or another. This is clearly not the case, since within all schools identified there are differences between authors. The Neoclassical exhibits the most uniformity, but even here there are differences of emphasis in policy discussions. Within the Radical school there are major differences of opinion, and some would see Dependency authors as forming a distinct sub-group. Furthermore, many important authors on industrialisation are difficult to place precisely in relation to these distinctions. None the less, bearing in mind the very broad and heterogeneous categories used, it is felt that these distinctions are helpful in setting out alternative views and the policies that arise from them.

SOME USES OF TERMINOLOGY

This book is concerned with industry in developing countries, where the latter group is comprised of a heterogeneous collection of relatively low-income economies with a wide variety of economic, geographical and cultural features. The term developing countries is used most frequently in this book, although other terms in the literature include less developed countries (LDCs), the Third World and the periphery. The basic premise behind the use of such terms is that despite this diversity there is still merit in considering developing countries as a group, for at least some purposes. The Industry sector is often defined as covering four divisions of the United Nations International Standard Industrial Classification (ISIC) — mining, manufacturing, construction and the public utilities, electricity, gas and water. In this book this is generally how the industry sector is defined in statistical comparisons, although in much of the discussion particular attention is given to manufacturing. In places the term industry is used in a narrower sense to refer to a collection of producers with a similar output; for example the steel or the fertilizer industry. Another term used for a sub-division of activities below the level of the sector is a branch of production. Here this term is used in places to distinguish between types of manufacturing. The ISIC classification, for example, distinguishes between manufacturing activities, and these sub-divisions are referred to here as manufacturing branches; thus transport equipment, electrical machinery and iron and steel, which are three-digit sub-divisions of manufacturing in the ISIC classification, are examples of manufacturing branches.

A BRIEF OUTLINE

Chapter 1 gives a statistical overview of industrial development in developing countries since 1960, noting some of the limitations of the published statistics, and the uneven spread of industrialisation between countries in the group. Chapter 2 examines attempts to categorise countries by the types of industrial strategies or policies they have pursued. It then considers whether it is possible to link economic performance, both in general and in industry in particular, with specific strategies and policies. Chapters 3, 4 and 5 discuss alternative theoretical approaches to industry in developing countries and the policy implications of each approach. Chapter 3 considers the Structuralist school, Chapter 4 the Radical, and Chapter 5 the Neoclassical. Several of the preceding chapters examine evidence on the economic efficiency of industry in developing countries. Much of this data is derived from the studies that have a Neoclassical perspective. Chapter 6 considers other sources of evidence on industrial efficiency. Chapter 7 takes up the question of reform of industry and considers both Neoclassical reform proposals, and some of the evidence available on their impact from countries where measures of this type have been applied. Finally, Chapter 8 examines some of the broad issues relating to future industrial development and gives a brief outline of an interventionist industrial policy. The policy discussion is intended to be suggestive rather than comprehensive and the difficulty of generalising for many different countries is recognised.

NOTES

1. See for example Herrick and Kindleberger (1983).
2. David (1986) p. 18 describes Structuralist, Neoclassical and Marxian approaches to economic development as competing paradigms. Foster-Carter (1976) introduced the paradigm concept to debates on development theory, but noted that it was not intended originally to be applied to the social sciences.

1

Industrialisation in Developing Countries since 1960: A Statistical Overview

This chapter summarises some of the basic data on the industrialisation that has taken place in developing countries since 1960. The conventional grouping 'developing countries' is very heterogeneous, covering countries with very different population sizes, income levels, resource endowments, and political and social cultures. Most statistical compilations work with income level as a criteria for membership of this group, although a relatively low share of industry in total economic activity is often assumed to be a key characteristic of such countries. This study uses the United Nations (UN) country classification for developing countries, whilst recognising the diversity of countries covered in this broad group.[1]

In international statistical compilations the industry sector is generally defined to cover not only manufacturing, but also construction, mining and public utilities. The focus here is primarily on manufacturing, but some sources give information only on industry in aggregate so that on occasions reference cannot be made to manufacturing specifically. As is discussed in later chapters, manufacturing is often seen as the most dynamic part of the industrial sector and given a leading role in planning strategies. The United Nations and the World Bank have both collected a substantial amount of comparative material on manufacturing in developing countries and this evidence is drawn on heavily in this chapter. However, at the outset it is important to note frankly some of the limitations of this data.

It is well known that economic data on developing countries can leave much to be desired, but there is a problem related specifically to the statistical coverage of manufacturing. This arises from the fact that by definition statistics refer to the 'enumerated' or 'formal' sector; that is to enterprises large enough to be covered by censuses of production. The activities of small workshops and household units of below a minimum size — that is the 'informal sector' — will go unrecorded, or at best their output will be estimated crudely. For most developing countries therefore, manufacturing statistics will underestimate total activity and will give a biased indication of its composition. It is normally the case that small-scale informal sector production has a much lower output per worker than in formal manufacturing. This means that small units are much more important in terms of their share in manufacturing employment than in manufacturing output, so that errors of under-recording are likely to be greatest in employment statistics.[2]

A separate problem with the data used here is that several important countries are excluded from the coverage of these statistics. UN data do not normally include Taiwan and China, nor several socialist developing economies of South East Asia. World Bank sources have similar gaps although they have some data on China, and countries like North Korea and Vietnam. These omissions make realistic comparisons between socialist and non-socialist developing economies difficult.

The period covered here is from 1960 to the mid-1980s, and it is important to stress that since 1960 the world economy has gone through several phases with the relatively high growth years of the 1960s, when output and trade expanded at historically high levels, a recession in the mid-1970s after the first oil price shock, a brief period of recovery in the late 1970s, followed by a more prolonged and severe recession after 1980. Although the downturn in world economic activity has been substantially less in the early 1980s than in the Great Depression period of the early 1930s, however, the fact that after a long period of more or less continuous growth since 1945, world trade actually declined in volume and value terms in the early 1980s shattered many illusions regarding the inevitability of economic expansion, and created a much less favourable international climate for the industrialisation of developing countries. It is well known that the level of economic activity in developed economies has a major impact on growth prospects in developing countries, particularly through changes in export demand. Developing country exports of manufactures, for example, whilst expanding strongly in the 1960s and 1970s, were stagnant in real terms in 1982, and although they recovered strongly in 1983 and 1984, showed only a modest growth in volume of just over 3 per cent in 1985.[3]

None the less despite a less favourable international environment in the 1970s and 1980s, the evidence is strong that a substantial degree of industrialisation has taken place in many developing countries. Although countries conventionally classed in this group still provide only a relatively small share of world manufacturing output, this share has risen and manufacturing has assumed a more central role in many of these economies.[4] In surveying the broad picture of industrial development since 1960 the discussion here is organised around two main issues:

- the extent to which the industrialisation of developing countries over this period has changed the economic structure of these economies;
- the extent to which industrial development has occurred unevenly within the group of developing countries.

The question of which developing countries can now be considered to be industrialised is discussed at the end of this chapter. Questions of industrial policy are not considered here, but are discussed in subsequent chapters.

INDUSTRIALISATION AND STRUCTURAL CHANGE

In many developing countries growth of national income and manufacturing output since 1960 has been high by most standards of comparison; whether in relation to historical rates in these countries before 1960, in relation to rates currently achieved by developed economies, or in relation to the growth performance of the developed economies at earlier stages of their industrialisation. Table 1.1 gives the growth of manufacturing production in developing countries, and developed countries for two periods after 1963. The impact of the first oil shock is apparent since in both groups growth is lower after 1973, but in both periods developing countries achieved a higher rate of growth of manufacturing; 8 per cent per year 1963–73, and just under 5 per cent 1973–83. It should be noted that at no stage in the nineteenth and early-twentieth centuries did manufacturing output in the UK, the USA or France grow

3

by around 8 per cent per year for any sustained period.[5] It is only in relation to the industrialised Centrally Planned Economies that the growth of developing countries appears less impressive.

Table 1.1: Annual average growth of manufacturing production by economic grouping[a] (1975 prices)

%	Developing countries	Developed countries	Centrally planned economies
1963–73	8.0	5.5	9.8
1973–83	4.9	1.4	5.2

[a]See sources for definitions of economic groupings.
Sources: United Nations Industrial Development Organisation (UNIDO) (1983), p. 24, and UNIDO (1984), p. 8.

Having noted the broad magnitude of manufacturing growth in developing countries as a group, it is important to consider the question of the impact of this growth on economic structure. Industrialisation is normally interpreted as a process whereby the share of industry in general, and of manufacturing in particular, in total economic activity is increased. A large number of studies have shown a clear tendency for industrialisation, defined in this way, to be associated with rising incomes. In other words, as incomes *per capita* increase, so too does the share of manufacturing in national income.[6] Naturally this statistical association cannot prove causation, and the issue of whether it is the increasing role of manufacturing in economic activity which causes higher incomes *per capita*, or vice-versa, is one to which we will return. However, an increase in the share of manufacturing in national income is conventionally taken as an important statistical measure of structural change at the macro-economic level. If one considers the sectoral composition of national income for developing countries as a group, one finds that over the period 1963–80 there has been a rise in the share of manufacturing, services and others at the expense of agriculture. However, the increase for manufacturing is only four percentage points, from 15 per cent to 19 per cent, and its share in gross domestic product (GDP) whilst surpassing that of agriculture remains significantly smaller than in developed economies. This is only the first of many statistical comparisons, however, where the use of the aggregate category 'developing countries' can obscure important trends within the

Table 1.2: Sectoral composition of GDP (1975 prices)

%

| | Developing countries[a] | | | | | | | | | | | | Developed market economies[a] | |
| | All | | Low-income | | Lower middle-income | | Upper middle-income | | High-income | | Large countries[d] | | | |
	1963	1980	1963	1980	1963	1980	1963	1980	1963	1980	1963	1980	1963	1980
Agriculture	28.4	17.4	47.4	38.0	40.4	27.4	16.2	9.5	9.2	5.1	9.4	6.4	6.5	4.3
Mining	11.6	10.9	1.2	1.4	6.1	8.7	11.2	6.9	32.0	28.1	3.1	2.6	2.7	2.1
Manufacturing	15.2	19.2	12.5	15.1	12.0	15.9	19.6	24.6	16.7	18.6	25.5	26.5	26.6	27.5
Services[b]	39.3	44.3	32.9	39.4	36.4	41.1	46.2	50.5	37.3	39.8	52.6	55.7	54.0	56.9
Others[c]	5.7	8.2	5.9	6.0	5.1	7.0	6.8	8.6	4.8	8.4	9.4	8.8	10.2	9.2

[a] For definitions of countries covered see the original source.
[b] Includes government services.
[c] Covers construction and public utilities.
[d] Developing countries with a population above 20 million in 1970. The figures for different income groups include large countries.
Source: UNIDO (1983), table IV.1, p. 83.

group. Structural change within different sub-groups of developing countries is illustrated in Table 1.2, where developing countries are shown by income level, with large countries also distinguished from the rest. It can be seen that structural change in terms of a shift of GDP towards manufacturing was greatest in the upper middle-income category and that whilst manufacturing was only 15 per cent to 16 per cent of GDP in the poorer countries, it was close to 25 per cent in the upper middle-income sub-group, a proportion not very different from that in developed economies.

Conversely, agriculture remained important in terms of its contribution to GDP in the poorer sub-groups. The figures for the high-income developing countries are distorted by the importance of mining covering petroleum extraction, in these countries, which reduces the role played by both agriculture and manufacturing. It is also worth noting the importance of domestic market size for economic structure; for the large developing countries, manufacturing already had a share of GDP close to that of developed economies at the beginning of the period. This share showed only a small rise between 1963 and 1980.

EMPLOYMENT GROWTH

Another approach to economic structure is to examine the share of different sectors in total employment. It can be argued that this is a more important indicator of structural change, since one of the main aims of a policy of structural transformation will be to shift employment from low to high productivity activities. This implies that the change in the proportion of the work force in developing countries engaged in manufacturing or industry in general, where productivity is high relative to the rest of economy, will be an important measure of structural change. Estimates of the proportion of the labour force engaged in manufacturing in developing countries are particularly prone to error due to the lack of coverage of small-scale household or workshop units by production or employment surveys, noted earlier. It is normally argued that this omission is particularly significant in terms of employment, since whilst in many developing countries unenumerated producers may contribute only a relatively small proportion of

Table 1.3: Distribution of the labour force by sector (%)

| | Developing countries[a] | | | | | | | | Industrial market economies | |
| | Low-income | | Lower middle-income | | Upper middle-income | | High-income oil exporters | | | |
	1960	1980	1960	1984	1960	1984	1960	1984	1960	1984
Agriculture	77	70	71	55	49	29	62	36	18	7
Industry	9	15	11	16	20	29	13	21	38	35
Services	14	15	18	29	31	42	25	44	44	58

[a] See source for definition of countries covered.

Source: World Bank (1984), table 21, pp. 258–9, and World Bank (1986), table 30, pp. 238–9.

output, they can provide a much more significant proportion of manufacturing employment.[7]

The share of either industry or manufacturing in total employment is often substantially less than their share in national income due to the low productivity of agriculture in many developing countries. However, notwithstanding the crudity of the data there is evidence of a rising share of industry in total employment in the majority of developing countries. Table 1.3 illustrates this trend using the income groupings for developing countries employed by the World Bank. Data on employment in manufacturing alone are not available from this source. However, agriculture still remains by far the most important employer in all but upper middle-income developing countries; in the latter there has been a significant shift in employment structure, so that by 1984 industry's share in employment was equal to that of agriculture. Nonetheless in most of these countries the employment share of industry still remains well below that in the developed countries.

In the context of employment growth, it is frequently asserted that manufacturing has generated relatively few new jobs, despite the substantial industrialisation that has taken place since 1960. On the basis of recorded employment statistics this view is questionable. For developing countries as a group, manufacturing employment appears to have grown by around 4 per cent per year during the 1960s and 1970s; a creditable performance in historical terms. For example, if one takes as a point of comparison the experience of developed countries in the latter part of the nineteenth century, the rough data available suggest that their annual growth of industrial employment was roughly half this figure. This more rapid employment growth in contemporary developing countries arises in part from their more rapid output expansion relative to that of developed countries in the latter part of the nineteenth century. However, it is also significant that the estimated employment elasticity of industrial output, that is the ratio of the percentage growth in industrial employment to the percentage growth of industrial output, is only slightly lower for contemporary developing countries than for the developed countries in the latter part of the nineteenth century.[8]

The basic problem is not the number of additional jobs created in industry relative to output expansion in the sector, but rather the number of these additional jobs relative to both the annual increase in the labour force, and the number of workers in low productivity activities in agriculture and services. Again a comparison with late-nineteenth-century experience may put the problem in perspective. In the 1960s in developing countries the industrial sector was able to absorb annually only around 22 per cent of the total increase in the labour force; the comparable estimate for a group of now developed economies in the 1880s is nearly twice this, at 42 per cent.[9] The substantial expansion of industrial and manufacturing output which has occurred in many developing countries since 1960 is still inadequate to generate the jobs required to absorb a high proportion of the new entrants to the labour force, let alone to offer work to large numbers of the under-employed.[10]

COMPOSITION OF MANUFACTURING OUTPUT

Structural change cannot be viewed simply in terms of the share of manufacturing or industry in total output or employment. It is important to know whether there has been a shift in the composition of output produced within manufacturing; in particular whether developing countries have moved from what is sometimes termed 'first-stage' import-substitution, involving the production of light consumer goods with relatively simple technologies, and no significant economies of scale, to the production of intermediates and consumer and producer durables. A diversified industrial structure which is capable of supplying a significant proportion of its own requirements of industrial inputs and capital goods is seen by many as a prerequisite of a self-sustaining programme for long-run growth. In this context structural change within manufacturing can be defined as a shift away from 'light', relatively labour-intensive industrial activities, towards 'heavy', more capital-intensive ones, and away from light consumer goods towards industrial intermediates, and durables both capital and consumer goods. Table 1.4 shows the extent of this shift for developing countries as a group. Evidence such as this must be treated with caution, since it gives no indication of the comparability, in terms of quality or technological sophistication of broadly similar output categories produced in developed and developing countries. Furthermore it does not distinguish between capital goods pro-

9

duction, often seen as a key element of a diversified industrial structure, and durable consumer goods. None the less it does indicate that in broad terms the manufacturing structure of developing countries has shifted from light consumer goods production towards more capital intensive activities, with the share of capital goods and consumer durables rising from just over 20 per cent of manufacturing output in 1963 to over 30 per cent in 1979.[11]

Table 1.4: Composition of manufacturing output — developing countries and developed market economies

	Developing countries		Developed market economies	
	1963	1980	1963	1980
By factor intensity				
Light industry	56.9	42.9	37.9	32.3
Heavy industry	43.1	57.1	62.1	67.7
	1963	1979	1963	1979
By end-use				
Consumer non-durables	51.9	37.6	37.0	30.8
Industrial intermediate	27.3	31.2	19.4	23.7
Capital goods and consumer durables	20.8	31.2	43.6	45.5

Source: UNIDO (1983), table III.1 and III.2, pp. 62–3.

Similar trends are found with employment data, although due to the more rapid growth of productivity in the heavy industry branches the employment shift within manufacturing is less marked.

COMPOSITION OF EXPORTS

The final broad indicator of structural change considered here is the composition of exports. Heavy reliance on the export of a small number of primary commodities was a key characteristic of many developing countries pre-1960, and a rising share of manufactures in total exports can be seen as desirable, not only to diversify the means of earning foreign exchange, but also as evidence of the international competitiveness of new manufacturing activities.

One of the dominant characteristics of world trade patterns

since 1960 has been the growth of manufactured exports from developing countries, although it is not always pointed out that developing countries' share of world trade is still no more than equal to their share in world production of manufactures. For developing countries as a group manufactured exports grew at just under 12 per cent per year in volume terms 1965–73, accelerating to just over 14 per cent per year 1973–80.[12] In both periods this growth exceeded substantially that of total world merchandise trade. The share of manufactures in total exports increased as a consequence of this rapid growth. If one excludes fuel from the comparison, the share of manufactures rose substantially from just under 13 per cent of developing country exports in 1960 to 53 per cent in 1982.[13] Success in exporting manufactures has been very unevenly spread between developing countries, a point to which we will return shortly, but even in many countries which remain highly dependent upon primary exports there has been some diversification, in the sense that they have become less dependent upon their single most important primary export.[14]

An examination of the commodity composition of manufactured exports from developing countries reveals that growth has occurred across a range of products, not simply the more traditional labour-intensive exports of clothing and textiles. Rapid growth has been achieved in products like consumer electronics, chemicals, iron and steel, machinery and transport equipment. However, exports of these latter products are still small absolutely so that in terms of the economic characteristics of manufactured exports for most developing countries, the majority of exports are still relatively labour-intensive, mature products, for which technology has become fairly standardised.[15] These characteristics are, of course, precisely those that would be predicted by theories of international trade, which attempt to explain trade flows between countries in terms of either factor endowments, or the life-cycle of products. However, in so far as the majority of developing country manufactured exports are of this type, this limits the degree to which the emergence of these exports since 1960 can be interpreted as a major departure from the earlier pattern of the international division of labour. Table 1.5 gives data on the growth of particular export categories for all non-oil exporting developing countries, and compares this with the expansion of total world trade for these categories. It can be seen that despite their rapid

11

rates of expansion by the early 1980s, developing country exports of iron and steel, chemicals and engineering products were still a relatively small proportion of total world trade in these goods.

Table 1.5: Exports of manufactures: growth by sector for non-oil exporting developing countries and the world 1973–1982[a]

Export sector	Nominal developing countries average annual growth (1973–82) %	World average annual growth (1973–82) %	Share of non-oil exporting developing countries in world exports 1982 %
Clothing	17.5	13.8	40.0
Textiles	12.6	9.1	23.0
Other consumer goods	19.2	14.2	19.4
Iron and steel	20.5	10.5	7.2
Chemicals	20.6	14.5	7.0
Engineering products	23.1	13.5	6.5

[a]See source for definition of non-oil exporting developing countries.
Source: Anjaria *et al*. (1985) table 59 p. 146.

To summarise, therefore, by any of the indicators conventionally used to gauge structural change at the macro level, as a group developing countries have shown important structural shifts. The share of manufacturing in total production has risen, as has its share in total exports. Furthermore within manufacturing there has been a tendency for intermediate and capital goods to grow more rapidly than light consumer goods. Employment data are particularly uncertain, but recent estimates suggest that the share of the labour force in industry and by implication manufacturing has also risen. Although one can question the accuracy of some of these statistics, the general conclusion is clear — manufacturing, and industry in general have played a much larger role in developing countries since 1960.

UNEVEN INDUSTRIAL DEVELOPMENT BETWEEN
DEVELOPING COUNTRIES

As pointed out earlier the group of developing countries is very heterogeneous. The main characteristic shared by most countries normally placed within this group is that their *per capita* income falls below a certain level. In 1960, at the beginning of the period with which we are concerned, there was a significant inequality between developing countries in terms of both income and manufacturing output. The evidence suggests that since 1960 this inequality between countries has increased rather than diminished, since the poorer developing countries have experienced lower growth of both income and manufacturing. Table 1.6 shows that when developing countries are grouped by *per capita* income the poorest group, which comprises over 50 per cent of the population of developing countries, had the lowest rate of growth of manufacturing value-added. Furthermore the next poorest group, the lower middle-income countries, also has a lower growth than the intermediate and middle-income groups. Table 1.2 above showed the mining sector — chiefly petroleum based — to have a key role in the high-income developing countries, but for this group manufacturing still grew more rapidly than in the low-income countries. These relative growth rates mean that the share of the two lower-income groups of countries in total manufacturing value added from all developing countries fell from 31 per cent in 1963 to 20 per cent in 1980.[16]

Table 1.6: Average annual growth of manufacturing value-added for groups of developing countries (1963–80)

Income group[a]	Annual growth of manufacturing value-added (%)	Group share in population of developing countries in 1980 (%)	Number of countries in group
Low	4.9	50.7	28
Lower middle	7.3	18.2	21
Intermediate	8.6	15.7	24
Upper middle	8.5	12.3	11
High	5.8	3.1	11

[a]For details of the income range in each group see the original source.
Source: UNIDO (1983), Table II.11, p. 36.

13

The additional manufacturing output and exports produced by developing countries since 1960 has been highly concentrated in a relatively small number of countries. For example, of the increase in manufacturing value-added in the developing country group 1973–80 over 70 per cent was provided by ten countries, with around 55 per cent of the population of the group.

However of these ten, four, Brazil, Mexico, South Korea and India provided over 50 per cent of the additional manufacturing value-added. Such a concentration of incremental production in a small number of countries was not unique to the period 1973–80. A similar exercise for 1966–75 found ten countries providing an almost identical share of additional value-added with the only difference in the composition of group being that in the more recent period Argentina is substituted by the Philippines.[17]

Although, many developing countries expanded their exports of manufactured goods over this period again the bulk of the increase was concentrated in a few countries. Data for the mid-1970s, for example, indicate that the ten chief developing country exporters took over 75 per cent of all manufactured exports from the group. The four major South East Asian exporters, Hong Kong, Taiwan, South Korea and Singapore accounted for over 45 per cent. Since the population of two of these leading exporters is relatively small inequality on a *per capita* basis is much greater in relation to the distribution of export growth than in the case of the expansion of manufacturing production.[18]

An important question is the cause of this uneven expansion of manufacturing. Naturally one should not expect all countries to grow at equal rates, since factors like natural resource endowments, current output levels, social systems, political and economic external links, and economic policies, will all influence the growth that can be achieved in a specific period. The explanation of this range of performance is clearly complex, and this chapter only sets out basic data, whilst the links between different aspects of policy towards manufacturing and performance are examined in Chapter 2. As one might expect with such a complex issue the evidence is rarely free from ambiguity.

NEWLY INDUSTRIALISING COUNTRIES

The uneven spread of manufacturing and export growth within the group developing countries has led to efforts to reclassify countries into the more dynamic and the rest. Terms like 'newly industrialising countries' (NICs), and alternatively 'semi-industrialised countries' have been used for the more dynamic group. Unfortunately there are no commonly agreed criteria for membership of this group. One approach is to define NICs as those countries with an export-oriented strategy for manufacturing; another includes as NICs those countries where manufacturing has reached some threshold share of GDP — either 20 per cent or 25 per cent. The countries most frequently included in lists of NICs are probably Hong Kong, Singapore, South Korea, Taiwan, Brazil, Mexico, Argentina, India, Egypt, Turkey, Malaysia, the Philippines and Yugoslavia.[19]

Data on some of the structural characteristics and economic performance of these countries, with the exception of Taiwan, is given in Table 1.7. Together they have around one-third of the population of all developing countries, including China. However this relatively high proportion is strongly influenced by the inclusion of India as a NIC; if India is omitted their share in the total population of developing countries is below 15 per cent.

From Table 1.7 it is difficult to identify common characteristics shared by the countries most commonly cited as NICs. With the exception of Argentina all had a growth rate of manufacturing in the 1970s in excess of both developed and the lower-income developing economies. Despite this poor performance Argentina is normally included in lists of NICs on the grounds of the absolute size and relative technological sophistication of its manufacturing sector.

The role of manufacturing in the economies of the NICs varies markedly between the countries in Table 1.7. In terms of its share in GDP all countries in the table have a share above 15 per cent, which Table 1.2 shows was the average for low and lower middle-income developing countries. In a majority of cases the share of manufacturing in the NICs is close to that in developed economies, and in three countries, Yugoslavia, South Korea and Hong Kong exceeds the average for developed economies. For exports, manufactures exceed 40 per

15

Table 1.7: Economic characteristics and performance[a]: NICs

NICs	Share of manufacturing in national income (%)	Manufacturing value-added per head of population (US$ 1975 prices)	Share of capital goods in total manufacturing[b] (%)	Share of manufactures in total exports (%)	Annual growth of manufacturing (%) 1975 prices	
					1963–73	1973–81
Argentina	25.8	394.0	33.6	57.8	6.5	−0.8
Brazil	28.2	403.0	32.9	70.9	9.7	6.2
Egypt	17.3	87.0	21.7	44.1	3.3	8.2
Hong Kong	30.8	966.0	33.8	97.0	12.3	12.3
India	17.2	27.0	27.4	65.3	3.7	5.1
Malaysia	18.4	189.0	26.0	47.4	9.1	9.2
Mexico	23.5	430.0	33.5	32.2	8.9	6.9
Philippines	25.7	115.0	16.4	55.0	6.5	6.6
Singapore	27.6	1144.0	63.6	79.9	18.0	10.0
South Korea	33.8	276.0	25.3	93.2	20.4	13.4
Turkey	18.6	177.0	22.6	55.7	9.9	3.4
Yugoslavia	36.1	621.0	34.4	92.0	6.7	6.2
Developed economies[c]	27.3	1925.0	43.8	84.7	6.1	1.6

a All percentage shares refer to early 1980s.

b Capital goods are defined here as ISIC branches 381, 382, 383, 384 and 385.

c Simple average for Canada, Federal Republic of Germany, Japan, UK and USA.

Source: UNIDO (1985b), various tables.

cent of total exports in all cases except Mexico, where oil distorts the comparison. In all but three countries manufactures are more than 50 per cent of total exports, which as we have seen was approximately the average share of manufactures in non-oil exports from developing countries in the early 1980s. Manufacturing value-added *per capita* varies substantially between countries from US$1,144 in Singapore to US$27 in India. In all cases the *per capita* figures are low in comparison with developed economies, but none the less are generally high by the standards of most other developing countries.

A diversification as well as an expansion of manufacturing is a characteristic of NICs. Some evidence of this is given in Table 1.7 by the share of capital goods in total manufacturing. Six of the twelve countries have a share above the average for all developing countries reported in Table 1.4, although it is likely that the capital goods sector is defined somewhat more widely in the earlier table, so that the comparison cannot be precise. However, with the exception of Singapore, where there is a very heavy specialism in machinery and transport equipment, the proportion of capital goods in total manufacturing is still significantly below that for developed economies. UNIDO (1979) provides more detailed evidence on the structure of manufacturing at the branch level, finding that whilst this structure is highly varied, a relatively small number of developing countries have a structure fairly similar to that of an 'average' developed economy. These countries include Argentina, Brazil, Mexico, South Korea and India.[20]

The trade pattern of the NICs also illustrates the extent to which their development since 1960 has differentiated them from other developing countries. On the import side, their increasing domestic production of capital goods has meant that several NICs have been able to reduce their dependence on capital goods imports. As a specific example of this pattern one can note that by 1980 imports of machine tools provided only around one-third of domestic use in India, Brazil and Taiwan, which is roughly the same proportion as in France and the UK. However, in other countries, such as Mexico, South Korea and Argentina this import-substitution in machine tools has been carried much less far.[21]

On the export side the NICs have been the main exporters of manufactures from developing countries. For example, countries listed in Table 1.7 provided around 80 per cent of all

17

developing country manufactured exports in the mid-1970s.[22] Furthermore in terms of the products they export the NICs have moved into higher value commodities involving greater processing of raw materials, and more use of capital as opposed to labour inputs. Also if one follows the product-cycle interpretation of trade flows a distinction can be drawn between new and mature industries, and NICs have been moving increasingly into new export industries.[23]

Manufactured exports from NICs, developed and other developing economies for the late-1970s are classified in Table 1.8. Exports are classed as either resource based, or non-resource based, depending on the level of processing of primary materials. Non-resource based exports are in turn broken down into mature and new industries, and within these two categories capital and labour-intensive products are distinguished. The composition of exports from the NICs by the late 1970s differed substantially from that of other developing economies. Resource based exports which involve relatively

Table 1.8: Distribution of manufactured exports[a] by industry categories[b]; late-1970s (%)

	NICs[c]	Other developing countries	Developed market economies
Resource based industries	33.0	76.4	28.8
Mature industries			
− labour intensive	38.5	14.8	15.5
− capital intensive	7.2	2.8	14.5
New industries			
− labour intensive	19.3	4.5	35.8
− capital intensive	2.0	1.5	5.4
	100.0	100.0	100.0

[a]The definition of manufactured exports is wider than that used conventionally. Here it covers 'industrially processed goods and intermediates'.
[b]The definitions of products and industry categories are given in UNIDO (1981), p. 108.
[c]The group of NICs is smaller than that given in Table 1.7. Here it covers only Argentina, Brazil, Hong Kong, Mexico, South Korea, Singapore and Turkey.
Source: UNIDO (1982), table 4, p. 15.

little industrial processing, were a much lower proportion of total exports. Furthermore, over 20 per cent of exports were from new skill-intensive industries as compared with just over 5 per cent for other developing countries. However, the move into capital-intensive exports had not been carried very far by the late 1970s, and both new industries and capital-intensive products remained less important in NIC exports than in those of developed economies.

The uneven pattern of industrial development can also be illustrated by contrasting the NICs with the 36 countries classed by the UN as 'least developed'.[24] Here manufacturing still has only a very small role in the economy and its growth since 1960 in this group has been below the average for all developing countries. In 1981 manufacturing value-added *per capita* in the least developed countries was on average US$13 in 1975 prices and had remained constant since 1970. This is in contrast with the average in 1981 for all developing countries, including NICs, of US$113 per capita. For the longer period from the early 1960s to the early 1980s, manufacturing value-added *per capita* grew at just under 2 per cent per year in the least developed countries compared with just under 5 per cent for all developing countries. However, in the early 1980s some of these poorer countries experienced major absolute falls in manufacturing value-added *per capita*. The NICs are becoming increasingly differentiated from this lower-income sub-group in both industrial structure and performance.

ARE ANY DEVELOPING COUNTRIES INDUSTRIALISED?

This chapter has surveyed the evidence on the spread of industrialisation within the group commonly referred to as developing countries. It has noted various measures of industrialisation, and the uneven development of industry between countries. In the light of this data the question must be posed as to how many countries normally classed as developing can now be considered to be 'industrialised'. A definitive answer is difficult, since there are no commonly agreed criteria for defining an industrialised economy. In very general terms it is an economy where the industry sector and manufacturing in particular, have come to play a 'critical role'; however, what constitutes a critical role is open to differing interpretations.

For example, Hughes, in a survey of industrialisation experience up to the end of the 1970s defines an industrialised economy by reference to the share of manufacturing in total commodity production, where the latter can be seen as GDP net of services. Following this approach, Hughes suggests that an industrialised economy is one where the share of manufacturing in commodity production is above 65 per cent. However, the application of this criteria to data from the mid-1970s in Hughes (1978) and (1980) gives counter-intuitive results, with the USSR and Canada not passing the test of industrialisation and Brazil and Argentina appearing industrialised. Hughes acknowledges that the criteria cannot be applied strictly without allowing for the circumstances of individual countries.

A wider set of criteria are put forward in Sutcliffe (1971) where three measures are used to define an industrialised economy, although Sutcliffe recognises the limitations of gauging what is essentially a qualitative change in economic structure by quantitative criteria alone.

The measures are:

- a minimum of 25 per cent of GDP originating in the industrial sector;
- at least 60 per cent of industrial output in the form of manufactures;
- at least 10 per cent of the total population employed in the industrial sector.

Together these criteria are intended to exclude those countries which have a large industrial sector due to the importance of mining rather than manufacturing, and those where only a relatively low proportion of the population earn their living from industry. These criteria are by no means the only ones that might be employed, but it is of interest to see how many countries pass these tests of industrialisation using data from the early 1980s as compared with the mid-1960s, the period with which Sutcliffe himself was concerned originally.

For the mid-1960s the only developing countries found by Sutcliffe to be industrialised under these criteria were Argentina, and Hong Kong, with a few others, Chile, Uruguay, Israel, Portugal and Yugoslavia being borderline cases. Data on Singapore were not available, but if they had been it is likely that it would also have passed these tests. It is clear that the third test relating to the numbers employed in industry is by far the most stringent. For the mid-1960s there were 15 other countries with relatively large industrial sectors, dominated by manufacturing, but where industrial employment had not spread widely enough for them to be classified as industrialised.[25]

Data from the early 1980s do not show a dramatically different picture. Large numbers of developing countries pass the first two tests, but again only a relatively small number pass all three. The borderline cases from the 1960s, Israel, Portugal and Yugoslavia now pass clearly, and probably most observers would now see these as having graduated out of the group of developing countries. The four South East Asian NICs, Hong Kong, Singapore, South Korea and Taiwan, now probably all pass. This judgement must be qualified slightly since comparable data are not available for Taiwan from international sources, but the first three pass clearly. Lack of data again prevents firm judgements on socialist developing economies, but North Korea might also pass all three criteria. Brazil is now the most obvious example of a borderline case.

What is of particular interest however is not simply the relatively small number of developing countries that qualify as industrialised, but the fact that several appear to have regressed in these simple statistical terms. The key examples are Argentina, which passed these tests in the mid-1960s, and Chile and Uruguay which were borderline. Now all three fail in terms of the employment impact of industry.[26] What is being reflected here is that industrialisation in Latin America has a relatively long history, hence the good performance of these countries by Sutcliffe's criteria for the 1960s. However, industrial expansion in these countries since that time has been slow, and has generated relatively few new jobs.

The overall implication of these results is a caution against reading too much into data such as that given in this chapter. Substantial industrial progress has taken place in many developing countries since 1960, but at least by one relatively well-known test, few of these countries, as yet, qualify for the description 'industrialised'. Sutcliffe himself also warns against placing excessive reliance on these figures, and his arguments are worth noting.[27]

First, he argues that despite the structural change that has taken place much of the industrialisation in developing

21

countries is 'premature', in the sense that, as we have seen, the value of manufacturing output per head of population is still very far below that in the developed economies. Therefore, whilst the share of manufacturing in national income in the NICs, for example, may be close to that in developed economies, labour productivity remains much lower. Second, he suggests that a rising share of manufacturing in GDP in some developing countries may reflect the weakness of agricultural performance as much as the strength of industrialisation. It is clearly the case that agricultural growth has been poor in many of the lowest-income developing countries. Third, he speculates that increasing polarisation may be taking place within the industry sector in many developing countries, so that whilst modern industry may be growing rapidly at rising levels of labour productivity, small-scale, more primitive industries may be doing much less well. This is related to the point, noted at the outset, that most of the statistics available fail to give a full picture of industrialisation since they either omit or under-record the informal industrial sector.

One can also add a further qualification: that developing countries still remain very far from self-sufficient in manu-factures. In the early 1980s, with the exception of South Korea, even the industrially successful NICs imported more manu-factured goods from the developed economies than they ex-ported to them. For developing countries as a group the trade deficit is far wider, with imports of manufactures from de-veloped economies nearly four times manufactured exports to these countries.[28]

CONCLUSION

Having noted these qualifications, however, the general con-clusion remains that from the available data it appears that a significant degree of industrialisation has taken place in many developing countries post-1960, although few as yet can be seen as 'industrialised'. Success in industrialisation has been dis-tributed unevenly between countries, and in most instances in the short period under review, has not been enough to trans-form social and economic conditions within these countries. Most studies on poverty, for example, indicate a rising absolute number of people living in poverty since 1960, although their

share in total population may have fallen.[29] Nevertheless, industrialisation cannot be expected to solve all economic problems and by historical standards the changes in many countries
have been impressive. Later chapters consider alternative industrial policies, their theoretical rationale, and their impact,
where it can be assessed.

NOTES

1. Kirkpatrick *et al.* (1984), pp. 2–4, discusses statistical definitions of industry. See UNIDO (1985a) p.v. for the United Nations
country grouping.

2. UNIDO (1985a), pp. 136–47, gives an indication of the importance of the informal manufacturing sector in several countries.

3. Data on export growth of manufactures come from World
Bank (1986), table 2.8, p. 26. Singer (1983) illustrates the possible
impact of lower growth in developed economies on prospects for
developing economies.

4. Developing countries share in world manufacturing value-
added rose from just over 8 per cent in 1963 to just under 12 per cent in
1984; see UNIDO (1985a) p. 5.

5. See Bairoch (1975), pp. 66–7. From 1938–50, a period of
economic dislocation due to the Second World War, manufacturing
output in developing countries grew by less than 4 per cent per year.

6. Kirkpatrick *et al.* (1984), pp. 25–39, survey some of this
literature. The general conclusion is that the relationship between the
share of manufacturing in gross domestic product (GDP) and *per
capita* GDP can be represented by an S-shaped or logistic curve with
the share of manufacturing rising sharply at low-income levels,
accelerating once a certain threshold income level has been passed, but
then stabilising. The implication of this pattern is that structural change
will be greater at intermediate income levels; see also UNIDO (1979).
UNIDO (1985), pp. 23–30, however, reports a weakening of the relationship between income *per capita* and manufacturing's share in GDP
in the period of slower growth post-1973.

7. Anderson (1982) surveys the evidence on household enterprises in manufacturing employment.

8. Comparisons between developing countries and the current developed economies 1880–1900 come from Squire (1981), pp. 24–5. The
employment elasticities are 0.45 for developing countries and 0.51 for
the developed economies in the nineteenth century. However the
confidence that can be placed on nineteenth-century data is unclear.

9. Squire (1981), p. 25.

10. UNIDO (1979) gives some rough orders of magnitude for the
problem: '. . . in order to absorb an annual increase of 3 per cent in the
total labour force a manufacturing sector employing some 15 per cent
of the labour force — which is generally the case among the develop-

ing countries — would have to expand at a rate exceeding 20 per cent per annum (in output terms) if allowance were also to be made for marginal increases in productivity.' UNIDO (1979), p. 223. Few countries have maintained manufacturing growth rates of this magnitude for a sustained period.

11. More disaggregated data show capital goods branches, particularly various forms of machinery and equipment, growing relatively rapidly in developing countries, as a group over this period; see UNIDO (1983), table III.6, p. 70.

12. Data from World Bank (1986), table 2.8, p. 26. Manufactured exports from developing countries fell in real terms by 0.1 per cent in 1982, although growth resumed in 1983. In 1984 the increase in export volume was almost 17 per cent, although by 1985 it was down to just over 3 per cent.

13. UNIDO (1985a), table III.1, p. 38. Definitions of manufactured exports can vary. The most common, which is used for the data cited here, is Standard International Trade Classification sections 5 to 8, excluding 68, non-ferrous metals.

14. Riedel (1983), p. 19–20. This is only true for non-African primary exporters, however, since African countries appear to have had little success in reducing the share of total exports taken by their single largest primary export.

15. Evidence on this is provided by Ballance, *et al*. (1982) who calculate 'revealed comparative advantage' measures for developing countries, and show these to be concentrated in labour-intensive products and standardised and mature industries; see Ballance, *et al*. (1982), pp. 150–2. Further data on the economic characteristics of manufactured exports from developing countries is given in UNIDO (1982), pp. 3–30.

16. UNIDO (1983), p. 37. The percentages refer to data at current prices.

17. See UNIDO (1983), p. 34, for the period, 1973–80, and UNIDO (1979), p. 42, for 1966–75. The total figures for developing countries omit China and Taiwan. This exercise picks out developing countries with large internal markets, since these dominate the absolute increase in manufacturing. Small, fast-growing countries like Hong Kong and Singapore are not included in this list because the absolute size of their manufacturing value-added is not large enough to make them one of the first ten contributors to manufacturing expansion by the group developing countries.

18. By the late 1970s a significant number of developing countries were exporting manufactures worth more than US$ 1 billion; see Keesing (1979), table 19, p. 27. This is still compatible with an unequal distribution of total manufactured exports from developing countries, however.

19. O'Neill (1984) brings together lists of NICs from various studies, and the listing given here is based on the countries cited most frequently by O'Neill.

20. UNIDO (1979), p. 72. More surprisingly some countries not normally listed as NICs — Kenya, Algeria, Peru and Colombia — were also found to have relatively similar structures to developed economies.

21. UNIDO (1983), p. 295. In Mexico imports of machine tools appear to have provided over 90 per cent of domestic use even in the 1970s, and in South Korea were 75 per cent of domestic use in 1979–80. China on the other hand has been highly successful in import-substitution in this area, reducing import dependence from 50 per cent in 1970 to less than 25 per cent a decade later.

22. Calculated from data in Keesing (1979), table 19, p. 27 and Annex B.

23. 'New' industries can be seen as those at an early stage in the product-cycle, requiring relatively high inputs of skilled as opposed to unskilled labour; 'mature' industries are at a later stage in the cycle where the ratio of skilled to unskilled labour will have fallen.

24. UNIDO (1985a), pp. 191–205, reports on industrial conditions in the least developed countries.

25. See Sutcliffe (1971), pp. 23–6.

26. Data for the first two tests come from World Bank (1984) and for the third from the International Labour Organisation (ILO) (1984). Employment data are likely to be the most unreliable. Sutcliffe (1984) reports his own reapplication of his earlier tests. He has broadly similar results to those reported here, but does not comment on the 'de-industrialisation', by his criteria, of Argentina, Chile and Uruguay.

27. See Sutcliffe (1984), pp. 127–9.

28. UNIDO (1985a), pp. 40–1.

29. See Adelman (1986) and Chenery et al. (1979).

2

Different Paths to Industrialisation:
Some Aspects of Policy
and Performance

This chapter considers different aspects of industrial policy and examines the possibility of classifying developing countries by the policies they have pursued. It then discusses the link between these aspects of policy and economic performance.

Industrial policy can be approached from a variety of perspectives, since governments frequently attempt to control or influence different areas of economic activity relating to the industrial sector. Consequently industrial policy can cover a broad range of questions, for example, relating to international trade in industrial goods, the allocation of finance between enterprises, the choice and development of technology, the competitive behaviour of producers, and the relative roles of large and small-scale firms. However if one wishes to generalise about the policies pursued across a large group of countries it is necessary to narrow the discussion to specific aspects of policy. This can allow a classification of countries in terms of their policies in these areas. In the literature on industrialisation in developing countries four major aspects of policy have received particular attention:

- the treatment of foreign trade, particularly the use of various forms of import taxes and trade restrictions to protect domestic industry;
- the use of direct controls, such as investment licences and price controls, to influence the allocation of resources both within industry and between industry and other sectors;
- the degree to which foreign investment by transnational firms is relied upon to provide foreign exchange and technology for new industrial projects;

– the relative roles attributed to the public and private sectors in industrial programmes.

Different intellectual perspectives have focused on different areas of policy with, for example, the Neoclassicals concentrating primarily on the first two, and the Radical literature on the last two. The theoretical basis for the approaches of alternative schools of thought is examined in later chapters. Here the aim is to consider attempts that have been made to classify the policies pursued by different countries in these broad areas. Such attempts normally work with simple dichotomies including:

– 'inward-looking' versus 'outward-looking' trade policies;
– 'distortionary' versus 'non-distortionary' policies towards the major markets of an economy;
– 'dependent' versus 'non-dependent' policies, particularly in relation to foreign investors;
– 'capitalist' versus 'socialist' policies on industrial ownership.

Generally such simple distinctions require major qualification but since they have been used widely in discussions of industrial policy, it is necessary to point to some of the ambiguities they involve. Furthermore it may be of interest to see how various countries have been classed by these different approaches and to consider whether it is possible to link particular policies with good or bad economic performance in general, and industrial performance in particular. The first part of this chapter considers the classification of developing countries by industrial policy, whilst the second part takes up the question of performance and its link with policy.

OUTWARD-LOOKING AND INWARD-LOOKING INDUSTRIAL POLICIES

Although, as we have seen, industrial policy can be considered from a number of different points of view many discussions start from the side of foreign trade, not only on the grounds that the choice of trade strategy will be important in its own right, but that it will also have a major influence on other areas of policy;

27

for example, the degree of competition in the domestic market, and the choice of technology for new investments. A distinction which has become conventional is that between inward- and outward-looking policies, where the former refers to policies aimed primarily at meeting the demands of the domestic market and the latter to those that do not discriminate against, and often encourage, export sales.[1]

In general, inward-looking economies are those that have pursued policies of import-substitution industrialisation, so that domestic industry is established to supply markets previously served by imports. Trade policy measures often employed in such economies include relatively high import tariffs, quota restrictions on imports and controls on access to foreign exchange. In such economies, the export sector is generally penalised relative to the sector producing for the home market. The definition used frequently is that inward-looking economies are those where in aggregate sales in domestic markets receive a higher rate of incentive than do sales for exports. Therefore on average the proportionate rise in the domestic price of importables relative to their world prices will be greater than the proportionate rise for exportables.[2]

In contrast following this approach outward-looking economies are those where the bias against exports is removed, and in the aggregate net incentives to domestic sales and exports are equal. Industrial policies of this type do not necessarily imply free trade in industrial goods since domestic prices and world prices can still diverge. However economies generally classed as outward-looking tend to have lower rates of import tariffs, and to rely much less heavily on import and foreign exchange controls, than the group of inward-looking economies.

The classification of countries in terms of trade strategies has proceeded in various ways. The most satisfactory approach in line with the definitions given above, is to examine the incentive structure for industrial goods to establish the direction of bias in the incentive system. Studies of this type are time-consuming and have been carried out in detail for only a limited number of countries. For example, Krueger (1978) reports on studies of ten developing countries and Balassa (1982) on six, of which only two had been covered by the earlier research surveyed by Krueger. Given this lack of comprehensive coverage there is no definitive classification of countries into those that have followed outward- or inward-looking industrial strategies. There is broad agreement, however, on some of the main members of each group. The leading outward-oriented economies are normally seen as the four South East Asian NICs — Hong Kong, Singapore, Taiwan and South Korea — that achieved an impressive growth of income and exports post-1960. These are sometimes referred to as the 'Gang of Four', and as we shall see, in the Neoclassical literature their success is held out as a model for other developing countries to emulate. Other countries, particularly Brazil for a period from the mid-1960s until the early 1970s, are also linked with this group although their inclusion is more contentious. The major inward-looking economies are normally taken to include India, China and some of the larger Latin American economies, such as Mexico, Argentina and Brazil in the later 1970s. Egypt, Turkey and the Philippines have also been linked with this group.

A relatively recent classification is given in Balassa (1984a) covering 24 countries and based on trade policies in force in the period 1974–78. Table 2.1 gives this grouping of countries. A major difficulty with this approach is that policies in this area can be transitory so that classifications valid for one period are not relevant for another. Also coverage is far from comprehensive; for example Hong Kong and India, clear examples of outward- and inward-looking economies respectively, are not in the original sample, and therefore are not in the grouping in Table 2.1. The transitory nature of trade policy is illustrated clearly by the fact that the outward-looking economies Chile and Uruguay were both protectionist and inward-looking pre-1973, and by 1980–81 both had re-introduced an exchange rate policy that diminished incentives to exports. Also Brazil is included in the group of inward-looking countries because a shift in policy in the early 1970s had re-introduced a bias against exports. Similarly several other countries classed as inward-looking have revised their policies generally as a consequence of balance of payments crises and pressures from the International Monetary Fund (IMF) and international creditors. These include Turkey, the Philippines and Jamaica, where devaluation and import liberalisation programmes have been introduced.

Another approach to the classification of countries is to use cross-sectional international data to compare the pattern of

Table 2.1: Balassa's division of countries into inward- and outward-looking: based on policies 1974–78

Outward-looking	Inward-looking
South Korea	Brazil
Singapore	Israel
Taiwan	Portugal
Chile	Yugoslavia
Uruguay	Argentina
Kenya	Mexico
Mauritius	Jamaica
Thailand	Peru
Tunisia	Tanzania
	Egypt
	India
	Morocco
	Philippines
	Zambia

Note: It is not clear from the original text how Balassa classifies four countries experiencing favourable external shocks in the 1970s; these are Indonesia, Nigeria, Colombia and the Ivory Coast.
Source: Balassa (1984a), pp. 955–6.

trade and production in an individual country with a typical pattern for a developing country of a similar size and income level. Outward- or inward-orientation can then be defined in terms of a divergence from a typical pattern.[3]

For example, using the cross-sectional regression analysis to estimate 'normal' patterns of trade and production Chenery (1979) gives a classification of developing countries on the basis of trade and production specialisation in 1965 in relation to the norm for a country of their population and income level. Four categories are identified:

– primary specialisation;
– import-substitution;
– balanced development;
– industry specialisation.

Countries in the first group retain a clear bias in both trade and production towards primary commodities, whilst those in the third show a pattern relatively close to that predicted by the regression study. On the other hand, those in the second group have a relatively low share of exports in national income, indicating an inward-orientation, and a relatively high ratio of manufacturing to primary production, indicating an industrialisation specialisation. They are relatively unsuccessful in generating manufactured exports however and are the closest to the inward-looking economies discussed above.

In the fourth group, countries show both a high orientation towards manufacturing and have generated more than expected levels of manufactured exports. This group corresponds to the outward-oriented or export promotion category. Table 2.2 gives Chenery's classification for 50 countries.

Table 2.2: Chenery's classification of developing countries (1965)

Primary specialisation	Import substitution	Balanced development	Industry specialisation
Tanzania	India	Thailand	Kenya
Nigeria	Ghana	Philippines	Egypt
Indonesia	Ecuador	Syria	Taiwan
Bolivia	Brazil	Morocco	Yugoslavia
Sri Lanka	Colombia	El Salvador	Hong Kong
Ivory Coast	Turkey	Guatemala	Singapore
Zambia	Chile	Peru	Pakistan
Algeria	Mexico	Costa Rica	South Korea
Dominican Republic	Uruguay	Jamaica	Tunisia
Iran	Argentina	South Africa	Portugal
Iraq		Spain	Lebanon
Malaysia		Greece	Israel
Saudi Arabia		Ireland	
Nicaragua			
Venezuela			

Source: Chenery (1979), table 1.3, pp. 30–3.

Since this approach to country classification examines actual production and trade structure, rather than the bias of policies, and considers the position of economies in the mid-1960s it is not surprising that there is not an exact match with the classification of Balassa in Table 2.1. Perhaps the main surprises in Chenery's grouping are the inclusion of Egypt and Pakistan in the outward-oriented industrial specialisation group, since at this time both were considered relatively protected economies. However both are borderline members of the group; Egypt only just qualifies on the basis of its trade orientation, and Pakistan's production specialisation deviates from the criteria required for membership. Chenery acknowledges that the distinction between the first and second group is one of degree, since most of the 'balanced development' economies used protection to establish industries producing for the home market, although this group were more successful in generating manufactured exports. Nevertheless, the balanced development group includes several countries, particularly Jamaica and the Philippines, which had relatively high levels of protection in the mid-1960s and which followed policies very similar or identical to those of the group of import substitution countries.

Qualifications to the simple distinction

Given changing policies and the difficulties of making valid comparisons across countries, it is clearly difficult to produce a definitive list of inward- or outward-oriented economies. Furthermore whilst the simple distinction may be useful in focusing on the bias inherent in various incentives to production, it needs to be qualified in several ways.

First, it is important to stress that outward-looking industrial strategies need not imply that import protection is removed. For example, of the four leading outward-looking economies — Hong Kong, Singapore, Taiwan and South Korea — only the first can be seen as a free-trade economy. In the 1960s and 1970s the others maintained varying degrees of import protection. This was generally low overall, but in the case of South Korea protection was relatively high for specific manufacturing branches, for example those producing transport equipment, machinery and consumer durables. Protection for these branches in Taiwan was lower than in South Korea, but was still significant for transport equipment and consumer durables.[4] Furthermore it should not be thought that import-substitution — defined as a falling share of imports in total supply — did not take place in these economies in several branches of industry. Although the incentive structure may not bias incentives in favour of home market sales, import-substitution can still take place without high import protection as domestic producers gain in experience and efficiency, and thus are able to compete with imports in the home market. There is evidence for example that during the 1960s and 1970s, in South Korea and Taiwan substantial import-substitution of this type took place, despite no overall bias in favour of the home market.

Second, a sharp distinction between inward- and outward-looking policies ignores the shifts in policy that have taken place in many countries. It is well known that some of the leading outward-looking economies — again South Korea and Taiwan are the clearest examples — pursued inward-looking protectionist policies prior to their shift towards a greater export-orientation in the early 1960s. However it is important also to note that even in many economies that remained predominantly inward-looking, some shift in policy in favour of exports took place in the mid-1960s, as the need to expand exports to overcome foreign exchange crises became increasingly apparent. Donges (1976), and Donges and Riedel (1977), for example, survey studies on 15 developing countries and argue that in most one could identify turning points in policy towards exports, either in the late 1950s or at some time in the 1960s. These policy changes either reduced 'the detrimental effects on the export sector of policies aimed at other objectives' or represented 'outright promotion of export expansion'. Whilst the sample of countries included the South East Asian 'Gang of Four', it also covered more inward-looking economies such as India, Pakistan, Egypt, Mexico and Turkey. During the 1960s, with the exception of Turkey, it appears that all the countries studied moved in some degree towards greater export-orientation, introducing various export promotion schemes; these included refund of import duties paid by exporters on imported inputs used in export production, tax exemptions for profits from exports, and preferential access to credit or import licences. This policy shift was taken much further in some countries than in others, and in many remained only a very partial offset to the biases against exports. However it would be incorrect to imply that even in highly inward-looking economies there was not a growing awareness of the significance of exports.

In line with a greater encouragement to manufactured exports in many countries, the period since 1960 has also seen both reductions in overall protection, and a shift in the way it is administered, with quotas substituted by tariffs. Crude comparisons between estimates of protection can be misleading because differences in methodology may mean that the results of studies for the same country at different times are not directly comparable. However there does appear to be evidence that the full incidence of protection has been declining, particularly in Latin America.[5]

Third, it should be noted that the term 'outward-looking strategy' may imply, somewhat misleadingly, that for all countries following such a strategy exports form a major proportion of manufacturing output. In general, exports of manufactures can be placed in four broad categories:

- exports of processed raw materials and primary products;
- exports of intermediates required as inputs into production processes located abroad;
- exports of industries established initially to substitute for imports in the local market;
- exports of final goods produced specifically for the international market.

In only the second and fourth of these categories is it inevitable that an outward-looking approach will involve a very high proportion of exports in total output. Empirical studies have demonstrated that, in general, exports play a much larger role in total demand in small as compared with large economies. This can be explained in that large economies are likely to have a much higher proportion of manufactured exports from industries established initially to serve the local market, and also if the local market is large a higher proportion of processed raw materials and primary products can be absorbed domestically rather than exported.

The key role of internal demand as opposed to external demand as a source of growth for manufacturing in large countries is demonstrated in Chenery (1979).[6] Here growth of output is broken down into that due to internal demand, export expansion, import-substitution, and technical change. Distinctions are drawn between the growth of primary activities, light and heavy manufacturing, and between countries of different income levels. The general conclusion is that in large economies the expansion of domestic demand is clearly predominant providing around 80 per cent of output growth for light industry and 65 per cent for heavy industry across countries at different levels of income. In smaller countries specialising in manufacturing, the role of export demand is greater, but even for these economies internal demand is found to account for around 60 per cent of output growth for light industry and 35 per cent to 40 per cent for heavy industry.

Ballance *et al*. (1982) utilising different data to that employed by Chenery find even stronger support for the view that internal demand 'stands in the forefront of the growth process'. In general they find internal demand to be more important than Chenery's results suggest. In only 6 out of 28 countries in their sample does export expansion account for more than 10 per cent of total manufacturing growth. Even in South Korea, the only one of the 'Gang of Four' covered, export expansion accounted for no more than 18 per cent of output growth for basic consumer goods, 10 per cent for intermediates, and 15 per cent for capital goods and consumer durables.[7]

Results such as these do not imply that exports need be unimportant for economic growth. Although in many larger developing countries they may provide a relatively small share of the total demand for manufactures, export earnings may still make a key contribution to growth by relieving a foreign exchange constraint. Thus if growth is held back by scarcities of imported inputs or by demand deflation used to remove excess demand for foreign exchange, additional exports can play a key role in allowing the expansion of economic activity. None the less it still remains the case that even for relatively outward-looking economies exports need not dominate sales of manufactures, so that a major proportion of output may still go to the home market.

To summarise, the inward- versus outward-looking distinction has a relevance in discussions of the biases arising from trade and other policies. However it cannot be taken to imply that outward-looking economies necessarily pursue free-trade nor that they are dependent on exports for their main source of demand. Furthermore policy shifts can take place fairly rapidly so that country classifications based on this distinction can easily become out of date.

DISTORTIONARY AND NON-DISTORTIONARY INDUSTRIAL POLICIES

A major theme in the Neoclassical literature on industrialisation is the degree to which policies in many developing countries have distorted market prices away from what are considered economically rational levels; that is levels that reflect the opportunity cost to the economy of the commodities or factors concerned. This topic is discussed in detail in Chapter 4. Here the intention is to consider how this approach has been used to classify countries on the basis of the extent of distortions created by government policies towards industry and other sectors. Many discussions link price distortions with the direct controls associated with inward-looking import substitution industrialisation policies. The implication is that one effect of such industrial policies is to create strong distortions in all major markets in the economy and therefore to create general economic inefficiency.

World Bank (1983) examines a sample of 31 countries, covering more than 75 per cent of the total population of developing countries, excluding China. An estimate is made of the degree of distortion in each country in several major markets, and a distortion index is compiled. Countries are then ranked using this index and placed in high, medium and low distortion groups.[8] To understand the nature of the country classification it is necessary to explain briefly the derivation of the index.

Six markets are considered for each country; those for foreign exchange, labour, capital, manufactured goods, agricultural goods and public utilities. In theory to apply this approach it is necessary to compare actual prices in these markets with an estimate of economic value, defined as the opportunity cost price of the commodity or factor concerned. Such economic values are not known precisely for the vast majority of countries in the sample, and therefore various proxy measures of economic value are used. In some cases these measures are rather crude, and in others clearly subjective. The data used refer to the 1970s, covering the whole decade.

For foreign exchange the degree of distortion is estimated by the annual average deviation of the real exchange rate from its 1972–73 level. High distortion in this case is defined as an annual appreciation above 15 per cent. It should be noted that theoretically what is required is a comparison of the actual exchange rate with its equilibrium level, although the concept of an equilibrium exchange rate is itself not free from ambiguity. For labour the treatment is particularly crude since the level of distortion is measured by the movement of real wages in manufacturing relative to productivity growth there, with an allowance for qualitative information on intervention in labour markets. In the case of capital the distortion is determined by the extent to which real interest rates were negative during the 1970s. A high distortion is defined as an average real rate of interest of −5 per cent or less per year. For manufacturing and agriculture the full incidence of protection is used as a measure of distortion. Effective Rate of Protection (ERP) estimates indicate the degree to which value-added in an activity under protection is in excess of what it would be under free-trade. For manufacturing a high distortion is defined by an ERP of 80 per cent or more, and for agriculture 30 per cent is used. For public utilities the rate of return on capital assets in the power sector is taken as a proxy for the return on assets in all public utilities. An average return of below 4 per cent per annum is taken as an indication that both power and public utilities in general are being priced below their full costs of production and is used as a measure of high distortion. Finally, in addition to behaviour in these six markets, the general inflation rate is included as an additional indicator of distortion in an economy, on the grounds that the higher is inflation the greater is uncertainty about future prices and the more attractive is non-productive investment. A high inflation distortion is defined both by the annual rate for the 1970s, and its relation with inflation in the previous decade.

The definition of distortions in this way raises questions as to the accuracy of the classification of individual countries.[9] Furthermore the effect of individual distortions may be in conflicting directions, and may thus partly counteract each other. For example domestic manufacturers may be able to charge prices above world levels due to protection, but may have to pay wages above an economic wage due to labour market distortions. In the presence of such potentially complex interrelationships a composite or overall measure of distortion is required.[10]

The ranking of the 31 countries by the distortion index is given in Table 2.3; a high figure for the index indicating a high degree of overall distortion. The table also shows how the countries in the sample are classed for the industry distortion alone, and whether any of the countries covered can be identified as inward- or outward-looking. Finally it also gives data on industrial performance, as measured by the expansion of industrial output over the 1970s.

Table 2.3: World Bank classification of countries by degree of distortion (1970s)

	Distortion index	Overall distortion classification	Industry distortion classification	Trade classification[a]	Growth of industry % per annum
Malawi	1.14	Low	Low	n.a.	7.0
Thailand	1.43		Medium	Outward	10.0
Cameroon	1.57		Low	n.a.	8.6
South Korea	1.57		Low	Outward	15.4
Malaysia	1.57		Low	n.a.	9.7
Philippines	1.57		Medium	Inward	8.7
Tunisia	1.57		Medium	Outward	9.0
Kenya	1.71		High	Outward	10.2
Yugoslavia	1.71		Low	Inward	7.1
Colombia	1.71		High	n.a.	4.9
Ethiopia	1.86	Medium	Medium	Inward*	1.4
Indonesia	1.86		High	n.a.	11.1
India	1.86		Medium	Inward*	4.5
Sri Lanka	1.86		High	Inward*	4.0
Brazil	1.86		High	Inward	9.3
Mexico	1.86		Low	Inward	6.6
Ivory Coast	2.14		High	n.a.	10.5
Egypt	2.14		Medium	Inward	6.8
Turkey	2.14		High	Inward	6.6

	Distortion index	Overall distortion classification	Industry distortion classification	Trade classification[a]	Growth of industry % per annum
Senegal	2.29		High	n.a.	3.7
Pakistan	2.29		Medium	Inward*	5.2
Jamaica	2.29		High	Inward	-3.5
Uruguay	2.29		Medium	Outward	5.2
Bolivia	2.29		High	n.a.	4.3
Peru	2.29	High	Medium	Inward	3.7
Argentina	2.43		High	Inward	1.8
Chile	2.43		Low	Outward	0.2
Tanzania	2.57		Medium	Inward	1.9
Bangladesh	2.57		Medium	Inward*	9.5
Nigeria	2.71		High	Inward*	8.1
Ghana	2.86		Medium	Inward*	-1.2
Overall average	2.01				6.1

[a] The classification in Table 2.1 was generally used. Asterisk indicates that the author's judgement was used in the classification of countries not included in Table 2.1. Where judgement could not be used n.a. (not available) is shown.

Source: World Bank (1983), table 6.1, pp. 60–1, Agarwala (1983), figure 1, p. 36, and Balassa (1984a), pp. 955–6.

The first point to note from Table 2.3 is that there is not an exact correspondence between inward-looking and high distortion economies, nor between outward-looking and low distortion economies. For example, Yugoslavia, and the Philippines, two countries classed as inward-looking on the basis of their policies in the mid-1970s are in the low distortion group. Similarly two outward-looking economies, Uruguay and Chile, are shown in the high distortion group. No doubt this is partly explained by the fact that trade policy can be accompanied by a range of policies in other areas, so that for example the level of export incentives cannot be used to predict how interest rate and wages policy will be pursued. However as we have noted it is also likely to reflect the transitory nature of classifications of trade orientation that can become dated quickly as a result of policy shifts. We have seen that Chile and Uruguay moved to a greater outward-orientation post-1973, but began to weaken incentives to exports by their exchange rate policy in 1980–81. Since the distortion measures are averages over a decade it is difficult for classifications based on policies at points in time to match classifications derived from estimates of the observed consequences for prices of changing policies, when price changes are averaged over a decade. However it is the case that a majority of the high distortion economies would be seen by most observers as being inward-looking. Therefore whilst the correspondence between inward-looking and high distortion is not exact, there is little doubt that there is some relationship.

The second point to note is that it is by no means inevitable that the overall level of distortion is a guide to distortion in the industry sector. For example, one finds two countries, Colombia and Kenya with a low overall distortion, but high rates of protection for manufacturing. Similarly Mexico and Chile, medium and high distortion countries respectively both have low measures of industry distortion. The implication is that the simple assumption commented on earlier, that distortionary industrial policy implies a distorted economy, and vice versa, does not hold.[11]

Third, a similar point is that the level of industry distortion is not necessarily related to classifications of trade policy. Two inward-looking economies (on the basis of Balassa's classification of the mid-1970s), Mexico and Yugoslavia, have low industry distortion figures reflecting a low effective protection for manufacturing. Also two outward-looking economies, Thailand and Uruguay, have a medium industry distortion, and one, Kenya, has a high distortion measure. These findings are not necessarily strange, if outward- or inward-looking policies are defined by the level of incentive given to exports relative to home sales, since it will be relative not absolute levels of incentive that matter. For example a country can have a low ERP for manufacturing in general, and still have an anti-export bias if the export sector is discriminated against. However one would expect such an economy to have only a relatively small degree of bias in its trade policy. What is significant here is that the simple generalisation that all inward-looking economies have highly protected industries, and that all outward-looking economies have little or no industrial protection does not hold.

Finally one must note an important point stressed by Agarwala (1983) that distortions are not necessarily the same as government interventions. In other words some governments can actively intervene in markets to bring prices in line with assumed economic values, whilst in other countries where governments do not intervene various disequilibrating forces in the economy can still cause prices to deviate substantially from such economic values. Agarwala cites South Korea as an example of activist economic management that avoided severe distortions, and Chile post-1973 as an example of how a non-interventionist policy created ex-post distortions.[12]

The relationship between distortions and economic performance is a central concern of World Bank (1983) and this will be considered in a later section of this chapter. Here it is necessary to note only that whilst notwithstanding the limitations in the calculation of the distortion index, there is evidence of a negative relationship between the level of distortion and economic performance in 1970s; so that the more distorted economies do appear to have grown more slowly, both in terms of GNP and industrial output. However this evidence is open to varying interpretations which will be considered below, after other classifications of industrial policy have been discussed.

DEPENDENT OR NON-DEPENDENT INDUSTRIAL POLICY

Authors working from a Radical perspective have argued that the major obstacle to the economic progress of developing countries is their dependent relationship with the rich developed countries. These views are examined in more detail in Chapter 4, and here the aim is to consider whether it is possible to identify countries that can be said to have followed dependent industrial policies. The concept of 'dependence' is itself both ambiguous and controversial, and can have both economic and non-economic dimensions. The economic characteristics of dependence in developing countries most commonly mentioned in the literature are probably:[13]

- a heavy penetration by foreign capital in the major sectors of the economy;
- the use of capital-intensive imported technologies;
- specialisation in exports of primary commodities or labour-intensive manufactures;
- consumption patterns of domestic elites copied from the rich countries;
- 'unequal exchange' in trade, defined in various ways;
- growing inequalities in income distribution.

The first of these characteristics relating to the role of foreign investment by transnational firms is generally viewed as central to the creation and continuation of dependence, and therefore a major cause of the other characteristics associated with dependence. Transnationals are the representatives of international capitalism and transfer capital, technology, management and marketing techniques between countries.[14] For the discussion here a dependent industrial policy is taken to be one where the government concerned invites or allows a heavy foreign involvement in industrialisation, through direct investment by transnationals.[15]

Unfortunately although this approach is relatively common in the Radical literature, it does not allow a comprehensive classification of countries, partly because of lack of accurate data on the magnitude of foreign involvement in many developing countries, and partly also because of the difficulty of determining what size of foreign presence is sufficient to create a dependent industrial policy. Critics of this approach have pointed out that by the criteria of the share of foreign firms in industrial activity many of the developed economies would appear to qualify for the description 'dependent', which appears paradoxical given the role dependence plays in explaining economic backwardness.[16] Nevertheless given the attention that the role of transnationals has received in the literature on industrialisation, and not simply from Radical authors, it is useful to summarise the data available on their involvement, and to identify the countries that have relied most heavily on foreign industrial investment.

Prior to 1970 the primary and extractive sectors were the main focus for direct foreign investment in developing countries. During the 1970s, however, there was a relative shift in foreign investment towards manufacturing and services. For manufacturing this partly reflected the aim of transnationals to establish local production in the markets of higher-income and rapidly growing developing countries. In many cases these domestic markets became closed to imports due to import substitution protectionist trade policies. Also some of this new foreign investment in manufacturing reflected a shift in location for some of the more labour-intensive aspects of the production carried out by transnationals. In this 'sourcing' investment transnationals established new production units with the explicit purpose of providing parts and components to sections of the corporation in other countries. Therefore this type of investment could contribute directly to an export-oriented industrialisation programme. Sourcing investment has been carried furthest in electrical goods branches, particularly in the production of electronic components. However it has been suggested that with the development of automation technology the cost advantages of developing countries in this field have been greatly reduced, so that this pattern may not continue past the mid-1980s.[17]

As with other indicators of industrialisation the flow of direct private foreign investment in manufacturing has been very unevenly distributed between countries with a clear tendency for those with a higher income to receive a disproportionate share.[18] The main developing country recipients of foreign investment in manufacturing in the 1970s are listed in Table 2.4. Many but not all of these countries are generally included in the group of NICs, and both inward- and outward-oriented economies are represented. The importance of this investment for total manufacturing activity clearly varies between economies. It is difficult to obtain accurate comparable data across a range of countries, but Table 2.5 summarises the position for twelve countries for which data are available, giving the share of enterprises — with full or part foreign ownership — in total employment and sales in manufacturing. A major drawback of this data is that it is not clear how foreign firms are defined — in terms of what share of equity is needed to constitute a foreign firm — in the different countries. Nonetheless the figures show a striking degree of foreign involvement in several countries. For example, the share of foreign firms in total sales is over 80 per cent in Singapore, over 40 per cent in Brazil, Colombia and Malaysia and over 30 per cent in Mexico, Peru and Argentina. On the other hand, it must also be noted that foreign firms appear to play a much smaller role in manufacturing in South Korea, India and the Philippines. If foreign involvement in industrialisation is taken as an indicator of a dependent industrial policy, the former group of seven countries — Singapore, Brazil, Colombia, Malaysia, Mexico, Peru and Argentina — are clearly some of the most dependent.

In terms of the distribution of foreign investments between different manufacturing branches, it is normally argued that

Table 2.4: Selected developing countries: stock of foreign investment in manufacturing (millions US$)

	(1) Early 1970s	(2) Late 1970s	Total change (2) − (1)
Brazil	2,802	13,005	10,203
Indonesia	1,622	4,202	2,580
Mexico	2,377	3,868	1,491
Singapore	665	1,773	1,108
India	1,261	1,238	23
Nigeria	575	873	298
South Korea	88	737	649
Philippines	46	716	670
Colombia	348	572	224
Hong Kong	133	434	301
Malaysia	137	433	296
Peru	310	350	40
Thailand	68	198	130
Ecuador	10	97	87
Morocco	9	92	83

Source: United Nations Centre for Transnational Corporations (UNCTC) (1983), table IV.I, p. 135.

Table 2.5: Share of foreign-owned or affiliated enterprises in manufacturing in selected LDCs (various years)

%	Employment		Gross value of production or sales	
Argentina	10–12	(1970)	31	(1972)
Brazil	30	(1977)	44	(1977)
Chile	n.a.		25	(1978)
Colombia	28	(1970)	43	(1974)
India	13	(1977)	13	(1975)
Kenya	30–35	(1975)	n.a.	
South Korea	10	(1978)	19	(1978)
Malaysia	34	(1978)	44	(1978)
Mexico	21	(1978)	39	(1970)
Peru	n.a.		32	(1974)
Philippines	7	(1970)	n.a.	
Singapore	72	(1980)	81	(1980)
Taiwan	28	(1976)	n.a.	
Hong Kong	10	(1980)	16	(1980)

n.a. = not available.

Source: For all countries except South Korea, Taiwan, Hong Kong and Singapore, UNCTC (1983), table IV. 2, p. 136. For South Korea, Koo (1985), table 4.16, p. 200 and table 4.17, p. 202. For Taiwan, Ranis and Schive (1985), table 2.7, p. 102. For Hong Kong, Lin and Mok (1985), table 5.18, p. 249, and table 5.19, p. 249. For Singapore, Yue (1985), table 6.8, p. 290.

they are concentrated in either technologically sophisticated capital-intensive branches, or those where the production process can be readily sub-divided to allow 'sourcing' investments. Foreign investments in developing countries tend to be greatest in the chemicals, machinery, electrical machinery and electrical goods, transport equipment and food processing branches.[19] Not surprisingly foreign firms often dominate production in recipient countries in the more sophisticated capital-intensive manufacturing branches. The pharmaceutical branch of chemicals is probably the clearest example of this, since in many developing countries foreign firms provide over 80 per cent of output. Foreign firms also tend to have a high share of output in branches like electrical machinery, metal products, transport equipment — particularly automobiles — and chemicals in general. However it is difficult to generalise about transnational involvement in manufacturing on the basis of simple dichotomies between light versus heavy industry, or new versus mature products. Whilst there is evidence that transnationals are particularly strongly represented in the technologically more complex branches, it is also clear that in some countries they are important in some of the traditional branches like textiles, tobacco and paper.[20] Furthermore it is by no means inevitable that the more complex manufacturing activities need involve heavy direct foreign investment. For example, in India and South Korea, two of the countries in which domestic production of capital goods has advanced furthest, government policy towards these branches has limited the involvement of transnationals. In these countries, direct transnational participation in capital goods production through either wholly-owned subsidiaries, or through joint ventures where they have a majority ownership, has been relatively low, in contrast, for example, with the situation in Brazil and Mexico.

Foreign firms have also participated in the expansion of manufactured exports from developing countries, and in some countries have come to supply a major proportion of these exports. Table 2.6, based on several different sources, gives data on the estimated share of foreign firms in manufactured exports for ten countries. The shares range from 93 per cent for Singapore to as little as 5 per cent for India, with these extremes reflecting the contrasting policies of the governments concerned towards foreign investors. It should be noted that foreign firms are important exporters of manufactures in all the Latin American countries covered and in South Korea and Taiwan

Table 2.6: Share of foreign firms in exports of manufactures: selected countries, various years

	%	
Argentina	42	(1973)
Brazil	40	(1974)
Colombia	50	(1974)
Hong Kong	10	(1972)
India	5	(1970)
South Korea	25	(1978)
Mexico	50	(1974)
Pakistan	10	(1975)
Singapore	93	(1980)
Taiwan	21	(1980)

Source: For Hong Kong, India and Pakistan, UNCTC (1983), table IV.3, p. 137. For Argentina, Brazil, Colombia and Mexico, Jenkins (1984), table 5.1, p. 115. For South Korea, Koo (1985), table 4.16, p. 200. For Singapore, Yue (1985), table 6.8, p. 290. For Taiwan, Ranis and Schive (1985), table 2.12, p. 109.

foreign firms take between 20 per cent and 25 per cent of total manufactured exports.

A process which appears to run counter to the logic of the dependency argument on the role of transnationals is the emergence of transnationals whose owners and headquarters are based in developing countries. This is not a new phenomenon but the numbers of such firms grew rapidly during the 1970s, although their size is still very small in relation to total direct foreign investment.[21] As is to be expected a majority — well over 60 per cent — of this foreign investment is made by firms from the NICs, particularly Hong Kong, India, Argentina and Brazil.

Despite the limited quantitative significance of such investments at present they can be interpreted as an interesting illustration of the depth of the industrialisation that is taking place in developing countries. Different explanations have been put forward for the advantages that underlie this foreign investment. Technological adaptation is stressed frequently — with the conventional view being that firms from developing countries can compete overseas using smaller-scale and more labour-intensive technology to that in use in developed economies. This adapted technology is seen as more appropriate for the market conditions of developing countries. The general applicability of this explanation has been questioned, however, and the need to identify more specific advantages is noted; for example, marketing and managerial skills in Hong Kong, and engineering capacity to modify product and process designs in India.[22] Much work needs to be done before the reasons for the emergence of foreign investment by developing country transnationals can be fully understood.

In terms of trade classifications noted earlier it appears that there is no direct link between 'dependence' in industrial policy, as defined by the degree of transnational involvement, and inward- or outward-looking trade policies. Several of the inward-looking economies, such as Brazil and Mexico, have relied heavily on foreign investments, whilst others, particularly India, have not. For the outward-looking group reliance on transnationals has varied; taking the 'Gang of Four', for example, transnationals have played a much more important role in Singapore than in the other three countries.[23] It does not seem possible therefore to link 'dependent' industrialisation, defined in this way, with a particular trade strategy.

The other classification considered above — of distortionary and non-distortionary policies also bears no close relationship with the degree of foreign involvement. To illustrate this one can compare the ranking of countries by the World Bank distortion index with that by an index of overall transnational penetration compiled by Bornschier and Chase-Dunn (1985).[24] A weak negative relationship holds, implying that countries with a high degree of foreign ownership tend to be less distorted. However the rank correlation coefficient is low and not statistically significant.

Some researchers have questioned whether there is an identifiable relationship between transnational involvement and economic performance and this is considered in a later section. Prior to a discussion of performance, however, it is necessary to consider the last of the four country classifications that have been identified here.

SOCIALIST INDUSTRIAL POLICIES

The data considered up to this point have not distinguished between countries on the basis of socio-economic system — whether capitalist, socialist or a form of 'intermediate regime' — and have been confined largely to capitalist developing countries. One might expect that policies in socialist economies would differ significantly from those in capitalist economies with a similar income level and resource endowment. However broad comparisons are difficult, partly because there is no agreed definition of what constitutes a socialist economy, and no universally acceptable list of socialist developing countries.

In considering which developing countries might qualify for the classification of socialist, it is clear that measures of the degree of public sector involvement in economic activity, for example in terms of its share in new investment or in manufacturing output, are inadequate on their own. World Bank (1983) brings together such data for a number of developing countries, and a relatively significant role for the public sector is identified in several, such as Egypt, Syria and Tunisia, that many would feel are far from socialist judged by the practice of their political regimes.[25] In addition the official statements of governments are also of little value in assessing the social base of their support and the overall direction of their policies. Most observers rely on judgement rather than on objective tests of socialism when attempting this type of classification. Table 2.7 summarises one recent attempt, that of White (1984). It should be noted that White employs the concept of an 'intermediate regime' to cover a relatively large number of ambiguous cases. These can be seen as regimes where the power of large private capital has been weakened very substantially and where state officials, often with the support of lower middle-class groups, play a major role in directing the economy. Socialism in the sense of full public ownership and widespread working class or peasant involvement has not yet been attained. The gains of such regimes may be eroded, particularly if economic growth recreates successful capitalist elements in society.[26] White's classification of countries would clearly not be acceptable to all, and is reproduced here, not to imply that it is in any sense definitive, but for purposes of illustration.[27] None the less it covers the most obvious cases of socialist developing countries on which there is likely to be general agreement.

Table 2.7: White's classification of socialist and socialist intermediate developing countries

Socialist countries	Socialist 'intermediate regimes'
Middle-income	Middle-income
Albania	Algeria
Angola	Iraq
Congo	Libya
Cuba	Nicaragua
North Korea	Yugoslavia
Mongolia	Zambia
Romania	Zimbabwe
Yemen P.D.R.	
Low-income	Low-income
Afghanistan	Burma
Benin	Guinea
China	Madagascar
Ethiopia	Somalia
Kampuchea	Tanzania
Laos	
Mozambique	
Vietnam	

Note: Countries on which White is doubtful — Syria, Tunisia, and Sudan — have been omitted.
Source: White (1984), table 1, p. 106–7.

The list in Table 2.7 reveals a wide diversity, with some countries, particularly Benin, Ethiopia, Somalia, Tanzania, Burma and Mozambique where little industrialisation has taken place. In others, however, particularly Romania, Yugoslavia, China and North Korea, both socialism and industrial development have a longer history.

As we have seen, Yugoslavia is commonly included in the group of NICs and from the data available on the growth of industry and its share in gross national product (GNP), there is a case also for including both China and North Korea in this group.

In terms of industrial policies, there is also diversity within the grouping of socialist developing countries. It is clear that industrialisation is likely to have a key role in socialist economic strategies. It is seen not only as a means of raising material living standards, but in addition as a way of reducing dependence on foreign trade and a hostile external environment, and of extending the political base of a regime through the creation of an industrial proletariat. In the early post-1945 period the Soviet model was highly influential, with the path to industrialisation viewed as that marked out by the USSR in the 1920s and 1930s. This protected inward-looking industrialisation, with a strong emphasis on the production of domestic capital goods, was a characteristic of the industrialisation programmes of the majority of socialist developing economies in the 1950s and 1960s. This inward-looking industrialisation created high growth in some countries — most notably North Korea and China — but at the same time created costs and inefficiencies that received increasing attention during the 1970s. The list of alleged inefficiencies included lack of access to modern technology, high cost production and low quality by international standards, imbalances between consumer demands and domestic supplies, and a scarcity of foreign exchange. There is a similarity here with many of the arguments on the inefficiencies of import-substitution industrialisation in capitalist developing countries, and similar issues appear to have been debated in the context of socialist planning with some differences of emphasis and terminology. The policy response to these arguments in countries like China, Vietnam and North Korea has been tentative moves towards a degree of foreign trade liberalisation, a more open policy on foreign technology and investment, and a shift towards greater use of markets as a means of allocating resources.[28]

Not all socialist developing countries have been so inward-looking, however. Yugoslavia is a notable exception expanding exports of manufactures rapidly post-1960. As Table 2.2 shows, Yugoslavia was placed by Chenery in the 'industry specialisation' group covering generally outward-oriented economies. Exports received substantial incentives, although Balassa (1984a) suggests that by the late 1960s incentives to home market sales had begun to outweigh those to exports. None the less export growth remains important to the economy, and this relatively high degree of outward-orientation can be put down, at least in part, to the country's independent foreign policy, and links with the capitalist economies.[29]

Furthermore several of the small, poor socialist economies in Central America and Africa have continued to rely heavily on traditional exports to provide foreign exchange. These include Cuba, and more recently Nicaragua, Mozambique and Ethiopia. Here the small size of the domestic market and the general poverty of the countries have meant that large-scale industrialisation programmes to establish integrated industrial sectors in these economies are largely inapplicable. Scarcity of foreign exchange is a key constraint and the traditional export sector continues to play a major role to allow the imports of plant and equipment necessary to restructure the economy. A clear example of a shift in policy orientation in these economies away from the conventional Soviet model is the Cuban decision in the early 1960s to abandon emphasis on import-substitution industrial programmes, in favour of a strategy based primarily on the expansion of sugar exports.[30]

One way of generalising about this diversity of experience is to follow White (1984) and distinguish between first and second waves of 'Third World Socialist Industrialisers', in the period post-1945. The first wave covers the 'mature' cases particularly China and North Korea, that largely followed the Soviet model, until the tentative moves towards reform in the late 1970s. The second wave refers to the small resource-poor countries that adopted revolutionary socialist policies in the 1960s and 1970s, with Angola, Mozambique, Ethiopia, South Yemen and Nicaragua cited as examples. Here industry remains only a small part of the economy and traditional exports remain critically important. White describes such economies as being at a stage of 'proto-industrialisation'.[31]

With reference to the other criteria discussed above, it should be noted that socialist developing countries inevitably have governments that attempt to plan and control markets — although the nature of planning will differ substantially between the countries in Table 2.7. By the criteria used to compile the World Bank distortion index it might be thought that such interventionist regimes would create large numbers of distortions. However, only three of the countries in Table 2.7, Yugoslavia, Ethiopia and Tanzania — are covered in the distortion study, and the results for these three do not bear out this expectation. Each falls in a different category — Yugoslavia in the low distortion group, Ethiopia in the medium, and Tanzania in the high. There is little doubt however that several socialist developing economies would appear highly distorted in the World Bank's sense, if data were available to allow a suitable estimate. On the question of dependence, one of the characteristics of the countries in Table 2.7 is that with only a few exceptions, they have nationalised the assets of foreign companies at an early stage after the new regimes had assumed power. Socialist developing countries, despite tentative moves to encourage foreign investment in recent years, generally rely relatively little on foreign private capital, and are therefore rarely dependent in this sense. However many still rely heavily on foreign aid and concessional foreign capital flows.

The comparative performance of socialist countries is discussed below. At this point it is necessary only to note that socialist industrialisation has emerged as a viable strategy even in very poor economies that at first sight might appear an unlikely base for socialism. As White (1983) points out, socialism in these countries 'has turned Marx on his head' by succeeding in relatively backward and peripheral contexts. In consequence rather than being an historical successor to capitalism, socialism has become an historical substitute.[32]

ECONOMIC PERFORMANCE AND INDUSTRIAL POLICY

The intention in this section is to examine some of the attempts to link the different classifications of industrial policy discussed above with measures of economic performance. In other words to consider whether there is evidence that countries pursuing particular types of industrial policy have been successful or unsuccessful by various criteria. The chief criteria used will be output growth, both for national income as a whole and industrial output, and income distribution, including poverty alleviation.

Trade policies and growth

A major concern of the Neoclassical literature has been to establish a link between trade policies, including trade in industrial goods, and economic growth. The economic successes of the export-oriented 'Gang of Four' are well known, but the argument is widened to imply that in general export-oriented economies do better than inward-looking ones. Typical of this approach is the work carried out at the World Bank that examines the responses of different developing countries to the international shocks of the 1970s, distinguishing between countries on the basis of trade strategy.[33] This analysis rests largely on the work of Balassa who examines the comparative performance of the groups of countries given in Table 2.1. Outward-looking economies, which Balassa divides into NICs and less developed countries, suffered greater external shocks during the period 1973–82 in unfavourable terms of trade movements, falls in export volume, and increases in interest rates, than did the more inward-looking economies. This stems largely from the higher share of foreign trade in national income in the outward-oriented group, and to some extent their higher foreign borrowing. However Balassa (1984a) demonstrates that in their adjustments to external shocks the outward-oriented economies were successful in both export promotion and import-substitution. It appears that gains in export market shares by the outward-looking group helped significantly in offsetting much of the unfavourable balance of payments effects caused by the oil price rises and the world recession. Perhaps more surprisingly this group was also more successful at import-substitution than were the inward-looking economies. Import-substitution in the outward-looking group is estimated to have offset nearly 40 per cent of the balance of payments effects of external shocks 1974–76, and 11 per cent 1979–81; the comparable figures for the inward-oriented group are 2 per cent and −8 per cent, with the negative figure implying a fall in import-substitution.[34] The major explanation for this apparent paradox — that less protectionist economies were able to lower

Table 2.8: GDP growth at constant prices — groups of countries — per cent per annum

	Outward-oriented NICs	Inward-oriented NICs	Outward-oriented LDCs	Inward-oriented LDCs	Outward-oriented NICs and LDCs	Inward-oriented NICs and LDCs
1963–73	7.1	6.9	7.2	3.7	7.1	5.7
1973–79	7.3	5.1	6.6	4.8	7.1	5.0
1976–79	9.0	4.9	6.8	3.8	8.4	4.5
1979–82	2.4	1.4	4.5	4.4	3.0	2.4

Note: See the original text for an explanation of the countries included in the different groups.

Source: Balassa (1984a), table 5, p. 968–9.

imports more substantially than more protected economies —
is likely to lie in the fact that the higher ratio of imports to
national income in the former group allowed greater scope for
curbing import demand than was available in countries where
non-essential imports were already tightly controlled. Balassa's
general summary of the policy responses of the two groups of
countries is that whilst the outward-oriented group were able to
pursue output-increasing policies — of both export promotion
and import-substitution — to overcome the negative balance of
payments impact of international developments, most inward-
looking economies reacted to the foreign exchange crisis initially by external borrowing and latterly by internal demand
deflation. These different policy responses, it is suggested, can
largely explain the growth performance of the different groups,
which is summarised in Table 2.8. It can be seen that in each
sub-period outward-oriented economies show higher rates of
GDP growth than do inward-looking economies, although the
gap between the groups is low in the most recent sub-period
shown.

This work rests on an examination of country performance
during a particular decade. Many other analyses have looked at
the link between exports and growth over longer time periods
and for much larger samples of countries. These studies generally involve rank correlation or regression analysis to establish a
statistical relationship between growth of exports and growth of
national income, with the assumption that the chain of
causation runs from exports to national income. Various
specifications of the relationship have been tried; for example
Michaely (1977) examines the relation between changes in the
export-national income ratio and growth of *per capita* national
income; Balassa (1978) looks at the relation between export
growth and the growth of both GDP and GDP net of exports;
Tyler (1981) using a larger sample than that of Balassa examines the relation between export and output growth, for all
output and for manufacturing alone; Ram (1985) looks at the
relation between export and national income growth in a production function model that treats exports as a production
input. In general these studies find a positive and significant
correlation between the export variable and some specification
of a variable covering overall economic activity, which they
interpret as evidence of the importance of export promotion
strategies.

55

It should be noted that the results of such studies appear to be sensitive to the samples used, with a tendency for the significance of exports for national income growth to be weaker in lower income developing countries.[35] Also where different time periods are employed it is found that the relationship has changed over time, with exports appearing to have a greater impact on growth in the 1970s than in the 1960s, presumably due to the increasing balance of payment crises in many countries in the later decade.[36] However what also emerges from this literature is that export shares in national income do not appear significant in explaining growth, despite the relationship between export growth and national income growth. Taylor *et al.* (1984) confirm this lack of relationship between export shares and growth, and point out that it is contrary to the conventional wisdom which argues that fast growing developing countries are 'export-led' in the sense that exports are a high proportion of national income. What appears to have happened in the 1970s is that the fast-growing developing countries were characterised by rapid export growth, chiefly in manufactures. However this group of countries appear to have reduced their shares of exports in national income as a consequence of their shift away from primary exports, so that a falling trade share accompanied rising *per capita* income.[37]

It appears from the evidence surveyed that claims for the superiority of outward-looking export-oriented strategies, over inward-looking import-substitution policies are well supported by the available evidence. However whilst there can be no doubt that some export-oriented economies have grown very rapidly post-1960, nor that countries that experience high export growth find it easier to maintain a high growth of national income, one cannot necessarily deduce from this evidence support for the generalisation that outward-looking trade strategies are inevitably the most effective policy for all developing countries. A number of qualifications must be noted concerning evidence on the link between trade policy and performance.

First, if one considers the data on GDP growth in Table 2.8 it is clear that in certain periods the performance of outward- and inward-oriented countries is not markedly different, although it must be acknowledged that in others, particularly 1976–79, the performance of the outward-looking economies is much superior. Of interest is the similarity in performance of the

NICs — both outward- and inward-looking pre-1973. Both groups achieved historically impressive growth of around 7 per cent per year 1963–73. It is this broad similarity in performance that led Chenery (1979) to suggest that choice of trade strategy does not appear to have been a major factor in explaining the divergence in growth rates between countries over the period 1960–75. Chenery prefers to stress the flexibility and skill with which a particular strategy is implemented rather than the initial choice of strategy *per se*.[38] If there is relatively little difference in performance — at least amongst NICs — before the mid-1970s, one can ask whether in periods when the external environment is less turbulent, greater similarity in performance may not re-emerge. In other words, how far are the results reported by Balassa (1984a) specific to the particular period of the 1970s?

However even focusing on the post-1973 period, where the arguments on the superior performance of the outward-oriented group are strongest, it must be noted that by no means all outward-oriented economies did well in economic terms. Chile and Uruguay, for example, clearly did poorly and demonstrate that simply freeing markets and raising incentives to the export sector does not guarantee high growth.[39]

On the interpretation of the statistical analysis relating growth of exports to that of national income, again the case remains not wholly proven. Since statistical association does not prove causation it is possible that an independent factor — such as technical progress or productivity growth — stimulates the growth of both exports and GDP. Having noted this, however, it is clear that there are several reasons why an increase in export growth should contribute to higher growth of national income. The real issue is how best to stimulate the long-run growth of non-traditional, chiefly manufactured, exports. Does one do it through high levels of incentives for exporters, hoping that resources will move into export manufacturing in response to these incentives? Alternatively, does one aim to build up a protected domestic manufacturing sector, which over time can become sufficiently competitive to sell abroad, provided incentives and support facilities are adequate? These are two different policy scenarios; the first can be interpreted as a simple export promotion view where potential exporters emerge in response to perceived profit opportunities, whilst the latter involves a gradual shift from import-substitution to more balanced policies. In interpretations of the statistical results linking exports and national income, export promotion strategies are identified by ex-post high rates of export growth. This evidence, however, cannot distinguish between the different routes to achieve export growth, so that import-substitution strategies that when modified produce successful export industries, are indistinguishable from simple export promotion. Furthermore the other side of this is that countries which fail to generate high export growth are not seen as export promoters, regardless of the levels of incentives they offer. Unsuccessful export promoters that disprove the hypothesis will simply not show up in the test. Therefore the possibility that there is a much closer link between initial import-substitution and later export success will not be picked out by this statistical analysis.

However, perhaps the most important general qualification to the case for outward-looking trade strategies is that if widely adopted they are likely to imply a major rise in manufactured exports, particularly to developed economies. The question is whether the world market could absorb this export expansion, or whether it would be forestalled by protectionist demands in the developed economies. The quantitative magnitude of the problem is illustrated by Cline (1982) who estimates that if all developing countries reach the same export-orientation as the four South East Asian NICs — the 'Gang of Four' — manufactured exports to developed countries would rise sevenfold, and the share of these goods in developed country imports would reach 60 per cent.[40] Even if only seven other NICs outside South East Asia reached this degree of export-orientation developing country exports of manufactures would still rise more than fourfold. This exercise can be criticised for neglecting the time aspect, since countries would not reach their new level of export-orientation instantaneously, and perhaps for not stressing sufficiently the feasibility of increased exports between developing countries.[41] However there is no doubt that it shows that the export-orientation and export growth rates of the 'Gang of Four' could not be replicated in large numbers of other developing countries without drastic changes in trade policies in the developed world. This does not disprove the importance of reforms in trade policy, but it suggests that the benefits often linked with export-led growth may be limited to a relatively small number of successful export economies.

To summarise, what is clear is that several outward-looking developing countries have achieved impressive performances in growth terms. What the evidence considered here has not proved conclusively, however, is that it is inevitably the case that this route will be the most effective for all economies or all sectors. The possibility that in some countries a period of import-substitution may be a necessary prelude to later export growth cannot be rejected. Also in some cases it may be sensible to distinguish between sectors and pursue inward-looking policies for some, and outward-looking ones for others. Furthermore the global dimension, that is the possibility of a limited market for a substantial expansion of manufactured exports from developing countries, should not be overlooked.

Market distortions and growth

World Bank (1983) argues that it can be demonstrated that the high distortion economies in the 1970s performed significantly worse in economic terms than those with lower distortions, thus supporting the emphasis on the need to reform markets and remove distortions. The main results are summarised in Table 2.9. Countries are grouped on the basis of the overall distortion index into high, medium and low categories, and the simple averages of the various performance indicators are calculated for each group. It is clear that the low distortion group has a superior performance on the basis of all indicators shown; for example, in terms of industry growth its annual growth of 9 per cent is 3 percentage points above the overall average for the

Table 2.9: Price distortions and growth performance[a] in the 1970s

Countries by distortion group	Annual GDP growth (%)	Annual growth of industry (%)	Annual growth of exports (%)
Low	6.8	9.1	6.7
Medium	5.7	6.8	3.9
High	3.1	3.2	0.7
Overall average	5.0	6.1	3.5

[a]All measures of performance are simple averages for the groups of countries involved.
Source: World Bank (1983), table 6.1.

sample, and almost 6 percentage points above the average for the high distortion group.

A further test of the relationship between distortions and growth is the use of cross-sectional regression analysis; this is intended to allow for variations between countries within each distortion group. This analysis shows a significant negative correlation between the distortion index and growth, with the index explaining about one-third of the variation in performance between countries. This is a reasonably high correlation for this type of analysis, but it should be noted that certain countries grew more rapidly in the 1970s than predicted by the equation — including South Korea, Brazil, Indonesia, Ivory Coast, Egypt and Nigeria — whilst others performed markedly worse than predicted — including Ethiopia, Jamaica, Ghana and India. World Bank (1983) acknowledges that whilst prices are important for growth, 'many other elements, not least natural resource endowment, as well as other economic, social and political, and institutional factors would need to be considered in a more complete explanation to account fully for the variation in growth rates'.[42]

Comment has been made earlier on the poor quality of some of the estimates of distortion used in the compilation of the index. Setting this aside, however, it is important to note that these results are open to more than one interpretation. World Bank (1983) sees the negative relation between distortions and performance as clear support for the view that if markets do not function effectively economic efficiency and growth will suffer. The argument is summarised succinctly by the statement that 'in short the statistical analysis clearly suggests that prices matter for growth'. The implication is that if prices can reach levels that reflect economic values performance will be much improved. There are many reasons advanced in the literature to explain why this may be the case. Protection, for example, may shelter high cost producers and create a bias against exports. Similarly, technology choice may be biased in an inappropriate direction, due to factor market distortions, and specialisation along the lines of existing resource endowments may be hindered. Such arguments suggest that causation runs directly from high distortions to low growth. However the evidence is open to another interpretation. Some would argue that in many developing countries growth is held back by various structural rigidities; for example, lack of domestic entrepreneurs and skilled workers may make it difficult to increase domestic supply of many commodities in the short-run; the inability of the government to raise revenue may restrict the level of investment, and export earnings may be held back by external constraints. In this view distortions can be the sympton of structural problems rather than the fundamental cause of low growth. It is interesting that World Bank (1983) finds the exchange rate to be the single most significant individual distortion. However one would expect an economy, with what may be termed a structural balance of payments problem — a small non-traditional export sector and a high propensity to import — to experience low growth, since whenever incomes rise significantly the absolute increase in imports will exceed the foreign exchange that the export sector can generate. In these circumstances growth may be curtailed for balance of payments reasons, and to conserve foreign exchange such an economy may have to establish an import controls system — inevitably raising the effective rate of protection granted to many producers. There may also be a real exchange rate appreciation, if structural bottlenecks create a higher rate of domestic inflation than in trading competitors. In such circumstances, low growth will be accompanied by distortions, as measured by high ERPs and exchange rate appreciation. However, such distortions are not necessarily the underlying causes of low growth, which in this view lie in the structural characteristics of the economy. One need not generalise this argument too far, since the interpretation of the relation between distortions and growth will be determined by a reading of the constraints faced by particular economies. There is no reason, however, why causation should always lie in a single direction. In some countries, at some times, distortions as defined here may contribute directly to poor economic performance, as World Bank (1983) suggests. In other circumstances, however, they may simply reflect more fundamental structural problems, so that removal of the distortions alone would not be a long-term solution.

To summarise therefore there is little doubt that the evidence can support the view that price policy has an important influence on performance, both in general and in the industrial sector in particular. However it certainly does not imply that only price policy is important. Furthermore a

Structuralist interpretation of the results would argue that there are reasons, relating to the structure of economies, that cause the observed trends that have been termed distortions. A narrow focus on distortions alone, in this view, would be simply a concern for symptoms not real causes.

Dependence and growth

Many studies consider whether a link can be established between a measure of dependence and economic performance. As noted earlier, probably the most common quantitative indicator of dependence is some measure of transnational corporation involvement in an economy. A large number of studies, for example, test for a statistical relationship between transnationals' penetration of an economy and growth in national income.[43] A majority, although not all, find a statistically significant negative relationship between foreign penetration and growth, which they interpret to mean that transnational involvement reduces the growth potential of developing countries. This result appears less frequently for smaller samples of countries, however, since some studies that concentrate on particular geographical regions do not report a significant negative relationship. Bornschier and Chase-Dunn (1985) have carried out a detailed re-examination of this question using a wider sample, and what they see as superior statistical techniques to those used in earlier studies, and their procedures and results are worth noting.

Bornschier and Chase-Dunn work with a sample of 103 countries, including 15 rich countries, and in some analyses divide their sample into sub-groups. They distinguish between short-term and long-term effects of foreign involvement, with the former represented by annual flows of direct foreign investment (1967–73), and the latter by a measure of the accumulated stock of foreign-owned capital in 1967 relative to the size of the total capital and labour force in the economy. This latter measure is what they term an index of penetration, and this index is calculated both for the whole economy and for individual sectors, including manufacturing. The variables covering transnational involvement are included in a multiple regression model to explain growth of GNP per capita for the period 1965–77.[44] The foreign capital stock refers to a year at the start of the period under consideration to avoid the charge that it is growth that determines foreign penetration and not vice-versa. The results indicate that both variables covering foreign economic involvement are statistically significant, when one considers the full sample of countries. The short-run variable — the annual flow of foreign investment — has a positive sign, and the long-run variable — reflecting foreign penetration — a negative sign. This is consistent with the authors' hypothesis, that the initial impact of foreign investment on growth will be positive, since foreign investment inflows will both increase foreign reserves and the funds available for investment. However, they argue, over time a number of effects harmful for growth will arise from transnational involvement in the economy. These results do not hold for the sub-sample of rich economies where the sign for the foreign penetration variable is positive but not significant. This is interpreted by the authors to imply an asymmetrical relationship, with foreign capital only creating negative growth effects in developing not developed countries. When foreign involvement in specific sectors is considered similar results are found. For example, for developing countries foreign penetration in the manufacturing sector is also found to be negatively related to growth and statistically significant.

These results can be seen as strongly supportive of much of the Radical and Dependency literature on development and industrialisation, that stresses the retarding effects foreign investment may have on developing countries. Chapter 4 discusses many of the arguments put forward to explain why there is likely to be a negative relationship between foreign involvement and growth. There it is stressed that many of these are not wholly convincing, in the sense that they do not demonstrate that foreign investment will inevitably have a negative impact. The evidence from careful cross-sectional studies, such as that of Bornschier and Chase-Dunn, cannot be dismissed lightly. However, as in the case of the distortions study, there can be varying interpretations of the evidence.

It is possible, for example, that the results may be transitory; that is, valid only for the period concerned. If the 1970s prove to be an unusual decade because of oil price rises and the deflationary policies pursued in many of the developed economies, it may be that relations valid from this decade will not hold in the future. This objection can be raised against any analysis of this type.

On the other hand, it may be that that foreign penetration and low growth are both explained by a third variable. What this third variable might be is an open question. It does not appear that the distortions considered in the previous section can play the role, since foreign penetration in an economy does not appear to be linked closely with the level of distortion.

Perhaps more important than these speculative comments is the point that a negative statistical association between high foreign involvement and growth cannot itself prove that foreign penetration caused individual countries to grow below their productive potential, which is what the Dependency argument implies. It might be that some relatively slow growing countries might have grown even slower without the level of foreign penetration they experienced. Foreign penetration may have been high in economies where growth potential itself was low, for example because of a specialisation in natural resources, or commodities, for which world market prospects were poor in the 1970s. In this case countries' growth performance, whilst low, may still not have been low relative to the potential of the economy over the period studied. This point is less relevant, however, where foreign investment in manufacturing is the main form of foreign penetration.

Even allowing for these qualifications these results must be taken as a clear caution against uncritical acceptance of arguments that stress the merits of foreign investment by transnational corporations as an effective means of stimulating industrialisation and economic development in general.

Socialist industrialisation — comparative performance

Broad comparisons of performance between socialist and non-socialist developing countries are difficult, not only because of the problems of obtaining reliable comparable data for many poor socialist economies, but also because performance within the group of socialist developing economies has been very uneven. In some cases poor economic performance reflects the fact that new socialist regimes emerged after a period of severe internal dislocation, and have encountered the hostility of powerful capitalist neighbours; the recent experience of Nicaragua, Mozambique and Angola illustrates this. However aggregate data for groups of socialist economies post-1960 indicate an economic performance at least comparable with capitalist economies. (Chapter 1 of this book has given figures on the rapid growth of industry in Centrally Planned Economies although these cover only the USSR and the East European socialist countries.) Gurley (1979) calculates the average annual growth of GNP *per capita* 1960–74 for a group of 13 'Marxian socialist countries'. The average for this group of 3.7 per cent per annum, can be compared with 4.2 per cent for the advanced capitalist economies, and 3.1 per cent for non-socialist developing countries.[45]

However because of the diversity of experience just referred to it is necessary to look a little more closely at the performance of individual countries. Table 2.10 covers the economies referred to earlier in Table 2.6 on which adequate data are available. Of the countries classed as socialist, four — Angola, Congo, Benin and Mozambique — have growth rates below the average for all developing countries of their income group. However the remaining six have above-average rates of growth. For the more ambiguous group of intermediate regimes six have below-average, and five above-average, growth for their income group. There are extreme performances within the group of countries covered in Table 2.10, with several, particularly Angola, Mozambique and Somalia experiencing real declines in income *per capita*, and a substantial real fall in manufacturing production. In others such as Romania, Yugoslavia, North Korea and China the record is very different with rapid growth in real income *per capita* and an impressive expansion in manufacturing. The case for including North Korea and China in the list of NICs has already been commented upon. It is worth noting that North Korea's growth appears to exceed that of its neighbour South Korea, whose performance has received so much attention in the literature on industrialisation. Also growth in China has been both above average for low-income developing countries, and substantially in excess of that of India, with which it is often compared due to their similarity in size.[46]

Socialist regimes in developing countries have been criticised for their record on human rights.[47] None the less

Table 2.10: Performance and structure: socialist and intermediate developing countries

	Growth of GNP per capita (1960–82) % per annum	Growth of manufacturing (1970–82) % per annum	Share of industry in GDP (1982) %	Share of manufacturing in GDP (1982) %
Socialist developing countries				
Middle-income				
Angola	−2.3	−12.0[a]	23.0[a]	3.0[a]
Congo	2.7	3.3	52.0	5.0
Cuba	—	7.9[a]	67.0[a]	—
North Korea	6.7[a]	15.9[a]	—	—
Romania	5.1	8.6	57.0	14.0
Yemen P.D.R.	6.4	—	27.0	
Low-income				
Benin	0.6	—	13.0	7.0
China	5.0	8.3[b]	47.0[a]	41.0
Ethiopia	1.4	2.9	16.0	11.0
Mozambique	−0.1	−5.8	16.0[a]	9.0[a]
Intermediate regimes				
Middle-income				
Algeria	3.2	10.9	55.0	10.0
Libya	4.1	14.7	68.0	3.0
Nicaragua	0.2	2.5	32.0	26.0
Yugoslavia	4.9	8.2	45.0	32.0
Zambia	−0.1	1.4	36.0	19.0
Zimbabwe	1.5	−4.1	35.0	25.0

	Growth of GNP per capita (1960–82) % per annum	Growth of manufacturing (1970–82) % per annum	Share of industry in GDP (1982) %	Share of manufacturing in GDP (1982) %
Low-income				
Burma	1.3	4.7	13.0	9.0
Guinea	1.5	—	23.0	2.0
Madagascar	−0.5	—	15.0	—
Somalia	−0.1	−3.8[a]	11.0[a]	7.0[a]
Tanzania	1.9	0.5	15.0	9.0
All developing countries				
Middle-income[c]	3.6	5.5	38.0	20.0
Low-income[d]	1.1	3.2	16.0	9.0

[a] Data from White (1984), table 1, pp. 106–7. Growth of GNP per capita covers 1960–80, growth of manufacturing covers 1970–80, and the shares of industry and manufacturing refer to 1980.

[b] Data refer to the growth of industry 1970–82.

[c] Socialist and non-socialist.

[d] Socialist and non-socialist, excluding India and China.

Source: World Bank (1984) except when otherwise stated.

where data are available they indicate that several have made impressive progress in the areas of poverty eradication and income redistribution. Countries where evidence of good performance in this area is available are China, Cuba and Yugoslavia, and in these countries, at least, there are strong grounds for believing that income redistribution and poverty alleviation have been carried much further than would be expected under an alternative economic system.[48] Chinese success in this area has been widely acknowledged and represents the clearest example of a socialist economy successfully combining an industrialisation programme with measures to raise living standards and to meet basic social needs.[49]

In planning of the provision of consumer goods and mass public services, it is argued that policies were effective in keeping down retail prices, and providing adequate health, education and welfare services. The Chinese system of rationing appears to have been much more successful than the system used in other socialist economies.[50]

To summarise this section, it is not possible to come to general conclusions on the comparative effectiveness of socialist as compared with non-socialist development strategies. The experience of socialist regimes — assuming that one can arrive at an acceptable working definition — is too varied for this type of conclusion to be drawn. A form of socialism has been pursued in a variety of material circumstances, and based on different combinations of class alignments. If socialism is an historical alternative to capitalism it is not clear that as practised in the Third World it is inevitably more progressive in material terms, nor that it is necessarily more humane. However it has proved to be a viable and relatively egalitarian model of development for some countries.

COMPARATIVE PERFORMANCE IN INCOME DISTRIBUTION

Most discussions of the relation between income distribution and development start with the hypothesis associated with Kuznets (1955) that as incomes rise income distribution worsens initially, but later improves after a certain income level is passed. This is often termed the 'inverted U-shaped curve' hypothesis. Most cross-section analyses of income equality and income *per capita* across a range of countries have found some support for the hypothesis, although in some cases the statistical relationship is only weak.[51] The theory behind the inverted U-shaped curve relation is that income *per capita* can be taken as a proxy for the level of development, and that changes in development will be associated with changes in the structure of an economy that are likely to have important distributional consequences. Changes in the economy at early stages of development that can worsen income distribution are thought to include an expansion of the modern, largely manufacturing sector relative to traditional activities, such as agriculture, and an increase in both the capital and the skill-intensity of production.

However, the implication of results such as these needs to be clarified. They are best interpreted to imply an average relationship across a range of countries of different income levels and characteristics, not an iron law. Individual countries can diverge from this pattern as a result of the policies they choose to pursue, or as a result of national peculiarities, such as resource endowments. Furthermore these studies do not support the view that it is a fast growth of income that creates greater inequality. The relationship appears to be a secular one between levels of income and inequality, and the speed at which a particular income level is reached does not appear to be a significant factor for income distribution. Some countries that have grown fast, such as Brazil in the 1960s, have experienced greater inequality than would be predicted by their level of income, whilst other fast growers, such as Taiwan in the 1960s and 1970s, have not.[52]

Since policy choice is an important element of performance in income distribution one can consider whether the distinctions relating to industrial policy used in this chapter are helpful in explaining comparative trends in income distribution. Reference has been made in the previous section to the relatively good performance in this area of certain socialist developing economies. Cuba, China and Yugoslavia are countries in this group for which detailed estimates are available, which indicate a degree of equality in income distribution well above that expected for the countries' income level.[53] A similar pattern is well established for the East European socialist economies, but relatively little is known about the trends in income distribution in the majority of socialist developing countries. However it would be misleading to imply that a simple dichotomy between socialist and capitalist development strategies can explain the different experiences of countries in this area. A small number of capitalist developing economies have also achieved a level of equality in income distribution well above the average for their income level. The 'Gang of Four' fall into this group, and in Taiwan, Singapore and Hong Kong rapid growth has been accompanied by an improvement in the distribution of income. In South Korea there was a moderate worsening from the mid-1960s to mid-1970s, although distribution is still relatively egalitarian.[54]

The distinction between trade strategies is also not particularly helpful in explaining performance in income distribution. As we have seen the outward-looking South East Asian economies have performed well in distributional terms, but this is not the case for Brazil in its outward-looking phase during the late 1960s and early 1970s. Further the inward-looking socialist economy of China has also done well in this area. Some of the complexity in judging country performance can be seen from the data in Table 2.11 on the twelve countries for which detailed comparisons over time are possible. Good performers are those with a level of equality (defined as the income share of the bottom 60 per cent of the population) above that predicted by their level of income. Intermediate performers are those with a more or less average level of equality, and poor performers are those where equality is below that expected for their income level.

The group of good performers include two members of the 'Gang of Four' for which data are available — Taiwan and South Korea — plus Yugoslavia, Sri Lanka and Costa Rica. Of these Yugoslavia was outward-looking, in terms of its incentive structure in the 1960s, but as noted earlier had begun to penalise exports by the end of the decade. Sri Lanka was a protected inward-looking economy for this period. Costa Rica's position is unclear. All of the intermediate and poor performers are generally associated with inward-looking strategies at this time. Brazil is the partial exception, starting the period under study as an inward-looking economy but shifting by the end of the decade to an outward-looking position.

Several explanations can be put forward to account for these

Table 2.11: Income distribution performance. Selected countries

Country	Period of observation	Share of bottom 60%			Growth of Income (% per annum)	
		Initial year	Final year	Incremental	Average	Bottom 60%
I Good performance						
Taiwan	1964–74	0.369	0.385	0.395	6.6	7.1
Yugoslavia	1963–73	0.357	0.360	0.365	4.2	4.3
Sri Lanka	1963–73	0.274	0.354	0.513	2.0	4.6
South Korea	1965–76	0.349	0.323	0.311	8.7	7.9
Costa Rica	1961–71	0.237	0.284	0.336	3.2	5.1
II Intermediate performance						
India	1954–64	0.310	0.292	0.258	2.3	1.6
Philippines	1961–71	0.247	0.248	0.250	2.2	2.3
Turkey	1963–73	0.208	0.240	0.279	3.6	5.1
Colombia	1964–74	0.190	0.212	0.240	3.1	4.3
III Poor performance						
Brazil	1960–70	0.248	0.206	0.155	3.1	1.2
Mexico	1963–75	0.217	0.197	0.180	3.2	2.4
Peru	1961–71	0.179	0.179	0.179	2.3	2.3

Source: Data taken from Chenery et al. (1979), table 11.5, p. 482.

performances. A point raised frequently in the Neoclassical literature is that export-oriented strategies encourage production based on labour-intensive techniques, and that this pattern of growth generates a strong demand for labour. For example, in the case of the 'Gang of Four' it is often suggested that over this period the labour surplus in these economies was removed, so that real wages and employment rose thus increasing the incomes of lower-income groups and thereby contributing to the relatively egalitarian trends in income distribution in these countries. Also it is argued that countries that introduce asset redistribution, particularly land, prior to the commencement of a period of rapid growth, tend to have a relatively equal distribution of the benefits of growth. This explanation appears to have a direct relevance to Taiwan and South Korea, where land reforms were instituted in the early post-war years, and also although the circumstances were different, to Yugoslavia and China.

Government commitment to equity as a policy objective cannot be overlooked, and it is important to note that the largest redistribution reported in Table 2.11 over the periods studied occurred in the relatively protected inward-looking economy of Sri Lanka. There the incomes of the bottom 60 per cent grew by more than twice the national average. Prior to the change of regime in the mid-1970s, the Sri Lankan government had operated a major subsidy programme, particularly for foodstuffs. One interpretation is that this programme reduced the potential investible surplus of the economy by transferring resources to consumption, and contributed strongly to 'slow growth with equity'.[55] Another view is that despite low overall growth the incomes of the bottom 60 per cent still grew by nearly 5 per cent per year (1963–73) which is a major achievement.

Poor performances in terms of income distribution have been found for some of the larger generally inward-looking capitalist economies where growth has been accompanied by a worsening of the distribution of income. The three poor performers in Table 2.11 illustrate this. The Neoclassical explanation for this inegalitarian development is that the capital-intensity of production in inward-looking economies, where capital costs are kept artificially low, slows the growth of employment and real wages. One can add to this explanation the high profits generated by the trade controls system, that in

72

these economies go to protected domestic or foreign capitalists. However it is also clear that within the group of inward-looking economies policy emphases will be important. For example, from Table 2.11 India is shown to have performed better, in terms of the share of incremental income going to the bottom 60 per cent, than any of the three Latin American countries. This is likely to be related to the greater emphasis placed on distributional issues by Indian governments, as compared with regimes in Latin America. None the less it should not be forgotten that despite a reasonably good distributional performance over this period, the incomes of the bottom 60 per cent in India still grew only slowly, because of the low overall growth of the economy. This brings one back to the question of whether in India over this period, as in Sri Lanka, there was a trade-off between growth and equity.

It is worth noting also that in terms of indicators of poverty alleviation, such as improvement in life-expectancy and literacy, the countries with the most impressive performances have very different socio-economic systems. Sen (1981), for example, calculates indices of longevity and literacy improvement for the 1960s and 1970s and finds the four most impressive performers in terms of the former to be Vietnam, Cuba, Taiwan and Hong Kong. For the latter the four best performers are South Korea, Hong Kong, Tanzania and Taiwan. The implication is that what in some countries can be achieved by market forces, can be achieved in others by government commitment and intervention.

It is also necessary to consider briefly whether the other distinctions discussed here, of distortionary and non-distortionary, and dependent and non-dependent policies, can be linked with country performance in income distribution. Since both the studies cited in relation to these classifications are based on cross-section regression analysis one can report whether the measures used, of either distortion or dependence, are significant variables for explaining the level of income inequality across countries. In the distortion study, the distortion index whilst positively correlated with inequality does not appear statistically significant. Thus for the period examined there are no grounds for linking performance in distribution with the level of distortion in an economy. On the other hand, Agarwala (1983) notes that a justification often given for government interventions that may result in distortions, is the beneficial effect of such interventions on income distribution. No evidence of this beneficial effect is found from these results. In the case of the dependency analysis, however, a statistically significant positive relation exists between the measure of dependence used — that is an index based on transnational penetration of an economy — and income inequality. In other words, dependent economies, by this definition, tend to have a relatively inegalitarian income distribution.[56] This relation holds only for developing countries, however, not for rich economies. Bornschier and Chase-Dunn (1985) interpret causation as running from transnational penetration to income inequality. It is suggested that transnationals create inequality through different mechanisms depending upon the sectors in which they are involved. For example, in export-oriented production transnationals need low wage costs, and with government collaboration wages may be held down to meet their requirements. As for import-substitute production for the domestic market, here it is argued that transnationals are concerned that there will be a domestic elite with an income sufficient to afford the type of goods in which they specialise. Income inequality becomes a prerequisite for selling their goods domestically, and transnationals will therefore support regimes that can guarantee this pattern of income distribution. The difficulty with this type of reasoning is that it rests on propositions from Dependency theory on the impact of transnationals on developing countries that are being questioned increasingly. An alternative explanation of the same data is that transnationals may be attracted to economies where income inequality is already high. Such countries may be attractive sites for transnational investment because of the size of their domestic markets or the natural resources they possess. Thus it can be argued that causation runs from inequality in income to transnational penetration, rather than vice-versa.[57]

To summarise, the policy implications of the evidence discussed in this section are ambiguous, in that it is clear that good performance in income distribution and poverty alleviation has been achieved under a variety of strategies and in very different social and political situations.

CONCLUSION

This chapter has considered different perspectives on industrial policy in developing countries, and discussed how individual countries have been classified on the basis of their policies. No universally acceptable classification is possible, given differences of definition between different studies, and the changing nature of policy in many countries. A major concern of studies that use these types of classification is to find a link between policy emphasis and overall economic performance. The evidence on this has been discussed at some length, although perhaps not surprisingly it is difficult to arrive at definitive conclusions.

A few points can be agreed however. In the period since 1960 a relatively small number of developing countries have performed well in terms of growth of both GNP and industry. Several of these countries have also done well in distributional terms. Up to the early 1970s it was not easy to distinguish between countries within this group on the basis of trade policy, but in the turmoil of the 1970s the outward-looking sub-group — whose performance was strongly influenced by the 'Gang of Four' — appear to have done considerably better than the inward-looking economies. However, this cannot be interpreted to mean that all outward-looking economies automatically do well, since there are well-known failures as well as successes, nor that many other countries can necessarily emulate the growth rates of the 'Gang of Four'.

Some inward-looking economies have a creditable growth record, particularly the socialist economies of China and North Korea, although for a number of reasons it is not meaningful to compare aggregate performance between groups of socialist and capitalist developing countries. Highly distorted economies have not, in general, done well in growth and distribution. Whilst the analysis on which this result is based has some limitations, this general conclusion stands. What is of more concern is how to interpret distortions. Are they fundamental causes of low growth or just symptoms of more profound structural imbalances in the economy? Finally on the question of dependence and transnational involvement, one of the unambiguous results to emerge is the negative correlation between degree of transnational penetration and economic performance in developing countries. Transnational penetration therefore tends to be highest where growth is relatively low; however, whether their heavy involvement reduces growth below its productive potential is not established clearly by this evidence.

The ambiguous nature of these results is such that they are unlikely to create converts from one school of thought to another. Most statistical evidence is open to varying interpretations, and legitimate areas of dispute remain. The purpose of the chapters that follow is to explore the theoretical arguments that underlie different analyses of industrial performance and policy. Of particular concern will be arguments on import-substitution and export promotion strategies; the role of prices and markets in industrial policy, and the scope for state intervention to control these; the efficiency of past industrialisation programmes and the possibility of stimulating improvements over time; and the significance of transnational corporation involvement in industrialisation in developing countries. The final chapter, Chapter 8, returns to the question of the different aspects of industrial policy.

NOTES

1. For example see the discussion in World Bank (1981).
2. Krueger (1978) defines this situation formally, as one where for year t, $B_t > 1.0$, and B_t is defined as below:

$$B_t = \frac{(1 + m + n + p)_t}{(1 + r + s)_t}$$

and m is the rate of import tariff
   n is the rate of import surcharge
   p is the rate of scarcity premium created by import licensing
   r is the rate of export encouragement schemes, other than direct subsidies
   s is the rate of export subsidies
   the subscript t refers to year t.

The numerator $(1 + m + n + p)$ gives the degree to which the domestic price of an importable is raised above its world price by a protective system that may involve tariffs, surcharges and licences for imports. Similarly the denominator $(1 + r + s)$ shows the degree to which domestic prices for an exportable are raised above world prices by subsidies or other forms of encouragement. Any export taxes would be treated as a negative subsidy. Where $B > 1.0$ domestic prices for importables will exceed world prices for the same goods, by more than the domestic prices of exportables exceed their world prices, and thus greater incentive will be given for import-substitution than for export. This ratio can be calculated at different levels; for individual commodities, for branches of a sector, for different sectors, or for the economy as a whole. At this last level one will be aggregating over all importables and exportables, and it is this calculation that will be most relevant for the classification of economies as inward-looking.

In contrast following this approach outward-looking economies are those where the bias against exports is removed, and in the aggregate net incentives to domestic sales and exports are equal. In Krueger's formal definition in outward-looking economies, $B_t = 1.0$. A value of $B_t < 1.0$, implies a pro-export bias in incentives and this is taken as an extreme case of outward-looking policies.

An alternative approach to anti-export bias is to use effective rate of protection estimates for home and export sales. This approach is discussed in Chapter 5.

3. This is the approach in the major studies Chenery (1979) and Chenery and Syrquin (1975).

4. These figures relate to the late 1960s; see Balassa (1982), table 2.3, pp. 28–9.

5. For evidence of this see Agarwala (1983), table 1, p. 14. Krueger (1978) points to the removal of import quotas and their substitution by tariffs in her survey of trade policies 1950–72 in ten countries.

6. Chenery (1979), pp. 108–40. Here 'large' refers to population size.

7. Ballance et al. (1982), pp. 56–7. Strictly the procedure used explains changes in output composition rather than growth. The precise explanation for the significant differences found by the authors and Chenery, when the latter uses the same procedures, is not clear.

8. Agarwala (1983) gives the detailed analysis on which the discussion is based.

9. Evans and Alizadeh (1984), p. 45, for example, question the classification of Chile as a high distortion economy. The treatment of Chile is of significance because of the attempt in Agarwala (1983) and World Bank (1983) to link high distortions with low growth.

10. For a discussion of the alternative approaches to weighting considered see Agarwala (1983), p. 34.

11. Agarwala (1983), p. 35, comments that: 'An analysis of distortion indices . . . shows, however, that the degree of collinearity among price distortions is not particularly high. Although some countries manage to distort almost all the major prices, in most cases, high distortions in some prices are associated with low distortions in others.'

12. Agarwala (1983), p. 37. This point acknowledges that markets alone cannot always find the 'correct' long-run price, and thus questions whether short-run market-clearing prices and economic values can be equated.

13. This list follows Lall (1975).

14. Transnationals can be defined as firms investing in more than one country and supplying more than financial capital; for example management, technology or marketing expertise. Investments of this

type are direct investments rather than portfolio investment where shares alone are purchased without the provision of non-financial inputs. Some studies define transnationals more strictly, however, requiring that they invest in a minimum number of countries, for example six, before they are sufficiently international to be termed transnational.

15. This is the sense in which the concept of dependence is used in Bornschier and Chase-Dunn (1985), for example. The authors distinguish between 'classic dependence' based on mining and primary goods, and the 'dependent industrialisation' that has arisen post-1960.

16. Lall (1975), p. 10, points out that: 'Canada and Belgium are more "dependent" on foreign investment than are India or Pakistan, yet they are presumably not in the category of dependent countries. The relative economic dominance of MNCs (multinational corporations) does not seem to vary on a consistent basis between dependent and non-dependent countries . . .'

17. See Kaplinsky (1984a) for example.

18. In 1978–80 developing countries with an income *per capita* of over US$3000 received 65 per cent of all foreign investment in developing countries whilst their share in population was only around 25 per cent. On the other hand the very poorest countries with an income *per capita* of below US$380 and roughly 60 per cent of the population of developing countries received below 5 per cent of foreign investment; see UNCTC (1983) p. 28.

19. Japanese transnationals diverge from this pattern, often investing in textiles and mineral processing. For textiles it appears to be a case of shifting traditional industries from Japan to lower wage sites; for minerals the objective of controlling raw material supplies seems the most important explanation; see Ozawa (1979).

20. See the data in UNCTC (1983), tables II.24 and II.25, pp. 351–2.

21. By 1980 it is estimated that 963 firms from developing countries had set up 1964 overseas subsidiaries and branches of which 938 were in manufacturing. The total direct foreign investment involved is put at somewhere between US$5 to US$10 billion, in comparison with a total stock of foreign investment in developing countries of US$119 billion; see Jenkins (1986).

22. Lall (1984b), pp. 1–18, and pp. 259–62, questions the conventional view as exemplified by Wells (1983).

23. Bornschier and Chase-Dunn (1985) give an index of transnational penetration for 103 countries for the year 1967 based on the relation between capital assets that are foreign owned, total capital stock and total population. South Korea and Taiwan are well below average for the whole sample by this index.

24. The Spearman rank correlation coefficient is -0.32, and is not significant at the 5 per cent level.

25. World Bank (1983), pp. 47–56.

26. White (1984) does not provide a definition of an 'intermediate regime'. However his use of the term appears to depart from the original definition of Kalecki (1976), since White writes of 'socialist

intermediate regimes'. In Kalecki's original discussion intermediate regimes are transitional, as yet neither capitalist nor socialist. The concept of an intermediate regime is discussed further in Chapter 4.

27. For example Jameson (1981) classes Guyana and Cuba as intermediate regimes, and Gurley (1979) questions whether Ethiopia and Benin can be classified as socialist.

28. Several chapters in White *et al*. (1983) cover reform proposals discussed in these countries in the late 1970s and early 1980s.

29. By the late 1960s around 20 per cent of additional manufacturing output was exported; see Balassa (1982), table 3.2, p. 46.

30. See Carciofi (1983), p. 198. Fitzgerald (1985) has a theoretical discussion of this general approach arguing that in such small 'peripheral socialist economies' capital goods should be seen as the product of the foreign trade sector. This is a major departure from socialist planning models, for example following the Russian economist Feldman, that assume closed economies.

31. White (1984), p. 114. This classification makes no reference to the East European regimes Yugoslavia and Romania that are listed in Table 2.7 nor to the majority of intermediate regimes. Also White has difficulty in placing Cuba and Vietnam. Cuba is a relatively long-standing socialist regime, but shares many of the characteristics of the 'second wave' countries. Vietnam also has had a socialist regime for a relatively long period, but has been prevented by war from following the path of China and North Korea.

32. White (1983), p. 3.

33. See for example World Bank (1981), pp. 65–83.

34. See Balassa (1984a), table 2, p. 960. In this context import-substitution is defined as savings in imports associated with a decrease in the income elasticity of demand for imports compared with the elasticity estimate for 1963–73, which is taken as the base period.

35. For example, Michaely (1977) finds no significant relationship for the sub-group of poorer countries in his sample, which leads him to conclude that 'growth is affected by export performance only once countries achieve some minimum level of development.' On similar grounds Tyler (1981) works only with middle-income developing countries.

36. Ram (1985) shows that the importance of exports for growth increased during the 1970s, and that the differential between its importance for higher income as compared with lower income developing countries diminished during this decade.

37. Taylor *et al*. (1984), pp. 19–22, and pp. 27–8.

38. 'Each of the four strategies for transforming the structure of production and trade [see Table 2.2] has produced its share of successes and failures in the period following World War II. Success in sustaining relatively high rates of growth has depended more on the ability to modify trade and investment policies in the light of the results achieved than on the initial choice of strategy.' (Chenery 1979, p. 44).

39. Fishlow (1984) raises some technical points on Balassa's methodology, and feels that despite the evidence presented 'the policy question is not closed'. The poor performance of Chile and Uruguay is discussed further in Chapter 7.

40. Export-orientation of the 'Gang of Four' is taken as their manufactured export share in GDP relative to the norm for countries of their population and income level. To calculate the growth of manufactured exports from other developing countries it is assumed that their deviation from their own norm is the same as that of the 'Gang of Four'.

41. See the debate between Ranis (1985a) and Cline (1985).

42. World Bank (1983), p. 63.

43. Bornschier and Chase-Dunn (1985), pp. 68–79, review this literature.

44. The levels of income, investment, exports and the size of the domestic market are controlled by including additional independent variables. See Bornschier and Chase-Dunn (1985), table 5, p. 95 for details of the main regression results.

45. Gurley (1979), table 2, p. 188. The 13 covered include the East European countries and China, Cuba, and North Korea but exclude several recently established socialist countries.

46. Directly comparable data are not available for all these four countries; however, recorded manufacturing growth for South Korea given in World Bank (1984) is 14.5 per cent per year 1970–82, compared with the figure of 15.9 per cent for North Korea in Table 2.10 covering 1970–80. Manufacturing growth in India is given in World Bank (1984) as 4.3 per cent per year (1970–82) compared with 8.3 per cent for China over the same period.

47. Jameson and Wilber (1981), p. 805, comment that '. . . the usual definitions growing out of an advanced capitalist context may not be appropriate for a Third World country following a socialist model. But even granting this performance by socialist countries is not impressive . . . the poor performance to date on human rights cannot be overlooked, even if it is seen against a backdrop of similar problems in Chile, Argentina or the whole capitalist sphere.'

48. In a survey of the evidence on income distribution in developing countries Bigsten (1983), p. 76, concludes that: 'As far as one can judge from the sparse data available on socialist countries in the Third World (e.g. China and Cuba) the income distribution in these seems to be more even than in the capitalistic (or mixed) economies about which more is known.'

49. Morawetz (1977), p. 49, suggests that by the 1970s health care in China had reached the standard of the USA in the 1930s; he describes this as a 'remarkable achievement'. See Singh (1979) for a general discussion of economic policy in China.

50. Griffin and James (1981), pp. 82–97, compare rationing systems in Chile (under Allende), Cuba and China, and find the greater selectivity of the Chinese system to have been more effective.

51. See, for example, Ahluwalia (1976), Chenery and Syrquin (1975) and Adelman and Morris (1973).

52. Morawetz (1977), p. 41.

53. For data on Cuba see Jameson (1981); for China, Bigsten (1983); and for Yugoslavia, Chenery et al. (1979).

54. Chenery et al. (1979) give data on South Korea and Taiwan.

Hsia and Chau (1978) give data on Hong Kong. Chenery (1980) asserts that distribution has also improved in Singapore.

55. There is some conflict between the income distribution data for Sri Lanka given in Chenery *et al.* (1979) and that in Morawetz (1980). The latter gives a much less favourable picture of the achievements of the Sri Lankan government.

56. This result has been found in most earlier studies in this area; see Bornschier and Chase-Dunn (1985), pp. 117–19.

57. There is evidence of this in relation to foreign investments in extractive activities. Adelman and Morris (1973) show that a greater endowment of natural resources is correlated with higher inequality. Foreign investment in mining will be correlated with natural resource endowments, and thus with income inequality.

3

Industry and Development:
A Structuralist Perspective

The previous chapters surveyed the broad empirical evidence on industrialisation in developing countries since 1960 and considered several general issues relating to policy and economic performance. It is necessary to go beyond this, however, and discuss the alternative theoretical approaches to the question of the role of industry in economic development, and of how best to encourage industrialisation. Early development economists in the late-1940s and 1950s were almost unanimous in stressing the importance of industrialisation and this chapter picks out some of their major arguments and attempts to qualify them in the light of both experience and subsequent theoretical developments.

The case discussed here can be seen as part of the Structuralist approach to development economics which, in the words of Hirschman, starts from the proposition that 'certain special features of the economic structure of the underdeveloped countries make an important portion of orthodox analysis inapplicable and misleading'.[1]

This approach covers a wide range of authors but can be seen as possessing several key characteristics:

- a belief that development is a process of major structural transformation with industry, and manufacturing in particular, having a major role: from this it follows that national income figures alone cannot be used to assess the level of development, since reference must be made to the production structure, that generates this income, and its capacity for creating future growth;
- a scepticism regarding the role of the price mechanism as a

means of allocating resources in developing countries, due primarily to the assumed low price elasticities of both supply and demand;

- following from this a belief in the importance of government planning and controls of various types as a means of allocating resources and achieving the structural shifts necessary for development;[2]
- an emphasis on the need to change the pattern of trade, and in particular to reduce the importance of primary exports. This implies the need to protect new industries in developing countries until they are able to compete on equal terms with producers overseas.

The Structuralist approach has diverse origins. In one sense it can be seen in the tradition of the Classical economists and Marx, who saw industry in general, and manufacturing in particular, as having a key role as an engine of growth. More recent antecedents can be identified however. There seems little doubt that the Keynesian system of macro-economics, developed to explain mass unemployment in the capitalist economies, greatly influenced writers like Nurkse and Rosenstein-Rodan. For the developing economies these authors stressed the existence of underemployment rather than open unemployment; however underemployment could also be identified with the failure of the labour market to generate adequate employment and could thus be used to justify active state intervention to raise investment and mobilise the underemployed.

Emphasis on the failure of the price mechanism to clear markets effectively has also been traced to both academic research and government planning in the UK in the 1930s and 1940s. Some of the individuals involved later visited Third World countries, and in particular, it has been suggested that the Latin American authors who worked in the 1950s on the so-called Structuralist theory of inflation for their own continent may have been influenced by these contacts.[3]

However despite representing the mainstream of thinking on development problems during the 1950s, Structuralist analysis and the policies derived from it came under increasing criticism in the 1960s and 1970s. Later chapters consider these critiques in relation to industrialisation. At this stage it is necessary simply to note that there are two broad lines of attack. One is associated with the Neoclassical school who stress the neglect in much of the early development economics of some of the fundamental precepts of conventional economic theory, such as the importance of prices for resource allocation and the role of comparative advantage in planning trade possibilities. On the other hand Structuralist analysis also comes under attack from what can loosely be termed the Radical perspective, chiefly for its inability to analyse class formations in developing countries, and for its insufficient emphasis on the constraints to development posed by the external economic environment.

Before turning to an examination of the Structuralist case for industrialisation, it must be stressed that the arguments that will be considered here should not be interpreted as part of a debate on the merits of giving priority to industry over other sectors, particularly agriculture. Some early discussions might have had such an emphasis, but it has long been recognised that simple notions of priority have to give way to an awareness of the interrelationships between sectors. There is no reason why all economic activities should grow at the same rate or require the same amount of resources. What is important is that bottlenecks should not emerge due to the neglect of particular activities. The simple industry or agriculture dichotomy has been replaced, in most discussions, by considerations of the contribution of industry to general economic goals, some of which can include the strengthening of other sectors.

Industry can strengthen agriculture, for example, by providing domestically produced inputs like fertilizers or farm equipment, or alternatively by generating the foreign exchange to import these. On the other hand, it is widely recognised that a strong agricultural sector can foster the expansion of industry by providing raw materials for processing and foodstuffs for industrial workers. In addition, growing agricultural incomes can be a source of demand for industrial goods and of savings for investment in industry. Industrialisation can be held back by a stagnant agricultural sector, so that over-emphasising industry at the expense of agriculture may lead in the longer-term to a rate of industrial growth lower than that possible under a more balanced investment strategy. What is required is that investment is allocated in line with expected returns in alternative activities, and the Structuralist case is that in most countries at relatively low-income levels, this will entail an increasing share of additional resources going to industry. This is not to imply that other sectors, particularly agriculture, should be neglected in the sense of being denied resources for viable investments. It is rather that because of the relatively high returns expected in industry the right balance in sectoral allocations will involve some shift towards industry, and manufacturing in particular.

In policy terms Structuralist authors are associated with the protectionist import-substitution programmes pursued in the majority of developing countries in the 1950s and 1960s, and which, as we have seen, have been criticised for leading to poor economic performances in several countries. The link between actual policy and the arguments considered here is not necessarily direct since, for example, protection often arose from short-run responses to balance of payments difficulties rather than from any long-run industrial strategy. None the less since there is at first sight a similarity between policies actually pursued and the apparent recommendations of many of these authors, it is necessary to consider the extent to which their views on the importance of industrialisation, based on some form of protection from foreign competition, remain valid in the light of experience.

The discussion here is not comprehensive, focusing selectively on what are seen as key contributions. Although there is some overlap the arguments are discussed under the following broad headings:

- foreign trade;
- externalities and linkages;
- infant industries;
- industrial specialisation and dynamic increasing returns.

FOREIGN TRADE

In the 1950s the majority of economists writing on development problems shared the widely held view of 'export-pessimism' regarding traditional primary exports from developing countries. At various times, some of the major economists, for example Nurkse, Prebisch, Lewis and Myrdal, working on development issues, all commented upon the difficulty of expanding rapidly developing countries' exports of these goods. Nurkse (1958) states the case clearly, arguing for the need to base growth on the home market:

Does it not mean turning away from the principles of comparative advantage? Why do these developing countries not push their exports of primary products according to the rules of international specialisation, and import the goods they need for a balanced diet . . . For fairly obvious reasons expansion of primary production for export is apt to encounter adverse price conditions on the world market, unless industrial countries' demand is steadily expanding as it was in the nineteenth century. To push exports in the face of an inelastic or more or less stationary demand would not be a promising line of development.[4]

Since traditional primary exports were seen as incapable of stimulating the domestic economy, local production of new industrial goods for the home market was an obvious alternative. New industries would inevitably be high cost in international terms, and would thus need some protection from import competition. This was generally viewed as an acceptable cost which had to be borne if domestic industry were to become established. Little (1982) is probably fair in his summary of the orthodox position in the 1950s on the issue of industrial protection:

I think that few academics among those who wrote mainly about development . . . would have accepted in the 1950s that developing countries should avoid direct trade controls and have at most a modest tariff . . . Certainly UN officials were not in this camp, and almost no LDC policy-makers would have endorsed such views.[5]

The prospects of significant manufactured exports to developed countries were not considered seriously at this time, given the relatively low level of industrialisation in developing countries, at least outside Latin America. However it is also clear that autarky was not widely advocated, and that the potential gains from trade were not overlooked. For example in the paragraph following Nurkse's quotation given above, he makes it clear that although the inward-looking strategy he is recommending may involve import controls, if national income grows, although the composition of exports and imports may differ from the pre-protection situation, the volume of trade is likely to be higher than it would be in the absence of trade controls, but with a lower level of economic activity. It is not that the significance of export demand was ignored, but that from the perspective of the 1950s exports appeared unpromising, as a source of demand for the newly established manufacturing activities of developing countries.[6]

In this section two distinct strands of the foreign trade pessimism case will be discussed. These have been singled out because of their impact on the perceptions of both economists, and in some countries also policy-makers. The first of these relates to the set of arguments put forward by the Latin American economist, Raul Prebisch, during the 1950s and 1960s when he held senior positions first at the Economic Commission for Latin America (ECLA) and then at the United Nations Conference on Trade and Development (UNCTAD). The second has rather more diverse origins, but is most closely linked with the growth models of the Russian economist Feldman and later the Indian planner Mahanalobis.

The Prebisch case

Prebisch has recently restated his case for industrialisation and placed it in the wider context of both the evolution of his own ideas and his responsibilities within international organisations. He comments revealingly on the polemical nature of some of his early work and the fact that in part it provided ex-post rationalisation for an industrialisation policy which was already being implemented in parts of Latin America.[7]

Prebisch's case for industrialisation is predicated upon a basic distinction, which has now become familiar from the Dependency literature, between the rich countries of the centre and the backward countries of the periphery.[8] Particular structural characteristics of these two groups of countries are seen as determining their trading relationship. Two key points of asymmetry between the two groups are stressed. First, due largely to the different functioning of labour markets, technology-induced productivity changes are seen as having different price effects for the exports of the two groups. Productivity growth in the centre is taken in higher wages, whilst in the periphery in the traditional export sector it leads to lower employment with a consistent downward pressure on wage rates. This asymmetry in reactions to technological progress,

Prebisch argues, is the key explanation for a long-run decline in the prices of the traditional exports of developing countries relative to their imports from the centre.[9]

Second, arising from the production structures in the centre and periphery, there is a clear disparity between the income elasticity of demand in the centre for the traditional exports of the periphery, and the income elasticity of demand in the periphery for the manufactured goods it purchases from the centre. The income elasticity of demand for the peripheries' imports is seen as exceeding substantially that for its exports.

Prebisch's policy prescription of industrialisation based on import substitution follows from these two assertions regarding the relations between centre and periphery. If a secular decline in the terms of trade was an accurate forecast of future trends, as opposed to simply an observation from a particular period, it clearly implies that the route of continued expansion based on traditional exports cannot be relied upon for sustained long-run growth. As Prebisch (1984) later points out it is rational to shift resources into new industrial activity even if this activity is high cost by international standards, provided that the losses sustained through the excess of domestic production costs over the costs of comparable imports, are less than the income losses, which would result from falling export prices as a result of the expansion of traditional exports.[10]

The establishment of new industries was also seen as a means of reducing the income elasticity of demand in the periphery for its manufactured imports from the centre. Prebisch (1964) illustrates the importance of different income elasticities of demand for imports in centre and the periphery with a simple numerical example. He assumes, for simplicity, equal rates of population growth in both areas, and an income elasticity of demand for imports of primary commodities in the centre of 0.8. The periphery exports only primary goods and the centre only manufactures. This means that if income in the centre grows at 3 per cent per year, its import demand for primary commodities, the peripheries' exports, will grow at 2.4 per cent per year. It is assumed also that in the periphery the income elasticity of demand for manufactured imports from the centre is 1.5. If a balance of payments crisis is to be avoided, in the absence of capital inflows, the sustainable income growth rate for the periphery cannot be higher than the rate which generates a growth of imports equal to the growth of exports. In this example, in the absence of favourable capital movements, the sustainable growth rate will be 1.6 per cent per year ($1.6 \times 1.5 = 2.4$). Therefore if income in the periphery were to grow at the same rate as the centre, that is 3.0 per cent, import demand would rise by 4.5 per cent (3.0×1.5) whilst exports of primary commodities would grow at only 2.4 per cent thus creating a balance of payments deficit. In this analysis if the periphery is to achieve a long-run sustainable growth rate, equal to that of the centre, either one or a combination of two changes must take place:

- the income elasticity of demand for manufactured imports will have to be reduced through import substitution; or
- non-traditional exports of manufactures will have to be developed along with primary exports.

It is worth noting that Prebisch does refer to the desirability of developing non-traditional exports, and notes the need to expand customs unions between developing countries as a means of widening their markets. He also comments on the undesirability of policies which create excessive biases against exporting.[11] However, given the relatively undeveloped manufacturing sector in many developing countries in the 1950s, his emphasis was on the role of import substitute industrialisation as the main means of overcoming the foreign exchange bottleneck.

In retrospect it is clear that Prebisch's views were influential in both reflecting and contributing to the foreign trade pessimism of the time. His empirical evidence on the trend in the terms of trade of developing countries was subject to much, often critical, comment, but none the less contributed to an atmosphere of scepticism concerning the potential gains from trade for developing countries. More recent analyses of the question have in fact found support for Prebisch's position, although strictly a decline in the terms of trade is not essential to his case for industrialisation, since a slow growth in world demand for the traditional exports to the centre is sufficient, regardless of the relative price effects.[12] In terms of the broader impact of Prebisch's work it can be argued that his emphasis on the disparity between income elasticities of demand for imports in the centre and periphery was highly influential in bringing the foreign exchange constraint on growth to the centre of the debate on industrialisation.

Prebisch's own definition of the sustainable growth rate, where exports and imports grow at the same rate, can be expressed as

$$g_p = \frac{x_p}{m_p} \qquad (3.1)$$

where g_p is the sustainable growth rate in the periphery

m_p is the periphery's income elasticity of demand for imports from the centre

x_p is the rate of growth of the exports of the periphery

and $x_p = g_c . m_c$

where g_c is the growth rate in the centre

m_c is the centre's income elasticity of demand for imports from the periphery, where $m_p > m_c$

This assumes no capital inflows, and all trade takes place between the centre and periphery only.

In this formulation, equation 3.1 is no more than an identity. However more recent work has expressed the sustainable growth rate in a non-tautological fashion with export and import functions which allow both income and relative price effects to determine export and import growth. The model can be reduced to equation 3.1 however, provided the 'law of one price' assumption is adopted. This implies that for internationally traded goods in all trading partners, divergences between the growth of domestic and world prices are matched over time by offsetting changes in exchange rates.[13]

This reformulation of the equation for long-run sustainable growth allows the simplicity of Prebisch's original argument to be maintained on a more rigorous basis. The balance of payments constraint can be overcome, therefore, either by raising exports, or reducing the income elasticity of demand for imports, or both. However, if developing countries cannot influence their export earnings, and if these grow only slowly, which is the assumption of the export-pessimism case, growth can only be raised by operating on the income elasticity of demand for imports. As we have seen in Prebisch's own policy prescription import-substitution industrialisation was to be the route for achieving this reduction in import demand.

Prebisch's argument provides a useful starting point for consideration of the critiques, raised frequently, regarding the practice of import-substitution. First, in many countries import-substitution has been unsuccessful in reducing the income elasticity of demand for imports in the aggregate. Therefore whilst the composition of imports may change, the overall import intensity of production may be relatively constant. Various explanations have been put forward to account for this, including the difficulty of extending import-substitution to intermediate and capital goods production, and the tendency where income inequality is growing, for shifts in consumer demand towards increasingly import-intensive commodities. Second, in addition, it is argued that import-substitution policies, because of the biases they create in the incentive structure, lower the growth of exports below what would be possible under a less biased system. This latter point is central to the argument on export promotion, and implies that export growth is not given exogenously to individual developing countries, but is open to their influence. In terms of equation 3.1, therefore, it is argued that import-substitution industrialisation in many cases has failed to lower m_p, whilst reducing x_p below its long-run potential.

There is little doubt that both of these points have a validity in several countries, and as a generalisation, it seems safe to argue that import-substitution has led to neglect of the export sector. However what is less certain is that as a strategy import-substitution will automatically create these effects, and one can argue that where it works effectively to reduce m_p, this may more than compensate for any fall in x_p. It is perhaps rather harsh to blame Prebisch for failures of policy that he himself warned of explicitly, and it is by no means certain that import-substitution as a strategy can be rejected for all stages of an economy's development.

Closed economy model

The aspect of the foreign trade pessimism case that will be discussed here is the growth model developed originally by the Russian economist Feldman, and taken up by the Indian planner Mahanalobis. The model was influential in planning circles in the 1950s and 1960s, and provided the theoretical rationale for what Little (1982) calls 'heavy industry fundamentalism'. It is also suggested frequently that the model helped determine public sector investment allocations in India, particularly in the Second Five Year Plan.[14]

In Prebisch's analysis discussed above growth is held back by the potential for import demand to outstrip export earnings, with no distinction made between types of imports. In the Feldman-Mahanalobis model a closed economy is assumed, but the general logic of the argument holds if one incorporates foreign trade, but assumes that exports are stagnant.[15] Here it is a scarcity of capital goods imports that will constrain growth.

Considering first the logic of the basic model the economy is divided into two sectors or departments — one producing investment or capital goods, and the other consumer goods. Each department is vertically integrated so that it supplies its own inputs.[16] The economy is closed, and critically important is the assumption that once capacity is installed in one sector it cannot be used to produce output in the other sector. The capital-output ratio is assumed constant and equal for both sectors. Under these assumptions the key parameter becomes the allocation of new investment between the two sectors. Consumer goods output will be higher in the short-run, with a higher proportionate allocation to the consumer goods sector, but it can be shown that by shifting the allocation of investment to the capital goods sector over time at some point a higher future level of consumption will be reached. In other words, one can either use machines to make consumer goods, or machines to make other machines; the latter strategy will raise the rate of investment and add to the capacity to produce consumer goods in the future.[17]

The policy implications of the model is that where there is little prospect of importing the capital goods necessary to expand capacity, in the allocation of investment priority should be given to building up the domestic capital goods sector. This will allow a higher rate of investment, and a higher rate of growth. Although it is generally recognised that the model is a helpful way of explaining the impressive growth rate of the USSR from the mid-1920s to the 1960s its use in the context of planning for developing countries has been questioned strongly. Focusing on the more fundamental points, three lines of criticism can be noted.[18]

First, the model is an example of the general category of 'bottleneck' models, which assume that the supply of one key resource or input cannot be expanded beyond a certain level regardless of the availability of other resources or inputs. The constrained item, in this case domestic capital goods, thus becomes the bottleneck holding back overall growth. It will be recalled that once installed, domestic capacity cannot be shifted between sectors, so that the capital goods installed initially to make consumer goods cannot later be turned to capital goods production. Furthermore, since the economy is closed, consumer goods cannot be sold as exports to pay for inputs of capital goods. In practice, resources often can only shift between sectors to a limited degree, and at rising cost, but a pure bottleneck of this type, is likely to be an extreme case.

The second line of attack comes from those who argue that the model focuses on the wrong bottleneck. Investment may be held back by a number of constraints, including not just the availability of capital goods, but also the domestic savings necessary to finance investment, the capacity to absorb these savings in productive projects, and the willingness of the private sector to invest their savings. If any of these other constraints are binding investment will be below the level allowed by the capacity of the domestic capital goods sector, and this capacity will be under-utilised. This point has been made particularly in relation to domestic savings, since the model assumes that savings will automatically adjust to the level of investment determined by the productive capacity of the capital goods sector, either as a result of government fiscal policy, or through a redistribution of national income from wages to profits. If workers, for example, can resist a cut in their real wage this will limit the extent to which savings can be increased at the expense of consumption. Some commentators on the Indian experience, for example Stewart (1976), have linked the government's failure to control domestic savings with the under-utilisation of capacity in the domestic capital goods sector.

Finally perhaps the strongest attack on the model is for its neglect of foreign trade possibilities. Once foreign trade is allowed the availability of domestic capital goods is not determined by domestic productive capacity in this sector alone, since consumer goods can be exchanged for capital goods through trade. A rigid capital goods bottleneck can only emerge if it is impossible to transform additional domestic resources into the foreign exchange needed to import these capital goods. In other words, if additional savings that reduce consumption and thereby free resources for the foreign trade sector can make available additional foreign exchange, even at a rising cost in terms of domestic resources per unit of foreign exchange, the strict capital goods bottleneck is removed.

Since it must now be widely accepted that individual developing countries through various policy measures can influence their foreign exchange earnings, the Feldman-Mahanalobis closed economy model seems relevant only for developing economies forced into autarky by various circumstances. This means that any demand for capital goods in excess of domestic capacity can be met by imports, as is the case for any other internationally traded goods. None the less this can mean a high import bill if investment is increased significantly, and if it is difficult to raise export earnings in line with the increase in import demand, then one is back to the more general argument of Prebisch on the case for industrialisation as a means of raising the growth rate. This is an argument for import-substitution in general, however, and does not specify priority to particular branches. It is significant that whilst the case for giving priority to capital goods production within an industrialisation programme is still argued, the emphasis is now more on the various external benefits and linkage effects associated with this type of manufacturing, than on the influence of domestic capital goods capacity on the rate of investment.[19]

In summary, it is suggested here that the case for industrialisation as a means of saving foreign exchange through import substitution, remains valid, although arguments on the need to give priority to capital goods production because of its effect on the rate of investment now appear dubious. However Structuralist authors have identified several other possible benefits from industrialisation apart from its foreign exchange effect, and these are considered below.

EXTERNALITIES AND LINKAGES

These concepts are central to many discussions of industrialisation, and although they are based on similar ideas they are conventionally discussed separately. Here externalities are considered first, before turning to linkages.

Externalities

Externalities are effects created by individual producers or consumers that are felt elsewhere in the economy. They have been a

central plank in the argument for the importance of industrialisation in developing countries at least since Rosenstein-
Rodan (1943) argued for a 'Big Push' — that is a co-ordinated
investment programme — that would attempt to maximise the
gains from these external effects.[20]

Central to the Structuralist position is the view that externalities are more significant in industry than in other sectors,
thus providing a major rationale for industrialisation. However
arguments on external effects can be put in very vague terms,
and it is necessary to clarify the issues by distinguishing between
different types of external effects. For this purpose the classic
article, Scitovsky (1958), remains one of the most helpful
starting points.

A more precise definition of externalities than that given
initially is that they are effects created by individual producers
or consumers, which have repercussions on other producers or
consumers, that are not reflected in the cost and revenue position of the original creator of the effect. They are examples of a
'distortion' since, for example, if a producer creates an effect on
another producer the market price of its output will not reflect
the cost or benefit to the other producer. Scitovsky (1958)
helped narrow down this broad concept by distinguishing between what he terms 'technological externalities' and
'pecuniary externalities'. He also helped to clarify the circumstances in which one or the other is likely to be relevant. The
following discussion draws on Scitovsky's article, and focuses
on examples of the interrelationship between producers largely
ignoring external effects on consumers.

Technological externalities are defined as direct external
effects that do not arise as a result of market transactions for
which prices are charged. Here the output of producer 1 will
depend not only on its own inputs, but also on the physical
quantities of the outputs or inputs of other producers. Externalities of this type are termed technological since the inputs
or output of a firm enter directly into the production function of
another firm.

Scitovsky suggests that externalities of this type are generally
of only theoretical interest. They are significant in a theoretical
sense because they demonstrate the inability of a competitive
market system to reach a socially optimum situation. However,
Scitovsky argues that there are few practically significant examples of this type of external effect, and finds only two which

seem relevant for industry. The first is a labour training effect where, for example, the training undertaken by producer 2 can create a skilled group of workers who, if they leave 2's employment, can bring their skills to producer 1; second, if several firms use a resource which is free, but in limited supply, the greater the inputs used by producer 2 the less there will be available to producer 1.[21]

Whilst technological externalities reflect direct interdependence between producers, pecuniary externalities on the other hand operate through the market mechanism, so that their effects are manifested in price terms. It is this second set of externalities which Scitovsky pointed out were seen as widely prevalent in developing countries:

> Interdependence through the market mechanism is all-pervading and this explains the contrast between the exceptional and often awkward examples of externalities cited in discussions of equilibrium theory (i.e. technological externalities) and the impression one gains from the literature on underdeveloped countries that the entrepreneur creates external economies and diseconomies with his every move.[22]

Scitovsky gave a formal definition of pecuniary externalities as arising whenever the profits of a producer are affected by the output and input levels of other producers. They are therefore a broader category than technological externalities which do not operate through the market and which, therefore, affect only output quantity; where technological externalities also raise profitability they are subsumed under pecuniary effects.

It is clear that there are numerous ways in which interdependence can affect profits; the examples given by Scitovsky are as follows:

(i) expansion of producer A may give rise to additional profits in B if the latter is a user of A's output, and A's production is subject to increasing returns to scale, so that its costs and price fall with expansion;

(ii) growth of A will create a demand for inputs used in A, and will create higher profits in these supplier industries, unless diseconomies of scale are important;

(iii) where other products are complementary to the output

of A, expansion of A can raise the demand for these goods and thus their profitability, again providing diseconomies of scale are not important;

(iv) producers whose goods are consumed by those whose incomes are raised by the expansion of A will also find demand for their products increased, and thus they will have the potential for higher profitability.

It should be noted that although Scitovsky does not dwell on the point, profit interdependence can be negative as well as positive.[23] Obvious examples of negative externalities of this type would be:

(a) where expansion of producer A substitutes for other goods thus lowering their demand and profitability;

(b) where expansion of A creates a demand for factors or inputs in limited supply and either reduces their availability or raises their price to others;

(c) where output of A is higher cost or lower quality than that of competitors, but after A's expansion users are compelled for various reasons to use A rather than alternatives.

The central importance of externalities, positive or negative, is that where they exist the net benefits to the economy as a whole, what we will term economic benefits, can differ significantly from the benefits accruing to private producers. The existence of externalities provides much of the rationale for appraising investments from a broad economic perspective, and for planning and co-ordinating investment activities.[24] Where firms act individually in response to their own private profit estimates their investment plans may be non-optimal in broader economic terms. Rosenstein-Rodan (1943) had this situation in mind when he suggested that external economies generated by individual firms could be 'internalised' by co-ordinating investment plans and bringing large numbers of producers under what he termed 'one huge firm or trust'. This is clearly an argument for a form of central planning.

As we have stressed, externalities are central to the early Structuralist view of industrialisation in developing countries, and Rosenstein-Rodan, at least, appears to stand by his earlier emphasis on their importance.[25] However, others, Neo-classical economists in particular, are sceptical of their significance. According to Little (1982), Scitovsky himself has commented on the misuse of his concept of pecuniary externalities to justify many economically unviable projects by vague references to their effects on the profits of other producers. Little and Mirrlees (1974) have also suggested that when considering the appraisal of individual industrial projects external effects are either very difficult to quantify or relatively minor where they can be measured.[26] They also challenge the assumption that externalities are more prevalent in industry than in other sectors, arguing that if the spread of learning and know-how is a major externality, this is more likely to be important in agriculture than in industry.

The empirical evidence on the role of externalities is limited, but a formal rationalisation of the greater potentiality of industry for the generation of external effects rests largely on the concept of linkages, popularised by Hirschman (1958). It is this concept to which we turn next.

Linkages

Linkages are closely related to externalities, and in some discussions appear to be almost synonymous. One of the difficulties is that linkages can be defined in a broad or a narrow sense. In the former a linkage is simply an inducement to activity on the part of one enterprise created by the actions of another; in the narrow sense it is more technical referring to a series of production relationships in an inter-industry framework. In his survey of the ideas of the early development economists Little (1982) argues that linkages can only be logically distinct from pecuniary externalities if they operate in a non-pecuniary way; in other words only if the inducement they create is not via additional profits. Where linkages have an effect through changes in profitability they will be identical to pecuniary externalities. For example, a linkage from firm A to B which induces the latter to expand production will only be distinct from an externality, if the additional production in B was already profitable prior to the linkage, but was either not recognised as such or ignored due to lack of entrepreneurial initiative. Put in these terms the claim for linkages to be a useful category separate from pecuniary externalities is not great.

However, if one focuses upon the narrower technical definition the concept appears more helpful in its own right. Hirschman (1958) identifies two categories of production linkages — backward linkages from a particular industry to its suppliers, and forward linkages from an industry to its users. These linkages reflect production interdependence, and are a mechanism through which some, but not all, pecuniary externalities can be transmitted. However, they are not relevant for pecuniary externalities created by demand complementarity, nor the multiplier effect of spending incomes generated by individual producers. The important point for the present discussion is that a focus on production linkages allows an assessment of the consequences of different patterns of investment, and thus the potential of particular forms of expansion for generating external effects in other productive activities. Clearly not all linkages create higher profits elsewhere, and as we have noted not all possible pecuniary externalities are covered by linkages of this type, but none the less one can argue that the activities with the highest linkages have the greatest potential for generating externalities.

Hirschman (1958) suggests as a measure of backward linkage per productive branch the ratio of the total value of purchases from other branches to the value of total production, and of forward linkage the ratio of the value of sales to other branches to the value of total demand. He terms these 'interdependence ratios' and argues the higher the ratio the greater will be the inducement to expansion elsewhere. This measure, as Hirschman himself recognises, captures only direct linkages, and estimation of total linkages, that is direct plus indirect, requires the use of the Leontief inverse of an input-output table. Subsequent attempts at identifying the linkage potential of different branches have followed this latter approach, although substantial difficulties in deriving accurate estimates have been revealed.

For illustrative purposes the results of Yotopoulos and Nugent (1973) in their assessment of the linkage potential of different branches are shown in Table 3.1. The authors construct separate input-output tables for typical developed and developing countries. The primary purpose of the exercise is to test for any relationship between a country's use of linkages as part of its economic strategy, and its growth record. However to do this they estimate the impact of linkages from different branches and sectors, and it is this part of their work which is of relevance here. Table 3.1 shows three measures of linkage, direct backward and forward linkages, defined as in Hirschman's interdependence ratios, and total backward linkages.[27] Since the latter should capture direct plus indirect effects it is probably the most significant. The interpretation of the total backward linkage measure is that it shows the total monetary units required per one unit of output expansion for the activity concerned. The figure of 2.239 for textiles, for example, implies that to meet a unitary increase in textile output requires 2.239 units of output for the economy as a whole. This will consist of 1.0 units of textiles itself, plus 1.239 of both direct inputs (such as cotton and electricity) and indirect inputs (such as fertiliser for cotton growing and fuel for electricity generation).

Table 3.1: Measures of linkage: developing countries

	Total backward linkage (LT_j)	Direct backward linkage (LB_j)	Direct forward linkage (LF_i)
Leather	2.393	0.683	0.615
Basic metals	2.364	0.632	0.980
Clothing	2.316	0.621	0.025
Textiles	2.239	0.621	0.590
Food, beverages	2.217	0.718	0.272
Paper	2.174	0.648	0.788
Chemicals and petroleum	2.130	0.637	0.599
Metal products and machinery	2.121	0.558	0.430
Wood, furniture	2.074	0.620	0.582
Construction	2.042	0.543	0.093
Printing	1.977	0.509	0.508
Other manufacturing	1.937	0.505	0.362
Rubber	1.931	0.481	0.453
Non-metallic minerals	1.826	0.517	0.870
Agriculture	1.592	0.368	0.502
Utilities	1.488	0.296	0.614
Mining	1.474	0.288	0.638
Services	1.413	0.255	0.378

Note: For definitions of LT_j, LB_j and LF_i see footnote 27.
Source: Yotopoulos and Nugent (1973), table II, p. 163.

Table 3.1 ranks branches by their total backward linkage effects. The important point for the present discussion is not the precise numbers shown, since they have been the subject of considerable debate, but that in general under all three measures most forms of manufacturing show greater linkage potential than the other major economic sectors — agriculture, mining and services.[28] This is particularly the case for the most rigorous of the measures, the total backward linkage index.

The greater linkages created by manufacturing, and therefore its greater potential for generating externalities, has been used as a major argument for the importance of industrialisation. Hirschman (1958), for example, argues that:

> The case for inferiority of agriculture to manufacturing has most frequently been argued on grounds of comparative productivity. While this case has not been shown to be entirely convincing agriculture certainly stands convicted on the count of its lack of direct stimulus to the setting up of new activities through linkage effects; the superiority of manufacturing in this respect is crushing.[29]

In opposition to this view it can be argued that agriculture can still raise the profitability of other activities, and therefore generate strong pecuniary externalities, when the incomes generated in agriculture are spent on consumer goods.[30] However the direct and indirect productive links between agriculture and other producing sectors are undoubtedly lower than for manufacturing.

If externalities are an important source of additional incomes and linkages are a useful measure of the potential for generating externalities, one might think that the policy recommendation is clear-cut; for example, within manufacturing one should give priority to the activities that create the maximum linkages. This is a simplistic view however, that Hirschman himself certainly did not advocate. The difficulty is that not all linkages will create economically desirable inducements; for example, setting up an automobile plant creates a demand for steel, and may encourage the setting up of local capacity. However if the domestic market is small, or local raw materials are expensive, the cost of producing domestic steel may be high by world standards. If local steel is not protected from foreign competition there will be no positive pecuniary externality, since due to its high cost it will not be possible to run a domestic steel plant profitably. However if protection is given, profits sufficiently high to justify domestic production may be generated. In this case the initial linkage has created the possibility of setting up local production by generating a demand for the product. However profits can only be earned through the intervention of the government. It is argued, particularly in the Neoclassical literature, that this sequence has been relatively common in protected inward-looking economies, and that linkages of this type have induced the establishment of many high cost supplying industries.[31] This does not mean that in many cases linkage effects may not be economically beneficial creating a market for goods which can be produced competitively, or which can become competitive over a period of time. The general point is that it cannot be assumed *a-priori* that simply because there is a domestic market for a commodity as a result of linkages, that this commodity should automatically be produced domestically. Furthermore where uneconomic suppliers are set up domestic users of the goods will be penalised and their cost competitiveness will be reduced.

The other important aspect of policy relating to linkages is that the inducements they create may not lead to positive responses even when there is a strong economic case for establishing backward or forward linkages. Hirschman (1968) has an interesting discussion of the forces that may encourage or discourage responses to the inducements linkages create. His main point is that the success of linkages in encouraging either investment by new suppliers, or further processing of goods, is determined not solely by objective considerations like the size of the market, or the sophistication of the technology involved. Subjective factors regarding the policies of governments and the perceptions and goals of industrialists, will inevitably be critically important in determining whether the inducements are taken up. There is evidence that government intervention has been important in encouraging linkages, particularly backward linkages, in many economies, although as we have noted, the economic wisdom of this policy has been questioned in many cases.

The linkage argument, therefore, remains ambiguous. There is no doubt that manufacturing has the potential for generating strong external effects through its links with supplying and using activities. Many of these effects may be positive in the sense that private profitability may be raised and new production encouraged. In some cases however the gain to private producers, and to the economy as a whole, may not coincide, so that the profits that are generated by the linkages do not reflect net economic benefits. In these cases the linkage effects are not economically justified, and government intervention encouraging 'premature linkages' is the reason why uneconomic industries can be set up. The argument illustrates some of the potential gains from industrialisation, but no more than that.

INFANT-INDUSTRIES

The infant-industry case for protection from imports has a long history in economics, providing a rationale for protectionism in the USA and Germany, for example, in the last century against the competition from British goods. It clearly has a relevance to discussions on the import-substitution industrialisation pursued in the majority of developing countries post-1945, and it was influential in the thinking of early development economists.[32] At the centre of the argument is the simple proposition that new activities can only be mastered effectively over a period of time — the 'learning period' — and that new industries therefore cannot be expected to compete on equal terms with established producers in other countries. The policy recommendation is for a limited period of protection from import competition whilst learning takes place. The expectation is that, over time, costs of production in these infant industries will fall to internationally competitive levels and the economy as a whole will gain from their protection. In principle the argument can be applied to any form of economic activity that produces internationally traded goods, but it has conventionally been associated most closely with manufacturing industry presumably on the grounds that the scope for gaining by experience, or 'learning-by-doing' is greater there than elsewhere.

In addition the infant-industry case has been linked with the question of the externalities generated by industrial investments. It is argued not only that the costs of individual producers will fall — which is an internal economy for them — but that the external benefits they create for others will also grow over time.[33] Positive externalities created by infant industries can arise at different levels. For example, they can be external to an individual producer but internal to the branch in which it operates; that is, the gains accrue to firms in the same branch. The labour training externality referred to earlier, where skilled workers possessing skills specific to a branch leave a producer for work in the same branch, is an example of this. Alternatively the externalities could be external to the producer but internal to the manufacturing sector; that is, benefits accrue to firms within manufacturing with no systematic distinction between branches. An example of this would be technical progress in the production of inputs, such as capital equipments, used in a wide range of manufacturing activities. If these equipments are either lower priced or higher quality there should be a gain in profitability in their user activities.[34] Finally at the broadest level externalities can be external to an individual producer and internal to the whole economy; that is, the extra incomes created by externalities can accrue anywhere in the economy. This would be the case, for example, if external effects are in the form of changes in attitude towards work or decision-taking, so that experience in manufacturing creates new attitudes that can be used productively in a wide range of other activities.[35]

These arguments are normally treated formally using diagrams that relate costs of production in infant producers to either time, or the cumulative output they have produced at any one point in time. Figure 3.1, for example, shows the real average cost curve AA of an individual producer over time, compared with the cost, insurance, freight (cif) price of comparable imports MM. Import prices are assumed constant in real terms, and domestic costs are shown falling as learning takes place. At the time t the infant 'matures' as costs fall to internationally competitive levels; beyond t costs are shown as continuing to fall so that exports should be possible. For the individual producer there will be a short-run cost up to t, in the absence of import protection, to be balanced against a longer-run gain for the rest of its operation. Where import protection is provided the short-run cost is borne by the consumers or users of the output since they must pay prices in excess of world levels. Externalities are introduced in Figure 3.2. Here it is assumed that not only do the costs of the individual producer fall over time but that other producers gain from the external benefits the original infant generates. In this situation a second cost curve is required EE, which shows the net unit cost to the economy of the production of the infant producer. This net economic cost is the infant's own cost of production minus the external benefits per unit of output that are created for others.[36] The consequences of the inclusion of EE in the diagram are that maturation occurs more rapidly at time t^1; that the initial losses are lower; and that the gains after t^1 are

Figure 3.1: Infant Industry: learning

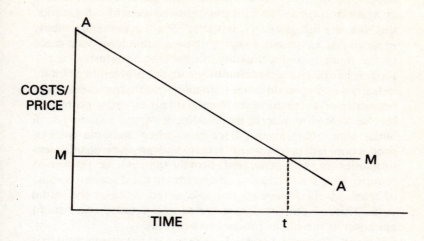

greater, since net economic costs are significantly below the
world price of comparable imports. In other words, what is
demonstrated is that the case for infant-industry protection is
strengthened wherever positive externalities are generated.

Figure 3.2: Infant Industry: learning and externalities

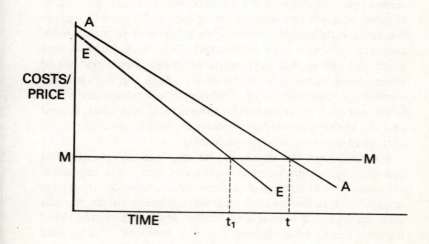

However experience with the result of import-substitution policies has created scepticism with the empirical validity of the infant-industry case. The empirical significance of both learning by and externalities from infants has been questioned. Data on this issue are discussed in Chapter 6. Here it is necessary simply to note some of the more important points that have been made in the more recent discussions of the infant-industry case.[37] First, it has been stressed that to justify the protection of infant industries one must do more than demonstrate that costs fall to internationally competitive levels. Infant-industry protection can be treated as a form of investment by the economy with initial costs offset against later gains when domestic costs of production fall below world levels, and possibly positive externalities are also generated. Strictly the case for protection requires over the lifetime of an investment the discounted value of later benefits outweigh the discounted value of the initial costs. This can only be demonstrated by a detailed cost-benefit appraisal of the infant producers' activities.

Second, Figures 3.1 and 3.2 are drawn on the assumption that prices of international competitors remain constant in real terms. This can be a dubious assumption when productivity growth in the developed economies is rapid, and the more import prices fall, the more difficult it will be for infants to mature and become internationally competitive.

Third, perhaps most fundamental, is that empirical case studies on firms in a number of developing countries have shown that learning is rarely an effortless or costless process. It is now common to distinguish between different forms of learning, with learning-by-doing as a result of production experience only the most elementary. The implication is that successful infants will need to purposefully pursue policies of raising their capacity to understand, adapt and improve the technology they are using. Only such technologically active firms will emerge as successful infants, and it is often argued that the shelter provided by protection provides no incentive to seek out these various improvements.

To summarise the discussion of this section, externalities, linkages and learning-by-doing, have been an important element of the Structuralist case for industrialisation. By setting up new industries even if they were initially internationally uncompetitive, it was argued that a whole set of additional benefits would arise elsewhere in the economy. The general empirical validity of this case has been questioned, as has the view that new infant-industries would soon become competitive with simply the passing of time. Whilst it is difficult to deny that externalities and learning effects can be important, now many question the likelihood that they will be associated with a majority of protected industries.

There is a related argument on the importance of manufacturing industry that draws on the concepts of linkages and externalities, as well as the historical experience of the now developed economies. This variant of the case for industrialisation is not as well known in the development literature as the arguments considered up to this point, but none the less should be seen as a major relatively recent contribution to a Structuralist interpretation of the role of manufacturing. This 'engine of growth' view of manufacturing is considered in the final section of this chapter, and since it has received less attention elsewhere, is considered in a little more detail than the other arguments discussed in this chapter.

INDUSTRIAL SPECIALISATION AND DYNAMIC INCREASING RETURNS

Growth of productivity has been a central feature in Structuralist discussions of the role of manufacturing industry. It is empirically well established that productivity per worker is higher in manufacturing than in other sectors, such as services or agriculture. What is of particular significance however is the trend in sectoral labour productivity over time, since a rising output per worker means more real income for distribution within an economy.

There is a view with a long tradition in economics that manufacturing is the only economic sector that in the long-run is subject to increasing returns; that is, rising productivity as output expands. This originates in the distinction conventional in the Classical economists such as Smith and Ricardo, between increasing returns in manufacturing compared with diminishing returns in agriculture, with commerce treated as an appendage of manufacturing. In more recent times the argument was set out by Young (1928) and expanded and elaborated upon by Kaldor (1966) and (1967). Most applied work following this approach has concentrated upon the historical role of manufacturing in developed economies, however this line of reasoning has been extended to developing countries. Weiss (1984a) surveys this literature.[38]

Kaldor provides the fullest statement of this approach and here attention will be focused initially upon his arguments; no single work gives a comprehensive statement of his views, but Kaldor (1967) probably comes closest to such a statement. Kaldor's case starts with an analysis of the relationship between growth of national income and sectoral output for developed economies. He finds a significant correlation across a number of OECD countries between the growth of GDP and the growth of manufacturing which he interprets to mean that growth of manufacturing causes growth of GDP. A significant correlation between GDP and sectoral output is not found for any of the other economic sectors, apart from distribution, and as we shall see, Kaldor argues that here causation is reversed.[39] Such an association is only important if one has a theory to explain what is special about manufacturing to enable it to play the role of an engine of growth. Kaldor's explanation is based on what he terms dynamic increasing returns in manufacturing. It is not just a question of higher levels of output being associated with lower inputs per unit of output and thus higher productivity; these are economies of scale in a static sense, and such economies are potentially reversible when output contracts. Kaldor acknowledges that economies of this type will be found in non-manufacturing activities, at least up to some minimum efficient level of output. What he has in mind in the special case of manufacturing is a dynamic relation between the growth of output and the growth of productivity, which in line with the arguments surveyed above he attributes to learning-by-doing and technological improvements. This means that the level of productivity is a function of cumulative output from the commencement of production, rather than the level of output at a point in time. Another way of putting this is that continuous reductions in inputs and improvements in product quality result from continuous increases in output over time. Economies of this type, resulting from the accumulation of production experience, and the technological improvements it allows should be irreversible.

As a means of testing the hypothesis of dynamic increasing returns in manufacturing, Kaldor uses cross-sectional regression analysis to estimate equations 3.6 and 3.7 below, for a number of different sectors across a sample of developed economies.

$$p_i = a + b.q_i \qquad (3.6)$$
$$e_i = a + b.q_i \qquad (3.7)$$

where q, p and e are logarithmic growth rates for output, productivity and employment respectively, in different economies and i refers to a given sector.

Equation 3.6 is the Verdoorn relationship between output growth and productivity growth, which has been found to hold for many branches of economic activity.[40] However since by definition $q_i = p_i + e_i$ it is possible for spurious correlations between q and p to be found, particularly when changes in employment are small. To allow for this Kaldor argues that the key test for the existence of dynamic increasing returns is not only that equation 3.6 holds, but that in addition equation 3.7 is statistically significant with a b coefficient of less than 1.0; implying that growth of output results from both productivity and employment effects, but that the growth in employment is less than proportionate to the growth in output. In Kaldor's original analysis industry is the only sector for which both equations are statistically significant.[41]

It should be noted that the validity of this test has been the subject of debate. First, an alternative interpretation of equation (3.6) would see causation running from productivity growth to output growth, and would place the explanation for differential rates of productivity growth on autonomously determined rates of technical progress. Kaldor rejects this on the grounds that if one is considering equation 3.6 across branches within a sector, it would imply that different autonomously determined productivity growth rates would be fully reflected in relative price movements, and that the price elasticity of demand for all the commodities produced by the branches concerned would have to exceed 1.0.[42]

Secondly, Rowthorn (1975) points out that ordinary least squares regression techniques when applied to models such as equations 3.6 and 3.7 will give biased estimates when the independent variable, in this case q, is not truly independent of the variables it is meant to explain. Rowthorn suggests that a more direct and satisfactory test would be to take e as the independent variable and to regress p on e. However in contrast Cornwall (1977) argues that for developed economies in the post-war period there is strong evidence that the growth of employment in manufacturing was determined by manufacturing output, so that e is itself not independent of the other parameters, and that Rowthorn's alternative is, if anything, less satisfactory.

There is agreement however that Rowthorn's procedure is inappropriate where surplus labour exists, since employment can adjust to demand changes, and whilst it is questionable how far the labour markets of OECD economies in the post-war period can be characterised in this way, it is generally accepted that such conditions are still widely prevalent in developing economies. The conclusion of this particular debate appears to be that whilst a simultaneous equation estimation procedure may give a more satisfactory test of the hypothesis, if ordinary least squares techniques are to be applied, the Kaldor test is probably as good as any other, and is clearly superior in the labour market conditions closest to those found in developing countries.[43]

Thus far it may appear that Kaldor's analysis is simply an empirical demonstration at a macro-economic level of the successful operation of learning and technical change within manufacturing. However the argument goes beyond the discussions of externalities, linkages and learning considered earlier, to suggest that the key element behind the productivity growth that historically has occurred in manufacturing in many countries is the scope for specialisation within manufacturing as the size of the market expands. This is an extension of Adam Smith's famous dictum that the division of labour is limited by the extent of market. However the argument also draws on Allyn Young's wider interpretation of the division of labour beyond the simple split of occupations into increasingly specialist activities.

One aspect of the division of labour, stressed particularly by Young (1928), is 'the growth of indirect or roundabout methods of production'. He sees this as responsible for much of the productivity growth in manufacturing, as increasing specialisation and differentiation between firms takes place, in particular as an increasingly complex network of supplier industries is established. The scale of operation of these specialist producers is dependent upon the size of the market for the products for which they provide inputs, so that as manufacturing in general expands firms have the opportunity to become more specialised and reap the advantages of specialisation.[44] However, Young stresses that this process is such that it is not always possible to observe a relation between productivity growth for an individual firm and the growth of its own output. Individual firms benefit from the external economies provided by the greater specialisation of their suppliers, and similarly at the branch level growth of one branch may have its immediate impact on the productivity of suppliers located in another branch. The important point is that, in principle, the expansion of the market for a firm or branch can have repercussions in terms of productivity and profits for a whole range of manufacturing activities. In these circumstances Young argues that it is necessary to see industrial operations as 'an inter-related whole', so new investments should not be planned in isolation from each other. This implies that the most appropriate level for testing the hypothesis of increasing returns in manufacturing is that of the aggregate of all manufacturing activities, which is the level at which Kaldor conducted his original analysis.

This interpretation of the role of manufacturing in development stresses what can be termed its distinctive structural features. Manufacturing unlike the other major sectors — agriculture and services — is characterised by increasingly inter-related and specialised branches of activity. To use Young's words it has the potential for a high degree of roundaboutness in its production structure, and thus when its aggregate output expands there is a far greater scope for the division of labour and specialisation within the sector itself, than is the case for other sectors. In the terminology used earlier manufacturing can create much greater intra-sectoral linkages, than other activities, and thus has the potential for greater positive externalities of a pecuniary kind. In addition, manufacturing is the sector that produces the capital goods used in a range of sectors, including agriculture, public utilities and construction. The existence of a domestic capital goods industry is a potentially powerful mechanism for transmitting and perhaps also initiating technical change. Endogenous technical progress arising from greater experience of and specialisation in the production of capital goods can be passed on as an external benefit, in the form of superior quality or lower priced goods, to all users of equipment, often in other sectors. Expansion of manufacturing thus has the potential for creating higher incomes both within

111

the sector itself, and in other sectors. Such externalities from individual manufacturing investments can be at different levels; both internal to manufacturing, or internal to the whole economy.

This analysis is not meant to imply that agriculture or services do not have linkages — backward or forward — with other sectors, although as we have seen there is evidence that their total impact is less than for manufacturing. The point is that the expansion of these sectors does not offer the same scope for specialisation and the division of labour within the sectors themselves: furthermore technical change in these sectors is not passed on in the same way as through the purchase of capital equipment. However it is important to make clear that this line of reasoning does not minimise the role which can be played by agriculture in the growth process. Kaldor (1967), for example, stresses the importance of agriculture at an early stage of economic development both as a supplier of wage goods and as a market for industrial products. Furthermore he does not deny that agriculture can experience rapid productivity growth: what he suggests however is that this productivity growth results from technical innovations or institutional changes which raise yields per acre. It does not require an acceleration in the growth of sectoral output to allow a greater division of labour within agriculture; in other words more specialised agricultural inputs are not required to allow the expansion of agricultural output. Kaldor takes as proof of this fact that equation 3.7 does not hold for agriculture in the sample of developed economies he examined. Therefore whilst there is a relation between output and productivity growth — equation 3.6 is statistically significant — this output growth does not require the employment of more workers in the sector. In developing countries there is clearly the possibility that productivity in agriculture may be negatively associated with employment growth, if surplus workers in agriculture are absorbed by an expanding manufacturing sector.

Kaldor points out that in the developed economies which have specialised in agriculture, the sector employs only a relatively small proportion of the working population. He argues that a developing economy which chose to specialise in agriculture alone, and to import its requirements of industrial goods, might achieve a high level of output per man employed in agriculture, but that agricultural expansion would employ only a small portion of the work force. This stems from the very limited possibilities for further specialisation within agriculture to supply its requirements of inputs from within the sector itself. Agricultural expansion, in other words, would generate relatively few jobs in supplier activities within agriculture. In the absence of a domestic manufacturing base its inputs would have to be imported, and jobs would be created abroad, not at home.

Similar arguments apply in the case of services. Most of Kaldor's comments are directed towards distribution; he finds a high correlation between the growth of the sector and that of GDP across the group of developed countries in his sample, but argues that the growth of distribution simply reflects the growth of commodity production, so that causation runs from growth of GDP to that of sectoral output. Furthermore, he suggests that even in developed countries, but clearly much more so in developing ones, there is a large potential for increasing the output of the distribution sector with a given labour force; this implies that productivity improvements in distribution will largely be a response to the growth of production in the primary and secondary sectors. As with agriculture, Kaldor accepts the possibility of productivity growth in services through static economies of large-scale production, such as those resulting from the introduction of supermarkets, but distinguishes these from the dynamic economies arising from an extension of the division of labour in manufacturing.

In summary, Kaldor sees manufacturing acting as an engine of growth since its growth will raise productivity not just in the sector itself, through an extension of the division of labour, but also in the other major sectors; productivity is likely to rise in agriculture through the absorption of surplus workers off the land, and in services because of the increased output of the distribution sector. Further productivity gains and technical progress arising in manufacturing will be passed on to other sectors through their purchases of capital and intermediate goods.

The argument on increasing returns in manufacturing has prompted considerable empirical work, although chiefly on the role of manufacturing in developed economies. Apart from Kaldor's original statistical analysis Cripps and Tarling (1973) and Cornwall (1977) amongst others, considered the validity of his generalisations for developed economies.[45] More recently however the approach has been extended to developing

113

countries. Mexican growth, in particular, has been examined from this perspective.

Brailovsky (1981) demonstrates the importance of manufacturing in the Mexican economy. He obtains similar results to those of Cripps and Tarling for developed economies, in that only for manufacturing and commerce is there a high correlation between sectoral output growth and the growth of GDP. In the case of manufacturing this is not due to it being an important component of GDP, since a significant correlation is also found between manufacturing growth and growth of GDP net of manufacturing. Brailovsky tests equations 3.6 and 3.7 using time series data on manufacturing and found both to be statistically significant. He comments that time series data on employment were not available to extend the analysis to other sectors: however a rough test was carried out by the present author using cross-sectional data on employment, output and productivity across 45 Mexican branches. For 1960–73 equations 3.6 and 3.7 are both statistically significant for 20 manufacturing branches, but only equation 3.6 holds for non-manufacturing. In other words, outside manufacturing there is no relation between the expansion of production and employment growth and thus, using Kaldor's test, there is no evidence for the existence of dynamic increasing returns.

Some work has also been done in this area for samples of developing countries, the results of which are summarised in Weiss (1984a). Whilst still no more than tentative they suggest that within developing economies where manufacturing has passed some threshold minimum level, there is evidence that the type of specialisation and associated productivity growth, that has been demonstrated to be important in developed economies, has begun to emerge. This conclusion needs to be qualified in that simple parallels between the behaviour and characteristics of manufacturing in developed and developing countries can be highly misleading since in the majority of developing countries intermediate and capital goods production is still relatively small. This structural imbalance in comparison with the position in developed economies may be due to a variety of factors, including difficulties in acquiring and assimilating foreign technologies, the relatively small size of the domestic market for these goods, and the lack of finance either in foreign or domestic currency. However since increasing differentiation in production and the accumulation of experience in these branches are the main mechanism through which Kaldor's dynamic increasing returns in manufacturing are said to operate, difficulties in establishing these branches in developing countries will obviously weaken the impact of the dynamic economies associated with manufacturing expansion. There are two possible reactions to this situation. One, which is based on calculations of short-run allocative efficiency, suggests concentrating resources only on the domestic production of the intermediate and capital goods in which a country has a reasonable chance of becoming competitive in the short-run, with other goods continuing to be supplied by imports. This is the Neoclassical response and Little and Mirrlees (1974), two of its most influential advocates, label it a strategy of 'trade intermediates'. The alternative approach is to override short-run efficiency considerations in the belief that in the long-run the establishment of a more integrated industrial structure will produce dynamic gains both for manufacturing itself and for the whole economy. Since these intermediate and capital goods firms will be uncompetitive initially they will require protection from imports. This is the logic of the arguments of Kaldor and Young, and can be seen as the Structural case for establishing an integrated manufacturing sector in developing countries, that can maximise the potential external effects from manufacturing, particularly through the specialisation associated with the increasing 'roundaboutness of production'. The argument that the manufacturing sector should be seen as an 'inter-related whole' implies not only that macro and sector level planning will be important, but that the familiar infant-industry case for protection, noted above, can be extended beyond the confines of individual producers. Whilst the conventional infant-industry argument relates costs and productivity in a producer to time, the Kaldor-Young approach adds the growth of manufacturing in the aggregate as a key explanatory variable. This can be seen as an argument for protection of the whole of manufacturing, so that the productivity of individual producers can grow more rapidly. It can be termed an 'infant economy' rather than a specifically infant-industry case for protection, since it relates to learning and specialisation at the sector level. The differences between the Neoclassical and Structuralist views on this issue are fundamental, and can be explained largely by a difference in time perspective and in the interpretation of the importance of externalities in manufacturing.

115

CONCLUSION

This chapter has surveyed what can be seen as some of the central Structuralist arguments on the role of industrialisation in economic development. They imply that industrialisation can be an important strategy for raising income levels through a number of mechanisms, including particularly foreign exchange savings or earnings, and the generation of externalities and learning effects. In many cases the original versions of these arguments can no longer be accepted without significant qualification, and evidence has shown that most of these arguments indicate no more than the potential for industry, and manufacturing in particular, to create these beneficial effects. There is a widespread disillusionment with much of the effects of industrialisation in developing countries, despite the broad relatively impressive performance, discussed in Chapter 1. In part this disappointment is likely to arise from excessive and unrealistic expectations as to what industrialisation could achieve. However the actual policies used to foster industrialisation, which often followed directly from the logic of the Structuralist case, have been strongly criticised for creating a wide range of short-term costs and for hindering the longer-term development of the industry they were designed to create. Chapter 5 examines the Neoclassical critique of the policies used to foster industrialisation, but prior to that Chapter 4 discusses Radical approaches to industrialisation in developing countries.

NOTES

1. Hirschman (1981), p. 375.
2. Little (1982) introduces the definition of the Structuralists as those who minimise the role of prices as effective policy instruments in developing countries. In contrast by his definition Neoclassicals are those who recognise the importance of prices.
3. Arndt (1985) traces the origins of Structuralism under Little's definition. He suggests that Kalecki and Kaldor may have been particularly influential in linking European and Latin American ideas on inflation.
Latin American Structuralists developed a theory of inflation based on an analysis of structural bottlenecks. Jameson (1986) examines their methodology, and several of his observations are valid for the wider group of authors that are linked here with a Structuralist approach. He stresses that in a Structuralist analysis each system must be studied as a

set of interrelated elements, and not broken down into individual components to be studied separately. Also he argues that Structuralists do not focus simply on surface phenomena, such as prices, but on the structure that lies behind what is directly observable.

4. Nurske (1958), p. 262.

5. Little (1982), p. 75.

6. For example, Lewis (1955), pp. 282–3, notes the importance of exports.

7. '. . . my policy proposal sought to provide theoretical justification for the industrialization policy which was already being followed (especially by the large countries of Latin America), to encourage the others to follow it too, and to provide all of them with an orderly strategy for carrying this out.' Prebisch (1984), p. 177.

8. Palma (1981) in his survey of Dependency theory acknowledges the influence of Prebisch, particularly in focusing attention on the differences in economic structure between the centre and the periphery.

9. See Baer (1971) and Bacha (1978) for surveys of Prebisch's views on the terms of trade for the periphery.

10. Couched in these terms the argument is close to the 'optimal tariff' case for protection, well-known in the conventional international trade literature; a point noted by Bhagwati (1984).

11. See for example Prebisch (1971). In a passage that anticipated much of the later criticism of inward-looking industrialisation Prebisch writes: 'The need for import-substitution and for consequent protection of substitution activities has been unavoidable. But there has been a failure to boost exports to the same extent. There has been a discrimination in favour of industrial substitution, and against exports, mainly industrial exports. The ideal policy would have been to promote exports in order to place them on an equal footing, again with substitution activities, but which does not necessarily mean equal incentives.' Prebisch (1971), p. 354.

There is some ambiguity as to what is meant by an equal footing in Prebisch's ideal policy, but the general statement is not very dissimilar from the views of many proponents of an outward-looking strategy.

12. Spraos (1983) concludes that for the period considered originally by Prebisch, that is pre-1945, there is evidence of a declining trend in the price of primary products. Thirlwall and Bergevin (1985) find evidence of a decline in the primary exports prices of the periphery relative to those of its manufactured imports for the post-1945 period.

13. Thirlwall (1980), pp. 250–4, gives a proof of this and a clear statement of the model.

14. See, for example, Bhagwati and Desai (1970), pp. 233–8. Radical critics of Indian planning usually question whether the logic of the model was followed consistently; for example Byres (1982).

15. Domar (1957) popularised the Feldman model. For a more elementary introduction see Jones (1975). Raj and Sen (1961) revise the model to take account of foreign trade.

16. This distinction has its origins in Marx (1967). However Feldman re-interpreted Marx's distinction between departments I and II, so that for Feldman the department covering consumer goods

117

consists not only of these final goods, but also of the inputs necessary for their production.

17. Following Domar (1957), consumption in year n can be shown to be

$$C_n = C_1 + K_{ml} \frac{(1 - \lambda)}{\lambda} (e^{(\lambda/v)^n} - 1) \tag{3.2}$$

where C_n and C_1 are consumption in years n and 1 respectively,
K_{ml} is the capacity in the capital goods sector in year 1
λ is the proportion of new investment going to produce capital goods
and v is the capital-output ratio assumed equal for both sectors.

With λ and v constant, in equation 3.2 the exponential term $e^{(\lambda/v)^n}$ will dominate, so that C_n and λ will be positively related.

18. The following discussion draws heavily on Stewart (1976).

19. See, for example, Thomas (1974) and Stewart (1976).

20. In a reflective piece Rosenstein-Rodan (1984) continues to stress the practical significance of externalities in developing countries, still arguing that they are more significant in industry than elsewhere; see Rosenstein-Rodan (1984), p. 211.

21. Scitovsky's own examples of this situation are: oil wells where output depends on the number and operation of other wells in the same field; fishing where the catch of one fisherman reduces that of others; and the use of a public road, where one firm is crowded out by others.

22. Scitovsky (1958), p. 300.

23. Fleming (1958) stressed this possibility in situations where factor supplies are not perfectly elastic.

24. Scitovsky (1958), p. 301, stresses that externalities should be taken into account in investment decisions . . . 'it is usually suggested that this should be done by taking as the maximand not profits alone, but the sum of profits yielded and the pecuniary external economies created by the investment.'

25. Rosenstein-Rodan (1984) stresses their key role and singles out two externalities for particular comment. The first is risk, if a range of new investments are started together, and the second is the labour training effect, which he feels Scitovsky dismissed too hastily.

26. Little and Mirrlees (1974), pp. 335–49.

27. Backward linkage for activity j (LB_j) is

$$LB_j = \frac{\sum_i X_{ij}}{X_j} \tag{3.3}$$

where X_{ij} is the number of units of input i used in the production of X_j units of commodity j.

Forward linkage for activity i (LF_i) is

$$LF_i = \frac{\sum_j X_{ij}}{z_i} \tag{3.4}$$

where $\sum_j x_{ij}$ is the total intermediate demand for input i and Z_i is total (final plus intermediate) demand for i.

Total backward linkages for activity j (LT_j) cover direct plus indirect backward linkages, so that

$$LT_j = \sum_i a_{ij}^* \qquad (3.5)$$

where a_{ij}^* is the ij[th] element of $[I - A]^{-1}$
and I is the identity matrix, and A the technical coefficient matrix.

See Yotopoulos and Nugent (1973), pp. 161–2.

28. Yotopoulos and Nugent (1973) have been criticised for their failure to use a weighting procedure (Laumas 1976); for their apparent neglect of foreign trade (Riedel 1976, Jones 1976); for excessive aggregation in their classification of economic activities and for omitting indirect forward linkages (Jones 1976). Their response is in Yotopoulos and Nugent (1976). The debate illustrates the difficulty in operationalising the linkage concept, and the variety of ways in which linkage indices can be constructed.

29. Hirschman (1958), pp. 109–110.

30. This seems to be the point that Mellor (1986), p. 80, makes in a critical comment on the above quotation from Hirschman.

31. See, for example, Little and Mirrlees (1974), pp. 335–57.

32. For example Mrydal (1957) and Lewis (1955).

33. It is sometimes argued, particularly in the Neoclassical literature, that falling costs over time do not justify protection, since producers can recover their early losses once they become competitive. In these circumstances it is suggested that only market imperfections, such as lack of access to capital markets, or imperfect information, can justify protection or promotion of infants; see Corden (1980), pp. 56–66.

34. This is what Stewart (1976) calls 'externalities to innovation in the capital goods sector'.

35. Corden (1974), p. 264, sees what he terms 'atmosphere creation' as the strongest argument for general protection of manufacturing.

36. This assumes that externalities are the only reason why market prices and economic values diverge. A fuller discussion would need to introduce shadow prices for the key inputs used by the infant producer, and possibly also use a shadow exchange rate to convert the cif price of competing imports to domestic currency.

37. For example, Bell et al. (1984).

38. This section draws heavily on Weiss (1984a); see also Singh (1982).

39. The obvious point that such an association may simply reflect a correlation between a whole, GDP, and one of its parts — manufacturing — is countered by Kaldor with the fact that there is also a statistically significant relation between the growth of manufacturing and that of GDP net of manufacturing.

40. For example, Salter (1966).

41. In Kaldor (1967) industry is defined as manufacturing plus

public utilities. Both equations hold for industry as a sector, and for its manufacturing and non-manufacturing components taken separately.

42. In a survey of this debate Kennedy (1971), pp. 182–3, concludes that the relative price effects necessary to negate Kaldor's interpretation are unlikely to occur in practice.

43. Kaldor (1975) acknowledges that the cumulative nature of growth makes it difficult to argue that q is wholly independent of p. He maintains however that whilst 'there is a two-way relationship from demand growth to productivity growth, and from productivity growth to demand growth . . . the second relationship is in my view, far less regular and systematic than the first.' Kaldor (1975), p. 895.

44. Young cites as an example the printing industry where early in the twentieth century a range of specialist producers took over the tasks previously handled by the printers themselves. The cost reductions, or increasing returns, resulting from this process are described as 'economies of capitalistic or roundabout methods of production'. Young (1928), p. 531.

45. Cripps and Tarling (1973) stimulated a major debate. Rowthorn (1975) points out that their conclusion on the validity of the increasing returns hypothesis is dependent upon the inclusion in their sample of Japan, a country which he claims should be treated as a special case of a latecomer economy. Kaldor (1975) replies that Cripps and Tarling's test, regressing productivity on employment, is inappropriate and that using his own test (equations 3.6 and 3.7) significant results are obtained even when Japan is excluded.

4

Radical Analysis of Industrialisation

Although agreeing on the importance of industrialisation for transforming the economies of developing countries, authors working in what is termed here 'the Radical tradition', stress a number of major obstacles to this industrialisation arising from a combination of the external international environment and the internal class and economic structures of developing countries themselves. The term Radical analysis is imprecise and can cover a wide range of authors who, whilst sharing a common perspective, may differ substantially in the emphasis and details of their argument. Here, following the survey by Griffin and Gurley (1985), Radical analysis can be described as 'that which is highly critical of capitalism, favours socialism, and often employs Marxian analysis'.[1] Several of the key characteristics of Marxian analysis can be seen as the view of the primacy of the production process in establishing class structures and other social relations, the importance of class struggle in the process of historical change, and often the application of the labour theory of value to explain exchange and trading relationships.

However it would be misleading to see the Radical literature on industrialisation as simply the application of Marxism to development problems, since in the last 30 years or so, much of this work has involved varying degrees of modification to what is generally recognised as the classical Marxian approach. The term Neo-Marxism has crept into the literature in recognition of this point.

It is common to identify 'Dependency theory' as an important and distinct approach within the Radical literature on development issues. Latin Americans played the leading role in the formulation of a Dependency perspective, but the broad approach has been applied in work on other continents. Several comprehensive surveys of Dependency theory are now available and there is no need to repeat here their discussions of its origins or its central themes.[2] The purpose of this chapter is to identify some of the main arguments in the Radical literature on the possibilities for successful industrialisation in developing countries. We have noted already several arguments linked with Structuralist authors that point to the importance of industrialisation. However much of the Radical literature stresses the obstacles to and the limitations of industrialisation in developing countries under existing international and domestic conditions. Dependency theory has been the most influential element in this literature, so that it is necessary to give a brief overview of the Dependency perspective as a background to the general discussion. It must be stressed none the less that Dependency analysis is not the only approach to industrialisation within the Radical literature, and some of the competing perspectives must also be noted. In addition, it must also be said that much of the original analysis of the major Dependency authors is now strongly questioned by many, including in some instances the original authors themselves. In surveying Dependency arguments therefore one must be aware that in some cases one is referring to positions that few would now hold without serious qualification. The very substantial critical literature on Dependency theory in recent years is evidence of its waning influence, and many now appear to take the view that the major contribution of Dependency authors lies in the questions they pose rather than in the answers they provide to those questions.[3]

DEPENDENCY THEORY: A BRIEF OVERVIEW

In the Dependency perspective developing economies are part of the world capitalist economy, whose current economic, social and political conditions have been determined by contact with the advanced capitalist economies. Following the terminology of Prebisch noted earlier — developing countries are the periphery and the advanced capitalist economies are the core. Relationships between core and periphery are such that the latter are 'exploited' in some sense by the former, and are 'dependent' upon them in a number of ways. It is contact with the core countries that has created the condition described as underdevelopment, so that implicit in this view is the argument that in the absence of this contact an autonomous nationally directed path to development would be feasible.

In what is generally recognised as one of the classics of the Dependency literature Cardoso and Faletto (1979) define a dependent economy as one which cannot grow on the basis of internal forces — 'a system is dependent when the accumulation and expansion of capital cannot find its essential dynamic component inside the system'.[4]

Running through this approach are a number of difficulties to which different Dependency authors have provided different solutions. Several of these problems should be mentioned to indicate the issues involved.

The definition of dependency

Dependency as a relationship is often unclearly defined. It is recognised, for example, that simple empirical measures of dependence, such as the share of foreign trade in national income, or of foreign investment in total domestic investment, are not helpful in identifying dependent economies. Furthermore the opposite condition to dependence is also ambiguous. In some works it is autarky within a nationally controlled capitalism, whilst in others it is socialism and with a limited participation in world trade.[5] The question of what is 'non-dependence' in an interdependent world economy needs resolution.

The extent to which external factors dominate internal

Crude versions of Dependency theory imply that it is external ties creating a flow of surplus from the periphery to the core that are of central importance in explaining both the poverty of the former and the wealth of the latter. More subtle analyses point to the importance of local responses to external links, so that economic and social change results from an interaction between external and internal factors. Whilst the latter position is more defensible, Dependency theory is often misconstrued as implying a simple dominance of external over internal factors.[6]

The nature of dependent capitalism

The capitalism that has emerged in the periphery is sometimes seen as a special type of 'distorted' or 'peripheral' capitalism, subject to its own laws of motion. Some try to identify the characteristics of peripheral capitalism that distinguish it from capitalism in the core countries.[7] Others dispute whether it is meaningful to consider this capitalism as a new mode of production, rather than as capitalism in the specific conditions of economic backwardness and dependence of the periphery.

The compatibility of dependence and economic growth

Associated with the early Dependency authors is a broadly stagnationist view that sees the periphery condemned to economic backwardness and low growth, as a result of dependence and its impact on domestic social or economic structures. In more recent years, however, it has become increasingly common to acknowledge that dependence and growth may not be incompatible, and to allow that some countries of the periphery who do not break their ties of dependence may none the less progress in economic terms.[8]

OTHER RADICAL APPROACHES

An inability to resolve these difficulties satisfactorily theoretically, combined with the incompatibility of some Dependency propositions with the evidence on recent economic trends in the periphery has led many to a rejection of much of Dependency theory.[9] The two main alternative perspectives in the Radical literature can be best seen as applications of Marxism to development problems. They are generally known under the headings of the 'modes of production' and the 'internationalisation of capital' approaches. The former examines the interrelationship between capitalism and pre-capitalist forms of production in the periphery, with the persistence of pre-capitalist forms providing the key explanation for economic backwardness.[10] This approach is not necessarily incompatible with some of the tenets of Dependency analysis with at least one commentator, Roxborough (1979), arguing for the need to see dependency as an internal structure different from that found in the developed or core countries, and arising at least in part from past and current external links. This internal structure in dependent economies, it is suggested, can be analysed by the modes of production approach.[11]

The 'internationalisation of capital' perspective, on the other hand, focuses on capitalism as the dominant mode of production in the world economy, and examines the implications of its global functioning for the periphery. Within international capitalism there is a clear tendency for capital to flow between economies in response to differential profit opportunities, and the drive of competition between firms. These international flows through the agency of transnational firms have implications for the periphery which this approach examines in detail. The analysis departs from the Dependency perspective however, in that economies of the periphery are not seen as dependent in a literal sense, but as part of an international economic system, and as such subject to its laws of motion. There is thus scope for seeing interdependence and mutual collaboration between capitalists in the centre and the periphery.[12] None the less some studies following this approach, for example Frobel *et al*. (1981), reach similar conclusions to Dependency authors on the limited development possible in the periphery through the operation of transnationals. Others, however, most notably Warren (1980) are optimistic that the extension of capitalism to the periphery will expand greatly the level of the productive forces in these economies and thus overcome obstacles to economic growth.

Having concluded this very brief survey, one must ask what this literature adds to the Structuralist arguments on industrialisation covered in Chapter 3. To anticipate the conclusion it will be argued here that the most tenable elements of Radical analysis in this field can be seen as a radicalisation of the Structuralist perspective. However this 'radicalisation of Structuralism' lays greater emphasis on the class nature and political base of developing countries, and the obstacles to development that they pose.[13] In general, at least until very recently, many Radical authors have been sceptical of the possibility of achieving successful industrial development in peripheral economies without major political and economic changes, both internally and in external relationships. The rest of this chapter focuses on some of the more important of the arguments from this literature on obstacles to industrialisation. For clarity these are discussed here under the following four headings, although many of the points raised under different headings are interrelated:

- surplus drain and unequal exchange;
- barriers to an integrated industrial structure;
- transnational corporations and dependence;
- the domestic bourgeoisie and the state.

SURPLUS DRAIN AND UNEQUAL EXCHANGE

A central argument in the Dependency literature is that developing countries are poor not primarily because of a lack of resources, but because of the major obstacles to the productive investment domestically of the resources available. The view popularised by Baran (1957) is that the economic surplus in these economies — defined as the difference between potential production and essential consumption — is either wasted on luxury consumption by domestic elites, or flows abroad to be invested in the advanced capitalist economies, primarily but not exclusively through the activities of transnationals and foreign banks. To quote Baran himself:

> The principal obstacle to rapid economic growth in the backward countries is the way in which their potential economic surplus is utilized. It is absorbed by various forms of excess consumption of the upper class, by increments to hoard at home and abroad, by the maintenance of vast unproductive bureaucracies, and of even more expensive and no less redundant military establishments. A very large share of it — on the magnitude of which more is known than on that of others — is withdrawn by foreign capital.[14]

The question of the unwillingness or incapacity of domestic classes in the periphery to undertake productive investments, particularly in manufacturing, is taken up in a later section.

Here attention is focused on the drain of surplus from the periphery as an explanation of economic backwardness. Attempts to analyse this drain can be divided broadly into two categories: those that see the drain as a loss of income measured at market prices, and those of the unequal exchange school, who view the drain as a loss of value measured in units of labour-time. The theoretical framework underlying the two approaches differs and each will be considered separately.

Income drains

Baran and those heavily influenced by him, such as Frank, discuss a drain of income, and thus work with a concept that is readily measurable, provided adequate data are available. One can infer from their arguments that the main mechanisms for income losses by the periphery will be:

- profits, declared or undeclared, transferred abroad by transnational firms operating in the periphery;
- interest and amortisation payments on loans to the periphery from financial institutions and governments of the centre;
- movements in the terms of trade of the periphery in its trade with the centre.

It should be noted that Frank (1967) and (1969) extends Baran's arguments to create a theory of the functioning of the world capitalist system in which appropriation of economic surplus takes place at different levels. Exploitation is seen as taking place not only between classes, but also between regions in a single country, and between groups of countries, as the centre exploits the periphery. Frank's version of the surplus drain argument has been the subject of intense theoretical criticism, and Frank himself appears to have shifted from his earlier position.[15] However, rejection of Frank's theoretical arguments does not disprove the views of Baran and others who stress the importance of income drains from the periphery. It is necessary to comment on the empirical evidence and its implications for the surplus drain argument.

It must be stressed initially that the available evidence does support the view that there is a drain of income from the periphery through the mechanisms noted above. It is well established that outflows of profits on direct foreign investments in the periphery outweigh considerably investment inflows; for example in the late 1970s outflows were more than 50 per cent greater than inflows.[16] It is clearly more profitable for many transnationals to invest in the periphery than in the centre, and recorded profit figures do not allow for 'hidden' transfers through transfer pricing. It is also well known that commercial borrowing has created problems for many debtor countries for whom in the early 1980s debt servicing came to take a significant proportion of export receipts. In addition as we noted in Chapter 3 there is now strong empirical evidence that in the post-1945 period there has been a long-term decline in the price of the primary exports of the periphery relative to the manufactures it imports.

Two questions must be raised in relation to evidence such as this however. First, is it compatible with theoretical perspectives other than the surplus drain argument of Baran and others, and second is the income loss that occurs large enough to be a major explanation for economic backwardness, as the surplus drain argument suggests? In relation to the first of these, the Neoclassical response to data on the excess of outflows over inflows either on foreign investment or commercial borrowings is that this is hardly surprising. Whenever positive profits are made on investment or a positive rate of interest is charged on loans in principle an outflow of funds greater than the original inflow can occur. This may not arise if there is significant reinvestment of profits, but even here this may be simply a postponement of the date at which funds are taken out of the country, since the reinvested profits will themselves earn profits which may be repatriated in the future. An excess of outflows over inflows on foreign capital does not by itself demonstrate that either the foreign exchange effects of such investments are negative nor more generally that the economic consequences are unfavourable. These can only be judged by a valuation of the effects of the projects which are financed by the foreign investments and foreign loans. For example, a foreign investment project that substitutes for imports will save foreign exchange through this output effect, and this foreign exchange saving may cancel out the net foreign exchange outflow created by profit repatriation. The full economic consequences of the use of foreign capital therefore requires the type of cost-benefit calculations discussed in Chapter 5, supplemented by an assessment of the broader impact of the projects financed by foreign capital. A simple comparison of outflows and inflows is inadequate. It should be noted that Radical critics have also attacked the use of such simple comparisons, for example arguing that an outflow of funds from foreign investment should be treated as a symptom of the lack of development of the productive forces of an economy rather than the cause, since at a higher level of development there would be sufficient profit opportunities to ensure that transnationals reinvested rather than repatriated their profits.

In terms of the economic consequences of the surplus drain that can be identified from official statistics it is difficult to conclude that it is of a sufficient magnitude to support the theoretical emphasis placed on such outflows by some Dependency authors. Foreign investment, as we have seen in Chapter 2, varies in importance between economies, but the published figures for aggregate income outflows on such investments in developing countries for the late 1970s given in UNCTC (1983) whilst large relative to direct investment inflows are none the less fairly small in relation to total financial inflows, including commercial borrowing and development assistance. As a measure of this, by the early 1980s assets owned through foreign investment in developing countries were on average below 20 per cent of the total external debts of developing countries.[17] This is not to deny that individual countries may have experienced adverse economic effects from such flows, nor that total outflows may not be much greater than published estimates. However the sums involved do not appear to represent a vast outflow of potential investible surplus. On the question of commercial borrowing, to argue that this has been a major form of surplus drain requires that either projects financed by such funds have had negative economic returns, or that macro-economic policies in debtor countries have been changed to allow debt servicing, but at a cost in lost national income. One or both conditions no doubt hold in several of the major debtor countries, but it is not clear that they are sufficiently general to support the broad surplus drain case. Finally on the declining terms of trade for the periphery it seems likely that this trend contributed to a worsening of world income distribution post-1945, and represents a significant loss for primary product exporters.[18] However, again it appears doubtful that this can stand on its own as a general explanation for economic backwardness, particularly with the shift towards manufactured exports in many developing countries in recent years.

In summary, therefore, despite the acknowledged drain of surplus from the periphery, it seems doubtful that a full theory of economic backwardness can be erected on these facts alone. The theory of unequal exchange, however, makes some striking claims that imply that inequality in trade is a fundamental factor in underdevelopment and this view also needs to be considered.

Unequal exchange

Unequal exchange can be seen as a strand of the Dependency theory literature that argues that the periphery is exploited in its trade relations with the centre through the international prices prevailing in the world market. The theory of unequal exchange is most closely associated with Emmanuel (1972), but has been used by others including Amin (1977). The central premise of the theory is that the Marxist theory of value as applied to domestic prices — that is 'prices of production' — can also be used to examine international trading relations. Briefly the argument is that value is given by the man-hours of labour-time necessary to produce a commodity. Actual market prices in a competitive capitalist economy will not equal values, but will be determined by them in a systematic way. Since the rate of profit will be equal between activities in competitive equilibrium prices of production must cover labour and other costs, and equalise the rate of profit on capital advanced for production.[19] In Emmanuel's original version the periphery produces 'specific' commodities; that is it specialises in goods different from those of the centre. Capital is assumed to be mobile internationally, so that internationally rates of profit are equalised. Labour is assumed not to be able to move freely, between countries, so that wage differentials are not removed by migration. Furthermore, and this is critical, labour in the periphery is assumed to be paid very much less than in the centre, so that the value of labour power, in terms of hours of labour-time is also much lower in the periphery. The consequence of these assumptions is that with a single rate of profit in the world economy, prices in low wage economies will be depressed relative to prices in high wage economies. In other words, if prices are determined by values, and the value of labour power is lower in the periphery than in the centre, the periphery will consistently receive lower prices than if wages and therefore the value of labour power had been equal in both areas. As Emmanuel puts it 'it thus becomes clear that the inequality of wages as such, all other things being equal, is alone the cause of the inequality of exchange . . . In relation to what is this exchange unequal? In relation to the situation where wages would be equalised. It is as simple as that.'[20]

Therefore, following Emmanuel and using the labour theory of value to explain international prices, it appears that if countries have different commodity specialisation and wage levels, prices will deviate systematically from values to the benefit of the countries with higher wages. Prices must be high enough to cover costs and give the ruling international rate of return, so that in this system an increase in wages in one group of countries is a means of redistributing to that group part of the total value produced in the world economy. Emmanuel argues that low wages are the key to understanding movements in the terms of trade of the periphery and that unequal exchange, in his terms, is a major drain of value, and thus of potential income, since man-hours expended in production go unrewarded. His own numerical examples, presumably for the late 1960s, imply that the magnitude of this drain is far greater than the other sources of international transfer discussed above. He suggests that if exports from the periphery to the centre are US$ 25 billion, wages are 50 per cent of export costs, and wage rates in the periphery are one twentieth of those of the centre, trade on an equal basis requires that the same volume of exports from the periphery rise in monetary terms to US$ 250 billion. The size of the drain in this example is therefore US$ 225 billion.[21] As a source of comparison this figure is nearly thirteen times total annual net financial flows to developing countries in the late 1960s and early 1970s.

Before commenting on the many critiques of this approach it is necessary to note that Amin also argues for the importance of unequal exchange, although using a different theoretical formulation.[22] Amin drops the assumption that the periphery produces only specific commodities, that is those different from the centre, and since similar commodities are produced, this in Amin's view allows a comparison between productivity in the two groups of countries. In his reformulation unequal exchange arises when differences in labour productivity between centre and periphery are less than differences in wages. In value analysis this implies unequal rates of surplus value, and in price terms, unequal rates of profit, per worker. Because similar or identical technologies are used in production of the same commodities in the centre and the periphery, Amin argues that productivity will be relatively close, whilst wages will be dramatically lower in the periphery. This creates unequal exchange since prices of the peripheries' exports will be lower than if the rate of surplus value were equal in centre and periphery. Workers in the periphery are seen as 'superexploited', since their wages are so much lower relative to the output they produce.

Amin gives an estimate of the magnitude of this drain. Referring presumably to the mid-1970s he estimates it to be around US\$ 300 billion, which is broadly comparable with Emmanuel's crude estimate referring to a few years earlier. Amin estimates the drain differently however by comparing the monetary value of production in the periphery with a notional value based on assumptions about comparative productivities in centre and periphery, and assuming that the rate of surplus value is the same for centre and periphery.[23] In other words, peripheral workers receive proportionately less of what they produce, than do workers in the centre and because of the tendency towards international equality of the rate of profit this surplus is not kept within the periphery but goes to raise profits in the centre.

Critiques of unequal exchange

Unequal exchange in both the Emmanuel and Amin versions has encountered such wide-ranging critiques that it is now difficult to take its policy conclusions seriously. An exhaustive discussion of the various points cannot be given here, but it may be useful to note some of the key issues.

- Wages are obviously the independent variable in Emmanuel's original version of the theory. However wage determination in his analysis is left largely unexplained, being attributed to 'historical and moral' factors — that is custom and institutional practice. Critics have pointed out the need to explain wages in terms of economic and class processes.[24] Amin has an explanation for low peripheral wages based on the co-existence of capitalist and pre-capitalist modes of production in these economies, however his view of wages in the centre is contradictory and confused.[25]

- The theory implies that countries can reduce the surplus drain arising from unequal exchange by raising their wage rates. However individual economies attempting this will run into balance of payment difficulties as their commodities become price uncompetitive, or as capital flows out in response to higher wage levels and reduced domestic profits. These balance of payment problems are likely to result in either devaluation, which will bring down real wages through higher inflation, or unemployment that will reduce the total wage bill and will probably also curb the growth in money wages.[26] The policy of raising wages to improve the terms of trade will only work, therefore, under the highly restrictive conditions that is applied by the periphery as a group, and all peripheral exports are non-competing with goods produced by the centre.

- Following the logic of the unequal exchange analysis there seems no reason why, if wages are lower in the periphery and capital is mobile internationally, capital will not flow to the periphery to take advantage of low wage costs. In the short-run, low labour costs will allow extra-normal profits to be earned, and if the capital export from the centre continues for long enough it can remove the labour surplus in the periphery and drive up wages to levels approaching those of the centre. The basis of unequal exchange will thus have been removed. Any attempt to explain why this process does not take place must rest on arguments external to the basic unequal exchange model.[27]

- Amin's specification of unequal exchange as the exchange of products whose production involves wage differences greater than those of productivity is imprecise in that it can apply equally to trade among countries of the centre.[28] Since a distinction between the groups of countries characterised as the centre and the periphery is essential to the theory, the possibility of unequal exchange occurring in intra-centre trade is a theoretical weakness.

- Most fundamentally one can question the applicability of the theoretical framework on which unequal exchange is based. The transformation of labour values to prices of production in Marxist economics is an abstraction relating to a competitive model of a national capitalist economy. In this system it is assumed that nationally there is free capital and labour mobility, so that standard hours of labour-time — socially necessary labour-time — can be identified as that necessary to produce a given commodity. A unit of this standard labour-time thus becomes the measure of value in the system. In the international economy, however, where there is immobility of labour, real wages differ, and different commodities are produced under varying degrees of market controls, it becomes difficult to argue that there is a single homogeneous unit of labour-time that can be used as a measure of value. If one takes this view, an hour of the labour of a peasant in the Sudan, for example, is not directly comparable with an hour of the labour of a factory worker in the UK, so that an hour given up by one does not necessarily create the same value as an hour given up by the other. If this is accepted international prices of production are an inadequate basis for explaining actual market prices.[29]

- Finally, in addition to these theoretical points, one can note that the empirical estimates of the magnitude of the drain arising from unequal exchange are crude and misleading. Emmanuel's calculation given earlier relates to a given volume of exports and takes no account of the impact of higher prices on the quantity traded. Not only are there substitution effects to be considered, but a ten-fold rise in the price of the peripheries' exports would have a depressing effect on incomes in the centre that would feedback as a lower demand for the peripheries' exports. Amin's calculations, on the other hand, have been shown to be confused in their lack of distinction between actual prices, labour values and what he terms 'effective prices', and in addition critically dependent on his assumptions regarding productivity differentials between centre and periphery. At a certain level of productivity differential the surplus drain from the periphery is reversed and actually becomes an inflow. Since no clear evidence is given to substantiate the assumptions used the result is dubious.[30]

In summary, therefore, the unequal exchange strand of the Dependency literature appears to add little to other versions of the surplus drain argument. Its starting point — the lower level of real wages in the periphery relative to the centre — is an acknowledged fact, but is probably best seen as a symptom of the problems associated with economic backwardness, and what is termed dependence, than their cause.

BARRIERS TO AN INTEGRATED INDUSTRIAL STRUCTURE

As noted earlier, many Radical authors would accept most of the points discussed in Chapter 3 on the key role indus- trialisation can play in economic development. Where some would reject the Structuralist case is over the feasibility of establishing an integrated industrial sector in the context of a capitalist development strategy that remains closely linked with the world market. In this section the arguments of two of the most influential proponents of this view — Samir Amin and Clive Thomas — are considered.[31]

Samir Amin — 'autocentric' and 'extraverted' growth

Amin, in line with other Dependency authors, sees the world system as divided into two distinct blocs — the centre and the periphery. Economic expansion in the centre is viewed as almost unproblematic — barring cyclical fluctuations. Growth there is seen as 'autocentric' or self-centred in that the internal not the external market provides the key demand stimulus. The growth of real wages of the proletariat is an important part of this process since wages are not only a cost to producers but also an income for workers, and thus a source of demand. A key characteristic of the self-centred growth in the centre, stressed by Amin, is the link between the sector producing consumer goods purchased by workers (wage goods) and the capital goods sector.

As the demand for wage goods expands it will create a market for the capital goods required for their production, and employment in the capital goods sector will in turn create a demand for wage goods, so that expansion can be cumulative.

In a simplified schematic discussion of this process Amin (1974b) divides an economy into four sectors. Sector 1 is the export sector; sector 2 produces wage goods (or goods of mass consumption); sector 3 produces luxury consumption goods (defined by Amin as goods purchased out of profits); sector 4 produces capital goods.

The determining relationship in a self-centred system in Amin's view is between sectors 2 and 4. This represents the logic of expansion in a closed capitalist economy as analysed by Marx (1967). However whilst the model of capitalism of the centre is based on a dynamic arising from links between domestic sectors, in Amin's analysis the situation in the periphery is very different. There he identifies a mode of production he terms 'peripheral capitalism'. Taking the capitalism of the centre as a norm he identifies a number of 'distortions' present in the peripheral variant. These are:

(1) a crucial distortion towards export activities which absorb the major part of the capital arising from the centre;

(2) a distortion towards tertiary activities which arise from both the special contradictions of peripheral capitalism and the original structures of the peripheral formations; and

(3) a distortion in the choice of branches of industry towards light branches, and also to a lesser degree towards light techniques.[32]

In other words, the economic structure of peripheral capitalism sees a heavy emphasis on the export sector, and services; within industry it is light — by implication non-capital goods industry — which is relatively more developed. The broader socio-economic structure is seen as one in which pre-capitalist modes, for example peasant production, coexist with capitalism, although the latter is dominant. The diversity of historical and cultural experience in different countries of the periphery is noted, but Amin is explicit that he sees an underlying unity — based on membership of the group of peripheral countries and the position of this group *vis-à-vis* the centre — behind this diversity.

Capitalism in the periphery is seen as resulting originally from external factors; the need for the centre to obtain raw materials and foodstuffs and the foreign investment that ensured that these goods would be provided for the world market. Amin acknowledges that with the growth of the export sector some linkages will be established with other branches, so that a form of diversification of the economy can take place. However, unlike the centre, where the key relationship is between the sectors producing goods of mass consumption and capital goods, in the periphery in Amin's analysis the main link is between the export sector and the sector producing luxury consumer goods. In terms of the schematic discussion noted earlier in the periphery the key link is between sectors 1 and 3, not between sectors 2 and 4, as in the centre.

The link between the export sector and luxury consumer good production arises from the structure of the peripheral system. The pre-capitalist branches of the economy provide cheap labour for the export sector and wages remain low because of the inability of the economic system to transform these pre-capitalist branches. The rising incomes of domestic classes and groups who support the system — domestic capitalists, traders, landowners, rich peasants, and bureaucrats — create a demand for the domestic production of luxury consumer goods. This is how Amin interprets the industrialisation experienced in the periphery since the 1950s.[33] However with the low incomes of the excluded classes there is no incentive for resources to flow into the production of basic wage goods.

Therefore, in Amin's analysis, even when industrialisation for the home market occurs in a peripheral capitalist economy the pattern of development remains 'extraverted' or dependent on external influences. External demand governs the expansion of the export sector, and thus indirectly the incomes of those domestic classes and groups associated with the export sector. It is the income of the latter that determines the expansion of luxury consumer goods production. This outward-oriented dynamic means that the demand from wage earners plays little part in the expansion of the system, and that wages are primarily a cost, which in the interests of capital accumulation and profitability should be kept as low as possible. Amin writes of the 'marginalization of the masses', by which he appears to mean their impoverishment in absolute terms, as an essential part of the functioning of a peripheral economy.

For Amin low wages in the periphery are necessary for the functioning of the overall world economy; in other words it is the role of the periphery to supply cheap labour to be used in the production of exports of essential primary products and raw materials to the centre. These low wages have a critical impact on the internal structure of peripheral economies, however, since they restrict the home market for mass consumer goods and thus prevent the emergence of an integrated industrial structure linking the wage goods and capital goods sectors. In addition, they also create the conditions for the unequal exchange of commodities between centre and periphery discussed earlier.

The importance of Amin's analysis for the present discussion is that he denies that an integrated industrial structure can be established currently in peripheral economies, since in his view such integrated structure can only be achieved under self-centred patterns of development. Amin concedes the possibility of the larger developing countries establishing their own capital goods production, but argues that these capital goods will be linked with the export and luxury consumer goods sectors, and not with the sector of mass consumer goods. As a consequence the market for such capital goods will be both limited and remain subject to the dynamic imposed by external demand. Therefore even where local capital goods production is established this is seen as simply an extension of extraverted peripheral development, and not as evidence of a move to a more autocentric path. The conclusion is that a radical break with existing international economic relationships is necessary to create the possibility for integrated industrial development. It should be noted that Amin appears to be advocating tight controls on trade rather than autarky, noting in Amin (1980) that the latter can entail heavy costs and is not necessarily synonymous with autonomous development. What he is implying is a system in which domestic production determines trade patterns for any individual economy, not as at present in the periphery where trade determines the structure of domestic production. Before commenting on the validity of these arguments it is necessary to examine the position of Thomas who, independently of Amin, put forward similar views on the difficulty of transforming the structure of developing countries without radical changes in political and economic relations.

Clive Thomas — the convergence strategy

Thomas, like Amin, sees the problem of underdevelopment in terms of a dependent relationship between peripheral economies and the advanced capitalist economies of the centre. He goes further than Amin in acknowledging that in the larger peripheral economies the development of an integrated industrial sector based on capitalist relations of production may be possible. However for the smaller countries that are the majority in the periphery he sees such a transformation as impossible without socialism. The material manifestation of economic backwardness is seen as the divergence between the use of domestic resources, domestic demand and domestic need. In other words, due to the outward-orientation of peripheral economies imposed by the international system, domestic resources are used in production to meet the demand and needs of other societies. Production is therefore unresponsive to and divergent from the needs of the indigenous population. An industrial transformation, in Thomas's view requires a convergence of domestic resource use, domestic demand, and domestic need; further what Thomas terms a 'vibrant indigenous technology' will be needed to ensure that available domestic resources can be utilised to meet domestic demand. An indigenous technology plays a key role in the argument since foreign technologies, designed in the light of resource availabilities in other societies, will not ensure the maximum use of local resources, both materials and labour.

Although the terminology is different much of the emphasis is similar to that of Amin. A successful industrial transformation must be inward-looking in the sense of linking the use of domestic resources and material inputs with demand, which must in turn reflect need. Whilst Amin writes of the link between capital goods and mass consumer goods sectors, Thomas sees the key relationship as between what he terms 'basic materials' and industries producing mass consumer goods, including agriculture. Basic materials are the inputs — such as steel, industrial chemicals, paper, plastics, cement, wood, glass, textiles and fuel — used in a wide range of activities. They are the goods which show the highest linkages — both backward and forward. Industrial transformation for Thomas requires that domestically available resources be used to produce these basic materials, which will then be used in the production of final goods to meet domestic demands. In this way an integrated industrial structure can be established, with far fewer linkages abroad in the form of import demand, than in existing industrial structures.[34]

Thomas sees the strategic sector of basic materials as wider than capital goods, as these are defined conventionally. However, there is a similarity with Amin, who identifies the capital goods sector through a simplified breakdown of an economy into only four sectors, and no doubt would include many of these basic materials under the heading of capital goods. Thomas writes also of the central role that the machine tools branch of capital goods can play, since indigenous technical innovations need to be embodied in machines. An economy without the capacity to produce its own equipment will be forced to rely on imported supplies which may stultify indigenous technical change and result in 'a pattern of production where the machines in domestic use are a by-product of forces elsewhere seeking to converge some other societies resources to their requirements.'[35]

However, Thomas's basic materials or basic industry strategy is not a restatement of the arguments for priority to capital goods production to allow a higher rate of reinvestment, associated with Feldman and Mahanalobis, and considered in Chapter 3. His case is distinct in that it is not capital goods *per se* that are important, but industrial inputs that can be used in a range of goods, and which will be required if the internal mass market for consumer goods is to be expanded. Not all of these basic materials will require heavy capital investment and it is argued that they will have the advantage of being based on locally available raw materials, which will not only increase local linkages, but also lower the production cost of these basic goods. The contrast is between the basic industry strategy aimed at a mass consumer goods market, and import-substitution of an import-intensive variety, that creates few domestic linkages and caters to the demands of the national elite for luxury consumer goods.

On the question of the role of foreign trade, Thomas also rejects a policy of autarky. In his strategy trade can play a role, although clearly one subsidiary to domestic demand. Imports, he acknowledges, are necessary to cover specific shortfalls, and foreign technologies may also be needed to supplement local technology. Furthermore as new production is established for the domestic market, and local producers gain increased experience, some output may be exported to cover the foreign exchange requirements for necessary imports. These exports, however, will be of a similar type to goods produced initially for the domestic market and will thus reflect the characteristics of that market. Therefore, as with Amin, under this strategy it is domestic decisions on production that determine the pattern of trade not vice-versa.

Low wages do not play the central role in Thomas's analysis as they do in that of Amin. In discussing the obstacles to industrialisation in small peripheral economies his main focus is on the difficulty of establishing major linkages within the industrial sector in the context of existing social and economic structures in the periphery. Three main arguments can be noted, all of which are raised frequently in the Radical literature. First, that much of the industrialisation in these economies will be dominated by transnational firms with no incentive to seek local suppliers. Second, that governments of these economies often will not have the capacity to plan for the establishment of such linkages. Third, that an indigenous entrepreneurial class capable of responding to the demand generated by linkages is absent. These arguments will be considered in more detail in following sections. Here some general comments will be made on the views of Amin and Thomas.

Some observations on Amin and Thomas

Both Thomas and Amin provide a case for the establishment of an integrated industrial structure that is compatible with the discussion of externalities, learning and productivity growth in Chapter 3. However whilst aspects of their arguments are no doubt valid in certain circumstances, they both put forward two key propositions that are questionable as generalisations; first that an export-orientation is inevitably inimical to the establishment of linkages within the domestic economy, and second that a successful capitalist industrialisation is not a viable option for the majority of developing countries. Successful capitalist development is seen as a possibility for only a few favoured countries with preferential access to foreign credits and export markets, because of their political ties with the hegemonic powers.[36]

The real issue is whether the authors can demonstrate both theoretically and empirically that these propositions hold. It is not clear, for example, why some forms of export growth cannot raise real wages as a result of higher demand for labour, and cannot stimulate the transformation of agriculture to the capitalist mode of production. With higher real wages or incomes for rural household producers the market for simple consumer goods will expand, and linkages can be established between domestic intermediate and capital goods suppliers and both the export sector and the sector producing basic consumer goods. Such a process may be gradual, but the question of the timing of the introduction of a basic industry strategy must be raised. It must be recognised that there are limits on the extent to which a strategy based on basic materials and capital goods can be pushed through in small countries in a short space of time. Thomas, for example, does not address fully the problem of market size, and its implications for economies of scale. Further he does not consider the increased dependence on imports of technology that is likely to be a short-run consequence of a shift in priorities towards basic materials and capital goods.

It is clear that not all basic material industries need be capital intensive, characterised by major economies of scale, nor dependent on best-practice foreign technology. For example mechanical engineering based production, such as machine tools, is often less capital-intensive than the average for all manufacturing and can be established in relatively small-scale production units, utilising local skills. However it is also the case that some basic materials, most particularly iron and steel, require to be cost competitive, heavy capital investment, relatively large-scale production and modern technology. It must be recalled that not all linkages are necessarily economically desirable, and that even if one can make a case for the establishment of a range of basic industries, based on local raw materials, this is not the same thing as demonstrating the validity of the immediate establishment of the local production of all basic materials that technically can be produced in a country. The question of sequencing, based on an assessment of the relative costs, benefits and learning effects associated with their production is critical. It is by no means obvious that the very rapid sequence envisaged by Thomas is the most desirable, at least in the small economies with which he is concerned.[37]

Empirical evidence can be used to question the authors' two main propositions and to demonstrate that basic industries have been established in a number of countries as a result of linkages arising from export or luxury consumer goods sectors. It has been shown, for example, that export growth in Taiwan and South Korea has generated both rising real wages and significant backward linkages to domestic intermediate and capital good suppliers.[38] Similarly Schiffer (1981) gives a detailed empirical rebuttal of Amin showing for the 1960s both the growth of real wages and of basic consumer goods production, in much of the periphery. This data refers not simply to the success stories of South East Asia, but includes countries in Africa, the continent with which Amin and Thomas are most concerned. Chapter 1 here also includes data particularly on the growth of capital goods production and exports of manufactures, that are contrary to the hypothesis of Amin, and also to a lesser extent Thomas. The important general point to stress here is that critiques of Amin and Thomas from within the Radical literature are part of a reappraisal that acknowledges the possibility of capitalist industrialisation in the periphery. This is a point to which we will return in the discussion of other arguments on obstacles to industrialisation in the periphery.

TRANSNATIONAL CORPORATIONS AND DEPENDENCE

In most of the Radical literature on industrialisation transnationals figure prominently. In particular in debates on the potential benefits from industrialisation in Latin America, the Dependency position was that much of these benefits will be lost if transnationals play a leading role.

As we have seen transnationals have been involved in industrialisation in the periphery in an uneven way — playing a major role in some countries and a smaller one in others. However the Dependency literature has been highly critical of this involvement stressing the negative effects of foreign ownership and control. Transnationals as global profit-seeking capitalist organisations with their own objectives and strategies, and the political backing of the advanced capitalist economies, were seen as draining away rather than expanding the resources available for development. This view implies that locally owned firms — either public or private sector — have different behavioural characteristics from transnationals and that these characteristics are more likely to lead to long-run growth and industrial transformation. Influential as this position has been, it has come to be questioned, particularly by what we have termed the internationalisation of capital approach.

From this perspective transnational firms are viewed not in isolation but as one, albeit highly important manifestation of the evolution of the world capitalist economy. It is argued that capital has become international in its search for profits and markets, and that international production is a response to wage rates and market opportunities in different countries. In this view the impact of transnationals on host developing economies can be contradictory — with the potential for both positive and negative effects. However one important implication is that dependence — in the sense of a heavy transnational involvement in the economy — can be associated with growth; what is now referred to as 'dependent development'. Furthermore this analysis sees a strong tendency for nationally-owned firms to become increasingly similar to transnationals; for example in the technology, marketing strategies, and product designs that they employ. In fact with the spread of non-ownership links between local and foreign firms — for example technology agreements and management contracts — it is argued that the distinction between national and transnational firms becomes blurred. This blurring is further reflected in the emergence of some transnational firms whose head-offices are based in countries of the periphery.

In the following sections these two broad alternative perspectives on transnational involvement — that of dependency and internationalisation of capital — provide the framework underlying the discussions. The next section examines the arguments that stress the negative effects of investment by transnationals and the following considers the extent to which these arguments need to be qualified or rejected.

CRITIQUES OF TRANSNATIONALS' INDUSTRIAL INVESTMENTS

Several arguments will be considered under the headings of:

- transnationals and surplus outflows;
- transnationals and restrictive practices;
- transnationals and denationalisation;
- other effects of transnationals on domestic industrial structure.

Transnationals and surplus outflows

As we have seen much of the work in the Dependency tradition follows Baran in stressing the importance of economic surplus and the way in which it is utilised. Transnationals are seen as draining this surplus from developing countries in a variety of ways, the most obvious being profit repatriations, royalty payments and fees for management and other services. Most studies of the direct balance of payments effects of foreign investments find these to be negative — implying that direct foreign exchange outflows associated with these investments exceed the original inflows.[39]

Furthermore this trend has been exacerbated by the tendency for transnationals to rely increasingly on local capital markets for the finance of their investments. In addition to direct outflows, however, it is also argued that transnationals have the ability to drain the economic surplus through the indirect means of transfer pricing. This involves setting prices on the inputs or outputs sold by a subsidiary to another enterprise within the same organisation at prices that differ from the 'arms-length' prices that would prevail in a commercial transaction. There can be a number of motives for transfer pricing and in some circumstances it may work in the interests of particular host economies. However it is normally argued that in developing economies transnationals will wish to keep their declared profits low, either to avoid high tax rates, or restrictions on profit repatriation. Therefore where profit tax rates are high or foreign exchange controls are tight they will have an incentive to shift their declared profits to another subsidiary or to their parent company, through the manipulation of transfer prices. It

145

is clearly difficult to estimate the extent of transfer pricing, but several studies suggest that it is important, at least in a selected number of industries, particularly pharmaceuticals.[40]

Transnationals and restrictive practices

It is also argued that when transnationals transfer technology, capital, and management skills to developing countries as either investment in wholly-owned subsidiaries or joint ventures with domestic partners, they impose both formal and informal restrictions on the activities of the new enterprise. These restrictions are imposed to preserve the monopoly or quasi-monopoly position of the transnationals, but it is argued that they work to reduce the net benefits to the host economy from transnational involvement.[41] The main areas of restriction on the new enterprise relate to export sales, technology development and local purchases of inputs.

It is clear that parent companies may not wish new enterprises overseas to compete with goods produced in other parts of their international organisation, so that restrictions on either exports in general or to particular markets have been found to be a common feature of agreements between parents and new enterprises within the same organisation. In the case of technology development, the argument here is that parent firms wish to maintain control over their own technology, and that it is easiest to do this by centralising research and development activities in a small number of locations, and not allowing subsidiaries or joint ventures in a range of countries to experiment with modifications and adaptations to the basic core technology; in addition sub-licensing of the technology domestically or collaborations with other local partners, which involve the domestic dissemination of the technology may be restricted. These restrictions, it is argued, inhibit local technological development.

The final major form of restriction relates to purchases of locally manufactured inputs or raw materials. Transnationals may have a preference for imported rather than local supplies on either grounds of quality or their own global profit objectives, where the inputs can be supplied from other branches of their own organisation. Formal restrictions on input purchases are most likely to be linked with quality standards that can only be met by imported inputs. Informal restrictions can operate through the guidance given by parent company headquarters to the local management of an enterprise. Where such restrictions are enforced they clearly weaken the backward linkages generated by transnational investments.

Transnationals and denationalisation

In a number of industries, particularly in Latin America, transnational firms have invested locally by acquiring nationally-owned firms. This process has been well documented particularly in pharmaceuticals, automobiles and electrical goods, and has been described as one of denationalisation since major industries have been brought under almost total foreign ownership.[42] Transnationals have used a variety of methods to weaken the competitive position of rival national firms, including in some cases cross-subsidisation by the parent firm to finance sales below costs of production, the establishment of control over supplies of key inputs and formal collusion between transnationals to weaken the position of particular competitors, as well as the familiar form of oligopolistic competition based on advertising and brand-names. In addition transnationals have often had favourable access to finance — either from within their parent organisation or from domestic financial institutions.

This process of denationalisation is viewed with concern for several reasons. First, domestic entrepreneurs are forced out of productive activities, and may not reinvest in industry, perhaps preferring to invest in shares or real estate. Second, take-overs are often the result of market power rather than greater efficiency, and are likely to contribute to greater market concentration in the industries concerned. In other words it is not obvious *a-priori* that the level of productive efficiency is raised as a result of such a take-over. Third, it is often argued that in several industries the 'style of development' will differ if transnationals come to dominate. This is a natural consequence of the view that the behaviour of transnationals differs from that of national firms, and more detailed statements of this argument will be considered below.

147

Other effects of transnationals on domestic industrial structure

A number of related points can be noted here. An argument often raised in relation to the industrialisation that has taken place in the periphery post-1945 is that it is 'prematurely oligopolistic'. In other words, in developed capitalist economies industry was organised initially on a competitive basis with a relatively large number of small producers competing for national markets, and only over a lengthy period did oligopolistic structures, dominated by a small number of firms emerge. The argument is that, in many branches, industry in developing countries has been oligopolistic from the outset of production. In part, this may be the result of technological factors, so that the small size of domestic markets in many developing countries means that with existing technology and plant scale only a small number of firms can coexist in the market. In support of this view is the tendency for small national markets to display the highest levels of industrial concentration.[43] It is also argued, however, that the activities of transnationals either through take-overs, or heavy advertising that raises barriers to entry for other firms, accentuate this process. The situation is complicated in that in some branches it appears that competition between transnationals to establish themselves in particular national markets may reproduce the international structure of the industry, in an individual country — the 'miniature replica' effect. This phenomenon will tend to reduce concentration in the industries affected, since all major international producers will aim to set up local production, although it may also contribute to substantial excess capacity. However, in general, the balance of the argument still tends to see transnationals raising rather than reducing industrial concentration.[44]

Oligopoly is seen as retarding the process of growth and accumulation largely because of the non-price competition with which it is associated. Measures such as advertising and minor design changes are seen as socially unproductive in the context of developing countries. In some industries, particularly automobiles, it has been demonstrated that frequent product differentiation through model changes reduces the potential for economies of scale and the development of local linkages.[45]

Another related argument on the style of development associated with a heavy transnational involvement stresses that transnationals transfer to host developing countries both technologies and products designed for the higher income markets of developed economies. The consequence is that the technology employed by transnationals is capital-intensive, creating only a small employment effect, and the consumer goods they produce are 'inappropriate' since only local elites can afford them. What is termed 'product taste transfer' has a key role in some versions of this argument since the initial choice of product, it is suggested, determines the technology to be used, the form of competition in the industry and the extent to which it will be possible to generate linkages with local suppliers. The point is that if production is seen as responding to the need for particular goods or services — such as demands for washing materials or transport — the involvement of transnationals can determine the manner in which these needs are defined. This definition may not be in the long-run interests of the majority of the population.[46]

Finally, a heavy transnational presence in an industry, it is argued, can make that industry vulnerable to changes that take place internationally and over which individual governments have little or no control. For example, mergers between transnationals internationally, or a poor profit performance in certain subsidiaries may lead to a restructuring of a transnational's production in an individual developing country. The dynamic of an industry, in these instances, is located externally.[47]

REASSESSMENT OF TRANSNATIONAL ACTIVITY

Common as these arguments are, they are held less widely now than ten or fifteen years ago, even by those sympathetic to a Radical perspective. For example Booth (1985) illustrates this reappraisal:

> . . . there is not much doubt that mainstream 1960s dependency theorists were taken in by a perfectly spurious correlation. Advanced import substitution was associated with an invasion of manufacturing multinationals, growing external vulnerability and regressive trends in employment and distribution. Plausibly but wrongly the last two things were laid at the door of the first.[48]

In other words, he is arguing that it is a mistake to blame transnationals for the inefficiencies and errors of past industrialisation in the periphery. Following this line several of the specific points noted above can be questioned. We have already considered the limitations of the surplus drain argument and pointed out that some form of cost-benefit calculation is needed to establish the full economic consequences of foreign investments. Whilst the available evidence shows considerable ambiguity on the question of the economic desirability of many foreign investment projects, neither is it possible to conclude that they are unambiguously undesirable.

A particularly important aspect of the surplus drain case refers to transfer pricing as a mechanism for draining resources from host economies. However the magnitude of this form of drain has also come to be questioned. Much of the available evidence comes from one industry — pharmaceuticals — which has several specific characteristics. Transfer prices in that industry are calculated by comparing transnationals' prices in sales to subsidiaries with the prices charged by firms who imitate the technology of the transnational, and who therefore do not observe patent restrictions in the industry. Whether or not this comparison between the prices of innovating and imitating firms is valid, it can be argued that the case of pharmaceuticals is exceptional.[49]

The argument on the impact of transnationals on industrial concentration in the periphery can also be viewed differently. The presence of transnationals in capital-intensive, concentrated branches is well established. What is less clear, however, is the issue of causation. To what extent is it possible to argue that it is transnational presence that causes concentration, or is it the case that the type of industries in which transnationals have the greatest competitive strength will tend to be relatively highly concentrated? In other words, is there a technological or institutional explanation for industrial concentration that is independent of the nationality of firms? The evidence on this remains ambiguous.[50] In addition, regardless of the causal factors at work, the negative relationship between industrial concentration, and economic efficiency and growth is less obvious than is implied by the argument noted earlier. A positive association between high concentration and high profitability has been found by most studies that have looked at this question. However if concentration through merger is necessary to achieve economies of scale, or if the higher profits resulting from concentration are reinvested, particularly in research and development, the implied negative effect of concentration on efficiency and growth becomes questionable. Therefore the argument that in the periphery concentration *per se* has a negative import on development prospects, remains to be demonstrated conclusively.

Perhaps one of the weakest aspects of the Dependency critique of transnationals, as outlined above, is the view that transnationals and national firms behave in significantly different ways when they are established in the same industry. As noted earlier the internationalisation of capital perspective challenges this view, and much of the data compiled over the last ten years or so provides little support for the argument that there are major behavioural differences between similiar firms that can be explained solely by nationality. When one compares firms of similar size and activity, but distinguished by ownership, it is generally difficult to detect a tendency for transnationals to be either more capital-intensive or more import-intensive than local firms. This latter point implies that transnationals can create important domestic linkage effects in the same way as national firms, although no doubt in some instances such linkages arise from government pressure rather than the commercial judgements of transnationals. Furthermore, as in the case of local firms, at least some transnationals have been flexible enough to adapt the technology imported from their parents in the light of operating conditions in host economies; generally, however, these adaptations are less common in core production technology than in ancillary activities. This apparent similarity of behaviour is explicable in terms of the need for capital, both foreign and domestic, to adopt similar technologies and market strategies because of the common international competitive pressures they face.[51]

None the less some studies have found major differences between transnationals and local firms; Langdon (1979), on Kenya, being one of the best documented. Langdon, as we have noted, links the greater import and capital-intensity of transnationals to the type of products in which they specialise. However he also finds that for the industries studied, transnationals have come to take a growing share of the domestic market, and that local competitors in several branches have been forced by competition to mechanise and advertise in the same way as transnationals. These findings are therefore not incompatible with the internationalisation of capital approach since they imply a tendency towards growing similarity between firms in some branches.[52]

Another important aspect of the critique of transnationals that must be qualified is the view, implicit in the de-nationalisation argument that transnationals inevitably are dominant in all relations with domestic groups. Evidence from Latin America, where this has been a major issue, suggests that this view is simplistic for several reasons. First, even in economies such as Mexico and Brazil, where foreign capital plays a key role in industrialisation, there are certain branches where local capital remains dominant. These are generally low-technology, labour-intensive traditional branches.[53] Second, even in branches dominated by transnationals, at least in the larger Latin American economies, local capital has not been displaced totally. Some local firms maintain a share of the market by adopting a role complementary to rather than competitive with foreign capital, and others enter into joint ventures providing local knowledge and government contacts for their transnational partners.[54] Third, the activities of the state in host countries cannot be ignored, since state intervention in several countries has forced transnationals to alter their behaviour: for example, in establishing backward linkages with local suppliers, in exporting to cover the foreign exchange costs of local production, and in setting-up joint ventures with local capital.[55] The state can also become a second partner along with domestic private capital, in alliances with transnationals, and because of the financial incentives it can offer is often seen as the senior local partner in such alliances.

Several authors working from a Radical perspective have built on the idea of collaboration between the state, transnationals and local capital to question the pessimistic conclusions of the Dependency literature on the scope for development when there is a major transnational presence in the economy. For example, Evans (1979) writes of the possibility of 'dependent development' based on a 'triple alliance' between transnationals, the state and local capital. The members of this alliance are seen as interdependent partners with a common interest in capital accumulation and the subordination of the majority of the population. The relative strengths of each member of the alliance will vary between countries, and between branches within countries. Although mutuality of interests exists, so too does the potential for conflict, so that it is difficult to predict *a-priori* how the alliance will react in particular situations. The potential of this alliance for generating growth and structural change remains ambiguous, although it is implied that growth and dependence — defined as a heavy reliance on transnationals — can co-exist. Evans suggests that this dependent development has not yet spread to many economies of the periphery, citing Brazil and Mexico as the most obvious examples of this pattern of development. By implication other developing economies are still in a situation of 'classic dependence' where the standard dependency arguments on the inhibiting impact of transnationals on growth and structural change still apply.

However Warren (1973) and (1980) goes considerably further in stressing the possibilities of successful capitalist development in the periphery, with a strong transnational involvement. He argues that just as the state in developing countries in the post-war period has been able to restrict the power of transnationals in extractive industries, so it can also control the activities of the transnationals who have invested more recently in manufacturing either for export or import substitution. In Warren's view contact with the advanced capitalist economies, through both trade and foreign investment, will greatly expand productive potential in the periphery and hasten the development of an indigenous capitalist class capable of playing a leading role in successfully industrialising these economies. In other words, in this view the local partners in the triple alliance will be sufficiently strong to counter any adverse tendencies, or conflicts of interest, associated with the activities of transnationals.

It is fair to say that this reappraisal within the Radical literature of the role of transnationals has not gone sufficiently far for these views, particularly those of Warren, to become a new consensus. However, as was stated earlier, it is coming to be recognised that many of the old arguments have been overstated. This does not mean that one can reject totally the view that there are dangers in a heavy reliance on foreign investment or that an independent national alternative is preferable. For example, as we have seen in Chapter 2, a number of statistical analyses using cross-sectional data from a large sample of countries have found support for the proposition that the level of transnational presence in an economy is negatively associated with both the rate of growth and equality in income distribution.[56]

This evidence is supportive of the general arguments discussed above, but it should be noted that it does not imply that transnational involvement creates stagnation. Furthermore it sheds no light on the feasibility of a non-dependent path, that is one involving a much lower degree of transnational involvement, for those economies where transnationals have played a major role.

It seems plausible to argue that transnational involvement in development remains contradictory with the possibility for both expanding and retarding the productive potential of a peripheral economy. There is evidence that well-designed government policies, backed by a strong state involvement, can raise the potential benefits to be obtained from transnationals. Furthermore the prospect of an independent nationalist development, either capitalist or socialist, appears increasingly illusory. This is perhaps best evidenced by the shift in policy in China and North Korea towards a much more encouraging posture *vis-à-vis* transnationals. It is clear that socialist governments cannot afford to ignore transnationals and the technology they can provide. The degree of transnational presence that makes economic sense will clearly vary between activities, for example, in some relatively less technologically advanced branches the necessary technology can be imported under licence without the need to allow foreign ownership of assets in the firm to be established using that technology. In others, where the pace of technological change is rapid and where transnationals are less willing to give access to their technology it may be neither possible nor desirable to 'unbundle' the foreign investment package and block foreign ownership. This approach, of course, implies falling back on case-by-case screening, rather than an open-door policy of acceptance, or a closed-door one of total rejection. In terms of the balance of arguments, however, Evans and Warren seem to be much nearer the reality than the earlier Dependency critics of transnationals.

THE DOMESTIC BOURGEOISIE AND THE STATE

If successful industrialisation is to be attained in developing countries some class or group must play a leading role in establishing and managing new industries. A question central to the

Radical perspectives is whether such classes or groups can emerge given the social and political, as well as the economic conditions in the periphery. An initial premise of most Dependency authors is that in the periphery the class seen as responsible for industrialisation in the advanced capitalist economies, the national or domestic bourgeoisie, is either small in number, or where it is numerically large, weak in influence. In other words, given the historical evolution of peripheral societies, and in particular their contact with the new developed countries through colonialism and trade, the domestic bourgeoisie cannot play the role of prime mover in the industrialisation of the periphery. The argument is a further aspect of the more narrowly economic points noted earlier in the discussion of surplus drain, structural change, and the role of transnationals.

Different Radical authors have characterised the middle class in the periphery in different ways. Baran (1957) in his influential work writes of a *comprador* bourgeoisie that is interested in trade rather than production, and where it is involved in manufacturing only maintains its position through its ties with foreign capital. Given the expansion of manufacturing in the periphery and the extent of local participation in this expansion, it is difficult to maintain the view that domestic bourgeoisies remain oriented towards trade to the exclusion of production. If one wishes to keep the concept of a *comprador* class it has to be seen as externally dependent in manufacturing, and thus unable to initiate an independent national industrialisation. This is the sense in which Frank uses the polemical term 'lumpen-bourgeoisie', and in which Amin writes of a '*compradorised* bourgeoisie'.

The trading origins of the bourgeoisie in the periphery plays a key role in one interpretation, Kay (1975), of the origins of underdevelopment. Here the argument is that it was foreign merchant capital that first opened the periphery to economic contact with the now advanced capitalist economies, and that unlike industrial capital, merchant capital was incapable of destroying pre-capitalist relations of production. In other words, merchants could rely on output from non-capitalist producers for the supplies they required, without needing to reorganise production along capitalist lines. Although the situation is recognised as different in the post-independence period, with national merchants and producers emerging to replace foreigners, Kay's analysis suggests that it is the historical evolution of the periphery — essentially the period when it was dominated by foreign merchants — that creates what is generally termed underdevelopment or economic backwardness. The implication is that even when national capitalists emerge they cannot shake off their historical origins.[57]

The general Dependency view is that the domestic bourgeoisie in the periphery is weak, and where it engages in production relies heavily on its ties with foreign capital. However, this class is privileged financially and socially in comparison with other national groups, and perceives its interests as lying in further foreign links. It is therefore a representative of foreign capital in domestic society, and is the central element of what Sunkel (1973) terms the 'transnational kernel'; that is, 'a complex of activities, social groups and regions in different countries . . . which are closely linked transnationally through many concrete interests as well as by similar styles, ways and levels of living and cultural affinities.'[58]

The validity of this general view of the domestic bourgeoisie is considered in the following section.

Evidence on the domestic bourgeoisie

Data on the origins and behaviour of domestic industrialists in developing countries remains scanty.[59] In terms of their origins it is clear that industrial entrepreneurs can come from a variety of backgrounds, including trade, agriculture, the professions and small-scale handicrafts. The first two source are likely to be particularly important since they offer scope for large-scale capital accumulation which can later be transferred to industry. The South Korean case is of interest due to the emergence of a relatively strong domestic capitalist class post-1945. There it appears that almost one-quarter of the 50 largest industrial groups arose out of the expansion of trading companies.[60] However the links between agriculture and industry should not be underestimated and there is evidence from a number of countries, particularly in Latin America, that families that initially accumulated wealth in agriculture invested subsequently in new industrial activities. In some economic groups, therefore, the links between agrarian and industrial capital can be relatively close.[61]

Considerable debate has taken place in recent years in the Radical literature on the question of the relative strength and independence of the industrial bourgeoisie. In large part this can be interpreted as a reaction against the Dependency view of a subservient *comprador* class summarised briefly above. The main geographical focus of this debate has been Latin America, with its relatively long experience of industrialisation, and rather more surprisingly, Kenya, a country where many of the authors interested in this issue have worked. The debate is not primarily about the size of the domestic industrial bourgeoisie, since it must be accepted that the assets of domestic groups will be very small in comparison with their transnational competitors. Nor is it about the ideological independence of the domestic bourgeoisie, since rarely do they appear to reject the life-styles and value-system associated with international capitalism; nor in general do they argue for a nationalist development path that closes the door to collaboration with foreign capital. The key issue is the degree to which in their links with transnationals the domestic bourgeoisie can be seen as subservient and wholly dependent on their foreign partners.

From this point of view the significance of the analysis of Evans (1979) on Brazil cited earlier lies in his rejection of the common Dependency position. Although the domestic private sector is seen as the weakest partner in the 'triple alliance', often depending on the state for finance and transnationals for technology, this analysis stresses the possibility of mutual interdependence. The local bourgeoisie can thus play an important integrative role in some branches helping transnationals to establish themselves in local markets, and set up links with local customers, suppliers and the bureaucracy. In other branches however, particularly where technology is less critical, one would expect the national side of the alliance to be more influential. Evans himself, for example, argues that 'from industry to industry . . . the leverage of local capital is inversely related to the importance of scale and technology . . .'[62] This approach therefore distinguishes between different sections of the domestic bourgeoisie and notes that whilst some may be subservient, as Dependency authors suggest, others may be both important partners for foreign capital and relatively independent. There is evidence, for example, from the larger Latin American countries that the large domestic industrial groups are in a position to strike relatively favourable deals on technology purchases and joint venture arrangements.[63]

Although the debate on the emergence of an indigenous industrial bourgeoisie in Kenya was conducted with little or no reference to Latin American experience, it is possible to interpret the central argument in terms similar to the 'triple alliance' view put forward in relation to Brazil.[64] Leys (1982) argues that an indigenous Kenyan bourgeoisie, with its roots in the pre-colonial period became increasingly strong economically in the 1970s, and began to play a more influential role in industry often through joint ventures and technology agreements with foreign capital. The latter might still dominate the relatively small manufacturing sector but the trend, Leys argues, shows an increasingly important role for national capital, bolstered by the support of the Kenyan state. It is clear that the claim that an independent national bourgeoisie was emerging in Kenya in the 1970s cannot be substantiated, but this is not Leys's position. He writes of the fundamental interests of capital, whether national or transnational, coinciding, and that 'the general form of this coincidence in Kenya is the general need of all fractions and strata of the bourgeoisie for further investment of foreign capital; and that what are in conflict are the interests of different elements of the bourgeoisie differentially affected by the specific forms this takes'.[65] In other words, one can interpret this to mean that national capital supported by the state needs to enter an alliance with foreign capital, but that the relationship within the alliance can vary between industries and over time. Kaplinsky (1982), the chief critic of Leys, appears to argue that any such alliance will undermine the position of national capital and recreate dependence on transnationals, but experience elsewhere suggests that this is not inevitable.

Kenya, a relatively backward economy, is not a very promising location for a strong national capitalist class and the existence of the Kenyan debate on this issue is symptomatic of the reappraisal that is taking place within the Radical literature. There are other studies that indicate the emergence of a relatively strong domestic industrial bourgeoisie; for example in India, South Korea and Taiwan and the larger Latin American economies, Brazil, Mexico and Argentina.[66] The success of domestic firms from the NICs in technology exports, and the emergence of foreign investments by such firms are further evidence of such a trend. It can be argued that this is a very brief list, given the numbers of developing countries. However what is at issue is an emerging trend that must be seen against the background of economic backwardness prevalent in most developing countries 40 years ago. Therefore whilst the available evidence is far from conclusive, it suggests that the common Dependency position on the weak subservient domestic bourgeoisie is becoming increasingly untenable. Domestic capitalists are rarely wholly independent of foreign capital, if they operate in the modern industrial sector, but this does not mean that they are not capable of playing a major role in the industrialisation of their economies.

The role of the state

A natural concomitant to an emphasis on the weakness of the national bourgeoisie in the Dependency literature, is a stress on the importance of the state and the state bureaucracy in peripheral economies. For example, Amin (1974a) writes of three essential features of peripheral societies, one of which is 'a tendency to a peculiar bureaucratic form of development' since 'owing to the weaker and one-sided development of the local bourgeoisie the weight of the bureaucracy in this society seems much greater.'[67] In terms of industrialisation strategy this implies that, where private capitalists have not emerged to undertake new investment, state sector enterprise managed by public officials must play a major role in industrialisation, if total reliance is not to be placed on foreign investment.

The question of the role of the state in economic development remains both complex and controversial, but a few background comments are necessary before the different alternative patterns of state involvement raised in the Radical literature are examined. The term state is used here in the sense of both a set of institutions covering the administrative bureaucracy, public sector enterprises, the military, police and judicial system, all co-ordinated by an executive authority — as well as a set of relationships of political control and domination exercised by these institutions. O'Donnell in writing on the state in Argentina provides a helpful definition:

The state is not merely a set of institutions. It also includes — fundamentally — the network of relationships of 'political' domination activated and supported by such institutions in a territorially defined society, which supports and contributes to the reproduction of society's class organisation.[68]

The key terms here are 'institutions', 'political domination' and 'the reproduction of society's class organisation', so that the role of the state as an institution is to facilitate the continuation of a particular economic and social system.

As this quotation suggests, any Marxist, or Marxist-inspired, analysis of the state must acknowledge that it cannot be seen as separate from the class organisation of a society; in other words its organisation and operation must reflect the balance of class forces. However, this is not to say that crude interpretations that view the state and all state activity as simple reflections of underlying economic struggles are widely accepted. It is now commonly argued that the state has a degree of 'relative autonomy' from the control of dominant classes, although the extent of such autonomy will vary from case to case.[69] One implication is that the state bureaucracy may pursue their own interests at the expense of those of the dominant classes, for example in military adventures or expenditures on economically irrational, but prestigious projects. Alternatively the state may intervene against the interests of particular sections of a dominant class in the interests of the system as a whole. An example of this would be the removal of protection from high cost domestic industries to allow other national producers to use cheaper imported goods. A further example of relative autonomy often referred to is the possibility that domestic classes may be divided or weak, and that the balance of class forces is not clearly defined. Here the state has much greater scope for autonomy and the consequence can be an authoritarian, military or quasi-military regime that lacks a clear social base.[70]

THE STATE AND INDUSTRIALISATION

With these few comments in mind we can turn to a discussion of the role of the state in the industrialisation of the periphery. Whilst some Radical authors reject the approach of categorising regimes by type, preferring to work in terms of historical forms of capitalism or socialism in particular economies, it is relatively common in the literature to find examples of such categorisation. Four categories are discussed here to illustrate the approach, although the categories given are by no means logically distinct. Furthermore it is not implied that any individual author would necessarily accept all categories as valid either theoretically or empirically.

Neocolonial regime

Here the state, although formally independent from the colonial power, pursues economic policies that serve the interests of transnational firms, and the *comprador* bourgeoisie allied with foreign capital. State functionaries can have interests of their own that they may pursue, but the dominant classes on which the regime relies for support are the transnational bourgeoisie and its *comprador* allies. This is the 'classic' dependent regime analysed by Dependency authors, and it is seen as committed to a pattern of accumulation that excludes both independent national capitalists and the mass of peasants and workers.

Intermediate regime

This category, as its name implies, refers to a state neither wholly capitalist nor socialist, where the dominant alliance is between the lower-middle-class, including in this group state functionaries and small domestic capitalists, and the rich peasantry. The weakness of the domestic bourgeoisie, that is the upper-middle-classes, and the nationalist orientation of such regimes, mean that the state sector assumes a major role in the economy creating what is often termed a system of 'state capitalism'. This may involve nationalisation of the assets of both domestic and foreign capitalists, and a heavy reliance on the state sector to carry out strategic new investments. However, given the class alliance on which the regime is based it is not seen as a form of socialism. None the less unlike a Neocolonial regime the intermediate regime is seen as generally hostile to big business, both in the form of foreign capital and its local allies.[71] It is an unresolved question whether the state functionaries that play a critical role in such a regime are seen as a new class or are simply an 'intermediary strata' whose authority rests on their position in the state machinery rather than on the ownership of property. It can be argued that such regimes are merely transitory, reflecting the weakness and division of existing classes. If they are successful in generating economic growth they may at the same time create a national capitalist class that, in alliance with state functionaries, will change the nature of the regime. In other words, with the growth of a private sector, capitalism may emerge to replace state capitalism. On the other hand, if growth does not take place and the mass of the population remains excluded from participation in the political system, the regime may be pushed to a more radical position that perhaps leads to a form of socialism.[72]

Developmental capitalist regime

Although the crude Dependency position implies that capitalist regimes in the periphery are Neocolonial, almost by definition, we have seen that alternative interpretations now stress the possibility of a more positive interventionist role for the state. A developmental capitalist regime can be seen as one where the state, in alliance with private national and foreign capital, plays such an active role. Here the state promotes capitalist accumulation in general, and adopts a degree of independence from fractions of capital whether foreign or local. Therefore where the objectives of foreign capital conflict with the requirements of accumulation in general the state is able to represent these wider interests in opposition to transnationals and their local representatives. This categorisation of the state underlies Evans's 'triple alliance' between state, foreign and national capital, and is consistent with Warren's view of an interventionist state, noted earlier. It differs from an intermediate regime, however, in the extent of state ownership and in the strength of private capital, although as has been suggested, if the intermediate regime is accepted as a valid category, some may evolve into developmental capitalist regimes.

National popular regime

This last category involves an alliance between state functionaries, who may have achieved their positions through a revolutionary struggle, and the popular classes of peasants, workers and lower-middle-classes. This regime often draws heavily on nationalist ideology and involves radical redistributive measures in favour of the popular classes. It differs from an intermediate regime in the degree to which it is committed to radical populist measures, and under certain historical circumstances may be a phase in the transition of regimes from the intermediate category to a form of socialism.

The most relevant aspect of this discussion for the concern of this chapter — obstacles to industrialisation in the periphery — is that the simple choice between Neocolonialism and socialism, often posed by Dependency authors, needs to be superseded by a more ambiguous interpretation of the functioning of the state. The recognition, for example, that developmental capitalist regimes may emerge in the periphery implies the possibility that states there may be able to foster industrialisation in ways not too dissimilar from the earlier interventions by states in the now economically advanced economies. It can be argued that Neocolonialism is only one possible pattern of state activity and one that may be increasingly inapplicable as a way of categorising states in the periphery.

Where developmental capitalist regimes emerge in the periphery the extent to which they assist domestic firms to challenge transnationals will vary, since often there may be a form of alliance between the state, foreign and local capital. As we have stressed, the balance within this alliance is limited by historical circumstances, and whilst on some occasions foreign capital can be controlled and in extreme cases nationalised, there are limits on the extent to which the state can go in antagonising foreign capital; partly because domestic capitalists may feel the interest of private capital in general is threatened, and partly because of the need for foreign technology and finance in particular industries.[73] As Jenkins (1984) points out, the state in the periphery has a dual and contradictory role: it is both national, since it represents the interest of national capital and at the same time international, since it participates in the process of the internationalisation of production through the activities of transnationals within its boundaries. This tension between the two roles of the state can produce vacillating and inconsistent policies with shifts over time between the interests of foreign and local capital.

The importance of this re-assessment in the Radical literature of the state's role in industrialisation is that it clears the way for an analysis of the scope for successful capitalist industrialisation in the periphery in collaboration with transnationals. The simple generalisation of a subservient Neocolonial regime incapable of supporting the interests of local capital can be rejected as the single explanation for the activities of the state in such economies. Naturally it is not inevitable that all developmental states, whether capitalist or socialist, will succeed in their industrial policies, but *a-priori* one cannot rule out the possibility of success. The policy implication is therefore in line with the general Structuralist arguments considered earlier. Active state intervention to support and direct industrialisation is a necessary condition for long-run economic expansion.

Where Radical analysis is used in this reformist sense to examine alternative economic policies that do not envisage a major break with the international economy and major internal social transformation its policy prescriptions overlap with those of Structuralists. For example Bienefeld (1981) lists various elements of an industrialisation programme inspired by what he sees as a Radical perspective. These are:

- major state intervention;
- protection against foreign competition, adjusted over time in accordance with changing efficiency;
- controls over direct foreign investment;
- policies to build up domestic technological capabilities.[74]

One can add a concern for basic materials, and mass consumer goods for low-income groups, as set out in Thomas (1974). The important general point is that once the possibility of growth within existing economic, social and institutional arrangements is acknowledged, much of the specific policy concerns of Radical authors are similar to those classified here as Structuralists.

CONCLUSION

The conclusion of this chapter must be that whilst several Radical authors have raised highly important points on the limits to industrialisation in the periphery, particularly on the role of transnationals and their relations with the state and local capital, both logically and empirically, however, the view that capitalist industrialisation in the periphery will inevitably be blocked or distorted seems untenable. There is ample evidence, some of it given in Chapter 1, to support the views of Warren on the emergence of capitalist industry. Quite how 'independent' this development is, is another question. If the 'internationalisation of capital' perspective is adopted the question itself is meaningless, since a national capitalism will be linked with other capitalisms through the various mechanisms of the world market, including the activities of transnationals. This is not to imply that the interests of individual governments and transnationals needs always coincide, nor that the activities of transnationals are always economically beneficial to the host economies. It is simply that a capitalist industrialisation in developing countries, closely linked with the world market, is feasible and in some countries has proved highly effective as a means of economic transformation.

NOTES

1. Griffin and Gurley (1985), p. 1089. For a much less sympathetic survey of Radical analysis see Little (1982) pp. 218–66.
2. Blomstrom and Hettne (1984) is probably the most comprehensive and balanced survey in English to date.
3. Blomstrom and Hettne (1984), p. 163, write of the 'demise of the dependency school' and of the need to move 'beyond dependency'.
4. Cardoso and Faletto (1979), Introduction, p. xx. The authors recognise that in the world economy there will be interdependence between economies. They compare this with the interdependence between a banker and his client; they may both need each other but there is a qualititative difference in the degree of need.
5. Gereffi (1983), pp. 21–36, identifies this problem and surveys the differing responses to it.
6. Frank, for example, is often interpreted in this way.
7. For example, Amin (1974a).
8. Cardoso (1977), for example, writes of the possibility of growth with dependence; what he terms 'associated dependent development'.
9. Some of the most influential radical critiques of Dependency theory are Palma (1981), Taylor (1979), Warren (1980) and Leys (1983).
10. See the surveys of Foster-Carter (1978), and Ruccio and Simon (1986). A mode of production can be seen as an abstract concept referring to a set of social relations between classes; see Brewer (1980), pp. 11–12.
11. Roxborough (1979), p. 68, argues: 'Must we then return to the notion of dependency as a social formation defined by the complex articulation, both internal and external, of several modes of production? It seems that we must.'
12. For example, Marcussen and Torp (1982) on the Ivory Coast, and Jenkins (1984) on Latin America, adopt this approach.

13. For example Bienefeld (1981), p. 80, argues that Dependency analysis is an extension of the Structuralist position that 'stresses the need to incorporate into the analysis questions concerning the adequacy of the political base from which policies aimed at national structural change must be complemented. The position broadly accepts the importance of the structuralist problematic but argues that in addition to establishing the need for such nationally defined policies, it is also necessary to analyse these factors which may stand in the way of their formulation and implementation.'

14. Baran (1957), p. 228.

15. Blomstrom and Hettne (1984), pp. 66–9, and pp. 81–90, summarise the position of Frank, and his major critics.

16. UNCTC (1983), p. 22; reported foreign investment inflows were US$ 8 billion compared with outflows of US$ 12.8 billion.

17. See IMF (1985), table A.2, p. 42.

18. Berry, et al. (1983) demonstrates a worsening of world income distribution (1950–77), as measured by the distribution of consumption.

19. This means that prices will exceed values for the more capital-intensive commodities and be below values for the less capital-intensive. This pattern of deviation of prices from values is treated as a normal form of unequal exchange, but is not of concern for the theory as applied to centre-periphery relations.

20. Quoted in Evans (1981a). Helpful expositions of Emmanuel's position are given in Brewer (1980), pp. 208–32, and Kay (1975), pp. 107–9.

21. Emmanuel (1972), p. 368. Emmanuel's policy conclusion is that developing countries should impose export taxes to offset their low wages; Emmanuel (1972), pp. 233–6. Data on net financial flows to developing countries are taken from IMF (1985), table A.1, p. 41.

22. Amin (1977), pp. 181–252.

23. Amin (1980), pp. 159–62.

24. Bettelheim (1972), pp. 287–9.

25. Smith (1980), p. 16.

26. Evans (1981b), pp. 126–7.

27. Brewer (1980), pp. 226–30 makes this point. He sees learning effects and external economies as the key explanations as to why such a capital flow to the periphery does not occur.

28. Smith (1980), pp. 15–16.

29. Roxborough (1979), pp. 61–2.

30. Smith (1983), pp. 80–5.

31. The discussion below draws on Amin (1974a), (1974b), and (1980), and Thomas (1974).

32. Amin (1974a), p. 170. The use of the term 'distortion' in the English translation of Amin's work is ironic given its frequent usage in the Neoclassical literature, which is so far removed from Amin's analysis.

33. 'Industrialization through import substitution will start from "the end"; i.e. the manufacture of products corresponding to the more advanced stages of development of the centre, in other words consumer durables.' Amin (1974b), p. 14. The capital intensity and reliance on foreign technology associated with these goods is also noted.

34. 'When the basic materials of industry are combined with our focus on agricultural production to satisfy the needs of the broad mass of the population, it can be seen that the convergence strategy requires a focus on the production of the goods which enter into the means of producing all other goods, whether indirectly (e.g. basic foodstuffs consumed by labour) or directly (e.g. the use of iron-ore in making steel commodities).' Thomas (1974), p. 198.

35. Thomas (1974), p. 215.

36. For example, in writing on the success of a number of small export-oriented countries, including the 'Gang of Four', Thomas comments, rashly in the light of hindsight, that in the absence of a socialist strategy 'there is no real possibility for these economies to develop beyond the misleading rises in *per capita* income or indeed of even sustaining such advances on a long-term basis'. Thomas (1974), p. 107.

37. Thomas wrote his study in Tanzania and his views have been influential in thinking about Tanzanian planning. The Basic Industry Strategy was articulated in the Tanzanian Third Five Year Plan in the mid-1970s. Barker *et al.* (1986) argue that this strategy has not been applied consistently; see also Green (1982) for a discussion of different interpretations of the Basic Industry Strategy in Tanzania. It should be noted that the establishment of an iron and steel industry in Tanzania was a central part of the early thinking on the strategy. Whilst not implemented, a feasibility study on an iron and steel plant is available and in the mid-1980s the government was still wishing to find international finance for the project. The present author looked into the economics of the project in 1986, and could find no rationale, either on the grounds of foreign exchange saving or external effects, for the commitment of the vast resources that would be required. It appears that in the present international and domestic conditions an iron and steel plant for Tanzania should be a long way back in the sequence for the establishment of basic industries.

38. See for example Amsden (1977) and (1985).

39. For example Dos Santos (1981), a leading Dependency author, cites studies on American direct foreign investment in Latin America that show over 1946–67 outflows of US$ 2.7 for every US$ 1 of new investments.

40. Vaitsos (1974) on Colombia is cited frequently as evidence of this view. Jenkins (1984), pp. 90–6, surveys the evidence on transfer pricing in pharmaceuticals in several Latin America countries.

41. Vaitsos (1974), pp. 42–65 surveys different types of restrictive clauses in technology contracts. Kidron (1965) pp. 281–96 in an early study of such restrictions attached to foreign investments in India.

42. For example, Evans (1976) on pharmaceuticals in Brazil, Jenkins (1977) for automobiles in several countries, and Newfarmer (1979a), (1979b), for electrical goods in Brazil. Evans (1986), however, stresses the increasing importance of national firms at the lower end of the computer market in Brazil. In this last case explicitly nationalist government policies supported nationally-owned firms.

43. Kirkpatrick, *et al.* (1984), pp. 46–85, survey the evidence on concentration in developing countries and find support for the view that concentration is greater there than in developed economies.

44. The original statement of the 'miniature replica' effect, Evans (1977) referred to pharmaceuticals in Brazil. Jenkins (1984), pp. 213–4, finds evidence of this effect in other branches elsewhere in Latin America, but argues that it is likely to be a pattern related exclusively to some consumer goods for whom competition is based on product differentiation, advertising and product changes.

45. Jenkins (1977) discusses model changes and their impact on economies of scale in the Latin American automobile industry.

46. Langdon (1979) cites the Kenya soap industry in the 1970s to illustrate this argument. Local firms concentrated on simple laundry soap that could be produced with non-mechanised labour-intensive techniques, utilising local resources. Transnationals however entered the market producing higher priced toilet soaps utilising mechanised technology and relying heavily on advertising.

47. Again the Latin American automobile industry provides a key example; see Jenkins (1984), p. 56.

48. Booth (1985), p. 746.

49. Lall, for example, has changed his views on the magnitude of transfer pricing arguing, in Lall (1985a), p. 78, that 'the pharmaceutical industry case seems exceptional. Few examples of gross misuse of transfer prices have surfaced from other sectors; indeed there are few other industries where highly firm-specific products can be copied easily and so provide a ready basis for comparison'.

50. In his survey of these issues Lall (1978) does not provide a clear answer. He argues, however, that where transnationals do not actually cause higher concentration, their entry to an industry may still speed up a process that would have occurred anyway, perhaps for technological or financial reasons. Blomstrom (1986), however, suggests that transnationals have raised industrial concentration in Mexico.

51. For example Fairchild and Kosin (1986) report the results of a survey of local- and foreign-owned firms in four areas of Latin America, operating in the 1970s. They find that in terms of several measures of performance there is no statistically significant difference between firms of different ownership, once factors like age, scale and location have been controlled. There are some important differences in the source of technology, however, with local-owned firms showing a greater tendency to rely on internal innovation, rather than on external sources. None the less the authors point out that in many industries foreign-owned firms do also undertake significant internal technological efforts.

52. The pharmaceutical industry is one where it has been demonstrated that where locally-owned firms exist they behave in ways similar to transnationals; see Chudnovsky (1979) for Argentina and Kirim (1986) for Turkey. On the other hand, for Brazil, Willmore (1986) finds evidence of significant behavioural differences from a large sample of matched pairs of transnational and local firms across different industrial branches.

53. For data on Mexico see Fajnzylber and Martinez-Tarrago (1975), and on Brazil, Evans (1979).

54. Jenkins (1984) cites automobile parts and components production in several countries as a clear example of a complementary role for local capital, since automobile production itself is dominated by

transnationals. Evans (1979) cites the Brazilian textile industry as an example of mutually beneficial joint ventures.

55. Lall (1978) surveys the linkage effects of transnationals and points to the establishment of major backward linkages in some of the larger semi-industrialised countries as a result of government pressure.

56. As was discussed in Chapter 2, Bornschier and Chase-Dunn (1985) survey previous work in this area and conduct their own analysis, finding a significant negative relationship between transnational presence and both growth and equality for the poor, but not the rich countries in their sample.

57. Although the terminology is different, Kays's analysis has much in common with the Dependency school. Blomstrom and Hettne (1984), pp. 166–9 describe his work as an example of the 'Marxification of Dependency' and note that his analysis is inadequate since merchant capital appears somewhat simplistically as 'the root of all evil'.

58. Sunkel (1973), p. 146.

59. Kirkpatrick, *et al.* (1984), pp. 129–39 give a useful survey.

60. Hamilton (1983), p. 152. Groups are defined here as firms linked through share-holdings and interlocking directorships.

61. Roxborough (1979), pp. 76–7, makes this point and comments that in some circumstances it can be misleading to talk of the landed oligarchy and the industrial bourgeoisie, as if they are two distinct classes.

62. Evans (1979), p. 159.

63. Jenkins (1984), p. 153 argues that the view of local firms as ill-informed and weak in their bargaining with transnationals 'is not consistent with the highly sophisticated economic groups which are such an important element of the local industrial structure.'

64. The chief protagonists are Leys (1982) and Kaplinksy (1982); see also Godfrey (1982) for a survey of the debate.

65. Leys (1982), p. 228.

66. For Mexico see Fairchild (1977); for South Korea and Taiwan, Hamilton (1983); for India, Kidron (1965); and for the Latin American economies Jenkins (1984).

67. Amin (1974a), p. 387.

68. O'Donnell (1978), p. 24.

69. Jessop (1977) surveys alternative Marxist theories of the state; see also Skocpol (1979), pp. 24–33.

70. Marx referred to this phenomenon as Bonapartism, and Roxborough (1979) analyses several Latin American political regimes in these terms.

71. As we have seen in Chapter 2 the term 'intermediate regime' comes from Kalecki (1976). The concept has been used by Skouras (1978) and Jameson and Wilber (1981).

72. It is from this perspective that Petras (1977) suggests that intermediate regimes, whilst increasingly common in the periphery, are none the less 'a transitional regime, a phase between one type of exploitation and another, or as a moment in the struggle for socialism'.

73. Gereffi (1983), pp. 132–63 gives a case-study from the pharmaceutical industry in Mexico illustrating the limits to state autonomy *vis-à-vis* transnationals.

74. Bienefeld (1981), p. 91.

5

The Neoclassical Resurgence

In contrast with the literature on industrialisation surveyed in the previous chapters, a clearly defined and logically consistent alternative view became increasingly influential during the 1960s and 1970s. This is what is now termed the Neoclassical approach to development. Ian Little, one of the foremost authors of this school, has defined its key characteristic as a belief in the importance of the price mechanism and of the role that market forces can play in development policy. Little's explanation of 'the Neoclassical vision of the world' is worth quoting, since it provides a clear statement of the Neoclassical position in the development context.

> . . . a Neoclassical vision of the world is one of flexibility. In their own or their families' interests, people adapt readily to changing opportunities and prices, even if they do not like doing so, and even though they may take their time. Businesses pursue objectives roughly consistent with the assumption that they maximize risk and time discounted profits . . . There is usually a wide variety of ways of making things such that production methods can be expected to shift when input prices change. Demand schedules are consequently curves, neither kinked nor vertical. Supply schedules are also smooth and rarely vertical. Although demand and supply always depend to a greater or lesser extent on expectations of an uncertian future, nevertheless most markets usually tend to achieve an equilibrium without wild price fluctuations. In short the price mechanism can be expected to work rather well.[1]

The paragraph that follows Little's quotation makes it clear that the possibility that markets may also fail to work effectively in some circumstances, is not ruled out. However a focus on the effectiveness of the market mechanism as a means of allocating resources is a central tenet of this approach. Coupled with this is also an emphasis on the potential gains from participation in world trade, and the neglect by developing countries of considerations of 'trade efficiency'; that is, the relative costs in domestic income foregone of earning or saving foreign exchange.

The Neoclassical approach to industrialisation is part of a wider perspective, some would say paradigm, that encompasses both price and capital theory, and broad questions of macroeconomic strategy. Neoclassical economic theory is characterised by a focus on market, or exchange, relations to examine fundamental issues relating to both the value of commodities and the distribution of income. In broad policy terms, in recent years, it has come to be linked with stabilisation and adjustment programmes applied in many developing countries. The reforms introduced as part of such programmes have been described in the Latin American context as 'Neoconservative experiments' in economic policy that aim not only to allow markets to function freely, but also to control inflation, primarily by monetary policy, and in general to reduce substantially the share of the state in economic activity.[2]

The discussion here has a narrower focus, considering market reforms as these affect industry specifically. To some extent this is an artificial distinction since policy towards government expenditure in total can have major implications for the industrial sector. An overall assessment of Neoclassical or Neoconservative economic policy is not the object of study, however, Chapter 7 comments on evidence relating to the broader macroeconomic implications of economic reforms in Latin America.

This chapter examines the Neoclassical critique of the industrialisation policies of many developing countries. Here two issues are the primary focus of attention. First the argument that government interventions have stifled the operation of markets and contributed to an economically inefficient form of industrialisation, and second the view that specifically in relation to trade patterns, policies have reduced export growth and ignored specialisation on the basis of comparative advantage. Since the concept of economic efficiency underlies much of this

171

analysis it is necessary initially to clarify what is meant in this context.

ECONOMIC EFFICIENCY

Efficiency is an ambiguous concept, since it must be related to performance in the achievement of particular objectives. As there can be different objectives pursued by a government it is often difficult to argue that a policy is unambiguously inefficient. An obvious example is a policy of subsidising commercially unprofitable industries because of the job losses that would arise if they were to close. Such industries may be described as 'inefficient', and will be so from the viewpoint of generating a financial surplus for the government. However they need not be an inefficient way of maintaining employment; inefficiency in this sense would have to be demonstrated in terms of costs per job, and it might be that new projects require higher expenditures to create the same number of jobs as the loss-making producers.

Theoretically the problem of multiple objectives must be overcome by placing weights on each objective, so that the total contribution of an activity to the overall set of objectives — termed the objective function — can be assessed. The Neoclassical literature focuses primarily, but not exclusively, on the objective of utilising existing resources so as to create the maximum possible national income; what is generally referred to as the objective of allocative efficiency. Efficiency in this sense, therefore, refers to the effectiveness of given resources in creating output and thus income. Additional objectives such as the growth of income over time, or the distribution of the benefits of growth, often via additional employment, have been incorporated in some studies. However, the most common use of the term efficiency is in the allocative sense.

As has been stressed the defining characteristic of Neoclassical analysis is its emphasis on markets as a means of allocating resources. The argument is that generally if left to operate freely markets will create a more efficient allocation of resources than would government interventions. Efficiency here refers to allocative efficiency, but many argue that interventions frequently fail to achieve growth and distribution objectives also. The theoretical model underlying Neoclassical policy discussions of industrialisation is illustrated frequently using a simple two commodity model incorporating foreign trade.

One considers an economy producing two goods, A and B, both of which are internationally tradable. The combinations of A and B that can be produced from given domestic resources are shown in Figure 5.1 by the concave curve A P_1 B, termed the production possibility frontier, and drawn assuming increasing unit costs. Potentially, efficiency can be achieved when production takes place at any point of this curve, since a given quantity of resources will be producing the maximum possible output. The economically efficient combination of A and B will depend upon the relative prices of these commodities. Relative domestic prices are shown in Figure 5.1 by the price line DD^1. It can be demonstrated that under perfectly competitive conditions, with given resources, domestic production will be at point P_1 where DD_1 is a tangent to AP_1B. At this point in technical terms the marginal rate of transformation in production, given by the slope of AP_1B equals the ratio of the two prices. In other words, the ratio of the cost of producing an extra unit of each commodity is equal to the ratio of the price of each commodity. This is allocatively efficient in that production of one good cannot be increased without reducing that of the other. Costs in this case will be opportunity costs, that is output lost elsewhere. The cost per unit of A is therefore the output of B foregone by producing an extra unit of A.

The possibility raised by international trade is reflected in Figure 5.1 by the introduction of an international price line II^1, which will differ from the domestic one where there is non-uniform tariff or quota protection. In other words, where the ratio of domestic prices for A and B differs from the international ratio, the efficient exploitation of trade possibilities requires that domestic production shifts to P_2, where the marginal rate of transformation in production equals the international price ratio. In this example, output of A is contracted whilst B is expanded implying that the country's comparative advantage lies in the latter. Allocative efficiency is increased by this move, since the country, whilst producing at P_2, can trade along the international price line II^1, and obtain any combination of A and B along that line. The actual combination chosen will depend on demand conditions, but there is the potential to obtain more of A and B than would be

Figure 5.1: Two commodity model representing allocative efficiency under trade

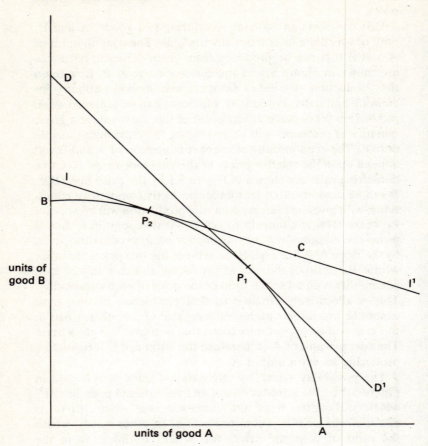

possible before trade. For example at C, the levels of A and B consumed are higher than at P_1, where they are supplied from domestic production alone. For the given amount of domestic resources, therefore, trade has allowed more of one commodity to be obtained without less of the other.

This simple model has been used to support various important propositions, including the following;[3]

– that a perfectly competitive domestic market can achieve an efficient allocation of resources;

174

- that no trade is an inferor strategy to free-trade;
- that once trade commences decisions on what to produce can be divorced from decisions on what to consume;
- that relative international prices should be used to guide domestic production for traded or tradable commodities;
- that the relevant domestic costs for planning are opportunity costs.

The criteria from the Neoclassical literature used to assess economic efficiency in production draw heavily on these propositions. In particular it is argued that internationally traded goods should be valued at their world prices, and non-traded goods and labour at their opportunity costs. However, the model as stated here is clearly a major simplification of reality, and any applied criteria must attempt to overcome these simplifications. Several simplifying assumptions must be noted, since they have important implications for the use of efficiency criteria.

First, as stated here, the model makes the 'small country assumption' for the economy concerned. In other words, world prices are given exogenously and are not influenced by the economy's level of imports or exports. Where this assumption does not hold, one has the 'optimum tariff' case for protection, as a country improves its terms of trade by imposing taxes on imports or exports. As far as the logic of the model is concerned economic efficiency requires the equality of the marginal rate of transformation in production with the marginal and not the average international price ratio. In this situation, therefore, it should be per unit marginal import costs and export revenues, that allow for the impact of price changes on the quantitites currently purchased or supplied, that should guide decisions on domestic production. However, relatively few developing countries will influence world prices and this qualification remains largely of theoretical interest.

Second, of considerably more practical consequence is the fact that in probably the majority of markets in developing countries conditions far removed from those of a perfectly competitive market will prevail. In addition to government interventions, domestic factors may be immobile, production may be dominated by a small number of oligopolistic firms, and external effects may be important. The existence of non-competitive market conditions implies that there will be two domestic cost structures; one for individual producers — often termed private costs — and another for the whole economy, what we will term economic costs. The domestic private marginal rate of transformation will differ therefore from the economic rate, and efficiency requires that it is the latter that is equated with the international price ratio.[4]

The theoretical problems posed by these 'domestic distortions' from perfect competition were considered at length in the international trade theory literature. The case had been argued that such deviations from competitive conditions provided a rationale for departures from free-trade, in the form of tariff or quota protection. For example, if labour market distortions meant that the private cost of employing a worker exceeded his economic cost, it was argued that this provided a justification for raising the profitability of domestic industry through protection to offset its disadvantage in labour costs. However the conclusion to emerge from these debates was that theoretically deviations from perfectly competitive conditions do not provide a justification for protection, since tax-subsidy measures are a more effective means of offsetting distortions. The logic of the argument is that whilst tariffs or quotas might counter some of the effects of distortions arising from non-competitive domestic markets, they would introduce additional costs of their own, in terms of deviations between domestic and world prices for traded goods. The 'first-best' solution is a set of taxes and subsidies aimed as directly as possible at removing the distortion concerned; in the labour case, for example, this involves paying employers a subsidy related directly to their wage bill, rather than raising profitability through protection.[5]

However whilst non-competitive domestic markets may not invalidate the theoretical conclusions of the model in terms of the superiority of free-trade, they do mean that prevailing domestic prices in these markets are no guide to economic costs. This provides the rationale for estimating shadow prices for commodities and factors. Shadow prices must be applied to estimate the economic costs of domestic production, and as we have seen efficiency requires that it is relative economic costs that are equated with world prices.

The third area of simplication relates to the omission of non-traded goods. Non-traded goods can be interpreted as commodities which an economy does not trade internationally, and whose prices are unaffected by world market trends.[6] The introduction of non-traded items raises both theoretical and practical difficulties. For these goods decisions on what to produce cannot be divorced from those on what to consume. Furthermore production decisions cannot be guided by world prices, since there is no relevant world price for these items. The economic valuation of these goods requires reference to domestic market conditions, either in production or consumption, which is often the most difficult aspect of the application of economic efficiency criteria.

Finally, and perhaps most significantly, there are a range of dynamic arguments not allowed for in the simple static formulation of the two commodity model. The most important of these relate to learning and technical change over time. There is no guarantee that the activities in which a country has a current comparative advantage will be those where these dynamic effects are most significant, so that a policy that focuses only on short-term cost considerations need not be in the longer-term interests of the economy. The Neoclassical approach treats these dynamic arguments as further instances of market failure or non-competitive conditions; for example, externalities in production arising over time, or lack of foresight on the part of individual producers. The first-best policy recommendation is therefore that these should be handled like all other distortions by tax-subsidy measures. For example, if technical progress stems from research and development this activity alone should be subsidised. The existence of major changes over time in the efficiency and technical level of activities makes the application of planning criteria particularly uncertain. The Neoclassical criteria discussed in this chapter, can be criticised for their failure to incorporate fully relevant dynamic effects, although one should not forget the intrinsic difficulty of doing so.

GOVERNMENT INTERVENTION AND DISTORTIONS

The argument concerning government interventions is that governments may intervene in markets for a variety of reasons; for example to conserve foreign exchange, to protect local producers from foreign competition, to guarantee a minimum wage, to encourage investment and to raise government revenue. These interventions will involve a range of policy instruments — including quantitative import restrictions, tariffs,

177

minimum wage legislation, credit subsidies, controlled interest rates and indirect taxes. In practice, the neat matching of one target (for example the balance of payments position) with one policy variable or instrument (for example the exchange rate), which is seen as the sole means of achieving the target concerned, is very rarely present. Government objectives are normally sought through a variety of instruments, often with the relative weights placed on the instruments varying over time. Whilst the basic objectives of government policy can be taken as given, the argument is that intervention in the operation of markets will force market prices away from economic values that reflect the scarcity of commodities or resources. Thus it is argued that significant losses in economic efficiency will be created if producers and consumers respond to distorted rather than 'efficient' market prices. Initially many market prices may not themselves reflect economic values, so that this original distortion is the reason for government intervention. However it is argued that, in many cases, intervention to remove one distortion is carried out in such a way as to create fresh distortions elsewhere in the economy. These 'by-product distortions' or side-effects, may be both unanticipated, and undesirable, and theoretically at least, could negate the beneficial effect of the removal of the initial distortion.

One of the major strands of the argument in favour of an overall reform of the price system in many developing countries is what is seen as the chaotic set of forces working to determine relative prices in these economies. Often, it is suggested, governments do not foresee the implications for prices of various policies, and if they could they would often feel unhappy with the consequences of many of their interventions in the functioning of markets. It should be noted that this type of argument has often been used as a justification for leaving many crucial decisions to the outcome of market forces. However the logic of the argument does not preclude government intervention. It simply suggests that if markets do not give the signals governments wish intervention will be necessary. However the implications of this intervention should be examined to ensure that desirable effects in one direction are not offset by undesirable effects in another.

Over the last 15 years or so a large number of empirical studies within the Neoclassical tradition have identified significant divergences between market prices, and economic values or shadow prices. In addition work on the systems of protection in developing countries has focused more narrowly upon the relative incentives which have been created by various forms of protection, and implications of these incentives for economic efficiency. For a large number of countries the general picture is of economies where the price system has been highly distorted through government intervention. The major areas of intervention will be discussed and their implications for industrial policy will be noted.[7]

Markets for traded commodities

It is well established in the literature on shadow pricing that for internationally traded commodities, that is those commodities for which an economy participates in world trade, opportunity costs will be given by the world prices, cif for imports, and free on board (fob) for exports, of the commodities concerned. These world prices will represent the terms on which an economy can participate in world trade. In an economy with protection from the world market — and most economies will be protected in some way — domestic and world prices will not be equal.[8] If import tariffs are imposed, once an import reaches its port of entry, its price will be raised immediately by the tariff. Quotas will also work to raise domestic prices above world levels, even if no tariffs are involved, since they restrict the supply of an import. The price of such a good in the domestic market will rise until demand is equated with the limited supply available under the quota. The excess of the domestic selling price above the import price is termed the scarcity premium arising from the imposition of a quota. The ratio of the scarcity premium to the world price is sometimes referred to as the tariff equivalent premium, since a tariff of this rate would create the same domestic price as the quota.

On the export side similar effects will be at work. An export tax on a commodity which can be sold domestically as well as abroad will create a domestic price equal to the export price minus the export tax. This follows since, other things being equal, producers will only sell abroad if they can obtain a net price, after tax payments, equal to that in the domestic market.[9] Export subsidies have the opposite effect however, since the domestic price must now equal the export price plus the subsidy.

These trade interventions will normally be introduced for a number of reasons, and in practice, one policy instrument often serves more than one purpose. Import trariffs may be imposed for revenue reasons, for example; however in many countries they may have an important role in either restricting the overall demand for imports, or raising the profitability of local import-competing producers. Import quotas are often introduced for short-run balance of payments considerations to restrict demand for the limited amount of foreign exchange that is available. However, it has been argued that frequently quotas introduced under such circumstances have been retained for protection after the original foreign exchange crisis has passed. Whilst theoretically quota restrictions and import tariffs can be shown to have identical effects on resource use, this argument rests on the assumption of competitive production conditions in the domestic economy. Under monopolistic domestic production, for example, supply and demand curves may be affected differently by a quota as opposed to a tariff. Of more practical importance is likely to be the fact that tariffs provide a known rate of protection given by the percentage tariff rate. The effect of quotas on domestic prices is more uncertain however, and will change with domestic supply and demand conditions. Therefore with tariff protection the domestic price is normally set by the world price plus the tariff, so that domestic prices alter in response to changes in world prices, with domestic demand and supply having little or no influence on domestic prices. With a fixed quota, however, the reverse will hold and it will be shifts in domestic demand and supply which determine domestic prices. The distributional effects of tariffs and quotas will differ also. Tariffs are a major source of government revenue, whilst the scarcity premium created by quotas will go to those traders or producers who obtain import licences under the quota system. Although in principle governments can auction import licences and thus capture this premium for themselves, in practice this policy is rarely followed.

Export taxes are used chiefly to raise government revenue and are normally applied to primary or mineral exports. They could be imposed, for example, to tax windfall gains due to sudden fluctuations in the world price for a commodity. In theory export taxes could also be imposed by an individual country for terms of trade reasons — what is described as the 'optimal tariff' case — the aim being to restrict supply and thus raise the export prices of goods with inelastic world demand. In practice this has not been a major motivation for most developing countries, who are generally price-takers for their exports. Finally, it should be noted that export subsidies can take various forms, and are means of raising the profitability of exporting, often as a counter to the level of official exchange rate which may provide an unattractive rate of return for exporters.

The extent to which many developing countries have used these interventions in markets for traded commodities is now well documented, and the undesirable consequences for economic efficiency of many protective measures are stressed frequently. Three separate strands of the argument can be distinguished.

- The varied and often unanticipated effect of protective measures in terms of the incentives created for different branches of the industrial sector; in other words not all branches will benefit equally and the relative levels of incentive may be unplanned and, in some cases, undesired.
- The general encouragement protection from import competition gives to high cost domestic production, and lack of stimulus it provides to reduce costs to international levels.
- The harmful impact of industrial protection on other parts of the economy, particularly agriculture and exports in general.

Variations in incentives

Considering the relative impact of protection on different industrial branches the essential point is that the final degree of incentive will generally not be known in advance, when the protective measures involved are being planned. This may be either because of the uncertain impact of quotas, or because of the effect of imposing different rates of tariffs, taxes or subsidies, on inputs as compared with outputs. The observed or Nominal Rate of Protection (NRP) is given by the ratio of the domestic price to the world price for a comparable commodity. However the full effect of a protective system can only be estimated by comparing the tariff or tariff equivalents on the output of a producer, with those on the inputs he must purchase. The logic of this is that if a producer's input prices are raised above international levels, by more than his output prices, he is being penalised rather than encouraged by the protective system, even though his own output may have a positive tariff. A comparison of the output tariff of a producer with a weighted average of the tariffs on his inputs, with the weights determined by the share of inputs in the value of the output gives the effective rate of protection (ERP). This measures the extent to which value-added of a producer, or the aggregate of all producers in a branch, at domestic, that is protected prices, exceeds what it would be in a free-trade situation where world and domestic prices for traded goods are assumed to be equal.

Formally ERP for activity i can be given in two alternative but equivalent definitions:

$$ERP_i = \frac{VADP_i - VAWP_i}{VAWP_i} \qquad (5.1)$$

where $VADP_i$ is value-added at domestic prices (VADP) in i and $VAWP_i$ is value-added at world prices (VAWP) in i, under free trade.

$$ERP_i = \frac{t_i - \sum_j a_{ji}\, t_j}{1 - \sum_j a_{ji}} \qquad (5.2)$$

where t_i and t_j are the tariffs, or tariff equivalents, for output i and input j respectively,

and a_{ji} is the number of units of j required per unit of i under free-trade.[10]

The argument is that those activities with the highest ERP will have the greatest incentive for expansion arising from the price effects created by protection. The degree to which resources will actually move in response to these incentives will depend upon supply elasticities, however, other things being equal, a relatively high ERP will mean an activity will have a relatively high output as compared with what its output would be in the absence of protection.

ERP measures have been used extensively in applied work on industrial development in developing countries, although they are not without both empirical and conceptual problems. For example, empirically there are difficulties in obtaining comparable world and domestic price data, and in achieving a sufficient degree of disaggregation to estimate separate ERPs for a large number of branches. Conceptually also there are difficulties in the treatment of non-traded goods, in the need to assume fixed input coefficients, and with the appropriate exchange rate to use in the calculations. None the less given these limitations it is generally felt that the ERP measure is useful for analysing the extent to which protectionist policies create incentives for resources to shift in different directions.

There is a substantial body of evidence on the wide range of ERP for different manufacturing branches in different economies. For example Balassa (1982) summarises data on the frequency distribution of NRP, and ERP in the six semi-industrial economies covered by his study. In the late 1960s the ERP on domestic sales exceeded 100 per cent for 24 branches in South Korea, 36 in Israel, 36 in Argentina and 11 in Taiwan. At the same time it was between 0 and −50 per cent in 67 branches in South Korea, 5 in Israel, 11 in Argentina and 27 in Taiwan.[11] The range of ERP estimates for individual branches and their divergence from NRP can be illustrated with data for a single country — Mexico — taken from the national plan document. Table 5.1 gives NRP and ERP by manufacturing branch in 1979. In general it can be seen that, with some exceptions, where nominal protection is positive, ERP exceeds NRP, and that where it is negative ERP is below NRP. The full range of ERP is from −77 per cent for soft drinks to 612 per cent for alcoholic beverages.

The important point about this wide variance in levels of protection is that activities which are given a relatively low priority in government policy statements may none the less receive above-average protection and thus resources may be encouraged to shift into these non-priority areas. Such a situation can arise because ERP estimates are not readily available in many countries, and where they are available are rarely up to date. Governments therefore are often not fully aware of the consequences for incentives of the structure of protection. A particular example of relatively unfavourable treatment for priority items relates to the protection afforded

Table 5.1: Nominal and effective protection by selected manufacturing branches, Mexico 1979

	NRP[a] %	ERP %
Coffee processing	9	67
Sugar products	−48	−51
Vegetable oils	−2	12
Other food products	8	23
Alcoholic beverages	43	612
Soft drinks	−60	−77
Tobacco products	−27	−27
Textile fibres and yarn	1	0
Clothing	24	63
Leather	7	8
Paper	20	57
Printing and editing	0	−7
Petroleum products	−53	43
Petrochemicals	−42	65
Basic chemicals	12	51
Fertilisers	−18	−15
Synthetic resins	29	200
Medical products	9	13
Soaps	4	11
Other chemical products	13	33
Rubber products	16	22
Plastics	40	481
Glass	3	9
Cement	0	21
Iron and Steel	1	12
Non-ferrous metals	11	76
Non-electrical machinery	20	36
Electrical machinery	17	34
Domestic electrical appliances	36	94
Electronic equipment	58	220
Automobiles	42	192
Other transport equipment	21	25
Other manufactures	21	52

[a]This is defined as the percentage difference between domestic and world prices, rather than nominal tariff rates.
Source: Government of Mexico (1984), table 6, 1.2, p. 218.

capital goods as compared with consumer goods producers. For example in their summary of the results of ERP studies of five countries in the 1960s, Little *et al.* (1970) find that in all but one capital goods in the aggregate received lower effective protection than consumer goods although the discrimination was only very substantial in Pakistan and Brazil. Broadly similar findings are also reported by Balassa (1971) using a slightly different classification.[12] Evidence from Mexico in Table 5.1 can also illustrate this point since priority branches such as electrical and non-electrical machinery, and iron and steel, receive an ERP below that granted to certain non-priority branches, such as domestic electrical appliances and automobiles.[13]

Lack of stimulus to cost reduction

The second strand in the attack on the use of tariffs and quotas in developing countries is that they provide a shelter for inefficient domestic producers who have no incentive to lower their costs to international levels. Local production at costs above world levels imposes economic losses, it is argued, since with the abolition of protection resources would be reallocated to more internationally competitive activities. The ERP measure discussed above must be seen primarily as an indicator of the relative degree of incentive received by producers in particular activities from the protective system. It is not strictly a measure of the efficiency with which resouces are employed.

Two related measures of economic efficiency that have been used frequently are cost-benefit (CB) returns at shadow prices and domestic resource cost ratios (DRC). The former compares the present value of economic costs with the present value of economic benefits; the test of economic efficiency is whether at shadow prices there is a positive net present value, or an internal rate of return above the economic discount rate. Application of this criteria requires both identification of all benefits and costs and their valuation at an appropriate set of shadow prices.[14]

Formally for per unit of activity i the cost-benefit estimate of returns can be expressed as

$$CB_i = PV(P_i + E_i) - PV(\sum_j a_{ji}.P_j + \sum_l a_{li}.P_l) \qquad (5.3)$$

where P_i is the shadow price of i:
E_i is the external effect from the production of i

185

(not captured in the valuation of inputs), which can be positive or negative;

a_{ji} is the number of units of non-labour inputs j per unit of i;

and P_j is the shadow price of j:

a_{li} is the number of units of labour input l per unit of i,

and P_l is the shadow wage for labour category l;

PV indicates present values discounted at the economic discount rate.

Economic efficiency requires that CBi>0.

Where output is a traded good, as will be the case with many industrial investments, and there are no additional external benefits, one will be comparing the world price of output with the domestic costs of production. The valuation of domestic costs, however, should allow for features of developing economies that justify the encouragement of new industry; for example surplus labour, learning effects as experience grows, and under-utilisation of capacity in input supplying sectors. However, using the CB criteria domestic production of a traded good will not be shown as economically justified unless either domestic costs at shadow prices are below the world price of the good, or there are strong additional external benefits generated by domestic production.

The domestic resource cost measure can be shown to be equivalent to the cost-benefit criteria, although it expresses the same information in a different way.[15] DRC ratio gives the domestic resources required to earn or save an additional unit of foreign exchange and is therefore an exchange rate for a particular investment or activity. Economic efficiency requires that a DRC is below the economic value of an additional unit of foreign exchange, so that a DRC must be compared with either the official exchange rate, or where this is felt to be an inaccurate guide to the scarcity value of foreign exchange, with an estimate of the shadow exchange rate.

The link between the CB and DRC measures can be demonstrated using equation 5.3. If i and j are traded goods, there are no external effects, and labour is the only domestic resource,

$$DRC_i = \frac{PV(\sum_l a_{li}.P_l)}{PV(P_i - \sum_j a_{ji}.P_j)} \qquad (5.4)$$

If i and j are valued in foreign currency, so that the denominator is a net foreign exchange figure, efficiency requires that DRC_i is less than the value of an additional unit of foreign exchange to the economy.[16]

A number of CB and DRC studies on developing countries have indicated substantial economic inefficiency, particularly amongst import substitute industries. The argument is that high cost sheltered producers can continue to make commercial profit only because of the protection they receive, and that in economic terms their costs of production are uncompetitive internationally.[17]

Relatively more published work has applied the DRC measure, although in many cases the procedures adopted are relatively crude and fall far short of a rigorous shadow pricing analysis. The shadow prices used to value domestic resources are little more than a form of sensitivity analysis to test how a different valuation of domestic resources will effect judgements on efficiency. DRC estimates are often carried out for a single year of operations, rather than over the full working life of an investment, and the results are highly sensitive to the degree of capacity working. This means that where capacity utilisation is determined by short-run factors, such as foreign exchange availability, DRC estimates can fluctuate substantially between years. Furthermore most DRC studies ignore or do not incorporate quantitative estimates of externalities, and are rarely carried out over a sufficiently long period of time to examine the long-run trend in DRC. Table 5.2 brings together DRC estimates for industrial activities from different sources for five developing countries.

All the studies suffer from the limitations noted above but none the less indicate a wide range of DRC estimates for activities in the same economy. The number of inefficient branches is shown to give a rough indication of the extent of inefficiency, by comparing DRC estimates with either the shadow exchange rate estimate referred to in the original study, or the official rate where this is judged to be appropriate. In one instance, India, an estimate of the shadow exchange rate from other sources is applied. Negative DRCs imply a loss of foreign exchange where the value of traded inputs exceed that of output.

The wide variations between DRCs for different activities is often interpreted as evidence of resource misallocation so that it

Table 5.2: Summary of DRC results: selected developing countries

Country	Year	Range of DRCs[a]	Number of branches studied	Number of branches with negative DRC[b]	Number of efficient branches[c]
India	1963–65	Rs 2.7/US$ to Rs 1049/US$	75	6	n.a.
	1968–9	Rs 5.9/US$ to Rs 259/US$	75	4	17
Chile	1961	28% to 1255%	21	0	6
Turkey	1965–69	TL 10.2/US$ to TL 93.9/US$	16	n.a.	10
	1981	50% to 1015%	14	1	4
Ghana	1967–68	19% to 2037%	39	8	9
Tanzania	early 1970s	2.9 shillings/US$ to 12.2 shillings/US$	24	0	17

[a]DRCs are either given in the normal fashion as exchange rates, or as percentages. Where the latter are used they refer to the ratio of domestic resources in local currency to net foreign exchange earned or saved expressed in local currency at the shadow exchange rate.
[b]Negative DRC implies a loss of foreign exchange.
[c]An efficient activity is defined as one where either
  – DRC is equal to or below the shadow exchange rate
or – the DRC percentage is equal to or below 100 per cent.
Shadow exchange rates are taken from the original source, except for India where it is estimated to be Rs 12/US$ for the late 1960s.
n.a. = not identifiable from the original source.
Sources:
  (i)   India: Bhagwati and Srinivasan (1975), pp. 177–83. For India data on the shadow exchange rate is taken from Beyer (1975) and Weiss (1975).
  (ii) Chile: Behrman (1976), pp. 137–46.
  (iii) Turkey: Krueger (1974), pp. 215–26 and Yagci (1984), pp. 85–96. For Turkey firms with negative DRCs are excluded from branch averages.
  (iv) Ghana: Steel (1972), pp. 223–39.
  (v)   Tanzania: Roemer et al. (1976), pp. 257–75.

is argued that efficiency in resource use would be improved by expanding activities with low DRCs — at the expense of those with high DRCs. The commonsense of this is that if it costs x per cent more to save foreign exchange in activity i as compared with activity j, it will be desirable to expand j relative to i. Theoretically the case is not as clear as this, since one needs to assume constant costs of production and given world prices, but in general wide variations in DRC between different activities can be taken as evidence of a misallocation of resources, which is likely to have been made possible by the differential set of incentives created by the import protection system.[18] Protection therefore allows firms with high costs in both economic and commercial terms to survive, and in the absence of reforms to the protective system they will have little incentive to lower these costs.

Effects on other sectors

Turning to the effect of trade controls on sectors of the economy other than import substitute manufacturing two important biases may be created by a protective system; one relating to exports, and the other to agriculture. The Neoclassical literature lays great stress on the importance of export markets for new industries in developing countries. The argument is not that all of the output of such industries need go abroad, but that as long as export possibilities are not neglected, a number of important benefits will ensue. These include:

- greater competition with resulting productivity gains as producers are forced to compete internationally;
- greater awareness of international standards and recent technical developments;
- greater equality in income distribution, if export growth is concentrated in labour-intensive activities;
- removal of market bottlenecks, where economies of scale are important and the domestic market is too small to allow these to be attained;
- alleviation of the foreign exchange constraint on growth.

However it is argued that by restricting the demand for imports, tariffs and quotas allow the maintenance of an exchange rate well above that which would obtain in the absence of such controls. This means that exporters receive less local currency for every unit of foreign exchange earned than in a free-trade situation, where a lower exchange rate would prevail. In addition further biases against exports can arise from

189

the effect of import controls in raising the price of goods sold in the home market, relative to those sold abroad, and in requiring exporters to use domestically produced inputs more expensive than, and perhaps inferior to, the alternatives available on the world market. It is recognised that subsidies to exporters, for example, in the form of access to low cost credit, or reductions in tax, can be used to offset this bias, and in theory there will be a rate of uniform import tariffs and export subsidies, which can create the same incentive effect as any level of the exchange rate. The argument is, however, that in many of the countries which adopted inward-looking industrialisation strategies in the 1960s and 1970s, export subsidies were no more than a partial offset to the biases against exports created by the protective system. Empirical attempts to substantiate this view have used an extension of the ERP measure — what is termed the effective rate of subsidy (ERS). The ERS allows for the fact that profitability can be affected by subsidies, as well as tariffs and quotas, and incorporates their impact on domestic value-added.[19] A bias against exports can be said to exist when either effective protection or subsidy on domestic sales exceeds that on exports. This is an alternative measure of anti-export bias to that of Krueger discussed in Chapter 2, so that anti-export bias exists where either

$$\frac{ERP_D}{ERP_x} > 1 \quad \text{or} \quad \frac{ERS_D}{ERS_x} > 1$$

where D and x refer to domestic and export sales, respectively. Where subsidies are significant it is clearly the latter measure that is more accurate.

These two alternative estimates of anti-export bias in the 1960s are shown in Table 5.3 for the six countries covered in Balassa (1982). It can be seen that the three members of the 'Gang of Four', South Korea, Singapore and Taiwan, have either a low or negative anti-export bias, in contrast with the three more inward-looking economies Argentina, Colombia and Israel. However, it is important to note the variations between branches, so that even in generally outward-looking economies discrimination against exports can still arise for some activities.

Table 5.4 summarises the available information on ERP for manufacturing in a large sample of developing countries. Since the data comes from different sources exact comparability is not

Table 5.3: Measures of anti-export bias. Six developing countries

	Argentina 1969		Colombia 1969		Israel 1968		South Korea 1968		Singapore 1967		Taiwan 1969	
	A	B	A	B	A	B	A	B	A	B	A	B
All-manufactures	3.41	2.92	1.42	1.20	1.63	1.32	1.10	0.93	1.06	1.05	1.26	0.97
Non-durable consumer goods	1.67	1.50	1.91	1.62	2.11	2.06	0.91	0.75	1.01	0.99	1.14	0.98
Durable consumer goods	n.a.	n.a.	n.a.	n.a.	2.27	2.18	1.73	1.35	1.16	1.16	1.55	1.12
Machinery	n.a.	n.a.	1.45	1.23	1.13	1.13	1.65	1.26	1.10	1.09	1.02	0.87
Transport equipment	n.a.	n.a.	24.01	10.10	2.88	2.81	n.a.	n.a.	0.98	0.98	1.80	1.51

Notes: A = ERP domestic sales/ERP exports. Anti-export bias is when A > 1.0.
   B = ERS domestic sales/ERS exports. Anti-export bias is when B > 1.0.
   n.a. = not available.

Source: Balassa (1982), table 2.4, pp. 32–3.

possible, so that the figures can only be taken as suggestive. Where data is available for more than one year it shows a tendency towards falling protection for manufacturing, particularly in Latin America. This can be seen for Brazil, Mexico, Uruguay, Bolivia and Peru, and would also be the case for Chile were estimates for the late 1970s available. Outside Latin America, Sri Lanka provides the clearest example of declining

Table 5.4: ERP manufacturing: selected developing countries (various years)

	Year	%	Year	%	Year	%
Ethiopia	1970	125				
Kenya	1967	92				
Tanzania	1966	116				
Ghana	1972	105				
Ivory Coast	1970–72	62				
Nigeria	1979	40				
Senegal	1972	70				
South Korea	1968	13[a]	1978	32		
Indonesia	1975	30				
Malaysia	1965	−6[b]	1971	38		
Philippines	1965	61[b]	1974	59	1978	44
Thailand	1974	37	1978	70		
Bangladesh	1976–77	144				
India	1968–69	125				
Pakistan	1963–64	271[b]	1970–71	181		
Sri Lanka	1970	118	1979	38		
Egypt	1966–67	42				
Turkey	1979	75	1981	181[c]		
Yugoslavia	1970	28	1974	9		
Argentina	1969	112[a]	1977	38		
Brazil	1966	68[b]	1980	46		
Chile	1967	217				
Colombia	1969	35[a]	1980	37		
Jamaica	1978	50				
Mexico	1960	16[b]	1979	11		
Uruguay	1968	300	1978	112		
Bolivia	1970	54	1980	24		
Peru	1970	90	1980	52		
Taiwan	1969	14[a]				
Singapore	1967	4[a]				
Israel	1968	76[a]				

[a]Refers to Balassa (1982).
[b]Refers to Balassa (1971).
[c]Refers to Yagci (1984).
Sources: Data comes from Agarwala (1983) except where [a], [b] and [c] are shown.

effective protection as part of a trade liberalisation programme, with the Philippines also showing the same trend. On the other hand rising protection over time is shown for Malaysia, and interestingly for South Korea, one of the 'Gang of Four', whose success has been commented upon earlier. The least protected economies in the sample, as far as manufacturing is concerned appear to have been Singapore, Taiwan, South Korea (in the late 1960s) and Mexico.

Finally, considering the case of a bias against agriculture, this may arise from the fact that agriculture is still the major export sector in many developing countries, so that it naturally suffers most from any anti-export bias. However this can also stem from the lack of protection afforded agriculture relative to other sectors. Cases of negative ERP for agriculture can arise if domestic prices for crops and livestock are broadly comparable with world levels, whilst the locally produced or imported inputs in agriculture are protected or taxed, and thus have domestic prices above world levels. In some instances this discrimination against agriculture may have been the unanticipated result of the separate policies of keeping down food prices for urban consumers, whilst at the same time protecting local manufacturing.

The significantly greater incentive normally granted to manufacturing as compared with agriculture-based activities, can be seen by comparing the ERP estimates for agriculture in Table 5.5 with those in Table 5.4 for manufacturing, although the same qualification regarding the lack of direct comparability of data across countries needs to be made. It is clear that in many countries, particularly in Africa, agriculture has been penalised quite strongly through relatively high negative ERP. In 15 of the 25 estimates covered in Table 5.5, ERP for agriculture was negative at some point during the period covered. Furthermore in only one country, South Korea, was the ERP for agriculture above that for manufacturing in general. Even in countries like Taiwan and Mexico where the negative protection experienced by agriculture was low, it still suffered relative discrimination in comparison with the positive protection received by manufacturing.

To summarise, therefore, in many countries where interventions in the markets for traded commodities are still widespread, it is frequently suggested that a number of harmful side-effects have been created; these include unanticipated

Table 5.5: ERP agriculture: selected developing countries (various years)

	Year	%	Year	%
Kenya	1974–75	−19		
Malawi	1977	0		
Tanzania	1979	−45		
Cameroon	1977	−64		
Ghana	1979	−90		
Ivory Coast	1970–72	−28		
Senegal	n.a.	−32		
South Korea	1968	18[a]	1978	57
Malaysia	1973	20		
Philippines	1965	0[b]	1974	18
Thailand	1973–74	− 7		
Pakistan	1963–64	−10[b]	1975–76	−30
Sri Lanka	1979–80	−10		
Egypt	1976	−11		
Tunisia	1973	50		
Turkey	1978	40		
Yugoslavia	1975–80	5		
Chile	1967	− 5		
Colombia	1969	−14[a]	1979	29
Mexico	1970	0.7[c]	1979	− 2
Bolivia	1970	77	1980	14
Peru	1970	51	1980	46
Taiwan	1969	− 4[a]		
Argentina	1969	−13[a]		
Israel	1968	48[a]		

[a]Refers to Balassa (1982).
[b]Refers to Balassa (1971).
[c]Refers to Ten Kate et al. (1979).
Sources: Data comes from Agarwala (1983) except where [a], [b] and [c] are shown.

effective levels of protection and profit incentives to particular sectors, a shelter to high cost producers, a bias against exporting in general, and in some countries, a bias against agriculture in particular. Therefore even if there may be a case for protection of manufacturing in developing countries along the lines argued by Structuralists there is a substantial amount of evidence from a range of countries, that in practice the way in which protection has been implemented has created a number of significant negative effects both within manufacturing itself and in other parts of the economy.

Markets for labour and capital

The second major market intervention which will be considered concerns the functioning of markets for labour in developing countries. A common pattern is for there to be a major divergence between rural wages for unskilled workers, and wages paid to unskilled or semi-skilled workers on new development projects in urban areas. In so far as these wages simply reflect differences in quality of labour or costs of training, no market imperfection need be present. However where these factors account for only a small part of observed wage differences the latter are normally put down to interventions in the operation of labour markets. In other words, in a smooth-functioning labour market workers could shift from rural to urban areas until the wage rates for similar skills were equalised. Nominal differences might remain due to variations in the cost of living in different areas, or to costs of movement, but after money wages had been deflated by the relevant cost indices real differences should be removed.

The picture which is normally painted in shadow price studies is one of relatively competitive rural labour markets for unskilled labour, so that daily wages for hired agricultural labour can be taken as broadly equal to the productivity of the workers concerned. The competitive nature of these rural markets can be taken to stem from their possession of the following characteristics; large numbers of employers chiefly small farmers, large numbers of potential workers normally poorly organised in terms of trade union activity, reasonably good information on prevailing wage rates, and geographical mobility of labour, at least on a regional basis.

On the other hand it is often argued that in urban labour markets for unskilled or semi-skilled workers conditions are non-competitive due particularly to trade union organisation, and government intervention in the form of minimum wage legislation. These factors it is suggested raise urban wages in the formal or organised sector significantly above rural wage rates. However it is the latter which are normally taken to define the economic cost of unskilled labour. In other words, if one adopts a view of the rural areas of developing countries as characterised by a surplus of underemployed workers, and assumes that the creation of new urban-based jobs draw additional workers out of agriculture, the opportunity cost of employing these workers on new projects will be measured by a drop in agricultural output. This is the output foregone, or the opportunity cost, associated with their new employment.

The divergence between market wages paid to unskilled workers on new projects, and their opportunity cost or shadow wage is often found to be substantial; a common result of shadow price studies, for example, is that the output foregone in agriculture may be less than half the urban wage.[20] The point of central importance for the present discussion however, relates to the role of government intervention. Government may intervene in the functioning of labour markets to establish minimum wages, to guarantee a certain minimum income level, or to support trade union activity to prevent the exploitation of workers by powerful employers. In some countries these interventions may be significant in raising urban wages above the levels they would otherwise reach. Many who might accept these interventions as desirable in their own right, none the less argue that they introduce major distortions in urban labour markets, and create a number of serious side-effects.

Several arguments are normally put forward in discussions of the harmful impact of labour market distortions, two of which are particularly important for discussions of industrial policy.

First, if the market wage paid to unskilled labour is substantially above the economic cost of employing these workers, the commercial profitability of new investment will be understated relative to its economic profitability. In other words firms will pay a wage bill determined by market wage rates, and other things being equal, their commercial or private profitability will be less than the economic returns they generate, to the extent that the shadow wage is below the market wage. If investment decisions are based on commercial criteria too little investment will be made. In addition labour-intensive activities will be particularly penalised, so that the composition of output in the economy will contain a lower share of labour-intensive commodities than if market and shadow wages were equal. This argument concerning the divergence between market wages and the economic costs of employing unskilled labour provided a major part of the initial theoretical rationale for protection of new industrial activity in developing countries, and was the clearest example of the need to introduce shadow price estimates into calculations of investment viability.

In addition to a problem of insufficient investment, it is

suggested that labour market distortions will have a harmful effect on the technology embodied in new investment. Therefore provided there is the possibility of substitution of capital or materials for labour, it is argued that urban wages above the economic cost of labour will encourage a shift in factor intensity in a labour-saving, rather than a labour-using direction. This will have undesirable effects in terms of both income distribution, since it is now recognised that the provision of employment is the most effective means of raising the living standards of low income groups in developing countries, and economic efficiency. In economic terms the argument is that there will be a loss of efficiency, since specialisation on the basis of developing countries' abundant resource, labour, will not be carried far enough. The impact of labour market distortions on technology choice will be compounded by additional factors operative in capital markets, which work to lower the market cost of capital below its economic level. The important point to stress is that the overall significance of both sets of distortions for the technology used in developing countries depends critically on the possibility of significant substitution between factors in the production of different commodities. There is probably now agreement however that there is at least some scope for factor substitution in most industries, although its magnitude will vary between industries, and substitution will be greater in peripheral and ancillary activities than in basic production processes.

Comparable arguments regarding the harmful effects of controls have been put forward in relation to capital markets. The term 'financial repression' is now used widely to refer to controls on interest rates, on either deposit or loan accounts, and can also be extended to other forms of intervention, such as a policy of discrimination in favour of particular sectors, who receive credit on favourable terms. The rationale for such controls is normally to encourage investment, either in aggregate or in priority activities. The critique of such measures rests on three main arguments.

First, it is argued that domestic savings are responsive to interest rates. This means that holding down or repressing interest rates has a negative effect on domestic savings, so that the total level of investment will be reduced below that possible under different interest rate policy. Secondly, it is argued that domestic savings are allocated inefficiently between competing

197

borrowers when rationing is by direct control rather than by the market. In other words, efficient potential borrowers are not permitted to bid resources away from the less efficient, since interest rate ceilings prevent a rise in rates, and available credit is rationed by non-price means either by government directive or by bank policy. Thirdly, it is argued that controls on interest rates along with an over-valued exchange rate, work to cheapen the cost of capital relative to labour. This has the harmful consequences for employment through technology choice referred to above.

For both labour and capital markets the general recommendation is clear, and it is that controls should be removed so that wages and interest rates are determined by demand and supply in the respective markets. Some estimates exist of the effect of labour and capital market distortions, in raising labour and lowering capital costs. Krueger (1984) reports data from eight countries in the 1960s and early 1970s, and these are given in Table 5.6. The key figures are the last column which show the increase in the ratio of wages to capital cost (termed the wage-rental ratio) for the protected industrial sector relative to the same ratio in the rest of the economy. It is difficult to generalise on the basis of data from only eight countries, but in two Pakistan and Tunisia, the combined effects of wage and capital distortions appear to have been very substantial and in all but Hong Kong and South Korea the cost of labour relative to capital increased by more than 30 per cent, due to distortions.

Table 5.6: Percentage estimated distortion in capital and labour costs[a]

Country	Year	% increase in labour costs	% reduction in capital costs due to Trade	Credit	Others	% increase in wage-rental ratio
Argentina	1973	15	8	9	n.a	38
Brazil	1968	27	0	4	n.a	31
Chile	1966–68	n.a.	37	n.a.	n.a.	37
Hong Kong	1973	0	0	0	0	0
Ivory Coast	1971	23	0	3	12	45
Pakistan	1961–64	0	38	53	10	316
South Korea	1969	0	0	8	2	11
Tunisia	1972	20	30	6	n.a.	87

[a]Percentage changes refer to costs in the 'distorted' or protected modern sector relative to costs in the rest of the economy.
Source: Krueger (1984), table 4.1, p. 556.

PATTERNS OF TRADE

Having examined some of the major arguments concerning interventions in markets, the Neoclassical interpretation of industrial trade possibilities will be considered. As implied by the simple two commodity model outlined above production specialisation, it is argued, should be on the basis of an economy's comparative advantage. This requires concentrating resources where activities are internationally competitive, with domestic costs defined in terms of the opportunity cost of the commodities and resources that go into production. There is said to be a comparative advantage in a particular line of production therefore, if domestic costs, that reflect the alternative uses of the input involved, are below the world price of competing production abroad.[21] Such activities will be economically efficient by the CB and DRC criteria noted earlier.

It is recognised that comparative cost advantages change over time, and this is incorporated in the argument on dynamic stages of comparative advantage. Here it is suggested that developing countries' cost advantages will initially be in simple labour-intensive goods, since the opportunity costs of employing unskilled workers in these economies will be low. Over time, however, as labour surpluses are removed and real wages rise, these countries can move to more sophisticated commodities embodying more skills and capital inputs. In other words, the opportunity costs of producing different types of commodity will shift over time.[22]

In Neoclassical discussions of patterns of trade specialisation a strategy of export-substitution is recommended in contrast with the more familiar import-substitution.[23] Export-substitution refers to a shift in the composition of exports, so that, for example new manufactured exports rise as a share of total exports. A simple descriptive sequence of stages is often used to illustrate alternative trade strategies. The stages are as follows:

- primary import-substitution;
- primary export-substitution;
- secondary import-substitution;
- secondary export-substitution.

The adjectives primary and secondary refer to the technological complexity and capital intensity of commodities; commodities that are primary are therefore relatively unsophisticated labour-intensive goods, the most obvious examples for manufacturers being textiles, clothing and toys. Commodities covered under the heading secondary are technologically more advanced, skill- and capital-intensive; both consumer durables, such as electrical domestic appliances, and intermediates and capital goods, like iron and steel and machinery of various types, are covered here. The argument is that new industries will generally commence production with sales to the home market of primary goods that were previously imported. This primary import-substitution can be 'natural' in the sense that it occurs as a result of transport and other cost advantages. Alternatively, and this is seen as the most common situation in developing countries, it can be policy-induced, as new industries are protected and encouraged by governments.

The Neoclassical view is that primary import-substitution if it arises from substantial protection will create the biases and distortions noted above. In addition, once the 'easy' stage is passed and all previous imports have been replaced, its growth will be limited by the expansion of the domestic market. An economically more efficient alternative for most developing countries is seen as a shift to a strategy of primary export-substitution. This involves the export of the simple labour-intensive goods, produced initially for the home market, or alternatively exports of parts and components for production located overseas. Commodities of this type draw on the unskilled labour resources of developing countries available at relatively low wages. A shift to a strategy of primary export-substitution involves at least the removal of the anti-export bias normally associated with protectionist trade policies.

Primary export-substitution will be relevant as long as wage costs remain sufficiently low for a country to maintain a comparative cost advantage in labour-intensive commodities. After a time, however, as real wages rise in response to growing demands for labour, it is argued that it will become economically efficient to shift into the production of secondary commodities, and establish a more sophisticated industrial structure. This may necessitate some encouragement for these new industries, either through protection or preferably through promotion via subsidies. Secondary import-substitution of these goods occurs as their local production supplants imports. However any anti-export bias at this stage should be short-lived and it is recommended that adequate incentives be given to encourage producers of secondary commodities to break into export markets. At this point secondary export-substitution will be reached. The time lag between secondary import and export-substitution will be determined not only by level of incentives offered for domestic and export sales, but also by the size of the domestic market and the importance of economies of scale in production, in individual branches of activity. For example the more important are scale economies relative to the size of the domestic market for a commodity, the greater will be the pressure to enter export markets to remain competitive.[24]

It must be recognised that this schematic sequence is an over-simplification of a complex sequence of shifts in industrial specialisation and orientation. The speed at which countries can and should move through these stages will vary with factors like national resource endowments, domestic market size, export market prospects, labour policies, and broad government priorities. At any one time the strategy of an economy might be considered a hybrid of at least two stages. None the less, this sequence has been considered sufficiently useful to be applied in a normative sense to suggest how developing countries could re-order their trade strategies.

For example, Ranis (1985b) in discussing the performance of South Korea and Taiwan in comparison with many of the larger Latin American economies argues that there have been two key differences in trade strategy between the two groups. First, the primary import-substitution phase in the two South East Asian economies was both mild in terms of levels of protection and short-lived — 10 to 15 years. In Latin America, however, protection was higher and the strategy of primary import-substitution was continued for much longer, thus creating more distortions and vested interests committed to the continuation of the system. Second, whilst the South East Asian economies shifted fairly rapidly to the primary export-substitution phase, and gained the benefits associated with rapidly rising exports, the Latin America economies moved to a further stage of protection — in the form of secondary import-substitution. Since the commodities produced at this stage are capital- and skill-intensive they are often high cost in international terms and thus require higher levels of protection than simpler primary goods. The distortions and biases of primary import-substitution it is argued are magnified at the secondary stage.

Therefore whilst South Korea and Taiwan are seen as passing through all four stages from the late 1960s to the late 1970s, in Latin America import-substitution dominated trade strategy until industrial exports began to emerge from secondary import-substitute industries in the 1970s. Ranis argues, however, that many of these exports arose not from the emerging competitiveness of domestic producers but from government willingness to subsidise high cost exports.[25] He sees the Latin America sequence as inefficient, since selective export promotion often of high cost industries, is grafted onto an unreformed secondary import-substitution strategy. The consequences of missing the primary export-substitution stage are not only that many distortions and biases remain, but also that the possibility of raising industrial employment through an expansion of labour-intensive exports is also lost.

This argument illustrates clearly the Neoclassical view of trade strategy. It is not that developing countries should remain as permanent exporters of labour-intensive goods, but that it will be economically beneficial at a certain stage of their development to focus trade strategy on these exports. At a later stage industrial diversification can take place.

The current position of an economy will determine the speed and direction of possible reforms. Most relatively unindustrialised developing countries have been, at least until recently, at the stage of primary import-substitution. However countries with a longer history of industrialisation have been moving to that of secondary import-substitution. Neoclassical discussions of policy reform have focused on ways of removing the biases and distortions linked with both of these stages. Where an economy is only at the stage of primary import-substitution the chief objective is to remove anti-export bias, and shift to primary export-substitution. Where a more sophisticated industrial base has been created at the secondary import-substitution stage, reforms will aim to encourage greater export, probably of both the primary and secondary type. Specific trade reform measures are considered below in Chapter 7.

CONCLUSION

This chapter examines the Neoclassical arguments on the inefficiency of industrialisation policies pursued in many developing countries. Two aspects of the Neoclassical case have received most attention — the impact of government intervention on the operation of markets, and the neglect of trade opportunities through the implementation of policies that discriminated against exports. An economically rational industrial policy, it is argued, is one that removes both of these sources of inefficiency. Chapter 7 discusses the Neoclassical proposals for industrial reform, and some evidence on the effectiveness of these measures. However prior to that Chapter 6 considers some alternative evidence on the efficiency of industry in developing countries, that to some extent is in contrast with the picture painted by the Neoclassical studies cited in this chapter.

NOTES

1. Little (1982), p. 25. Authors like Viner, Myint and Bauer can be seen as earlier exponents of this approach.
2. See Foxley (1983).
3. There are exceptions to these propositions under conditions not specified in the model. Some of these exceptions will be commented on below. See Bhagwati (1968) for a fuller statement of the model.
4. In the figure a new production frontier must be added reflecting economic not private production possibilities.
5. See Corden (1974), pp. 28–31.
6. Commodities can be non-traded either because of their physical nature or because of government trade controls. A formal definition is of commodities whose domestic price is below the cif price of imports, and above the free on board (fob) price of exports of comparable goods. For a discussion of non-traded goods see, for example, UNIDO (1978), pp. 22–7.
7. The following sections draw heavily on Kitchen and Weiss (1987).
8. In this statement and elsewhere in the discussion the deviation of domestic from world prices due to domestic transport and distribution costs is ignored.
9. Strictly this assumes that export demand is perfectly elastic so that exporters have no problems selling more at the prevailing price, and that competitive conditions prevail domestically.
10. Corden (1971) gives a comprehensive survey of the ERP measure, and on pp. 35–40 gives a proof of the equivalence of equations (5.1) and (5.2).

11. There is often a correlation between the ranking of activities by effective and nominal rates of protection, which implies that the latter may give a rough indication of resource pull. Balassa (1982) calculates the rank correlation coefficient for NRP and ERP on total sales for six economies, and finds it to be above 0.75 and statistically significant in five out of the six cases; see Balassa (1982), table 2.2, p. 26.

12. See Little *et al.* (1970), table 5.2, p. 174, and Balassa (1971) table 3.2, p. 56. Balassa (1982), table 2.3, pp. 28–9 distinguishes between capital goods branches and reveals more ambiguous results, showing that some capital goods activities were relatively highly protected in some of the countries examined.

13. Weiss (1984b) discusses government industrial priorities in Mexico at this time.

14. There is a vast literature on shadow pricing. The most significant texts are UNIDO (1972), Little and Mirrlees (1968) and (1974) and Squire and van der Tak (1975). Irvin (1978) is a survey of the field.

15. For a demonstration of the equivalence of the CB and DRC measures see Krueger (1972) and Balassa (1974). Schdlowsky (1984) argues that DRC can be used as a measure of dynamic comparative advantage.

16. The treatment of foreign exchange in CB can vary depending upon whether world or domestic prices are used as the overall numeraire or unit of account. If shadow prices for domestic factors are already world price equivalent values, economic efficiency simply requires a DRC of less than 1.0. Any external effects can be incorporated in DRC calculations by adding or subtracting them from the domestic resources used, so that including Ei, equation 5.4 becomes

$$DRC_i = \frac{PV\ (\sum_{l} a_{li}.P_l\ \pm\ E_i)}{PV\ (P_i\ -\ \sum_{j} a_{ji}.P_j)}$$

17. Industrial CB case-studies are given for example in Little *et al.* (1970), Page (1976), Lall and Streeten (1977), UNIDO (1980) and Adhikari (1986a).

18. Strictly it is incorrect to rank activities by DRC unless foreign exchange is the binding constraint on growth; see Warr (1983).

19. Formally the ERS can be expressed in a similar way to equation (5.1), except that VADP now includes the effect of subsidies, as well as tariff and quota protection.

20. See Weiss (1985) for a discussion of the shadow wage in Jamaica.

21. This is in the absence of additional external effects that can justify local production even if costs exceed the world price of competing output.

22. See Balassa (1977). The stages of comparative argument is considered further in Chapter 6.

23. See for example Ranis (1985b).

24. Fei *et al.* (1985), p. 56 stress this point in discussing the evolution of trade patterns in South Korea, Taiwan and Japan.

25. Teitel and Thoumi (1986) trace the growth of exports from secondary import-substitute industries in Argentina and Brazil, and question Ranis's conclusion that they were simply the result of export incentives. One can also query the extent to which Latin America economies with higher wage levels could have competed effectively with labour-intensive South East Asian exports in the 1960s and early 1970s.

6

Alternative Approaches to Industrial Performance

The previous chapter has focused on Neoclassical criteria for judging economic efficiency, and considered the results of studies that have used these criteria in an examination of industrial operations in developing countries. These criteria rely, however, on estimates of notional shadow prices to value the costs and benefits of industrial operations. Estimation of such prices is both complex and controversial, and the practical difficulty of obtaining realistic figures may limit the usefulness of these criteria. This chapter, therefore, considers an alternative set of indicators of economic performance that whilst not always free from ambiguity are conceptually and empirically easier to estimate than the measures examined in Chapter 5. The discussion focuses on the utilisation of plant capacity, the diversification of exports, productivity growth and technical progress.

UTILISATION OF PLANT CAPACITY

The level of capacity utilisation in industry is a direct measure of the extent to which assets are productively employed. It is obvious that changes in utilisation rates over time are of relevance to discussions of the efficiency of industrial operations in developing countries, and that the existence of high levels of under-utilisation, in economies where investment funds are scarce, is likely to be evidence of significant resource misallocation. Much has been written on the theoretical issues relating to capacity working in developing countries, and in recent years empirical evidence has emerged to modify some earlier views on the extent of under-utilisation. At one time it was commonplace to encounter discussions that stressed the magnitude of idle industrial capacity in developing countries. For example, Little, *et al.* (1970) stated that:

> Just as the too fast migration of labour creates urban un-employment, so too great a diversion of investible funds creates more industrial capacity than can be utilized. Indeed, the chronic under-utilization of manufacturing capacity is as common among developing countries as urban un-employment.[1]

This picture of widespread idle industrial capacity across most developing countries arose partly from the availability of statistics from countries, such as India and Pakistan, where the problem appeared particularly severe. However it can be argued that it stemmed also from a confusion in some estimates regarding the concept of the capacity output with which actual output should be compared. In some cases full capacity output was defined loosely as the maximum output that could be produced under normal working conditions. What was considered normal, particularly with regard to the number of shifts worked per day, could vary between studies, thus making comparisons of results difficult. There now seems to be agreement that the best means of gauging capacity working is to estimate the time utilisation of plant; in other words, the maximum number of hours plants can be operated per year allowing for multiple shifts and necessary maintenance time, must be compared with actual operating time. The major empirical studies of recent years, whose results are discussed below, employ this approach.[2]

Most theoretical discussions of capacity working in developing countries have been influenced by the pioneering work of Winston, who adapted theoretical arguments from the analysis of the problem in developed economies.[3] A number of alternative definitions of full capacity can be used and it is necessary to clarify these at the outset. One is technical capacity relating to the maximum output achievable in a given time period. This must be distinguished from optimum capacity, in either the financial or economic sense. In other words the maximum feasibility output may not be the one desired, from either a private or an economic point of view. The financial optimum output will be where firms maximise profits, assuming that this is their overriding goal, and neglecting any ambiguity in the specification of profit-maximising output. Optimum capacity in economic terms, on the other hand, will be the output where net economic benefits are at a maximum, and this will differ from the financial optimum whenever market prices and economic values differ. These capacities can be illustrated diagrammatically in Figure 6.1 using time as the measure of capacity. Taking 8,760 hours per annum as the maximum working time of a plant, technical capacity U_T will be this figure minus the minimum necessary maintenance time.

If U_E is the economic optimum, and $U_E < U_T$, the difference $(U_T - U_E)$ can be termed economically optimal idleness; in other words this level of under-capacity working is

Figure 6.1

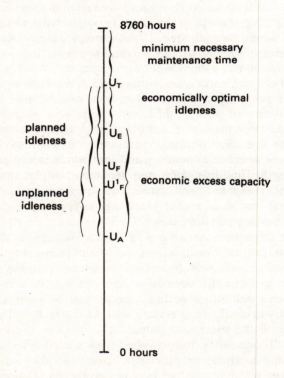

Source: Adapted from Winston (1981).

208

justified, since an expansion beyond U_E will add more to costs than to benefits. The financial optimum U_F, where firms maximise profits is shown below U_E in Figure 6.1, implying that firms desired capacity working is below the economic optimum. However, in principle, there is no reason why this need be the case, so that U_F can exceed U_E. If firms plan to produce below U_T, $(U_T - U_F)$ gives planned idleness from a private point of view. It has been pointed out that private producers need not necessarily aim to maximise profits.[4] If they wish to produce an output below financial optimum, shown as U^1_F in Figure 6.1, the logic of the argument is not disturbed, although private planned idleness is now $(U_T - U^1_F)$. Actual capacity working is shown as U_A, and the difference between actual working and a firm's own target or planned rate gives unplanned capacity idleness; assuming profit maximisation this is $(U_F - U_A)$. Total economic excess capacity is the difference between economic optimum and actual capacity working $(U_E - U_A)$.

The significance of this analysis for discussions of capacity utilisation in developing countries is two-fold. First, it brings out the point that there may be a divergence between technical capacity and the economic optimum level of output. The commonsense of this is that it may not be economically rational to run plants for the maximum time possible technically. Second, it allows a distinction between two categories of under-capacity working; that which is planned by producers — desired idleness — and that which is unplanned or undesired. This distinction may be important for policy discussion, since if the causes of excess capacity differ, so too will the policy measures to reduce excess capacity.

At this point a link can be made between the two categories — desired and undesired excess capacity — and the Structuralist and Neoclassical views on industrial development discussed in earlier chapters. Undesired excess capacity can be interpreted as a situation where various features of an economy prevent producers from reaching their target level of capacity working. The normal explanations for this form of excess capacity are taken to include:

- inadequate domestic demand;
- inadequate foreign exchange, creating a scarcity of key imported inputs;

- various bottlenecks in non-traded sectors, such as power and transport;
- a scarcity of skilled labour;
- difficulties in assimilating foreign technologies.

In one way or another all of these explanations can be linked with structural features of developing economies, where for example, the size of the domestic market may be limited by the pattern of income distribution, and where bottlenecks in the supply of foreign exchange, and non-traded inputs may arise from the pattern of production in the economy. Undesired excess capacity will be a symptom therefore of many of the problems identified in Structuralist discussions of industrialisation.

Desired excess capacity, on the other hand, can be explained by the Neoclassical focus on the importance of relative prices. As we have seen it is argued that producers face prices of labour and capital that are distorted away from economic values, so that the price of labour is raised relative to that of capital. If decisions on the level of output firms wish to produce are sensitive to relative prices, this can have significant implications for capacity working. It is argued specifically that the key distortion relates to the cost of night shift work, and that institutional or other factors that create premia for night work above normal day-time wages raise the nominal cost of night employment well above the real cost, in either economic or broader social terms. It is argued, therefore, that producers have a strong monetary disincentive to work night shifts, and that this is a major explanation for the absence of multiple-shift working in many developing countries. To put the same point in a slightly different way, firms faced with a growth in demand may either choose to meet this by building a new plant, or by running their existing plant more intensively. The costs of capital equipment relative to that of night shift payments will be the major influences on the cost calculations of producers in determining the least cost of these two alternatives. With high night shift premia it may be that it is financially unprofitable for firms to work multiple shifts despite the fact that from society's point of view the cost of night work may be little more than that of day work.[5] Despite the focus on labour, capital costs that are kept below economic levels, for example by interest rate ceilings or an over-valued exchange rate, are also part of the

Neoclassical explanation of planned excess capacity. If capital assets are kept relatively cheap, it is argued that producers will have less incentive to utilise them fully.

Empirical evidence on under-capacity working

The empirical evidence on capacity working is not free from ambiguity. International comparisons are difficult due to differences in the definitions of excess capacity used in different studies. However one major study, Bautista *et al.* (1981), on capacity utilisation in four developing countries — Israel, the Philippines, Colombia and Malaysia — provides consistent comparative material. Since this is the most significant work in recent years on capacity utilisation in industry it is worth discussing its major conclusions.[6] The country studies generally employ a time utilisation measure of capacity working, and involve detailed surveys of manufacturers in each country.

The degree of capacity working found in all countries studied was higher than would have been expected from earlier work on those economies, and the results generally do not support the view of widespread under-capacity working in the industrial sectors of developing economies. Of the four countries, capacity utilisation, both actual and desired, was lowest in Israel, where it is argued, labour shortages were important in the early 1970s.

A number of different definitions of capacity working are used, and it is notable that in the four countries unplanned capital idleness or excess capacity was relatively low. In other words, capacity working based on the ratio of actual output to planned output was high in all of the countries.[7] This implies that unplanned excess capacity was much less important than planned excess capacity. Similar results on the greater importance of planned as opposed to unplanned excess capacity have been found elsewhere; for example Nigeria and Sri Lanka.[8] Table 6.1 summarises some of the more important results of Bautista *et al.* (1981) for manufacturing as a whole in the four countries.

Whilst averages for all-manufacturing may be helpful for purposes of international comparisons they may hide significant variations both between branches within manufacturing and between plants within a single branch. The results indicate a substantial variety of experience within particular countries.

211

Although the authors are reluctant to generalise too far across countries they suggest not surprisingly that there is a tendency for industrial chemicals, a capital-intensive continuous process industry, to show high utilisation rates everywhere, and for some highly labour-intensive consumer goods, such as footwear, to have low utilisation rates in all countries.

The studies use multiple regression analysis in an attempt to identify the major variables explaining the level of actual capacity working. Whilst the results of this type of exercise are rarely conclusive some of the findings, both those which prove significant and those which do not, are worth noting. The Neo-classical arguments on the inefficiency of import-substitution programmes imply that export-orientation should be associated with a high level of capacity utilisation. This would be rationalised in terms of both the greater efficiency of producers who have to compete internationally, and the removal of a demand constraint on production once firms can break into export markets. However, the results provide only partial support for this hypothesis. The share of exports in output at the plant level is statistically significant in Colombia, the Philippines and Malaysia, but not in Israel. Furthermore where it is possible to include the level of effective protection as an explanatory variable it is not significant. The authors place the most weight on the links between exports and demand, and

Table 6.1 Measures of capacity utilisation in manufacturing: four developing countries (early 1970s)

	Colombia	Philippines	Israel	Malaysia
Actual to possible capacity working[a](%)	79	61	43	71
Actual to desired capacity working[b](%)	88	78	48	73

[a]This is a time measure that appears to correspond broadly with U_A/U_T in our notation. It is a weighted average for all-manufacturing with capital stock as the weight.
[b]This is a time measure that appears to correspond broadly with U_A/U_F in our notation. It is a weighted average for all-manufacturing with capital stock as the weight. The figure for the Philippines is calculated on a different basis from those for the other countries.

Source: Bautista *et al.* (1981), table 9.1, p. 242, table 5.8, p. 117, table 6.4, p. 151, table 7.4, p. 195, and table 8.7, p. 224.

imply that in so far as exports do contribute to higher utilisation this is likely to be as a result of their impact on the scale of production. They also point out that Israel, the country with the highest ratio of exports to total manufacturing production, has the lowest utilisation rate of the four countries studied.

The two consistently most significant variables explaining the level of capacity utilisation are found to be measures of the capital-intensity, and the scale of production. The link between capital-intensity and utilisation appears straightforward. Once capital-intensive plants have been installed, it is argued, there will be strong pressures to utilise them as fully as possible, because of the high fixed costs involved. In the case of scale of production the argument is that large firms will find it easier to take advantage of economies of scale in production; a piece of equipment capable of production at the minimum level of unit cost may be under-utilised in a small firm due to lack of complementary inputs. Furthermore large firms can use a division labour between managers to ensure that multiple shift working can be adequately controlled and supervised, whilst this may be difficult for small firms run by their owners, or where the managerial team is small.[9]

Whilst relative capital-intensity clearly figures in the Neoclassical theory of planned excess capacity, the other key variable in that theory, the wage premium for shift work does not perform well. In the cross-country analysis, for example, the coefficient of the wage premium has the wrong sign in two of the countries, and where it has the correct sign is not statistically significant. The results are a little better in the individual country studies with one of the measures of shift premium significant for Malaysia, and two measures significant for the Philippines, but with each having only a very weak effect on utilisation. This relatively poor performance of what is a key explanatory variable in the Neoclassical analysis can be attributed to different causes. One is the poor data on wage differentials with which the studies had to work. The problem is particularly serious where firms had never operated more than one shift. In these circumstances it was difficult to estimate the largely hypothetical wage that would be payable for night or overtime work. Another explanation however is that decisions on shift working and overtime are not strongly influenced by wage costs, but more by attitudes towards night work by both workers and management, and by lack of infrastructure and housing facilities to support work outside normal hours. The authors acknowledge that these latter considerations are likely to be far more important in developing than in developed countries.

Age of plants is not a significant explanatory variable for capacity utilisation in any of the countries. Thus no evidence of any learning-by-doing effect on capacity working could be identified.[10] In only one of the countries, Colombia, is there adequate data to allow a meaningful comparison of changes in capacity utilisation within manufacturing over a substantial period. It is clear that utilisation rates rose over the period 1945–73, but more recently from the early 1960s to 1973 the slight upward trend that appears in the data is described as too small to be accepted with any confidence.

The results of Bautista *et al.* (1981) clarify several important points on the question of capacity under-utilisation in developing countries. However there are a few important qualifications which should be made to the summary of results presented above. First, statistical analysis of this type clearly cannot capture all of the factors explaining the degree of capacity working. The study on the Philippines, in particular, points to the low explanatory power of the regression equations that have been estimated, and draws from this the implication that whilst factors like relative costs and scale matter, there will be a number of other influences, for example, social attitudes and the poor quality of supporting infrastructure, that may also be important. Second, in terms of the earlier discussion of the theoretical concepts of capacity, no attempt is made in these studies to compare actual utilisation with the economic optimal rate of utilisation; in our earlier terminology U_E is not estimated. The omission of this definition of capacity is not surprising, given the difficulties involved, but it does mean that it is not possible to draw conclusions on the magnitude of economic excess capacity.[11] Third, and perhaps most important, the four countries studied, shared a key characteristic in the period for which data were collected; that is they were not suffering major foreign exchange crises with the associated scarcity of imported inputs. In countries where a foreign exchange constraint is critical unintended excess capacity is likely to be much more significant than in the four economies covered in Bautista *et al.* (1981).

On the question of unintended surplus capacity a number of

studies have linked this with a scarcity of foreign exchange. Winston (1971), for example, in his analysis of capacity working in Pakistan finds the share of imported raw materials in total raw materials, to be statistically significant and negatively related to capacity utilisation; this is a result which appears to accord with much anecdotal evidence on capacity working.[12] India is another economy where foreign exchange scarcity has been critical, particularly in the 1960s and 1970s. A number of government reports examined the question of capacity utilisation in public enterprises and surveyed the possible causes of excess capacity. A scarcity of crucial inputs, many of these tradeables, was identified as the factor in a majority of cases.[13] An institutional feature of the import licensing system used in India over this period has also been linked with excess capacity. Since import licences for raw materials and other inputs were allocated on the basis of existing installed capacity, it is argued that this created an incentive for producers to install capacity in excess of their current needs since this gave them access to essential imports.[14] Following this argument, a scarcity of foreign exchange generated excess capacity indirectly, through the incentives to capacity expansion ahead of demand that arose from the institutional arrangements used to allocate foreign exchange.

Whilst the cases of India and Pakistan are relatively well documented it is clear that many other developing countries also experienced substantial under-capacity working in the industrial sector as a result of foreign exchange scarcity. There is evidence on this for economies as diverse as Jamaica, Tanzania, Ghana and the Sudan.[15] For example, the Jamaican study shows not only that the vast majority of manufacturers operated only one shift in the 1970s, but that even taking only 1.5 shifts as the definition of full capacity, on average producers in Jamaica were operating at just over half of full capacity output. When questioned on the causes of excess capacity the single most common response was non-availability of imported inputs.

Conclusion

This survey of evidence on capacity utilisation has not been able to identify precisely the merits of competing explanations, and there is no reason why a single explanation should be valid for all countries. In some countries, it appears that unplanned excess capacity, normally explained by various structural bottlenecks, was relatively low. However in economies where a foreign exchange scarcity has been important there is strong evidence that actual industrial output has been well below target levels. Econometric work has not always been able to substantiate the full Neoclassical explanation for capacity utilisation, even where most excess capacity is planned rather than unplanned. However it is likely that relative prices are one of a number of factors at work.

In terms of drawing conclusions on the efficiency of plant operation in developing countries this type of data is inconclusive. Certainly in some countries reported utilisation is close to that in developed economies. However in others, particularly those constrained by foreign exchange, it has been much lower. Furthermore this evidence gives little information on changes over time, and the reasons for them.[16] None the less it is important to note that in some countries at least industrial capacity working has been relatively high.

MANUFACTURED EXPORTS FROM DEVELOPING COUNTRIES

Chapter 1 has already pointed to the rapid growth of manufactured exports from developing countries post-1960. This section examines some of the characteristics of and explanations for this export growth, and in particular its implications for discussions of industrial efficiency.

In terms of the commodities that have been exported as part of this mini-export boom, it is now well documented that the majority have been labour-intensive, have involved mature as opposed to recent technologies, and have been standardised in the sense that relatively few changes in specifications have been introduced for these goods in recent years.[17] Studies that focus on the pattern of export specialisation of developing countries, using a version of the 'revealed comparative advantage' (RCA) measure, find that specialisation is predominantly in such products, and that the trend at least from the 1960s to the mid-1970s was for an intensification of this pattern of specialisation.[18] For example, commenting on their results over the period 1962–63 to 1972–73 Donges and Riedel point out that:

216

The industries exhibiting the strongest comparative advantage according to 1972/73 data were cotton fabrics, footwear, textile clothing, tanneries, canned fruit, household equipment, jewellery and wood products. Not surprisingly, these are all labour and/or raw material intensive products. Interestingly however the sample countries appear to have developed a comparative advantage in a number of light manufacturing products of which electrical equipment, metal containers and telecommunications are the most prominent.[19]

The latter category of goods to which they refer can be seen as covering non-traditional relatively labour-intensive items, generally using mature technologies.

An important point, which must be considered before passing to the question of the relevance of these exports for discussions of industrial economic efficiency, is the degree to which the dynamic version of the Neoclassical approach to trade — the stages of comparative advantage argument — can explain this export performance. The stages argument implies that countries' resources and factor endowments will change over time, so that their comparative advantages will shift from existing to new patterns of specialisation. The 'stages' of comparative advantage are generally seen as commencing with traditional labour-intensive commodities, followed by a shift to goods-intensive in skilled, as opposed to unskilled labour. The third stage involves specialisation in physical capital-intensive commodities, and the final highest stage is where high technology, human capital and knowledge-intensive goods are those in which economies develop a major specialisation. New exporters of manufactures will enter export markets at the lower end of the spectrum with unskilled labour-intensive goods. Over time if they can graduate to the next stage by shifting to more skill-intensive commodities they can free export markets for traditional goods for new exporting countries. The real significance of this argument is that it challenges the view that developing country exports will run into a demand constraint, particularly in the markets of developed economies. Balassa, the chief proponent of this view, puts it thus:

The stages approach to comparative advantage also permits one to dispel certain misapprehension as regards the foreign demand constraint under which developing countries are said to operate. With countries progressing on the comparative advantage scale, their exports can supplant the exports of countries that graduate to a higher level. Now, to the extent that one developing country replaces another in the imports of particular commodities by the developed countries, the problem of adjustment in the latter group of countries does not arise. Rather the burden of adjustment will be borne in industries where the products of newly graduating developing countries compete with the products of the developed countries.[20]

However the evidence on the validity of the stages approach as a means of explaining developing country export performance is by no means clear-cut. Balassa's seminal article relates revealed comparative advantage in a large number of products for a sample of developing and developed economies to the characteristics of those products.[21] Furthermore the regression coefficients obtained from this analysis are themselves related to the characteristics of the sample countries. Capital intensity of both physical and human capital is generally found to be a significant independent variable explaining the revealed comparative advantage of different countries in different products. In other words countries with an estimated high capital endowment — in physical and human terms — tend to have an export specialisation in capital-intensive products. Balassa interprets this as clear support for the stages of comparative advantage argument, since if capital endowment rises over time with the accumulation of physical and human capital, and the regression results of the study hold, countries will tend to shift towards a greater specialisation in capital-intensive goods.[22]

Evidence of this nature can be no more than suggestive, however, particularly as there can be different methods for valuing the critical variable capital stock. A key question is the extent to which the export success of the NICs, described in Chapter 1, has been followed recently by other developing countries, since a central plank of the stages argument is that other countries should be able to follow the route of the NICs. There is now some fairly firm evidence that a 'second tier' of successful exporters emerged in the 1970s. These can be defined as countries with

- a rate of growth of manufactured exports in the 1970s equal to or above that of the NICs; and
- a concentration on similar export commodities to those in which the NICs made their greatest market gains in the 1960s and early 1970s.

Havrylyshyn and Alikhani (1982) identify twelve countries in this group which they term 'new exporting countries' (NECs), although it must be remembered that in several rapid export growth reflected expansion from a very low base in the early 1970s.[23] Perhaps of greatest interest is the composition of the manufactured exports from these countries. A comparison of the top seven product categories exported by this group in 1979 revealed that 5 out of the 7 — clothing, textile yarns and fabrics, electrical machinery, non-metal mineral manufactures, and miscellaneous manufactures — were in the top seven list for the NICs in 1970. The chief development in the exports of NICs during the 1970s was the reduction in concentration on the more traditional labour-intensive items — such as clothing and textiles — and a shift towards engineering products requiring greater skilled labour inputs. In the NECs however this trend had not been carried very far by the end of the 1970s, although electrical machinery exports had begun to assume importance. Havrylyshyn and Alikhani argue that in terms of the type of commodities exported, the NECs appeared to be following the NICs with a lag of 5 to 10 years.[24]

In terms of the growth and composition of manufactured exports, therefore, from the experience of the 1970s it appears that some countries have begun to follow the path first set by the NICs, and to shift gradually from success in the export of traditional labour-intensive commodities towards those with a higher skill content. This must be seen in perspective however since, as stressed in Chapter 1, the majority of manufactured exports from developing countries are still dominated by a relatively small number of NICs.

Another part of the stages of comparative advantage argument is that over time some of the more rapidly growing developing countries will develop an export specialisation more closely in line with that of the currently developed economies — that is a specialisation in more capital-intensive and high technology commodities. The technology exports from developing countries, to be discussed in a later section, provide some evidence of the emergence of such a trend, although these exports are still relatively small and cannot be seen as a major departure from existing patterns of specialisation.

In terms of commodity exports, at least for the period up to the late 1970s, it appears that the NICs pattern of specialisation was still quite a long way removed from that of the developed economies. Evidence on this is provided by Ballance *et al.* (1982) who calculate revealed comparative advantage measures (which they term export performance indices) for groups of countries in 134 industries, over the period from 1965 to 1976. Four groupings of countries are used — industrialised, recently developed, NICs and other LDCs — and within each country group industries are ranked by their export performance index. Rank correlation coefficients are used to test the degree of similarity between the rankings in each of the four country groups. The major result to emerge from this analysis is that the export performance ranking of the industrialised countries differs markedly from that of all the other groups, and that this difference accentuated rather than weakened over the period studied. Furthermore there was a significant similarity between the export performance in the NICs and other LDCs, which was constant over the period. It is unwise to place too much weight on evidence such as this since the period covered only goes up to 1976, and the statistical procedure used is not very sophisticated.[25] However taken at face-value it clearly does not support a stages interpretation, since there is no evidence that NICs moved away markedly from the pattern of specialisation of other LDCs, and towards that of industrialised countries. The authors themselves make this point explicitly arguing that their results are more compatible with a dependency interpretation, which suggests that developing countries will have great difficulty in changing fundamentally their patterns of trade specialisation.

A key question is how far things have changed since the mid-1970s, and how they will evolve in the immediate future. The most that can be said on the stages of comparative advantage argument is that there is evidence that some developing countries are beginning to follow the NICs, although it is clear that all are not. However the export composition of the NICs is unlikely — even in the mid-1980s — to be close to that of developed economies. This need not, of course, invalidate the argument over a longer time period, but at present one has really only the evidence on the evolution of Japan's exports in the period since 1945, as firm support for the stages view. The Japanese experience is discussed further in Chapter 8.

Manufactured exports and government policy

Given that a rapid growth of manufactured exports from developing countries has taken place since 1960 what are the implications of this growth for government trade policy? There is substantial evidence, particularly from the results of the country studies by the Kiel Institute and the US National Bureau of Economic Research, both conducted in the 1970s, that government policy changes were instrumental in stimulating export growth. The policy changes concerned can be seen as falling into three broad categories:

- changes in the nominal exchange rate;
- changes in tax and subsidy policies affecting exporters;
- changes in direct controls affecting exporters, such as procedures for the allocation of foreign exchange and credit.

In their survey of the results of the Kiel Institute studies on trade reforms in 15 developing countries up to the mid-1970s Donges and Riedel (1977) use time series regression analysis to test the importance of policy shifts in favour of the export sector. The time trend for growth of manufactured exports is estimated for each country, and a dummy variable is introduced for all years after the policy change. Three out of the 15 sample countries showed no clear change in trade policy over the period studied, and therefore are excluded from the analysis. Of the remaining 12, however, in 8 the dummy variable is statistically significant with a positive sign, implying that export growth was above the trend rate in the years after the policy change.[26]

This type of analysis cannot distinguish between the effect of different policy measures, but the parameter, the real effective exchange rate, is used to capture the effects of changes in either nominal exchange rates, or taxes and subsidies affecting exporters. The real effective exchange rate can be defined as the nominal rate adjusted for differences between prices for similar goods in domestic and export markets. Taking manufactures as a commodity group

221

$$E = r. \frac{P_x}{P_d}$$

where E is the real effective exchange rate for manufactures:

r   is the nominal exchange rate in local currency per unit of foreign exchange

P_x is the price in local currency received by exporters of manufactures inclusive of subsidies, or net of taxes:

P_d is the price for domestic sales of manufactures inclusive of subsidies, or net of taxes.

A price index is normally used for P_x and P_d.

A rise in E, which raises the relative profitability of exporting can come either through an increase in r, that is a nominal devaluation, or through a rise in P_x relative to P_d; this latter situation can arise as a result of a shift in tax-subsidy policy for export as compared with domestic sales.[27]

In both the Kiel Institute and National Bureau studies regression analysis shows a measure of the real effective change rate to be a significant explanatory variable for the growth of manufactured exports across a range of developing countries.[28] Since there is a significant positive correlation this is taken as evidence that policy shifts in favour of the export sector — either devaluation or higher export subsidies — do stimulate export growth.

However it also seems clear that devaluations on their own are generally a fairly weak means of stimulating exports. The role of devaluation as an economic policy remains controversial. Much of the difficulty stems from devaluation's impact on internal inflation, which will erode the rise in the real effective exchange rate through its impact on domestic prices. There is substantial evidence, summarised in Krueger (1978), that in the countries covered by the National Bureau studies even substantial nominal devaluations to a fixed parity were followed by only brief periods in which the real effective exchange rate rose significantly. Internal inflation eroded relatively rapidly the improved price incentives for the export sector. The conclusion drawn by Krueger and now probably fairly widely accepted is that it is not simply a case of changing the exchange rate, either periodically or on a 'crawling peg' basis. Restraint of internal demand, must be combined with increased incentives to the export sector. To give exporters confidence in the long-run attractiveness of selling on the international market it is argued that a sustained commitment to the export sector must be maintained. This commitment will be in terms of providing exporters with the equivalent of the full set of incentives available for domestic sales. An increase in export incentives, *ceteris paribus*, will raise the real effective exchange rate, and can work to compensate for the inflationary effects of devaluation on domestic prices. Krueger's conclusion on this point is that:

> All the 'success' stories involve not only a lack of bias towards import-substitution but also positive incentives for export. In addition they involve a government commitment to sustaining the export drive, so that it is not only at times of formal exchange rate changes that incentives are attractive to exporters. All the evidence (and theory) points to the conclusion that maintaining a sufficiently high real exchange rate *and* providing an environment in which producers can expect this commitment to continue are necessary conditions for rapid export growth.[29]

Manufactured exports and transnational firms

If as it appears shifts in government policy have been an important feature explaining export growth, a relevant question is the extent to which this growth has been led by transnational rather than national firms. If the former have been the dominant suppliers it is difficult to interpret this export growth as a sign of the emerging competitiveness of national producers. Chapter 2 gives some information on the role of transnationals in industrial development post-1960, and as is pointed out there most indications are that this involvement has been very uneven both between countries and industries.

To clarify the role of transnationals in the growth of manufactured exports it is necessary to distinguish between different groups of manufactures. Excluding processing of raw materials from the definition of manufactures, one can identify three broad groups of exports where transnationals have played a major role.[30]

(i) Labour-intensive standardised products, with relatively simple technologies. Goods classed under this heading normally include toys, sports goods, travel goods, clothing and footwear. In this type of commodity transnationals have not been very

223

active in production, although they have been involved as major purchasers and distributors of these goods. Transnational trading houses and retail firms have provided the marketing outlets and often the brand names for these exports.[31]

(ii) Capital-intensive, non-standardised products, often with relatively sophisticated technologies. The goods normally included in this category are industrial chemicals, steel, engineering goods and transport equipment. They are the type of item produced initially for the domestic market, as import-substitutes, which transnationals began to export in the 1970s. The reasons for this shift to the export market, include the changes in policy towards exports in some countries, noted above, in some cases direct government pressure to export was also important, and in others, exports were a response to the opportunities provided by regional trading arrangements, most notably the Latin American Free Trade Association. It is in Latin America that this type of export by transnationals has assumed the greatest importance, with firms specialising in different products in different countries and exporting from there to the rest of the free-trade area.[32]

(iii) Labour intensive components the production of which can be separated from that of the final product. For these goods the production process is non-continuous so that components that can be produced labour-intensively can be 'sourced' from developing countries to take advantage of low wage costs. The industry where this process has been carried furthest is electronics, with transnational firms supplying parts and components from their subsidiaries or joint ventures to other production units within their international organisation. International sourcing by transnationals is not restricted to electronics however, nor simply to labour-intensive inputs. For example, in the automobile industry it takes place in response to government pressures and broader corporate strategies.[33]

Of these three categories transnationals provide the bulk of exports under (iii), but themselves own relatively little of the assets responsible for producing exports of category (i). Category (ii) is the smallest of the three, and for these goods transnationals probably provide a share of exports roughly equal to their share of domestic production in these goods in the exporting country.[34] In terms of total manufactured exports from developing countries there is no accurate estimate for the share taken by transnationals. It has been argued that up to the mid-1970s, at any rate, their share was relatively low. Nayyar (1978), for example, puts it at no more than 15 per cent. This is consistent with data on the export specialisation of developing countries in manufactures, which indicates that transnationals played a major role in only a relatively small number of products.[35] (There is however a wide diversity between shares for particular countries which is illustrated in Table 2.6.) It has already been noted that transnationals have dominated exports from certain manufacturing branches; particularly chemicals, electrical machinery and transport equipment. However in some countries transnationals have also played a major role in more traditional exports, like clothing, wood, pulp and paper and food.[36]

Clearly, therefore, one cannot ascribe the majority of manufactured export expansion post-1960 to the activities of transnationals, although they may well have played a key role in certain, often dynamic, branches. How this pattern has changed in more recent years is not yet clear, although one frequently encounters the argument that international sourcing, that is category (iii) exports, may be a less important form of export growth in the future. This is on the grounds that the new electronic-based automation technology is reducing dramatically the labour element in many lines of production, and is thus undermining the cost advantages of developing countries as a site for parts and component production. There appears to be evidence that sites for the assembly of electronics circuits, for example, are shifting back to developed countries, and that a similar trend is emerging for the production of electronic consumer durables.[37] The degree to which these radical technical changes will affect developing country exports in the future remains to be seen.

Efficiency and manufactured exports

Whilst shifts in government policy, and the activities of transnationals played a part in export growth post-1960, they are unlikely to be the only explanations. It seems intuitively obvious that rapid export growth must to some degree reflect improved international competitiveness, arising from higher economic efficiency. Evidence on this is difficult to establish, but seems to be in line with this intuitive reasoning.

One approach attempts to distinguish between the different causes of export growth, breaking these down into the effects of the growth of overall demand, the commodity composition of exports, the distribution of exports between different markets, and the improved competitiveness of exporters. This is termed a 'constant market share analysis' and is applied by Ballance *et al.* (1982) to explain the export growth of both developing and developed countries 1966–76. The competitiveness factor is both positive and relatively high for virtually all developing countries studied, in direct contrast with the results for developed countries, where growth of demand is the most important factor. For example, several developed economies had a negative competitiveness effect for all manufactures, implying that they lost market shares in their main markets; on the other hand, for example, 91 per cent of the growth of South Korean exports, 82 per cent of those of Brazil and 94 per cent of those of Thailand are put down to improved competitiveness. The authors conclude that:

> . . . export performance in the industrialized countries and the LDCs were again subject to distinctly different sets of factors. Internal factors related to the supply-side made a positive contribution to export growth in the LDCs, while external factors pertaining to the demand side were the major determinant in the industrialized countries . . .[38]

It must be acknowledged however that evidence such as this can be no more than suggestive. The competitiveness effect is simply a residual term which picks up the growth not explained by the overall expansion of demand, and the product composition and market effects. There are well-known difficulties in placing too much emphasis on residual effects. Further even if the residual is a reasonable proxy for competitiveness, one cannot distinguish between different aspects of competitiveness, such as price or non-price factors, and the impact of different government policies.

Another approach to the identification of improved export competitiveness at the aggregate level is to estimate the relationship between income growth in developed economies, and the expansion of developing country manufactured exports. If this relationship is unstable over time, so that the income elasticity of demand for manufactured exports from developing countries rises, in the absence of major shifts in trade policy such as lower barriers to imports, this can be interpreted as the result of the improved competitiveness of developing country exporters. This is the procedure of Reidel (1983), who using regression analysis finds a statistically significant difference between the developed country income elasticity of demand for these manufactured exports in the 1960s, and that in the 1970s. In the aggregate for all developing countries this income elasticity is just under 2.0 in the 1960s, but rises to over 4.0 in the 1970s. The analysis is used to support Reidel's more general thesis that developing country manufactured exports are governed more by internal supply conditions in these economies, than by market growth in the developed countries. This focus on the importance of improved supply conditions in developing countries is in line with the results of Ballance *et al.* (1982).

This type of evidence provides general support for the view that export growth has arisen at least in part through improved efficiency, and thus greater competitiveness. However it need not be the case that higher exports inevitably imply greater efficiency. For example, it has been argued that some manufactured exports from industries initially established as import-substitutes are high cost, and that export has only been possible due to strong government incentives.[39] There is no doubt that there have been instances of this, demonstrated by studies that estimate the domestic resource cost of earning foreign exchange through exporting. These studies identify not only a wide range of DRCs for different export activities, but also a number of activities where the DRC ratios are significantly above any realistic assessment of the value of foreign exchange to the economy. It will be recalled that these are precisely the results often cited for DRC studies of import-substitution programmes. It is an important qualification therefore to the general view of the inefficiency of inward-looking industrialisation to note that in some countries exporting has also been given incentives that create economic inefficiency. This evidence on DRC ratios for exporting is particularly well documented for India and Pakistan in the 1960s and 1970s, two countries where export incentives were generally only a partial offset to the incentives available for home sales.[40]

In these countries there is also no evidence that the degree of incentive to export given to different activities was linked with the efficiency of production as reflected by the DRC ratio. It is difficult to know how widespread the phenomenon of export inefficiency has been. Donges and Reidel (1977) also report results that show high DRC ratios for exports in several countries including Brazil, Colombia, Egypt, and Israel. None the less it is unlikely that this evidence can weaken substantially the general conclusion that much of the export growth post-1960 has reflected improved competitiveness. This is because high export subsidies will be required if high cost inefficient exporters are to break into international markets, and in many developing countries over this period the rate of export subsidy was relatively low. None the less this qualification to the link between exports and efficiency must be noted.

PRODUCTIVITY GROWTH AND INFANT-INDUSTRY EFFECTS

Productivity growth can be an important indicator of changes in economic efficiency and international competitiveness, and a guide to technical change. Productivity growth can be calculated on the basis of either single or total factor productivity, where the former refers to output or value-added per unit of a single input, normally labour; the latter relates output or value-added to a composite index of factor inputs, normally both labour and capital. Given the practical and conceptual problems in valuing capital, the majority of empirical estimates focus on labour productivity alone.[41]

It is well known that in many activities absolute levels of labour productivity in developing countries are substantially below those in similar lines in developed countries, although in some branches this is likely to be due less to a lack of skills in particular tasks, than to causes like lack of management capacity, and an inability to attain economies of scale in production.[42] However for an assessment of dynamic changes in an industry and their implications for international competitiveness, it is necessary to have data on productivity trends over time. Aggregate data on labour productivity by industrial branch for developing and developed economies as groups is available from UN sources, and is set out in Table 6.2. As we have noted employment statistics in developing countries are particularly unreliable, so that evidence such as this can only be suggestive. However the picture which emerges is of a relatively poor productivity performance for developing countries as a group, particularly in the post-1973 period.

Table 6.2: Labour productivity growth by manufacturing branch: developing and developed countries, 1963–73, 1973–80

branch or major industrial group	Annual percentage growth			
	Developing		Developed	
	1963–73	1973–80	1963–73	1973–80
Food, beverages and tobacco	2.2	− 0.9	3.1	2.7
Textiles	2.0	− 0.1	5.2	3.2
Wearing apparel, leather and footwear	− 0.2	2.6	1.2	1.7
Wood products and furniture	− 0.3	1.4	3.4	1.7
Paper, printing and publishing	4.0	− 0.3	3.6	2.4
Chemical, petroleum and plastic products	4.4	− 0.4	6.1	3.5
Non-metallic mineral products	2.7	1.2	4.3	3.1
Basic metal industries	1.3	1.7	4.6	1.9
Metal products	4.4	2.4	3.7	2.8
Machinery and equipment				
Total manufacturing	2.8	0.7	4.0	2.8

Source: UNIDO (1983), table III.10, p. 75.

Infant-industry effects

This rather unsatisfactory general view is consistent with the results of most attempts to test for infant-industry learning effects in developing countries. Productivity growth at a more rapid rate than in competing industries in developed economies can be seen as a necessary but not sufficient condition for the infant-industry case for protection set out in Chapter 3. As we have seen, protection of infants can be interpreted as an investment by society with short-run costs, contrasted with longer-run benefits that arise when infants mature and become internationally competitive. It is clear that the achievement of high rates of productivity growth in itself does not guarantee that initial disadvantages relative to international competitors are overcome, nor does it say anything about the size of the longer-run benefits once competitiveness or maturation is reached. However without achieving a growth of productivity superior to that of countries whose producers are already internationally competitive, maturation will never be achieved. Bell *et al*. (1984) stress this point, and assemble data on productivity growth for a range of activities in a number of developing countries. This productivity data varies substantially from very high annual rates found in steel in Brazil, and electrical machinery, metals and chemicals in Argentina, to the negative growth in cotton textiles in Tanzania, and chemicals and electrical machinery in India. However given the productivity growth of 3 per cent to 4 per cent recorded in developed economies across a wide range of branches, on the evidence presented, it seems unlikely that many of the activities in developing countries would achieve international competitiveness, at least in the short-run. Bell *et al.* argue that 'few of the infant enterprises studied in less developed economies appear to have demonstrated the high and continuous productivity growth needed to achieve and maintain international competitiveness'.[43]

This lack of evidence on successful infant-industry effects is borne out by studies that adopt a slightly different approach to testing for such effects. The results of Islam (1972) for Pakistan, and Krueger and Tuncer (1982) for Turkey are worth noting. Islam calculates comparative cost ratios (defined as domestic ex-factory to cif prices) for import-competing goods, and examines the relation between the number of years firms have been in operation and their comparative cost ratio. If industry learning effects are present there should be a tendency for the longer established firms to have lower ratios. This trend does not appear however.[44] Krueger and Tuncer examine whether in Turkey there has been any tendency for costs of production in protected firms or industries to fall more rapidly than in less protected ones. This test, like that of Bell *et al.*, can be seen as a necessary but not sufficient condition for infant-industry effects to be operative. No tendency for more protected activities to experience faster productivity growth is identified, however, even though data over a 14 year period 1963–76 are used.

Qualifications to the infant-industry argument

Results such as these clearly cast serious doubt on the extent to which the benefits asserted by the infant-industry case for protection have emerged in practice. However before one dismisses the infant-industry argument altogether it is important to consider some alternative evidence.[45] First there is considerable ambiguity as to the timespan that should be associated with infant-industry protection. Several commentators suggest that if new activities are not capable of achieving competitiveness in a short period such as five to eight years they should not be supported as infant-industries. However this short-run view is in direct contrast with some of the historical evidence on the length of time required for competitiveness by industries in more industrialised economies. It has been suggested, for example, that cotton textiles in Japan took 20 to 30 years to reach maturation, with Japanese automobiles taking at least three decades.[46] Even in the mid-1960s Japanese automobiles had significant tariff protection in their domestic market. One can argue that infant-industries that do not achieve competitiveness in the short-term, in say up to eight years, will never be socially worthwhile investments, given that the effective operating life of many plants may not exceed twenty years, in the absence of substantial retooling and maintenance expenditures. In other words, if costs are high initially, relative to world levels, will not the early learning period have to be followed by a lengthy period during which time costs are well below those of international competitors? Thus, for a given plant life, the longer maturation is postponed the more unlikely it will be that the initial infant-industry investment was justified. This view is persuasive provided that international competitiveness does not require the early start of production, so that the experiences of the original producers, who themselves may take a long time to become fully competitive, are available to later entrants to the industry. If the experience and learning of the early entrants allows the later establishment of competitive domestic production in the longer-term, perhaps by different firms, the basic infant-industry case may still hold. In this version, however, the time period required for competitiveness has been lengthened, and may exceed the life of the plant installed by the original producer. Furthermore the argument rests squarely on the external effects generated at the branch or industry level. In this view Japanese automobile production in the 1930s, at relatively small output scales and uncompetitive in cost terms, was necessary to lay the ground for the emergence of internationally competitive production in the 1960s.

A second qualification to the attack on the infant-industry case is that the conditions for achieving international competitiveness become less stringent, if it is acknowledged that the exact product quality and specifications of imports need not be reproduced in domestic import-competing production. The

231

argument is valid most obviously for consumer goods, where provided domestic import-substitutes can meet the same broadly defined needs as imports, there is no reason why the same production techniques or product specifications should be involved. This allows import-competing producers freedom to adjust the technology they use in the light of both domestic factor costs, and the income levels, and demand characteristics of the local market. If these adjustments can create cost savings the scope for cost competitiveness is enhanced. From this perspective the fact that productivity may grow at x per cent per year in exporting competitor economies need not be of great relevance if the product specifications and the technology used in local production are sufficiently different from imports to give a 'natural' competitive advantage. However it is not always possible to extend this argument to intermediates and capital goods, where product design and quality may be of central importance, and where local alternatives may be much less efficient than imports.[47]

Finally, an interesting reassessment of the infant-industry argument is provided by the recent experiences of some of the NICs, particularly South Korea and, to a lesser extent, Brazil. Westphal (1981) draws attention to the fact, the full implications of which were ignored by many other commentators on South Korean industrialisation, that in South Korea there had been a significant and apparently explicit policy of infant-industry protection. What is important for the present discussion is that many of these protected industries achieved international competitiveness very rapidly, in direct contrast with the results from Pakistan, Turkey and elsewhere, noted above. Westphal points out that South Korea in common with many other developing countries, used quantitative restrictions on imports to guarantee a secure market for local producers, and that the ERP generated by these controls was in some cases in excess of 100 per cent. This does not imply that such measures and levels of protection are the best or most economically efficient means of encouraging infant-industries, but it does raise the important question as to why such a policy should have been apparently so successful in South Korea, and unsuccessful elsewhere. Westphal identifies two distinctive features of Korean policy on infant-industry protection which throw some light on this question.

Protection was on a selective basis, so that potential infants were singled out for special treatment relative to the rest of industry. Westphal argues that in trade regimes which are highly protectionist in a non-discriminatory manner it is difficult to grant infant-industries sufficient incentive to draw resources to them rather than to other protected, but potentially less promising, activities.

In addition Korean infants were strongly encouraged to break into export markets at an early stage. Domestic sales were normally more profitable than exports because export subsidies were insufficient to offset the relatively high levels of import protection granted in the domestic market. However the government encouraged exports through, for example, the system of indicative export targets and the allocation of credit between firms, and Westphal argues that many infant producers found it both possible and profitable to act as discriminatory monopolists, taking lower prices on their export, as compared with their domestic sales. This export-orientation he suggests brought substantial benefits both to the domestic producers themselves, and to the economy as a whole. These arose not only through the relatively familiar channels associated with export growth — such as competitive pressures and access to larger markets and thus economies of scale — but also through export-related technology transfers. It appears that buyers of Korean exports provided virtually costless access to a wide range of technological improvements, covering not only product design and quality control, but also the wider areas of production organisation and management techniques.[48]

The link in South Korea between export growth and productivity growth, as a proxy for improved competitiveness, is verified by the econometric results of Nishimizu and Robinson (1984) for the period 1955–73. The latter find that in South Korea, and also in Turkey and Yugoslavia, growth through export expansion is more often associated statistically with positive productivity growth than is growth through import-substitution. This evidence is of interest since it implies that the positive relationship between output growth and productivity growth discussed in Chapter 3 in relation to the case for infant-industry protection may differ depending on the market for additional output. In other words, there may be a greater positive impact on productivity growth for a given rate of output expansion if sales are directed to the export as opposed to the home market, due to the various efficiency

233

effects that are said to be linked with export expansion. Support for this view is provided by Goldar (1986) in an analysis of productivity growth in Indian manufacturing in the 1960s. Whilst he finds a positive statistical association between growth of total output and factor productivity, a measure of growth through import-substitution is negatively associated with productivity growth. This is an important area of research that requires further testing. It is an extension of Kaldor's case on productivity growth, discussed in Chapter 3, and if substantiated further would be strong support for the argument on the intrinsic merits of export growth.[49]

It is not surprising that Brazil is the other main NIC for which evidence of the emergence of successful infant protection policies is becoming available. Given its large domestic market many manufacturing activities are able to reach something close to minimum efficient scales of production. Steel, metal-working and automobile production have been singled out by recent commentators. In steel the main national producer, Usiminas, has reached the point of developing its own technology and providing technical assistance to other firms, both nationally and internationally. A survey of the metal-working sector in Latin America concludes that in the use of continuous flow production technologies only Brazilian firms have achieved internationally competitive production. This is explained by the access such firms had to a large protected domestic market during the 1960s and 1970s.[50] Similarly automobile production in Brazil is described explicitly by Dahlman (1984) as a 'success story of infant-industry development'. Despite being highly uncompetitive in the 1960s, the industry appears to have achieved price competitiveness by the early 1980s. In addition it provides Brazil's main manufactured export, and it is argued, has stimulated the development of domestic component suppliers through its backward linkages. A full assessment of the import protection policy for automobiles must allow for the dominance of transnational firms in the industry, and compare the costs of protection in the early years with later benefits. However the point of interest here is that this major branch of Brazilian manufacturing has reached a stage of maturity. In the case of steel, metal-working and automobiles however the Brazilian experience is by no means typical of Latin America, since in most other countries these industries remain uncompetitive.[51]

Interpreting the South Korean experience

Given the size of Brazil's domestic market, and its relatively advanced level of industrial development, its experiences may be less relevant to the majority of developing countries than those of South Korea. However at first sight the version of the infant-industry argument presented by the South Korean case — with an emphasis on a dual policy of promotion for both domestic and export markets — appears to turn the conventional argument on its head. In the latter, protection is required because producers are initially uncompetitive, and therefore are not expected to sell outside the protected domestic market. In the new version, however, it is justified in both private and economic terms, for new producers to aim to export as early as possible. Given the initially uncompetitive position of the industry such exports will require subsidisation either by the government, or by the producer himself, if profits from domestic sales are used to cross-subsidise exports. However 'premature' exports from an infant-industry are expected to generate benefits in the form of productivity growth and technical change.

Despite the apparent novelty of this version of the infant-industry case it can be made compatible with earlier views, if one argues that, even allowing for subsidisation, new industries will only be able to meet the quality standards of the export market, if a minimum threshold of domestic 'technological capability' has been achieved. This level of technological development applies not only to the producer concerned, but also to his suppliers of parts and components, and of the marketing and after-sales services that are required. One has here, therefore, another variant of the argument for building an integrated industrial base to allow producers to benefit from the range of externalities generated within the manufacturing sector. It can be argued that only after this integrated structure and the associated technological capacity have been created will the policy of breaking into non-traditional export markets with a range of manufactured goods be viable. If this view is valid it implies the need for protection whilst the industrial base, from which a later export drive can be launched, is being built up. One is back therefore to the familiar debate on the extent to which initial import-substitution policies are a necessary prerequisite for later export promotion. This interpretation is in fact compatible with South Korean experience. Nishimizu and Robinson (1984), for example, illustrate the importance of import-substitution behind relatively high protection 1955–63, and link it with the post-1963 export boom.[52] This is not to suggest that such a sequence is always essential for export growth, and certainly it appears to fit the facts on the experience of Taiwan, less well. However it seems one route to industrial competitiveness that has achieved considerable success at least in South Korea, and may hold lessons for other countries.

The conclusion of this examination of the evidence on productivity growth and infant-industry effects is that as yet successful cases of internationally competitive industries emerging from previously highly protected infant-industries are still relatively rare. However the experience of South Korea and Brazil indicates that productivity growth and export success in such industries can be achieved. Furthermore there is also a growing body of evidence from a wider range of countries, which shows that significant indigenous technical changes have been introduced in various lines of manufacturing. This does not necessarily demonstrate the use of best-practice technology nor the attainment of international competitiveness in price or quality terms, but it does indicate successful domestic efforts to introduce technical change, reflecting greater economic efficiency. This material is considered in the next section.

INDIGENOUS TECHNICAL CHANGE

Before focusing on case-study evidence on technical changes within manufacturing it is necessary to comment in general terms on the treatment of technology in the development literature. Until relatively recently technology was discussed by reference to two main questions:[53]

- the appropriateness of the technology transferred to developing countries; for example, the degree to which techniques use labour or capital, and the extent to which they can produce output suitable for the socio-economic environment of developing countries;
- the relative costs of the various institutional means of

affecting this transfer, for example, the merits of obtaining foreign technology through licensing agreements, direct foreign investment or capital goods purchases.

The issues involved are not wholly resolved but perhaps the most contentious — the scope for technology choice between capital- and labour-intensive techniques — has been clarified. The 'technology determinism' view, that there is relatively little practical scope for choice between techniques, has been shown to be invalid across a range of industries, although the scope for choice and the employment consequences of different choices vary substantially between industries.[54] Following from this it has also been shown that in some industries it is desirable in economic, and sometimes also in private terms, to shift to greater labour-intensity in production.

However recently the focus of attention has shifted to a question directly relevant to the present discussion on the long-run efficiency of industry; that is the extent to which manufacturing technology transferred to developing countries is adapted, modified and later improved as a result of indigenous effort in these countries. The capacity to carry out such activity is often described as 'indigenous technological capability'. Whilst technology is seen as covering both physical processes for transforming inputs into outputs, and the social arrangements for organising this transformation, technology capability is defined as the ability to make effective use of technology and arises from the knowledge and skills embodied in persons.[55]

Understanding the emergence of indigenous technological capability within developing countries becomes of central importance if one accepts the view, now current, that the main source of technical change in most economies is not major or radical innovation, but the cumulative effect of a large number of minor incremental changes to known technologies. In the context of industry in developing countries, technological capability is necessary to allow modifications and adaptations to technology largely transferred from abroad. Growing technological capability is evidence therefore of an increasing capacity to introduce economically beneficial technical change, and thus indicates a potential for longer-term economic efficiency.

For the purposes of the later discussion on technical change, it may be helpful to distinguish between technological capability in relation to different technology-related activities, by identifying a simple five-stage division of the process of technical change:[56]

(i) search for new products and processes, which for developing countries may often involve identifying foreign-made commodities and foreign technologies;

(ii) adaptation of the new products and processes to local conditions;

(iii) improving products and processes in the light of experience in local production;

(iv) developing new products and processes in some way superior to the e currently available, either locally or internationally;

(v) conducting basic research.

Mastery of these different stages requires different levels of capability with the last two normally associated with the need for greater capability than the first three. This must be qualified, however, by reference to the activities involved, since adaptations to sophisticated products may be more demanding technically than developing new simple products. None the less the distinction between the first three stages — associated with the simpler form of technical change — and the last two with the more complex, is both common and generally helpful. It also corresponds broadly with the distinction in Lall (1985b) between 'know-how' — largely knowledge of production, and necessary at the first three stages — and 'know-why', knowledge of basic processes, and necessary at the last two. It is clear that most technical change activity in developing countries is restricted to stages (i) to (iii), and little basic research is carried on at present, although as we shall see some significant new products and technologies have emerged in a few developing countries in recent years.

One important area clarified by recent research on technical change relates to the impact of 'learning-by-doing' in infant producers on productivity growth and technical change. As was pointed out in Chapter 3, learning is often seen in the infant-industry argument as a costless automatic process which arises as a by-product of production. However work on case studies of technical change at the firm level suggests that it is necessary to distinguish between different forms of learning and to consider how these relate to increasing the technological capability of

238

domestic producers. Bell (1984) identifies six categories of learning; of these only two 'learning-by-operating' and 'learning-by-changing' can be seen as a by-product of output and investment activities. The other four — 'learning-by-systems performance feedback', 'learning-by-training', 'learning-by-hiring', and 'learning-by-searching' — all involve conscious efforts to accumulate knowledge and skills. This effort requires expenditure, for example, on management controls systems, on labour training, or on technical assistance contracts. As far as the stages of technical change used here are concerned, costless learning-by-doing — Bell's learning-by-operating and-changing — is likely to be important at stages (i) and (ii), but is likely to be less helpful at stage (iii). On its own it will be totally inadequate for the more complex changes at stages (iv) and (v). The implication of this argument is that sustained technical change and productivity growth will involve active policies on the part of producers to raise their own technological capability. Automatic learning-by-doing will only be a partial and limited means of acquiring such capability. Studies of indigenous technical change must therefore identify the dynamic firms in developing countries and attempt to explain why they and not others have acted in a positive assertive manner to raise their technological capability.

Firm level case-studies

A number of case-studies at the firm level have created a rather different picture from the stereotyped view of technologically dependent developing countries, relying heavily on imported and often inappropriate technology. Most work has been done on the NICs where the greatest indigenous technological capability has emerged; within this group Latin American producers have received the most attention.[57] The case-studies reveal both formal and informal mechanisms of technology transfer between developed and developing economies, as well as significant domestic efforts at technological change. The formal mechanisms of transfer are the familiar channels of foreign investment, turnkey projects, management contracts and technology licensing. The informal mechanisms are less well studied and include imitation of imported models and informal contacts, for example, between exporters and buyers in developed economies. Domestic efforts, on the other hand, can be conducted at different levels; some small-scale firms that started production initially on the basis of simple copying of previously imported designs have been able over time to move to what is described as 'adaptive imitation', where imported designs are modified to suit local conditions. This corresponds to stage (ii) of our classification of technical change.[58] At a higher level more progressive firms may establish their own design and engineering expertise and move to stages (iii) and (iv).

Even where technology is received from abroad through formal mechanisms there is evidence from a range of countries that significant efforts have been made to adapt it to the prevailing economic conditions of the recipient countries. Such adaptation and modification should come as little surprise when the difference in economic environments between recipient and supplier economies is acknowledged. Typically, efforts at technical change are directed towards the solution of problems created by the difference between these environments. Problems mentioned frequently include:[59]

- use of local rather than imported raw materials, due to foreign exchange scarcity or import controls;
- scaling down of plant size to cater for a small domestic market;
- diversification of the product mix or change in product design to meet the needs of the local market;
- use of simpler and lower capacity machinery because of the poor ancillary services available;
- stretching the capacity of existing equipment because of constraints on the ability to invest in new equipment.

Many of these technical changes can be seen as arising from the establishment of production in the industry concerned, and are necessary to allow the successful application of the imported technology. However they are not simply the result of learning-by-doing of the costless or automatic variety, since they require the expenditure of effort and resources to overcome various bottlenecks and constraints. They are akin to Bell's learning-by-training, -hiring or -searching categories. Their successful introduction in some industries has led to the development of new products or processes, so that relatively simple technical change arising from production experience using imported technology can contribute to more complex higher stage technical change.

Evidence from Latin America suggests that it is difficult to generalise about the type of firm most likely to undertake such changes; simple distinctions between large and small, foreign and national, public and private sectors do not appear helpful. Furthermore in terms of policy debates, it also appears that both inward and outward-looking trade regimes have fostered firms that undertake significant technical change and have therefore developed an indigenous technological capability. However it has also been argued that the type of technical change that arises under an inward-looking protectionist policy is often economically inefficient.[60] The argument is that trade controls can force technical change in an undesirable direction; for example, if restrictions on imports of raw materials force producers to base production on higher cost or lower quality domestic substitutes, or in the presence of economies of scale, if policy imposed barriers to export force plant size to be scaled down to a level sufficient for the domestic market alone. Whilst such effects are clearly plausible direct evidence on the significance of this point has to be inferred from other work, rather then emerging directly from the technology case-studies under discussion. In general there is relatively little direct data on the economic merits of the type of technical change under discussion and on the extent to which it has increased economic efficiency, where it has been introduced. Probably the most convincing evidence on this is where industries that have been shown to have undergone indigenously induced technical change have been able to commence exporting, both commodities that embody the new technology and in some instances even the technology itself and related technical services. The limited evidence on technology exports from developing countries is considered in the following section. Prior to that, however, some of the experience of individual countries in this field should be noted briefly.

Country experiences

In Latin America, Brazil and Mexico are the countries most studied from this perspective. Steel production in Brazil is cited frequently as a major example of successful indigenous tech-

241

nical change. The firm concerned, Usiminas, was able to raise its capacity output very substantially without additional investment, through indigenous technical efforts supplemented by foreign technical assistance. A situation of initial dependence on foreign technology at the start of production in 1962 had been transformed by 1975 into one where all engineering work for further expansion could be done internally and technical assistance could be provided to other domestic steel producers. This is seen as an example of how foreign technology can be a complement to domestic efforts to create technical change.[61]

Despite its less advanced industrial sector there is also evidence of significant indigenous technical effort in Mexico, with domestically-owned firms often relying on local sources for technology. One survey found local engineering consultants to be a major source of technical assistance, but with a significant part of technological capability coming from firms' own efforts.[62] The relatively strong scientific and engineering infrastructure in Mexico reflected in the results of this survey may help to explain why some significant new technologies, that are not simply modifications of imported technology, have been developed by national firms. The most important of these include a process to provide sponge iron from natural gas, a process for non-woven textiles, and a process to manufacture newsprint from the sugar by-product bagasse. These technologies are of interest because they reflect a high level of technical change, either stages (iv) or (v) of our framework, and are on or close to, the international technology frontier. As we shall see, as a reflection of this they have been exported to a number of countries, including some developed economies.[63]

Outside Latin America, South Korea and India provide two relatively well documented and contrasting experiences. The Korean case is important not only because of the country's very rapid industrial growth over the last 25 years, but also because of its emergence as a major exporter of certain types of technology. For the present discussion what is most noteworthy about the Korean experience is that it is now conventional to argue that in Korea substantial adaptations and modifications to foreign technology were introduced first without major reliance on direct foreign investment — although transnational firms are important in certain sectors like electronics — and second without a very profound depth of technical knowledge

242

within the economy. What this latter point means is that the indigenous technological capability that has undoubtedly emerged in South Korea does not yet extend to all aspects of technical change. Mastery over technology, at least in the 1970s, was chiefly in the area of production engineering rather than in the more complex areas of plant and product design. This is close to the distinction of Lall, noted earlier, between mastery over production 'know-how', as opposed to 'know-why', relating to design capability. To the extent that capability does not yet reach to the underlying principles of design this will limit the extent to which technical change can develop beyond stage (iii) of our framework. However the implication of South Korean experience is that this limitation of the country's technological development was not a major obstacle to rapid growth.[64]

In contrast in India the depth of technological knowledge appears to be much more profound than in South Korea, and probably more so than in any other NIC. It is argued that this can be linked directly with the government policy of protecting not just domestic production, but also domestic efforts at technological mastery. In other words, India is the NIC where imports of foreign technology have been most tightly restricted, partly no doubt to conserve foreign exchange, but partly also for protectionist reasons to encourage indigenous technological efforts.[65] The consequences of a policy of protecting not just production, but also 'know-why' is that India has developed a capability to both manufacture and design a wide range of industrial products. It is interesting that a comparative study of capital goods production in three NICs found that in foreign technology agreements Indian firms relied far less on foreign sources for detailed designs than did Korean firms, although for both groups much basic design was provided by foreign suppliers.[66]

An indigenous Indian technology based on adaptations and modifications to imported technology in the light of Indian conditions has emerged in many industries, and in some has been exported, chiefly to other developing countries. In general, with a few exceptions, it is seen as well behind the technology frontier, but this does not mean that it may not be economically efficient for Indian or other developing country environments. Examples of recent Indian technological developments include rayon technology, truck design, and at a smaller scale of production, the open-pan sugar process.[67] There is controversy over the long-run benefits of the Indian policy of protecting domestic technological efforts. A broadly based, and in many branches, technologically self-reliant industrial sector has been established, but there is some question as to whether the adaptations and modifications to foreign technology are always in an economically efficient direction, and whether Indian industry could compete in a more liberalised domestic market without further substantial inflows of foreign technology.[68] This is a major unresolved issue, but it is worth noting that policies on technology need not be treated as immutable; as with protection of production, in some circumstances, it can be a sensible strategy to protect for a period, whilst building up a domestic capability. Once this has been established later liberalisation can allow foreign technology to complement and modernise the indigenous technological base. Viewed in this light it may well be that the Indian strategy has been highly effective in developing this domestic base.

Having completed this summary of evidence on indigenous technical change it is important to stress that most of the data refer to a relatively small number of NICs. These trends are clearly significant, and indicate that even with relatively protected economies important progress has been made. However in other less industrialised countries several studies reveal relatively little adaptation and modification of imported technology. There are illustrations of disappointingly poor performance from a range of countries, including Egypt, Thailand, Ivory Coast, Nigeria and Kenya.[69] It is necessary therefore to caution against generalising too far from the experience of a small number of NICs.

Technology exports from developing countries

Most commentators see the emergence of technology exports from developing countries as clear evidence of the establishment of an indigenous technological capability which in certain branches is not only economically appropriate for domestic conditions but is also internationally competitive. Although the share of developing countries in total world trade in technology is very small, and as far as one can judge from the available data is heavily concentrated in the group of NICs, these technology exports are generally taken as an important indicator of the emergence of a dynamic comparative advantage in certain developing countries arising out of the process of indigenous technical change.

Technology exports are conventionally defined to include four broad categories, although the coverage of these categories can vary between studies:

- 'project exports', where these are normally defined widely to include the export of plant and equipment, as well as various services, including plant design, detailed engineering, construction work, training and commissioning. Project exports are sometimes described as turnkey plant exports. Sales of capital goods which involve no element of technical or managerial services are normally excluded;
- 'consultancy exports' — covering sales of technical and managerial services;
- 'licensing' — covering sales of patents, brand-names, technical know-how and technical assistance;
- direct foreign investment, where this is not simply equity participation, but includes technology in the form of product or process knowledge and technical or managerial services.

Different countries collect and publish their data in this area using different categories, which makes international comparison particularly difficult. Probably the single most important issue of definition to be resolved is the extent to which it is appropriate to include exports of capital goods — which do not fall strictly under the definition of project exports — as part of technology exports. Some studies include a category 'plant exports' which cover all capital goods exports above a minimum value, regardless of whether or not additional technical services are also associated with their sales. Such a procedure has been justified on the grounds that a significant proportion of these exports will be likely to be based on locally improved or locally developed designs, and therefore embody domestic technological capacity.[70] In this discussion capital goods exports are treated as commodity exports so that the four categories of technology exports given above provide the definition of technology exports used here.

In explanations of the emergence of a competitive advantage

in certain technology exports in several NICs four reasons are normally stressed. First, there may be cost advantages over developed economies in certain types of products or processes; such cost advantages are seen most commonly in terms of unskilled and skilled labour costs, but could also refer to raw materials.

Second, producers in NICs may be able to supply technologies more suited to the needs of other developing countries than the technology currently available from developed countries. The technology concerned is likely to be based on either modifications to currently available developed country technology, or on older processes no longer used in developed economies. The advantages of this type of technology are seen as including greater scope for applicability at small scales of production, greater labour-intensity, and the ability to produce relatively unsophisticated products suited to markets in poor countries. Technologies of this type are often referred to as 'idiosyncratic technologies' in recognition of their individual characteristics.

Third, producers in NICs may derive an advantage from production experience in their domestic markets with the technology concerned. Here conditions specific to an individual country — such as resource availability, and government promotion of the technology — are seen as creating a competitive advantage — either in cost terms, or in the general suitability of the technology for use in other economies.

Fourth, exports may arise from major technical breakthroughs. In this case alone will the technology exports of developing countries represent international best-practice technologies, or as they are sometimes termed 'technologies at the international production frontier'.

The bulk of technology exports from developing countries are based on the first two of these four advantages, and the vast majority do not involve major technological breakthroughs. The industries in which these technology exports are most common tend to be steel, textiles, pulp and paper, chemicals and various capital goods branches. These can be seen as relatively mature industries in which most NICs now have significant production experience. Also they are industries where international technology has not been changing rapidly, which has enabled developing country producers to keep pace with technical developments internationally. However it should be noted that a simple distinction between industries on the basis of the level of sophistication or maturity of the technology involved can be misleading. There may be complex or innovative technologies within some traditional industries which it is still difficult for developing country firms to master.

In terms of the type of producers responsible for technological exports there is evidence that these are often nationally-owned firms whose technology exports are an offshoot of activities performed initially for the domestic market. This view of technology exports as an extension of domestic activity appears to hold across the spectrum of exporters — including construction firms, engineering and consulting firms, and manufacturers.[71] The importance of nationally-owned, as opposed to foreign firms in technology exports appears to hold even for NICs like Brazil and Mexico where transnationals play a major part in the industrial sector.

Country performance in technology exports

Although several studies have recently been completed in this area of technology exports, and further work is going on, it is difficult to obtain an accurate comparative picture across a range of developing countries. This stems from the lack of comparability in much of the data that is available. However, Lall (1984a) brings together material from a number of NICs and adjusts the original data to make it roughly comparable. Table 6.3 reproduces Lall's estimates, using his classifications. The values for technology exports refer to the cumulative totals from roughly the mid-1970s until the end of 1981, although there is some ambiguity as to the precise period covered. Lall distinguishes between industrial and non-industrial technology exports, chiefly it appears on the basis of whether or not the exporting firm is primarily a manufacturing enterprise; if it is its exports are classed as industrial. The major exception to this procedure is in the treatment of licensing and other services where insufficient data are available to allow a breakdown of earnings by manufacturing and non-manufacturing enterprises. Lall uses the definition of 'project exports' given above, and thus excludes exports that are no more than capital goods. He aggregates licensing, consultancy and technical services into a single category.

247

Table 6.3: Summary of technology exports by NICs. (Cumulative values[a], US$ million)

		Country					
	Taiwan	South Korea	India	Mexico	Brazil	Argentina	Hong Kong
A. Industrial							
project exports	n.a.	802[b]	2200–2500	n.a.	285[c]	106	—
direct investment	83	67	95	23	n.a.	49	600–800
licensing, consultancy and technical services							
(i) actual receipts	n.a.	n.a.	322	51	n.a.	0.3	n.a.
(ii) contract values	n.a.	472	500[d]	n.a.	357	22	n.a.
B. Non-Industrial							
civil construction project exports	n.a.	43,953	6024	984	4284[e]	696	—
direct investment	18	256	21	n.a.	252	n.a.	n.a.

[a] Period covered unclear, but appears to cover mid-1970s to 1981.
[b] Rough over-estimate, since data contains some capital goods exports.
[c] Under-estimate, since full data on all contracts are not available.
[d] Rough under-estimate.
[e] Under-estimate, since full data on all contracts are not available.

n.a. not available.
Source: Taken from Lall (1984a), table 1, p. 474.

The most striking feature of the data in Table 6.3 is the extent to which technology exports are dominated by construction activity rather than by industrial technology exports. This is most obvious in South Korea the most successful NIC in this field, but in the other major exporters — India, Brazil, Mexico and Argentina — non-industrial exports are also significantly more important than industrial exports. Successful construction project exports are based chiefly on cost advantages relative to competitors in developed economies; these advantages are not simply the result of wage cost differences however, but include, at least in the South Korean case, managerial and organisational competence. In general, it appears that most non-industrial project exports are not based on designs developed by the developing country exporters themselves. The majority reflect what is termed 'embodiment activity' — defined as 'the activities of forming and maintaining physical capital in accord with given and complete design specification.'[72] In other words developing country firms are responsible for a number of aspects of projects — including construction, erection, training and the supply of equipment they produce themselves, but not for the basic design technology.

Industrial project exports are much smaller than non-industrial civil construction project exports. Further, from the data available they are very small relative to total domestic manufacturing in all countries except India and South Korea.[73] However it is in these industrial exports that one sees the clearest evidence of indigenous technological capability since a significant proportion of these exports appear to arise from the advantages incurred by idiosyncratic technologies developed in the exporting economy. India is the leading exporter of industrial projects, and its exports reveal a high content of domestic technological capability, since Indian firms are able to both design and supply the capital equipment used in their project exports. This is also the case with Indian direct foreign investments overseas which can be interpreted as a means of exploiting indigenously developed Indian technologies.[74] Although the scale of project exports and foreign investment is lower in Brazil and Argentina — firms from these economies also appear to have a high indigenous content in their technology exports — both in terms of design and equipment; it has been suggested that this is due to the substantial capital goods sectors in these economies.[75] South Korean firms typically appear to provide relatively less of the designs embodied in their new industrial projects than in India, Brazil and Argentina. None the less there is evidence that a substantial proportion of Korean industrial project exports also have used domestic basic design engineering and have transferred locally developed process technologies.[76] However, as Table 6.3 reveals, such industrial technology exports are still small in comparison with Korea's construction projects, where embodiment activity, not design, is the key advantage.

The aggregate category in Table 6.3 of 'licensing, consultancy and technical services' covers payments for a range of activities. It is here that sales of original proprietary technology in the form of designs and patents would be captured. However most exports under this category appear to be based on either the cost advantages of NICs, stemming from their much lower salaries for scientists and engineers relative to developed economies, or alternatively from experience in domestic production and problem-solving relevant to conditions in other developing countries. None the less there are some sales of licences for best-practice technologies originating from developing country exporters, of which the best-known examples come from Mexico and Brazil.[77]

To conclude this discussion, what are the implications and significance of the technology exports described here? Our chief concern is with evidence of indigenous technical change, and through such change, of the emergence of international competitiveness in new lines of production. It is clear that technology exports reflect the depth of the industrialisation that has taken place in several NICs, and indicate that over time comparative advantage can shift even into relatively capital- and technology-intensive activities. However at present it seems more accurate to interpret such exports as indicative of a shift in direction rather than a major departure from existing international patterns of specialisation. The values involved are still small in terms of total world trade in technology and most exports are limited to a small number of NICs. Even within this group some countries have been considerably more successful than others.[78]

CONCLUSION

This lengthy chapter considers various alternative indicators of industrial performance that do not involve the type of detailed estimates discussed in Chapter 5. Four broad areas are examined relating to capacity utilisation, export growth, productivity growth, and technical change, including technology exports. It is clear that some of the over-simplified generalisations on poor industrial performance in developing countries must be qualified in the light of this material. For example, in several countries industrial capacity working has been relatively high, manufactured exports have grown rapidly and the more advanced economies have even commenced exporting technology. There is also data from firm-level case-studies to demonstrate that in some lines imported technology has been adapted, modified and improved, and that this has helped build up internationally competitive production, after an initial learning period.

However this progress has been both studied unevenly, and it appears also distributed very unevenly between countries. In this sort of evidence one is seeing the micro-level data that is a counterpart to the macro figures on country performance considered in Chapter 1. In a relatively small number of the more industrially advanced economies — and the evidence does not cover fully all of the countries in Table 1.7 — these trends appear both well documented and important. Elsewhere, however, in the majority of developing countries one suspects that they are much less significant. For example, whilst a relatively large number of countries have expanded their manufactured exports, arising at least in part from improved economic efficiency, the total value of these exports from developing countries is still dominated by a relatively small number of NICs. In the non-NIC economies the evidence on capacity utilisation, learning and technical change, whilst not always as detailed, appears generally much less favourable. This raises a basic question as to the extent to which it is possible for the majority of developing countries to follow the industrial success of the NICs in these areas. In other words, are there lessons for industrial policy in other countries to be learnt from the experience of the NICs? The following chapter discusses issues of industrial policy, bearing in mind both the evidence on performance post-1960, and the various theoretical approaches considered in earlier chapters.

NOTES

1. Little *et al.* (1970), p. 93.
2. Betancourt and Clague (1981) survey both theory and evidence on capacity working. Lim (1976) discusses the limitations of estimating capacity working by the number of shifts or total electricity consumption.
3. The seminal article is Winston (1971); Winston (1974) is a survey of the field.
4. Lecraw (1978) stresses the significance of non-profit maximising behaviour for measurement of capacity working.
5. Farooq and Winston (1978) survey the preferences of workers in Pakistan for employment at different times of the day, and argue that whilst workers prefer day-time employment, the majority prefer night work to unemployment.
6. The research, carried out for the World Bank, refers to the early 1970s, although it was not published until 1981.
7. The figures for actual to planned capacity working found for Colombia, Malaysia and the Philippines are similar to those reported for producers in the USA. U_F was defined subjectively by the producers themselves for the purpose of the survey.
8. See Winston (1981) on Nigeria, and Betancourt (1981) on Sri Lanka.
9. Betancourt and Clague (1981), pp. 92–7, discuss the main results of Bautista *et al.* (1981). They point out that a positive statistical association between scale and utilisation rates need not imply that the higher plant size causes higher utilisation, since the relation could run from higher utilisation to higher levels of output, that require larger plants.
10. Lecraw (1978) in a study on Thailand finds a negative relation between plant age and capacity working. He argues that new plants embodying new technology are likely to work at higher utilisation rates than older plants with older technologies.
11. Winston (1981) attempts to estimate U_E for Nigeria in the mid-1970s. He concludes that actual output is about 8 per cent below firms' planned rates, and that economically desirable output is between 15 per cent to 21 per cent above actual output. However this latter estimate is little more than a guess; see Winston (1981), p. 135.
12. Winston (1971) also uses a number of other explanatory variables, but Bhagwati (1978) in commenting on his results argues that the ratio of imported to total raw materials is the most plausible theoretically.
13. Merrett (1972) is a detailed case-study of the Indian fertilizer industry that brings out some of the specific links between foreign exchange scarcity, and production shortfalls.
14. See Bhagwati and Desai (1970). This pattern has also been considered for other countries, but was found not to be very significant in either Colombia (Diaz-Alejandro 1975) or Turkey (Krueger 1974).
15. For Jamaica, see Ayub (1981); for Tanzania, Wangwe (1979);

for Ghana, Steel (1972); and for the Sudan, Yassin (1984). Killick (1978) discusses alternative causes of under-capacity working in Ghana.

16. In one of the few studies that examine dynamic changes, Kim and Kwon (1977) show that utilisation in manufacturing grew rapidly in South Korea during the 1960s, reaching levels above those in the USA and UK by the end of the decade. The authors do not address the question of causation explicitly, but link this performance with the price reforms of the early 1960s. This explanation is asserted not demonstrated however.

17. See for example, UNIDO (1982). Tuong and Yeats (1980) also show that developing country export performance has been superior in labour-intensive products.

18. Different measures of revealed comparative advantage (RCA) can be used. The simplest is

$$RCA_{ij} = \frac{X_{ij}}{X_{wj}} \bigg| \frac{X_{im}}{X_{wm}} \qquad (7.1)$$

where RCA_{ij} refers to country i in industry j

        X_{ij} is the value of exports of j by country i

        X_{wj} is the value of world exports of j

        X_{im} is the value of total exports of manufactures of country i

        X_{wm} is the value of world exports of manufactures.

Here RCA is the ratio of the share of a country in world trade for an industry to the share of that country in total world trade in manufactures. $RCA_{ij} > 1.0$ is taken as evidence of comparative advantage in industry j.

More sophisticated versions of RCA are possible; see Donges and Reidel (1977), pp. 68–9, and Ballance *et al.* (1982), p. 167.

19. Donges and Reidel (1977), p. 69.

20. Balassa (1977), p. 26.

21. The simple measure of RCA, equation 7.1, is used.

22. The experience of Japan post-1945 is cited as an illustration of a country passing rapidly through the various stages; see Balassa (1977), pp. 24–7.

23. The NECs identified by Havrylyshyn and Alikhani are Colombia, Cyprus, Indonesia, Jordan, Malaysia, Morocco, Peru, the Philippines, Sri Lanka, Thailand, Tunisia and Uruguay. Table 1.7 shows that some of these countries have been included as NICs in other studies.

24. It is worth noting that most NEC countries have been far less successful than the NICs in terms of income growth, so that the link between rapid export growth and GNP growth is far from automatic.

25. A counter-intuitive result not commented on by the authors is that there is more similarity between the ranking of export performance indices in the groups, other LDCs and recently developed countries (such as Israel, Portugal and Greece) than between the latter

and the NICs. This result casts doubt on the validity of the test employed. For the results of these rank correlation tests, see Ballance *et al.* (1982), table IV.2, p. 143.

26. Donges and Reidel (1977), pp. 61–3. In most of the countries studied the policy shift was not sufficient to grant equal incentives for sale in domestic and export markets, so that anti-export bias still remained.

27. There is a further possibility, since a difference in inflation rates at home and abroad, not matched by a corresponding change in the nominal exchange rate will also change E.

28. See the surveys in Donges and Reidel (1977) and Krueger (1978). Morawetz (1981) gives a case-study of the effect of the real effective exchange rate on clothing exports from Colombia to the USA, concluding that although it was significant, it was not the only important influence on exports.

29. Krueger (1978), p. 208.

30. This classification follows that of Nayyar (1978).

31. This point was first stressed by Hone (1974), particularly in relation to exports from the South East Asian NICs.

32. Jenkins (1984), pp. 112–41 gives a detailed analysis of manufactured exports from Latin American transnationals. Olivetti is cited as a clear example of a transnational pursuing a regional trading strategy since it specialises in calculators in Argentina, electric and standard typewriters in Brazil, and semi-portable typewriters in Mexico.

33. Jenkins (1984), p. 120, points out that General Motors have supplied international affiliates with engines in Mexico, and Fiat exports engines from Brazil to Italy.

34. In Latin America, for the goods in (ii) there is no clear evidence that transnationals are more export-oriented than national firms in the same branch or industry; see Jenkins (1984), p. 116.

35. Dunning (1981), p. 350, footnote 39, points out that for data from the early 1970s where developing countries had a RCA of > 1.0 in only 6 out of 36 product categories were transnationals' exports important.

36. Lall (1981), pp. 207–9 gives data on the share of foreign firms in exports of different branches in selected countries.

37. Kaplinsky (1984a), p. 81, cites evidence of this. For example the cost of assembly of semi-conductors in Hong Kong was 33 per cent of that in the USA in the early 1970s. In 1983, with the introduction of automatic assembly in the USA Hong Kong's cost was 92 per cent of that of US-based producers.

38. Ballance *et al.* (1982), p. 139.

39. See the argument of Ranis (1985b) for Latin America, referred to in Chapter 5, a view disputed by Teitel and Thoumi (1986).

40. See Staelin (1974) for India, and Hufbauer (1971) for Pakistan.

41. Nelson (1981) discusses the conceptual and empirical problems associated with studies of productivity growth.

42. Pack (1981) and (1982) gives evidence on capital goods and textiles respectively. Teitel (1981) compares productivity in Latin America with that in the USA for the early 1970s.

43. Bell *et al.* (1984), p. 22. Their results are incomplete in that they use market not shadow prices, and ignore externalities. In some countries use of a shadow exchange rate in the comparison between domestic and foreign costs might make some industries appear competitive sooner.

44. Several of the DRC and CB studies referred to in Chapter 5 fail to find a relation between the age of a firm and its DRC ratio: see, for example, Steel (1972), Page (1976). See also Adhikari (1986b).

45. Fransman (1985) covers many of the issues raised in the following paragraphs.

46. See Bell *et al.* (1984). In Japan, ERP on automobiles was 67 per cent in the mid-1970s; see Weiss (1986a).

47. On the other hand, it is now well documented that highly competitive machine tool production has emerged in a number of NICs, particularly South Korea, Taiwan and Hong Kong. In these industries output is geared to relatively low quality price-competitive tools, which perform similar functions to higher quality imports. See Amsden (1977), Fransman (1982) and Jacobssen (1984). Only in South Korea, however, does it appear that these producers grew up under significant protection.

48. See also Westphal *et al.* (1981).

49. The comparative experience of several NICs in machine tool production is also relevant in relation to the dynamic effect of an export-orientation. A study on lathe production in Argentina, South Korea and Taiwan, for example, shows that producers in Argentina who had relatively little incentive to sell outside the domestic market, and as a consequence operated at much lower scales of output, were in a much weaker position than the more export-oriented firms of Taiwan and South Korea to respond to the new technology involved with computer numerically controlled lathes; see Jacobssen (1985).

50. For steel see Dahlman (1984), and for metal-working Katz (1984a).

51. Katz (1984b) suggests that batch production activities that produce quasi standard, or custom-made goods, and therefore are less dependent on market size, have the potential for international competitiveness in a number of Latin American economies. He cites capital goods production in Brazil and Argentina, shipbuilding in Colombia, and pharmaceuticals in Argentina and Mexico.

52. Nishimizu and Robinson (1984), p. 199.

53. Stewart (1977) covers the main issues in the technology literature of the 1970s; Fransman (1985) surveys the newer literature.

54. See for example the survey White (1978), and the empirical estimates of Pack (1980) and Amsalem (1983).

55. Dahlman and Westphal (1982) and Westphal *et al.* (1985) give definitions of the many specialist terms used in this literature.

56. The discussion draws heavily on Fransman (1985), pp. 585–6.

57. See the surveys of Teitel (1984) and Katz (1984b).

58. Chudnovsky *et al.* (1983), pp. 48–60, give examples of adaptive imitation in capital goods production, from the starting-point of crude copying. They describe this as the 'evolutionary' form of entry into capital goods production.

59. This list comes from Teitel (1984), p. 41.

60. Teitel (1984) makes this point, for example.

61. Dahlman (1984), p. 328, who researched this case-study originally argues that: 'The evolution of USIMINAS shows a technological strategy that rather than seeking to resist foreign technology, as is currently advocated by some, sought to pull itself up by it. USIMINAS started by being completely dependent on foreign technology using that as a base from which to selectively absorb more advanced technology, through which it progressively developed its potential. From a technologically dependent firm it has evolved to the point where it is developing technology of its own and selling technical assistance both nationally and internationally.'

62. See Fairchild (1977) who finds locally-owned firms to be at least as technically dynamic as foreign-owned firms. Fairchild uses this evidence to challenge the Dependency view on technological dependency. More recently Fairchild and Kosin (1986) report similar results from four areas of Latin America — Mexico, Brazil, Colombia and Central America. They draw attention to the relatively greater emphasis on internal innovation as a source of technology in local- as opposed to foreign-owned firms in these countries.

63. Dahlman and Cortes (1984) survey eight Mexican technologies of this type embodying high level technical change, although probably not all at the world technology frontier. They identify three main motives for the development of these technologies: a need to scale down foreign technology; the desirability of using cheap local raw materials; and the non-availability of foreign processes.

64. This interpretation of South Korean development follows that of Westphal et al. (1981) who argue that:'. . . it is not too great an overstatement to say that Korea has become a significant industrial power simply on the basis of a proficiency in production. There is an important lesson here; a high level of technological sophistication is not required to attain substantial industrial competence.' Westphal et al. (1981), p. 72.

65. See Lall (1982). This does mean that technology imports were not allowed, but that imports were restricted where domestic alternatives could be developed.

66. See Chudnovsky et al. (1983), pp. 121–3.

67. For details of the first two see Lall (1982), and for the third Kaplinsky (1984b).

68. Lall, one of the first to draw attention to the Indian strategy on technology appears to have shifted his position. In Lall (1982) he writes positively of the long-run benefits of technology protection. However, in Lall (1984c) he seems far more sceptical, characterising Indian industry as dominated by large areas of technological backwardness with only a few dynamic branches that are still behind world frontiers.

69. For Egypt see Forsyth (1985); for Thailand, Bell et al. (1982); and for Kenya, Langdon (1984). Langdon distinguishes between foreign- and locally-owned firms and argues that in his survey the latter showed far greater moves towards an indigenous technological capability. Mytelka (1985) examines textile production in the Ivory Coast, Nigeria and Kenya.

70. See Dahlman and Sercovitch (1984), p. 67. The authors summarise the results of a major comparative study and the following paragraphs draw heavily on their analysis.

71. As a specific illustration Dahlman and Cortes (1984) link Mexican construction exports with experience derived from domestic irrigation and pipeline projects.

72. Westphal *et al.* (1984), p. 511. The authors comment on South Korean construction exports that: 'The bulk of this export activity appears to have been performed in accord with detailed specifications provided by the purchaser. We may thus conclude that Korea's revealed comparative advantage in exports of capital goods and related services is in project execution, mostly in embodiment activities in the form of construction and metal-working.' Westphal *et al.* (1984), p. 527.

73. Lall (1984a) shows cumulative industrial project exports to be around 15 per cent of manufacturing value-added in India in 1979, and 8 per cent in South Korea. The percentages are insignificant for other NICs.

74. Lall (1982) gives information on Indian foreign investment, and Lall (1984d) on Indian industrial project exports. Lall (1982) also points out an interesting example. The manufacture of Cummins diesel engines in India in the 1960s was the subject of a highly critical study by Baranson (1967) which stressed the high cost, low output level of operations in India. Within a decade, however, the Indian licensee was established as an overseas investor producing engines on an internationally competitive basis.

75. Lall (1984a), p. 476.

76. Westphal *et al.* (1984), pp. 523–6 refer to Korean technologies in textile machinery, cement and plywood manufacture.

77. Dahlman and Sercovitch (1984), pp. 81–2 list these, and place most emphasis on Mexican examples, particularly in steel, petrochemicals and textiles.

78. Taiwan is the NIC where it appears technology exports are low relative to the overall level of industrial development; in the 1970s most of its technology exports were mechanical engineering capital goods with a low technology content; see Amsden (1984).

7

Neoclassical Market and Trade Reforms: Proposals and Evidence

The discussions examined in Chapter 5 can be seen as part of a wider debate on economic reforms in developing countries. This chapter considers the reform proposals that relate most directly to the industrial sector. It then examines evidence on their effectiveness, from both studies of individual reforms and from the general experiences of specific countries.

Neoclassical economic policy reform, or as it has been termed in the Latin American context, Neoconservative economic experiments, has several important aspects, all of which will influence the industrial sector.[1] Three main elements can be identified:

- the liberalisation of both foreign trade and capital flows, with the removal of quantitative import controls, reduction in tariffs and the freeing of capital movements;
- the deregulation of many markets, including those for foreign exchange and domestic credit;
- a major reduction in government expenditure and the general role of government in economic activity, for example by privatisation measures or by phasing out subsidies particularly to unprofitable state enterprises.

This type of package has been introduced in a number of developing countries in recent years normally as part of stabilisation and adjustment programmes aimed at coping with foreign exchange and debt crises, and orientating economies to a more outward-looking economic policy. Although theoretical discussions in the Neoclassical literature have influenced thinking in powerful international institutions such as the IMF and the World Bank, actual reform packages have rarely followed theoretical recommendation precisely. The reforms introduced in the mid-1970s in Chile come very close, and there is no doubt that both foreign and national advisors, working from a Neoclassical perspective, were instrumental in devising the reform programme. The unfortunate results of the Chilean experiment are discussed below.

NEOCLASSICAL REFORM AND INDUSTRY

Although there is some disagreement between Neoclassical authors on the exact details of policy, there is unanimity on the general outline of reform.[2] Freeing markets means the removal of government controls on prices and an end to government direct intervention to allocate supplies between competing users or consumers. Therefore specific recommendations include the removal of minimum wage legislation, interest rate ceilings, and price controls for public utilities. However it is in the area of trade reform that most discussion has occurred, and it is reform in this area that is likely to have the greatest direct impact on industry.

As we have seen the central conclusion of the Neoclassical literature on industrialisation is that the level of protection in most developing countries has been both excessive in absolute terms, and highly discriminatory in its impact on different branches and sectors. There is general agreement that levels of protection should be both reduced significantly and made more uniform between different activities, although there are differences of detail in the exact policy prescriptions that have been put forward.

A major point of difference is the degree to which authors are willing to allow some import protection as a means of encouraging manufacturing industry. The theoretical recommendation, as we have noted, is that if particular activities are to be encouraged, this should be done by a system of subsidies, that raise the profitability of producing that output, but which do not involve the costs to consumers of the good in question that arise when tariffs or quotas are used to protect domestic industry.[3] Also subsidies should be granted for all output, regardless of where it is sold, so they will not discriminate between domestic sales and export. Encouragement through subsidies is termed promotion, as opposed to protection through tariffs and quotas. Subsidies have to be financed and administered, however, and it is now recognised that for financial and administrative reasons it may be very difficult to fully substitute protection by promotional measures.

Balassa, for example, one of the leading advocates of policy reform along Neoclassical lines, recognises that there is a case for giving some special encouragement to manufacturing on grounds like externalities and the excess of market wages over the economic cost of unskilled labour. However he argues in favour of abolishing import quotas and of setting a relatively low uniform rate of tariff protection of around 10 per cent, since a widespread subsidy scheme is likely to be inapplicable, due to either fiscal or administrative constraints.[4] Balassa argues that protection should normally be uniform between manufacturing activities so that through the operation of competition the more efficient producers can expand relative to the rest. None the less he accepts that on infant–industry grounds there may be a case for granting a higher rate of protection to new firms. This he argues should still be at only a relatively modest rate — no more than 20 per cent with no distinction drawn between different infant firms, so that all producers classed as infant-industries receive a uniform above-average rate of protection. In addition to avoid the danger of high cost infants never growing up, Balassa suggests that this infant-industry protection should last for no more than five to eight years.

This reform package is in contrast with schemes based on subsidies. Little *et al.* (1970), for example, argue that import tariffs should be reduced to modest levels, and used chiefly to bring in revenue. Whatever special encouragement is required by manufacturing, they suggest, can be given through either production or labour subsidies. Labour subsidies will be required if the aim is to offset a divergence between the market and the shadow wage for unskilled labour, and subsidies to production in general will be relevant if promotion is justified on grounds of the external effects from the activity.[5] The revenue required to finance such subsidies is to come from commodity taxation, and it is envisaged that similar domestically produced and imported commodities would be taxed at equal rates. The feasibility of such a scheme is critically dependent on the ability of the government to raise additional tax revenue, and specifically to tax domestic and imported items at equal rates. Despite the authority with which subsidy measures have been recommended, widespread subsidy schemes have rarely been applied, and few would now see them as a practical alternative. However this does not mean that selective and limited subsidies cannot be used, since on a selective basis subsidies are widely employed. It is the total replacement of a policy of protection by one of promotion that appears infeasible.[6]

The Balassa programme can be taken as fairly representative of the Neoclassical position on trade reforms. However despite their apparent simplicity it should be noted that the proposals are not without ambiguity. Balassa envisages that the uniform rate of protection of 10 per cent should be in effective, not nominal terms, since it will be the effective rate (ERP) that has the greater influence on production decisions. This raises the practical problem of calculating current detailed ERPs. In addition however there is a theoretical difficulty in the recommendation for uniform ERP. There are two conflicting goals, depending upon whether one approaches the problem from the side of supply or of demand. Uniform ERPs are required to establish equal incentives to production, whilst uniform nominal rates of protection (NRP) are required to avoid distorting consumer choice between different commodities; in other words with uniform NRP consumers can choose between traded consumer goods facing relative domestic prices that correspond to relative international prices. The problem is that if one sets tariffs to establish uniform ERP, and thus to equalise production incentives between branches, one will automatically create a system of non-uniform NRP, and thus create consumption distortions, in the sense that relative domestic prices for traded consumer goods will deviate from relative world prices. The recommendation for uniform ERP assumes implicitly that the producer effects of protection are more significant than the consumer effects. In noting the incompatibility of these two goals Corden (1980) suggests the simple practical compromise of starting with the objective of setting either uniform ERP or NRP rates, and adjusting whichever is chosen, if it creates wide variations between branches in the other rate.[7] Given the complexity involved in the calculation of ERP, it seems more practical to take nominal rates as the starting point, and adjust these if they create unacceptably wide variations in effective rates.

The Neoclassical stress on uniformity in tariff-setting is in direct contrast with much of the practice of tariff authorities in developing countries, who often make efforts to calculate the tariffs required by individual producers or branches. The latter, termed conventionally 'made-to-measure-tariffs', have the advantage that in principle they can be linked directly with the cost structure of domestic producers, so that tariffs need not be set at a level that allows extra-normal profits to be earned. However, this individual approach to tariff policy is generally viewed with suspicion by most Neo-classical authors. For example, they point out that the detailed cost data necessary for this approach to be applied may not be made available; that where more than one domestic producer is involved there is an ambiguity as to whose costs of production should be used — those of the average or the marginal producer; that setting individual import tariffs at a level sufficient to earn a normal profit on domestic production provides no incentive for producers to lower costs over time; and that such a policy is an obvious target for the pressures of interest groups.[8] It is of course, fully consistent with a belief in the effectiveness of market forces to stress that protection, where it is granted, should not differentiate between branches or producers, so that relative expansion can be determined by the competitiveness of individual firms.

Where protection is to be continued the Neoclassical reform proposals stress not only uniformity in tariffs, but that if protective measures are to be used, tariffs are superior to quotas. A number of reasons are normally given for this. Tariffs are preferred since they operate through the price mechanism, whilst quotas impose a physical or value limit on imports. Unless tariffs are prohibitive, so that imports cease altogether because of the increase in price resulting from the tariff, under tariff protection domestic producers are not fully insulated from world competition. Domestic prices cannot be set above the world price plus the tariff and any fall in world prices is a competitive threat unless tariffs are raised to compensate domestic producers. It is also argued that the operation of an import licensing system will introduce bureaucratic judgement to the question of what inputs are necessary for production. If a licensing authority has to give its opinion on whether imports should be allowed, where domestic substitutes are available, it may mean that important decisions are taken on the basis of inadequate data. Tariffs, it is argued, avoid this, since the final decision to import will be taken by the user who is in a better position to judge the need for the item than any licensing authority. Finally in distributional terms quotas are also seen as inferior. Tariffs provide revenue for government, whilst under a quota system the holders of import licences earn extra-normal profits, since they obtain imports at prices that do not reflect the excess demand for these goods.

The advantages normally attributed to quotas, such as their directness, their ability to discriminate between different types of import, and the certainty they grant domestic producers in terms of their future market share, are viewed as unconvincing. Import quotas are seen chiefly as short-run measures to curb a serious balance of payments problem, and the recommendation of the removal of quota protection is normally one of the first aspects of Neoclassical trade reform programmes.

As we have noted the need for greater awareness of export possibilities is a common theme in the Neoclassical literature on industrialisation. A major policy recommendation is that anti-export bias be removed. Exporters are seen as penalised for a number of reasons; for example, tariff and quota protection allows domestic sales at prices in excess of world prices for comparable goods, whilst exporters receive only world prices; the exchange rate is maintained artificially high in terms of the value of local currency relative to foreign exchange by the restrictions on import demand, thus reducing the local currency earnings of exporters; and exporters are often forced to use locally available intermediate inputs that are higher cost or lower quality than alternatives that can be obtained from overseas. Removal of the anti-export bias involves equalising the incentives for the sale of a given commodity in both the home and the export market. In policy terms this can involve two broad alternatives; if the import protection system is not to be reformed radically it will mean introducing large and wide-ranging export subsidies, to offset the incentives to domestic sales arising from import protection. Alternatively where import controls are reformed significantly removal of anti-export bias requires a devaluation of the exchange rate and the introduction of more modest export subsidies to offset the effects of whatever tariffs or quotas remain. In both cases exporters would no longer be forced to use locally produced inputs in preference to imported alternatives, if use of the former reduced their competitiveness in overseas markets.

263

It should be noted that devaluation is essential to a major trade reform package. It is judged to be critical not only to improve the competitiveness and profitability of exporting, but also to offset the fall in prices of imports in domestic currency that results from abolition of quotas and reduction of import tariffs.

To conclude this discussion on trade reform there is a general agreement in the Neoclassical literature on the need to introduce a number of measures, including:

- removal of import quota protection;
- reduction of both the level and the variability of import tariffs;
- continuation of some modest protection for key activities, that can be phased out gradually;
- introduction of export subsidies where necessary to offset the effect of whatever import protection remains;
- devaluation of the exchange rate.

The whole package could not be introduced overnight, but would have to be phased-in over a period of three to five years. However as we shall note further below there is now discussion on the timing and sequencing of the reform package which implies that the order in which markets are liberalised can have an important bearing on the effectiveness of the reforms.

Whilst the implication of Structuralist and Radical analysis considered in earlier chapters is that government should intervene directly to influence the level and composition of industrial activity in an economy, Neoclassical analysis suggests a much less active industrial policy. Trade is to be liberalised, and markets are to be decontrolled so that firms and households can largely take their own decision on what to produce and consume.

EVIDENCE ON MARKET REFORMS

Although there are major differences of theoretical approach between Neoclassical and other writers on industrialisation particularly those linked here with a Radical perspective much of the policy debate focuses on the empirical issue of the effectiveness of specific policy changes. Little (1982), for example, criticises early Structuralist authors for asserting that prices had little effect on resource allocation decisions, because of low supply and demand elasticities, in the absence of evidence to substantiate this view.

However it is somewhat surprising that the empirical evidence on the significance of distortions is rather less convincing than would be thought from the clear statements of their importance in both the academic and policy literature.[9]

Chapter 2 has discussed the cross-sectional analysis of Agarwala (1983) on the link between distortions and economic performance, and noted that despite the negative association the evidence is open to varying interpretations. This section first examines data on particular markets from a range of countries. It then considers the experiences of particular countries whose cases are often taken as evidence of either the success or failure of Neoclassical policies.

Markets for traded goods

Most work on the quantitiative impact of distortions has been devoted to the costs of protection and general interventions in international trade. Two broad approaches can be identified; the first involves what is termed 'partial equilibrium' analysis, since it does not rest on some consistent macro-model of an economy; the second, however, uses such a model, and can be seen as a 'general equilibrium' approach. It is significant that early attempts to estimate the cost of protection in a partial framework found this cost to be only a small proportion of current national income. The approach was basically to estimate the production and consumption cost for goods produced domestically under protection, but which would be imported if the protective system were abolished. The production costs are defined as the difference between domestic costs for the importable items, which would be imported under free-trade, and their import value. Consumption costs are the difference between what consumers are willing to pay for the importable products under protection, and the price that would be established once free-trade is introduced.[10] In combination these two effects are described as the 'allocative inefficiency' associated with protection, and are generally found to be rather small. However, partial equilibrium approaches to the cost of protection have been extended significantly by Bergsman (1974) who incorporates 'X-inefficiency' effects into the calculations. X-inefficiency implies that firms are not producing at their minimum possible unit costs, and can arise, it is argued, due to a lack of competitive pressure in an environment protected from world competition. Bergman's extension of the earlier approach allows for the possibility that many protected commodities might still be produced domestically after the move to free-trade, but that in the new competitive environment X-inefficiency would fall thus bringing production costs down to international levels. The existence of X-inefficiency creates an additional cost of protection not captured by the earlier production and consumption costs.

Bergman's main work was on Brazil, but he also extended his analysis to several other countries using data for the 1960s. In all cases allocative efficiency cost of protection is small, but in Brazil and Pakistan he finds the total cost of protection to be 7 per cent and 6 per cent of GNP respectively. In the Philippines and Mexico it is less than 4 per cent, and in Malaysia the cost of protection is negative implying that protection is in fact economically justified, largely it appears for terms of trade reasons.

Of course what is a high cost in this context is not clear. Bergsman himself argues that the figures for Brazil and Pakistan are high enough to matter. Others may feel that given the emphasis often placed on the irrationality of the protective system in many developing countries results of this order of magnitude are hardly convincing evidence that distortions arising from protection really are significant.[11]

The general equilibrium approach to estimates of the cost of protection has also been employed in recent years. Krueger (1984) summarises the types of models which have been used, stressing their demanding data requirements and pointing out the econometric techniques involved. The work of de Melo on Colombia is frequently cited as an important example of this approach. What is significant is that although his results generally produce higher cost of protection estimates than the partial approach, they appear highly sensitive to key assumptions, thus illustrating the uncertainty attached to exercises of this type.[12]

The major point to stress regarding any attempt to capture the macro-economic costs arising from an import protection system is that for most countries experiencing relatively high protection, free-trade is no more than a hypothetical situation, and little confidence can be placed in projections for an economy which moves from a highly protective to an open policy. It is significant that only by incorporating dynamic factors, such as cost reductions due to lower X-inefficiency, can quantitatively significant cost of protection estimates be derived, at least in a partial equilibrium framework. However these improvements are only one possible scenario resulting from the removal of trade controls. Those less optimistic concerning the benefits associated with freer trade could construct an alternative with high cost domestic producers closing down, and the resources freed by their closure not finding their way into dynamic export activities. In these circumstances it would be free-trade which introduces the costs, in terms of a loss of potential national income, not protection. The difficulty is that once one allows for the central importance of dynamic rather than static considerations, estimates of costs will depend largely upon judgements concerning the viability of alternative growth strategies. Naturally opinions differ on such broad questions, and those sceptical of the merits of free-trade are unlikely to be convinced by cost of protection calculations.

A more fruitful approach to the question of the impact of trade distortions on growth is likely to be through reductions in exports due to the anti-export bias created by protection. As we have seen there is evidence that manufactured exports respond to both export incentives and exchange rate changes. The role of devaluation as a policy measure remains controversial, although there is evidence from a number of studies that devaluations generally improve the trade balance, at least in the short-run; this implies that exchange rate over-valuation can hold back exports and thus tighten the balance of payments constraint on growth.[13]

However, a number of qualifications need to be made. First it is often the case that the period over which the real exchange rate is devalued is relatively brief. Often this follows in part from the inflationary consequences of devaluation itself, which will be heightened where workers can resist a cut in real wages. Following from this the relative internal price effect of devaluation, in increasing the price of traded *vis-à-vis* non-traded goods, is also normally transitory. Evidence from a number of countries suggests that the price advantage for tradeables is largely eroded in a period of up to three years, as a result of

267

internal inflation.[14] The favourable effects of devaluation on the trade balance can be at a short-run cost of higher inflation and a reduction in real domestic expenditure, and the favourable effects can be weak in economies where import demand and export supply are inelastic so that neither respond strongly to the price effects of devaluation, and where labour's resistance to real wage cuts is strong.

Probably of greater importance than the actual level of the exchange rate is the overall trade-bias of policy. In other words what is likely to be of central concern is the relative levels of incentives for sales in domestic and export markets. Several of the successful export economies of the 1960s, for example, Japan, South Korea and Brazil, maintained various forms of import protection, whilst export growth was taking place. The important point was that the incentives created by import protection were offset by various combinations of export incentives and exchange rate changes.

Labour and capital markets

As we have seen in Chapter 5 estimates exist of the magnitude of labour and capital market distortions, in terms of raising labour and lowering capital costs. However, again it is unclear what constitutes a significant level of distortion in cases such as this. Krueger (1984) reports that in studies of the impact of trade policy on employment efforts to simulate the level of employment in the protected sector in the absence of distortions produced a 10 per cent increase in Argentina, 15 per cent for Brazil, and as much as 271 per cent for Pakistan. The realism of such projections is unclear, but even allowing for the fact that they refer to once-for-all increases, and disregarding the Pakistan result as extreme, the results for the other two countries are still substantial.

Others have judged labour market distortions to be less significant for employment, however. Squire (1981), for example, in a survey of evidence on the operation of labour markets in developing countries argues that government intervention is often not in support of a high wage policy; minimum wage legislation is seen as ineffective in many countries, and in others government intervention is to keep down urban wages rather than to increase them. A number of countries where a high wage policy has been pursued are identified, but Squire suggests that not only is experience varied, but that only a limited number of countries would have much to gain from a major change in government policy towards the labour market.[15]

As noted earlier there is now general agreement that scope for technology choice, in terms of degrees of labour-intensity, exists in a fairly wide range of industrial activities. Several firm-level studies have indicated that for particular branches the gain in employment arising from the use of more labour-intensive techniques can be substantial. One of the most comprehensive of these is by Pack (1980), and his results are worth noting. Pack examines the range of technologies in use in nine manufacturing branches, and contrasts the characteristics of what he identifies as the most economically appropriate and the most capital-intensive technologies. In total for an equal investment in each branch use of the economically appropriate technologies generated approximately four times the number of jobs associated with the most capital-intensive technologies. Naturally this result depends upon the branches selected for study but the nine chosen are all likely to be important, particularly for the less industrialised developing countries.[16]

However, this evidence on the scope for technology choice does not demonstrate that particular labour or capital market distortions will be sufficient to block the adoption of economically efficient technologies. Distorted prices are un-likely to be the only reason why more labour-intensive techniques are not adopted. Additional explanations, whose importance will vary between industries, include lack of information on alternatives, lack of spares for older vintage equipment, general preferences for up to date technologies, and lack of supervisors required for the labour-intensive alternative. Simply reforming markets alone is unlikely to be sufficient to create a major shift in technology choice.

Regarding the importance of capital market distortions, for reasons other than their impact on the choice of technique, most empirical studies concentrate on the relationship between real rates of interest and domestic savings and investment. Regression analyses have generally produced mixed results with some studies finding a significant positive relationship between interest rates and domestic savings, whilst others are more inconclusive. For example, in a study of a large sample of

269

developing countries Fry (1980) finds savings to be negatively affected by the real deposit rate of interest, and that credit availability is an important determinant of investment. He estimates that for his sample the cost of financial repression is approximately a loss of 0.5 per cent in GNP growth for each 1 per cent by which real interest rates are below a market-clearing level.[17]

Few studies are available for economies where major liberalisations of the interest rate structure have taken place. However, for Sri Lanka post-1977 Roe (1982) finds that interest rate reforms had little effect on either the level of investment, or its allocation between sectors. The South Korean reforms of the mid-1960s are often cited as a clear example of a highly successful capital market liberalisation. However, even here this interpretation has been challenged by the argument that much of the increase in savings deposits with the commercial banking sector after the capital market reform, came from a shift of money from the informal or 'kerb' market, rather than from an increase in total savings. The short-run effect of the reform was to tighten credit in the informal market on which many smaller firms were highly dependent.[18] Similarly in their analysis of the impact of financial liberalisation in Uruguay in the 1970s de Melo and Tybout (1986) find real interest rate changes played no role in explaining the behaviour of private domestic savings.

However the Neoclassical view on capital market controls can be modified to allow for the possibility of the inelasticity of savings with respect to interest rates. Little (1982), for example, accepts that it is a more questionable proposition that savings respond significantly to interest rate changes, than that a free functioning capital market can improve the quality of investment by allocating funds more efficiently than would either banks or the government, using non-market means. A weaker variant of the Neoclassical case on capital market reform would be therefore that total domestic savings and investment might be affected only slightly, but that the efficiency of a given investment would improve. On this latter point, however, there is still relatively little evidence.[19]

To summarise the discussion on evidence relating to reforms of markets, one can argue that the evidence is not as conclusive as bold statements of the Neoclassical case might suggest. There seems little doubt that in many countries reforms of the system of trade controls, and in particular greater emphasis on the export sector, could improve growth performance, although this need not imply a move to free-trade. However, there is less support for the view that the removal of labour and capital market distortions would have a major impact. The experience of specific countries is considered next, turning first to the South East Asian 'Gang of Four', whose impressive growth has been discussed extensively.

THE 'GANG OF FOUR': ALTERNATIVE INTERPRETATIONS

In some Neoclassical discussions it appears as if the four South East Asian NICs have become a model for other developing countries to follow, in much the same way that early 'modernisation theory' envisaged that the transition from traditional to modern societies would proceed along a path similar to that first traced by the now developed capitalist economies of Europe and North America. The South East Asian NICs are thus seen as providing an intermediate stage in a simple stages theory with other developing countries following their route before reaching modernity and an advanced economic structure.

Two versions of the Neoclassical argument on the relevance of the 'Gang of Four' can be distinguished. The weaker of the two, in the strengths of its claims, is that the experience of these countries demonstrates the potentiality of export-led growth, based on labour-intensive manufactures, at a relatively early stage of industrialisation; as we have seen, this is often termed export-substitution and in policy terms is associated with the removal of incentives biased against exports. The second version, on the other hand, argues not only for the importance of export expansion, but adds also that the performance of these economies is explained largely by the application of 'sound' economic policies, that allow markets to function freely and in general reduce substantially government activity in the economy. Stress is laid particularly on the freeing of labour markets from government legislative controls and union-imposed distortions.[20] In this version, therefore, the 'Gang of Four' are seen as providing empirical justification for the full set of Neoclassical policy prescriptions discussed above.

Any careful examination of the experiences of the 'Gang of

Four' must recognise both the differences between the four countries and the historically specific features that help explain their growth.[21] A distinction is often drawn between the two small city states of Hong Kong and Singapore, and the larger economies of South Korea and Taiwan. The former pair are seen by many as too unique for their experience to have a major relevance for other countries.[22] Whilst the two larger economies are seen as more representative of developing countries as a group, critics of the Neoclassical interpretation stress the historical specificity of their experience. The Radical literature in particular has several analyses of the 'Gang of Four', that are concerned to explain their performance in the context of the evolution of the world economy post-1945, and the specific class formations in these economies.[23] An explanation of the growth of the 'Gang of Four' is important for Radical analysis since as we have seen, until recently, the Dependency perspective with its emphasis on obstacles to capitalist industrialisation in most developing countries was highly influential in this literature, and the experiences of these countries is in direct contradiction to this stagnationist position. Several important features of South Korea and Taiwan are identified, whose absence elsewhere, it is argued, helps explain the impressive growth of these economies.

First, in the early 1950s despite being relatively poor with large agricultural sectors, both had a significant industrial base, much of which had been built up in the 1930s under Japanese colonial rule. While some of this industrial sector was destroyed in the Second World War, it is suggested that this early industrialisation laid the basis for later development by creating a relatively large industrial proletariat, particularly in South Korea. Second, it is argued that Japanese colonial rule altered the class structure in another way by destroying the legitimacy and power base of agrarian capital, thus paving the way for the dominance of domestic industrial capital from the 1950s. Third, given their sensitive geo-political position in South East Asia both countries benefited substantially from the availability of US aid. These funds, it is argued, played a key role in building up industrial and infrastructure assets in the 1950s and early 1960s.[24] Fourth, the authoritarian and repressive political regimes in these countries are seen as necessary to emasculate labour organisations and thus hold down real wages during the early stages of growth in the 1950s and early 1960s. What

Neoclassical discussions term freedom of labour markets, is viewed here as 'political unfreedom'.[25] Finally the educational traditions, cultural homogeneity and sense of nationalism in these countries, it is suggested, explain the emergence of a state bureaucratic strata that could administer effectively the set of government policy measures used in these developmental capitalist regimes. The range of measures employed in these economies will be commented on further below, but it seems the case that such levels of government intervention could not have been sustained effectively in the absence of a highly capable bureaucracy imbued with a sense of national purpose.

These features of South Korea and Taiwan, it is argued, made it possible for them to be among the major beneficiaries of the major expansion in world trade in manufactures of the 1950s and 1960s. Despite low wage costs other developing countries were less well placed to do so, and in less favourable international conditions in the 1980s, the South Korean and Taiwanese experiences are likely to have only a limited relevance for others. It should be noted that this interpretation cannot deny the depth of industrialisation that has taken place in these economies, since they have been moving into more capital-intensive branches of manufacturing, with the production of intermediate and capital goods. Nor can it explain these achievements simply as the result of collaboration with transnationals, since it has been demonstrated that the involvement of such firms in these countries is by no means high by the standards of other developing countries. What it does query strongly, however, is the view that these countries provide a direct model for others to follow.

In evaluating these Radical and Neoclassical interpretations of the experiences of the 'Gang of Four', it should be noted at the outset that they are not wholly incompatible. There are strong grounds for believing that much of the recent economic performance of these countries can be explained by historically specific factors. However, at the same time there is also convincing evidence, that what can be termed the weaker version of the Neoclassical case is also valid. In other words, the export promotion policies pursued in these countries, based on the removal of biases against exports, and in some product lines the introduction of pro-export biases, via significant export subsidies, were a major factor in stimulating both the growth of manufacturing exports and the economy as a whole.

273

What is at issue is the degree to which similar export supply responses would be forthcoming in other countries, if similar policies are applied. The extent to which producers will be able to respond to export incentives will vary with a range of factors including their accumulated production experience, technological capability, access to credit and inputs, knowledge of foreign markets, and also government policies towards labour. In so far as conditions, both internal and external, were particularly favourable for the 'Gang of Four' one would not expect such dramatic responses elsewhere, although this is not to deny that some increase in manufactured exports would result from a shift in trade policy.

The stronger version of the Neoclassical interpretation of the experience of the 'Gang of Four' appears far more questionable however. This relates to the domestic policy environment most likely to stimulate export growth. The free functioning of markets is at the centre of the argument, however it is now generally recognised that only in Hong Kong and to a lesser extent Singapore, is this an wholly accurate interpretation of the way in which resources were allocated in these economies.[26]

For South Korea and Taiwan several major deviations from Neoclassical policies can be noted. First, regarding trade policy, despite the emphasis on export growth, import protection was not removed from major parts of manufacturing. The overall ERP was very low in comparison with other developing countries, but this aggregate figure hides wide variations between sectors and branches within sectors. In South Korea in the 1970s there was relatively high protection for manufacturing branches producing transport equipment, consumer durables and machinery and full steps to liberalisation were only taken in the mid-1980s. However, it is significant that when protected firms sold goods as inputs to export production these sales were generally at or close to world prices, since exporters were allowed tariff-free access to the inputs they required.[27] In Taiwan a similar variation in effective production was experienced, although the absolute level of protection was lower than in South Korea. The implication is that selective protectionist import-substitution policies were still pursued in these economies, during the period when in general anti-export biases were being removed. However, the link between domestic and export sales was close, and many protected new industries were expected to break into export markets at an early stage.

Second, financial markets have been tightly controlled in both these economies. Rather than allowing interest rates to allocate credit, governments have intervened to ensure the flow of funds to priority activities. It is significant that one of the major forms of export incentive was selectivity in credit allocation and interest charges. Although South Korea's financial reforms of the mid-1960s, with the freeing of interest rates and an apparent rise in private savings in response, have been cited often as an example of a successful capital market reform, they were in fact short-lived, and were reversed after 1972. Of the 'Gang of Four', South Korea is the country where selective credit policies have been used most extensively, with as much as 60 per cent of bank lending being subject to government control. However, even in Hong Kong and Singapore capital market controls have been used.[28]

More generally, intervention in these two economies has been incompatible with the stronger version of the Neoclassical interpretation of their experience. Government investment in productive activities was important in the early stages of industrialisation in the late-1950s and early-1960s.[29] However in both countries state involvement extends beyond public ownership. Governments have been active in influencing private sector decisions, not only through trade and credit policy, but also through direct measures that have included the licensing of foreign investment proposals and technology imports, and in South Korea a system of export-targets. Furthermore unofficial interventions similar to the Japanese practice of 'administrative guidance' are also accepted as normal. Here civil servants make known informally to private firms and their industry associations the government's views on specific issues. The aim is to influence events in the light of what is perceived as the national economic interest. Enterprises both foreign- and locally-owned can be given precise instructions as to the products they are to produce and the shares of these that should be exported and sold domestically. Various combinations of financial incentive, legal sanction and informal guidance are used to implement government priorities.

This is not command planning in a legally binding sense, but interventionist planning, often on an *ad-hoc* basis, that influences decisions through discussion and interaction. Perhaps the best illustration of these links between the state and the private sector is the South Korean system of export targets.

Here annual targets, often further broken down by quarter and month, were set for commodities and firms. These targets emerged through discussions between firms themselves, their industry associations and government officials. The system was intended to be flexible, so that targets were revised to take account of changing circumstances. It is often argued that because good performance in meeting targets by individual firms was linked with preferential treatment in dealings with the government, the system helped sustain export growth.[30]

The general picture of these two economies therefore is one where government intervention of various types has been important, although, and this is where the Neoclassical case has merit, this intervention was generally successful in combining elements of both direct controls and price measures to pursue national industrial priorities. Import-substitution was selective and not excessive; export growth was pursued by a range of measures, including complex financial incentives, credit policy and direct targetting; labour costs were held down in the early stages of industrialisation by the repression of labour organisations, and the role of foreign investors and technology imports was screened in an attempt to control these in the national economic interest. This is an interventionist scenario, but one that, as noted in Chapter 2, in practice appears to have generated relatively fewer distortions than the measures used in many other developing countries.

However, this interpretation of the evidence has allowed critics to argue convincingly that far from demonstrating the Neoclassical case on the importance of market reform, the experience of South Korea and Taiwan illustrates the key role of government intervention in stimulating industrialisation.[31] It is a natural conclusion from this interpretation that in other countries also well thought-out government intervention can have a major role in future industrialisation. Whilst wishing to support this view, it should also be recalled however that the historically specific features of these economies — particularly their highly competent nationalist bureaucracy and their patterns of private-public sector collaboration — mean that it is difficult for any simple model of policy to be derived from their experiences. Forms of intervention effective in one context are not necessarily effective in another.

CHILE AND OTHER LATIN AMERICAN EXPERIMENTS WITH MARKET REFORMS

Whilst the degree to which at least, two members of the 'Gang of Four' have pursued consistently market-oriented policies is open to serious doubt, what is clear is that in the 1970s several Latin American economies adopted a series of wide-ranging economic reforms that in many respects corresponded closely with the set of Neoclassical policies discussed earlier. The main countries concerned were Chile, Argentina and Uruguay. Recent assessments of the performance of these economies are now available and this section attempts to draw out the implications of the experiences of these countries for the debate on industrial policy reform. The Chilean case, which is the clearest example of market liberalisation in practice, and the best documented, receives the most attention.[32]

As is well known the reform experiment in Chile was undertaken post-1973 after the military coup removed the socialist Allende government. In the initial stages the main focus was on economic stabilisation, with a major reduction in government expenditure; on privatisation of state-owned enterprises, the vast majority of which were sold to the private sector; and on de-regulation of prices, including the exchange rate, which was devalued soon after the coup. Tariff reforms were introduced over a five-year period with the average nominal rate falling from around 100 per cent in late-1973 to a uniform rate of 10 per cent in 1979. Therefore protection, which had been both high and with a wide variation between activities, was reduced fairly rapidly to a low and uniform rate.

It is important to note that after an initial failure to curb inflation through monetary controls the exchange rate began to be used as an instrument of stabilisation policy rather than to guide resource allocation. To break inflationary expectations and lower costs the exchange rate was revalued; this was at a time when import tariffs were being reduced so that competitive pressure on import-competing producers was intensified. Exchange rate revaluations could not be sustained in the face of a deteriorating balance of payments position, and were replaced by a system of pre-announced devaluations at rates below prevailing inflation; again the objective of breaking inflationary expectations determined exchange rate policy. Finally in 1979 after the major tariff reforms had been introduced official

277

thinking was strongly influenced by the so-called 'monetary approach to the balance of payments'; this being monetary theory for an open economy, which by then Chile had become. At this stage the exchange rate was fixed so that, it was argued, domestic inflation could come down to the inflation rate of the world economy.[33]

The outcome of these major reforms is now widely acknowledged as a failure, although not surprisingly, different interpretations have been placed on this experience. To clarify the subsequent discussion it is necessary to go over some of the main facts of the Chilean case:

- a short period after the initial reforms the economy entered a major recession in 1975, partly due to declining world prices for copper, the country's main traditional export, but also induced by the major reduction in government expenditure. Real GNP *per capita* fell by almost 14 per cent in 1975;
- 1977–81 saw a significant recovery with historically high growth rates, none the less this was a recovery from a very deep recession so that real *per capita* GDP only regained its 1971 level in 1980;
- there was success in reducing inflation, since the increase in consumer prices which had been over 350 per cent annually in 1974 was down to around 30 per cent in 1980;
- non-traditional manufactured exports grew rapidly over the period of liberalisation increasing threefold 1974–79;
- despite this impressive growth of the non-copper export sector, import demand particularly for high income consumer goods also increased rapidly in response to the trade reforms leading to a widening trade gap by the end of the 1970s;
- the deregulation of domestic capital markets created extremely high domestic interest rates by historical standards, and this, combined with the liberalisation of international capital flows and the availability of international funds, led to a major inflow of foreign capital in the late-1970s; this accumulation of foreign debt allowed the continuation of an open trade policy in the face of rising imports;
- specifically in relation to manufacturing, there was a decline of around 3 percentage points in its share of GDP

over the reform period, and a substantial shift in its structure, with as would be expected, a relative decline in the branches that had been most highly protected; however recovery in manufacturing was much less impressive than in sectors like construction, commerce and financial services, and manufacturing output *per capita* declined by 2 per cent per annum 1974–81, with a major fall of 23 per cent in 1982;

– the economy was in another major recession by 1982, when GDP *per capita* declined by over 16 per cent, and from which it was only just recovering in the mid-1980s; a combination of increasing foreign indebtedness at rising real interest rates, adverse movements in the terms of trade, and a domestic financial crisis with an accumulation of bad debts by the banking system, precipitated a major reversal of policy. The currency was devalued, foreign exchange controls were reimposed, and the liberal import policy was abandoned temporarily; import tariffs were raised to a uniform 35 per cent, due to be lowered to 25 per cent by mid-1986. Even in 1985 GDP was still below the level of 1980.

The Chilean experiment has been attacked strongly by many critics.[34] Whilst success in curbing inflation and raising non-traditional exports is acknowledged, it is argued that this was at a high cost in unemployment and lost output. The technical prescriptions of both the closed and open economy monetarist approach to inflation are challenged on the grounds that they ignore the effects of supply-side shocks and expectations in generating inflation. By focusing only on the demand-side through monetary policy, it is argued that the recessionary impact of anti-inflationary policies was magnified. The political economy of the Neoconservative experiment is also stressed, with the argument that market-based policies are not neutral between classes and social groups, so that opening an unequal society to market influences only serves to magnify initial inequalities. In support of this argument there is clear evidence that the reform period saw a major concentration of wealth. The large financial and industrial groups strengthened their position in the economy, partly because they were allowed to purchase privatised state enterprises at subsidised prices, and partly because they, rather than smaller borrowers, had access to the international capital market, where interest rates were significantly lower than those for domestic loans. On the other hand, poorer groups appear to have suffered substantially during the liberalisation period; for example from reductions in government social expenditure, in areas like education and housing; from the reversal of previous reform policies with the return of expropriated land to the previous owners; and most critically from high unemployment rates and falls in real wages. Market freedoms were not extended to organised labour so that strikes were forbidden and no collective bargaining allowed until 1979. After that date trade unions could operate, but only in an emasculated form. Throughout most of the reform period wages were controlled and indexed to official estimates of past inflation. The exact decline in real wages is open to dispute, with significantly different estimates from different sources, but there seems agreement that by 1982 real wages were still below their pre-reform peaks of 1971 or 1972.[35]

In terms of the impact on manufacturing, critics must acknowledge the major response of manufactured exports to the greater incentives to export in the early years of the reform programme. However several important arguments should be noted. First, in some instances this export growth may be a reflection of an 'easy stage' of export promotion; in other words where plant capacity is under-utilised, due to domestic recession, it will be fairly easy to achieve a rapid short-run growth of exports, when incentives are changed. Sustaining this growth in the longer-term when the under-utilised capacity is no longer available may be more difficult. Also it is important to note an asymmetry in the incentives created by the reforms. Whilst there was ample reason for firms to move out of previously highly protected manufacturing activities there was much less reason for them to shift within manufacturing. The very high cost of domestic credit, over 40 per cent in real terms in the late-1970s, and the opportunities for speculative gains in non-productive activities, made investment outside manufacturing a more attractive proposition. The productive activities that could earn real rates of return above 40 per cent must have been very limited. Related to this latter point on the domestic cost of capital is the argument that if the deregulated domestic credit market produced artificially high interest rates, in the sense of temporary rates that did not reflect the long-run return to real investment, firms that could not compete with imports, when faced with these interest charges need not be economically inefficient. In other words, these interest rates, even though they were market rates, might still be distorted and thus would give the wrong allocative signals.[36] If this view is valid, some of the import-competing producers forced out of business by the high cost of credit need not necessarily have been economically inefficient.

The general conclusion of this critique is that the Chilean experiment was both costly in lost output and employment, and highly divisive and inegalitarian in social terms, whilst largely ineffective in overcoming the long-run obstacles to sustained economic growth. As such it is scarcely an attractive advertisement for market-oriented policies.

The Neoclassical interpretation of events in Chile, and also in Argentina and Uruguay is somewhat different. There is recognition that the reforms failed ultimately, but less emphasis is placed on the costs of the experiments, and their successes in reducing inflation, stimulating new exports, and raising productive efficiency, are stressed. Failure is put down to policy inconsistencies, and adverse external events, rather than more fundamental problems with market-oriented strategies.[37] In the Chilean case it is argued that the manufacturing sector benefited significantly from trade liberalisation, as efficiency was increased with the contraction of high-cost protected firms and the expansion of new competitive manufactures. Job losses specifically from trade liberalisation are estimated to be relatively small, although it is recognised that when liberalisation occurs in a recessionary environment, it is difficult to disentangle the job losses created by stabilisation policies from those created by trade reforms. It is also necessary to stress that there is little doubt that the trade liberalisation reforms would have been accompanied by far higher unemployment had it not been for the massive inflows of foreign loans.[38]

However Neoclassical analysis of the reforms in Chile, Argentina and Uruguay, is faced with major paradoxes. First, despite the declared intention of boosting the export sector, and thus moving away from an inward-looking development strategy, in all three countries the real value of the exchange rate appreciated significantly thus reducing the incentives to export, and discouraging the production of traded as compared with non-traded goods. This real appreciation resulted from domestic inflation in excess of world inflation, when the nominal exchange rate was either fixed or depreciating at a rate insufficient to offset the difference in inflation. Second, despite very rapid increases in real interest rates domestic private savings remained low, demonstrating a major and unexpected inelasticity with respect to interest rates.[39]

The contradiction between the objectives of the reform programmes and an appreciation of the real exchange rate, is central to the Neoclassical view of the policy inconsistencies that ultimately doomed these experiments. If one takes the Chilean case, the key inconsistency is seen as that between the policies of a fixed nominal exchange rate, wage indexation when inflation was declining, and free capital movements. The large spread between domestic and international interest rates encouraged a heavy inflow of foreign borrowing, which raised domestic expenditure particularly on non-traded activities like construction. In the face of internal demand pressure on prices, and a rise in the domestic relative price of non-traded goods, the alternatives were either devaluation or a further major decline in real wages. By the continuation of a fixed exchange rate and a wage indexation policy, it is argued that both were postponed for too long.[40] In Argentina and Uruguay the key inconsistency is seen as that between the size of the government budget deficit and the policy of pre-announced devaluations designed to reduce inflationary expectations.[41] In all three cases it is argued the common error was to use the exchange rate as an instrument of anti-inflation policy, to the detriment of its role as an allocative parameter influencing the size of traded and non-traded sectors.

The implication of this interpretation is that if certain policy inconsistencies can be removed, liberalisation reforms can still be effective in raising the efficiency and growth of economies. However the difficulties experienced in these Latin American cases have raised new issues in the Neoclassical literature on the timing and sequencing of reforms.[42] It is now recognised that the recommendation to free markets is not as simple as might have been thought from earlier discussions. The speed and sequence of reforms must be influenced by the current conditions of an economy; for example, whether it is in recession, suffering from inflation or vulnerable to external shocks. The question of the appropriate mix of macro-economic policies to accompany market liberalisation raises complex issues of macro-economic management relating particularly to the role of the exchange rate, to the freeing of international capital movements, and alternative approaches to price stabilisation. One conclusion that is drawn increasingly from the reform experiences examined here is that in general it is desirable for the liberalisation of the capital account of the balance of payments to be phased to follow trade liberalisation with a substantial time lag. This is to avoid the possibility of major capital inflows creating an appreciation of the real exchange rate, that can threaten the basic objective of such reforms by penalising new export industries.[43]

Therefore even if one accepts the Neoclassical view that a well designed market-oriented reform programme is an economically efficient strategy, where short-run social costs can be minimised, it is now clear that such programmes can be difficult to implement and carry through effectively. There can be no disputing the difficult economic circumstances of the Latin American economies discussed here, in the immediate period in the 1970s preceding the introduction of the reforms. None the less other aspects of their situation were relatively favourable to the introduction of such programmes. A significant industrial base already existed, so that entrepreneurs and their capital could shift into new lines of activity in response to the changed set of incentives. International borrowing was available to these countries to finance transitional costs of the programmes. The authoritarian nature of their political regimes made it easier for the reforms to be persevered with despite apparent inegalitarian shifts in wealth and income. Finally the technical expertise of the bureaucracy and the high professional competence of the economic advisers to these regimes meant that the theoretical basis of the policies to be implemented was much more thoroughly understood than would be the case in many other developing countries. The failure of the reforms under these circumstances casts doubt on their applicability elsewhere, particularly in most of Sub-Saharan Africa, where this type of policy package has been proposed recently.[44]

CONCLUSION

This chapter has examined the details of the Neoclassical case for economic reform, looking particularly at the arguments

283

addressed to trade policy. In addition it surveys some of the evidence on the consequences of specific policies. The most significant point to emerge from this discussion is that whilst the Neoclassical concern that prices and the functioning of markets have been neglected in many industrial programmes is no doubt valid, this does not mean that market-based reform strategies that dismiss the role of direct government interventions are necessarily an adequate basis for successful industrialisation. There can be little doubt that prices matter, but so do a number of other factors, some which will require government intervention. Recent historical evidence provides little support for the view that market forces alone can be left to determine the size, composition and characteristics of a country's industrial sector. It can be argued that governments in at least the majority of developing countries ought to retain some responsibilities for the process of industrialisation. The final chapter examines different aspects of an interventionist industrial policy.

NOTES

1. Foxley (1983) examines Latin American examples, and the categorisation given below follows his analysis.
2. Some of the most influential statements of the Neoclassical case for industrial reform are Little *et al.* (1970), Corden (1974), Balassa (1982) and Little (1982).
3. Corden (1974) pp. 9–57 explains the reasoning behind this recommendation. It should be noted that even use of a total subsidy scheme to encourage industry would necessitate some tariffs on imports, since subsidies must be financed by higher taxes some of which will be taxes on trade.
4. Balassa (1982) argues that: 'The advocates of production subsidies disregard budgetary considerations on the assumption that government intervention is a costless operation; in other words there is no cost attached to the choice between a tax and a subsidy. But while such an assumption is "in accordance with the conventions of theoretical analysis" it does not conform to the conditions existing in most developing countries.' Balassa (1982), p. 67.
5. Little *et al.* (1970) recognise that there is a case for non-uniform rates of subsidy, for example, as a percentage of value-added, since different activities will have different shares of unskilled labour in total costs, and different capacities to generate externalities.
6. Squire (1981), for example, dismisses in one sentence the feasibility of a widespread labour subsidy scheme. Mexico is a country where such a scheme was tried, in the later 1970s, although it appears

that its effect in encouraging greater labour-intensity is very doubtful; see Weiss (1984b).

7. Corden (1980), pp. 74–6.

8. Corden (1974), pp. 220–3 gives a critical discussion of made-to-measure tariffs.

9. Krueger (1984), p. 555 comments that: 'Despite the importance of distortions in theory relatively little empirical work has been undertaken to estimate their magnitude or their effects.'

10. Corden (1975) gives a brief exposition of the approach. It should be noted that a number of qualifications may have to be made to the simple definition of producer and consumer costs given above. In particular the expansion of exports associated with a move to free-trade must be allowed for. This expansion may have a negative terms of trade effect, if international prices for exports fall, and may also encounter rising production costs if there are diminishing returns to scale. On the consumption side, if domestic prices of exportables rise with the move to free-trade this will create consumption costs of free- trade to offset the removal of the consumption costs associated with protection.

11. Balassa (1975) amends Bergman's calculations to produce somewhat higher figures for the cost of protection, including 6.2 per cent of GNP for Pakistan and 9.5 per cent for Brazil.

12. See de Melo (1978). The cost of protection he finds for Colombia ranges from 3.8 per cent of GNP assuming a quota on coffee exports and an upward sloping labour supply curve to 11.0 per cent with an optimal tax on coffee exports and the same labour market conditions. These results are reported in Krueger (1984), p. 547.

13. See Bird (1983) for a survey of the effectiveness of devaluation in developing countries.

14. See Warr (1984) for evidence on this relative price effect.

15. High wage economies where government intervention has been important are listed as the East African countries, plus Nigeria, Puerto Rica, Colombia, Sri Lanka and Pakistan; see Squire (1981), pp. 129–30. Berry and Sabot (1978) also take the view that the economic cost of labour market distortions is not great.

16. Pack defined economically appropriate as the technology which generates the highest net benefit to capital ratio, at market prices. Stewart (1977) and White (1978) are surveys of the literature on the scope for technology choice.

17. Less conclusive results are reported, for example, in Galbis (1979), Brodersohn (1981) and Vogel and Buser (1976).

18. See van Wijnbergen (1982).

19. Little (1982), p. 204, argues that the most general effect of financial repression is that large operations are favoured at the expense of smaller competitors, since with interest controls banks will channel funds where their perceived risks and transactions costs are lowest.

20. As an illustration of the stronger case see Little (1981) and of the weaker Krueger (1985).

21. Krause (1985) illustrates differences between the four.

22. Since neither have a rural sector their income and productivity *per capita* is high by developing country standards. Furthermore, since

agriculture as a sector rarely grows as rapidly as manufacturing or services over sustained periods, its absence makes it easier for those countries to show a rapid increase in total GDP.There are also specific social factors; for example, Hong Kong benefited from the immigration of professional and business groups from mainland China.

23. For example, Hamilton (1983), Evans and Alizadeh (1984) and Browett (1985).

24. US aid covered around one-half of Korean government revenue until the 1960s; and around one-third of gross total investment in Taiwan in the 1950s; see Hamilton (1983), p. 158. Foreign commercial borrowing and foreign investment only became significant after the mid-1960s, after export growth had established both countries as credit-worthy.

25. White and Wade (1984), p. 2.

26. Singapore has had a far more open trading policy, and policy towards foreign investors, than South Korea and Taiwan. For industry there are virtually no controls on the private sector, although the government uses tax allowances and subsidies to influence activity. However, most observers see the Singapore government as playing an important interventionist role in the economy; for example, through investment in infrastructure, and financial institutions, and particularly through its regulation of wages and controls over trade unions; see for example Fong and Lim (1985) pp. 89–93.

27. Suppliers of inputs to exporters were seen as producing 'indirect exports' and thus were eligible for similar incentives to those received by exporters themselves. These incentives might offset any losses caused by selling at world prices; see Dahlman et al. (1981), p. 24. Estimates of ERP in South Korea and Taiwan in the 1960s are given in Balassa (1982), table 2.3, pp. 28–9. Estimates for South Korea in 1978 by Chong are cited in Fransman (1984). The timetable for import liberalisation in South Korea introduced in the early 1980s, envisages a major reduction in protection to the levels of some OECD countries by 1988. In 1984 average nominal tariff rates were around 20 per cent; see Anjaria (1985), p. 76–9.

28. Fry (1985) surveys financial policies in the 'Gang of Four' and concludes that: 'In general, real institutional interest rates in the Gang of Four were held below their competitive free market equilibrium levels during the period 1960–82.'
Leite and Vaez-Zadeh (1986) examine the effectiveness of government credit controls in South Korea, and find that it has been relatively effective in channelling resources to efficient small to medium enterprises.

29. In Taiwan in the late-1950s state enterprises produced over 50 per cent of industrial output, although some of these enterprises were later sold to the private sector, see Hamilton (1983), p. 151.

30. It appears that targets and performance were close in the 1970s; see Rhee et al. (1984).

31. See for example Sen (1981) from a generally Structuralist perspective, and Bienefeld (1981) from a Radical one.

32. The following paragraphs draw heavily on Foxley's account of the Chilean reform sequence and its theoretical rationale. Data are also taken from Ffrench-Davis (1983) and Edwards (1985).

33. Put simply the argument was that in an open economy with free capital and trade flows and a fixed exchange rate, should domestic inflation outstrip world inflation, a balance of payments problem would emerge and international reserves would decline thus reducing the domestic money supply. This monetary contraction would raise interest rates, encouraging an inflow of foreign capital and reduce domestic expenditure, thus curbing pressures both on the balance of payments and on internal prices. The economy would adjust to a new equilibrium, where, with a fixed exchange rate world and domestic inflation rates would be equal, and there would be no undesired loss of foreign reserves. In this view domestic monetary policy has no independent role in economic management and the money supply is assumed to adjust passively to changes in the international trading position.

34. See the critiques of Foxley (1983) and Ffrench-Davis (1983), which are drawn on in the discussion below.

35. One can compare the estimates of real wages in Foxley (1983) table 15, p. 69 and in Edwards (1985), table 3, p. 229. Foxley gives three alternatives that use different price deflators, and all are well below the estimates given by Edwards.

36. Very high real interest rates in Chile have been a concern of Neoclassical authors. For example, Harberger (1985) explains such high rates by the weakness of the Chilean banking system, since banks accumulated a stock of bad debts, which were rolled over rather than recognised as bad loans. This, he argues, produced a strong 'false' demand for credit in addition to the 'true' demand generated by new productive investment. The supply of credit for the latter category was therefore squeezed, with the consequence being high real interest rates of 3 per cent to 4 per cent per month. Edwards (1986) explains high rates by both internal and external factors, where the latter include movements in international interest rates and the exchange rate.

37. See for example the survey of Corbo and de Melo (1985) which reports on the results of a World Bank research project on liberalisation experiments. Evidence on improved productive efficiency arising from the reforms is admitted to be still 'sketchy'; see Corbo *et al*. (1986), pp. 617–8, who argue that the reforms improved resource use in Chile and Uruguay, but not in Argentina.

38. Edwards (1985), p. 234 suggests that the maximum un-employment created by trade liberalisation was 3.5 per cent of the work force. Cortes Douglas (1985), p. 175, supports this view of a small total impact on job losses but acknowledges that 'if the availability of credit had been less enormous than it was the results of the commercial reform could have been significantly different.'

39. Edwards (1985), p. 238, discusses some explanations for poor savings performance in Chile. The socialisation of private banks in these countries as governments took over their bad debts in the financial crises of the early 1980s, is also paradoxical, given government commitment to financial deregulation and withdrawal from economic activity.

287

40. Edwards (1986) gives this interpretation in detail.

41. See Corbo *et al.* (1986).

42. See for example several of the papers in Choksi and Papageorgiu (1986).

43. See for example Bruno (1985).

44. Sandbrook (1986) questions whether African political systems could incorporate such a reform package, arguing that the patronage that direct economic controls bestows is an important factor legitimising many African regimes.

8

Government Industrial Policy: Issues and an Outline

The case that is argued in this chapter is that an active industrial policy defined broadly as a conscious attempt by government to influence the size, composition and activities of the industrial sector through various interventions, using both price and non-price policy instruments — is likely to remain an important area of government responsibility in most developing economies.[1] Naturally the nature and degree of government involvement in industry will be far higher where there is an official commitment to socialism, but in any economy the balance between government intervention and private sector initiative will vary with factors like: political commitment to public ownership; the administrative competence of the government bureaucracy; the strength and influence of the domestic capitalist class; the role of foreign capital; and the resources available to the economy. No simple blue-print for intervention can be specified, since it must be recognised that policies that are effective in one economic environment need not be so in another. The comments given below are directed primarily at the majority of developing countries, where public ownership is likely to arise more from the weaknesses of the private sector than from an ideological commitment.

An active industrial policy is most closely associated with Structuralist, and to some extent Radical, arguments on the importance of industrialisation. This chapter considers first aspects of the Neoclassical critique of past industrialisation that need to be incorporated in industrial planning. It then turns to the familiar debates on inward- versus outward-looking industrialisation to ascertain how current thinking on these issues may influence industrial policy. Finally recognising the difficulty of sketching any ideal policy in the abstract, some of the major areas for government activity are considered in general terms.

NEOCLASSICAL CONTRIBUTIONS TO INDUSTRIAL POLICY DEBATES

Despite some overstatements of the significance of market distortions, and the relatively poor record of market reform programmes in some countries, there is little doubt that much of the Neoclassical critique of inward-looking industrialisation must be taken seriously. Three general contributions can be noted. First, the importance of not neglecting the export sector, and of granting equal incentives to exporters and import competing producers. Secondly, the effectiveness of policy interventions that act through the price mechanism rather than involving a form of rationing by direct controls. Thirdly, the importance of assessing quantitiatively the economic costs and benefits of interventions, particularly in relation to new investments and protection policy.

Policy towards exports has been touched on at various points in this study, and will be referred to again later in this chapter. Greater use of price measures as opposed to direct controls has been justified in terms of their greater speed, transparency and lower information requirements.[2]

None the less it must be remembered that direct controls may still be more effective in particular circumstances; for example import quotas have an important role in cutting off inessential imports quickly and in granting domestic producers certainty regarding their share of the domestic market; price controls for key wage goods may be necessary on income distribution grounds, and investment licences may be essential to avoid over-capacity in an activity or to direct firms to priority locations. It is well known that direct controls can also generate significant costs, including delays, arbitrary discrimination between producers, loss of government revenue in the case of import quotas, and disincentive supply effects, particularly from price controls. An effective industrial policy is one that balances these costs and benefits and utilises direct controls and price measures where each can be most effective. Just as it has been a mistake for some countries to make excessive use of direct controls, one should not go to the opposite extreme and assume that price measures alone can guide and co-ordinate industrial policy. Recent policy shifts in China that combine a limited use of market prices with a mandatory planning system of quota production is an interesting illustration of a combination of policy measures.[3]

An emphasis on the quantification of economic costs and benefits should be an important aspect of industrial policy. This will involve the type of cost-benefit criteria examined in Chapter 5, supplemented where appropriate by judgement on more intangible issues like learning effects and externalities. 'Picking winners', in the sense of identifying potential infant-industries, is central to an active industrial policy, since the aim of such a policy is to alter the pattern and level of industrial development, by channelling resources to priority activities. These priorities may not be those of the private sector, nor of public enterprise managers acting independently of broader government objectives. However if winners or potential infants are to be picked and encouraged, some systematic criteria must be applied to test the reasonableness of the set of activities that are judged to be priority. The approach of cost-benefit and domestic resource cost analysis has been the subject of much critical discussion, but nonetheless can be seen as providing a practical planning tool that provides important information relevant to such decisions. Since it is argued here that cost benefit techniques can have a useful role in industrial planning it is necessary to comment briefly on the debate regarding their use.

Cost-benefit techniques

First, it must be recognised that the shadow prices used in most applied cost-benefit studies are based on partial or 'piecemeal' analyses. Theoretically accurate estimation of shadow prices requires a general model of the economy where government objectives and resource constraints are clearly specified. Within the framework of such a model shadow prices are the dual values derived from the maximisation of the objective function subject to the relevant constraints. However the difficulties of estimating economy-wide programming models are widely known so that the central issue is whether approximate shadow prices, derived from partial analyses, can give a more accurate guide to resource allocation than can market prices. In some instances use of shadow prices will involve an 'act of faith', but in others the potential they hold for improvements in economic efficiency may be obvious.[4]

Practical objections have also been raised. For example even the apparently straightforward rule that internationally traded goods be valued at their world prices can be difficult to interpret where world prices vary between different suppliers and quality differences make strict comparisons between domestic and foreign goods inapplicable. Non-traded goods can cause even greater problems, since a detailed analysis requires that they be disaggregated into traded inputs and domestic factors. The data requirements for this exercise are high, and short-cut procedures may give misleading results. Probably the major practical objection, however, refers to the difficulty of incorporating the externalities, linkages and dynamic learning effects, that are central to the Structuralist case on industrialisation. In cost-benefit analysis the use of world prices to value traded output is not, in itself, evidence of a 'free-trade bias', but such a bias can emerge if the practical problems of quantifying any positive dynamic or external effects mean such effects are ignored.[5]

It is worth pointing out that some of the external effects discussed in Chapter 3 can be handled readily in a cost-benefit framework. Probably the most significant and easily quantifiable will be the additional income effects arising out of backward linkages between an activity and its input suppliers. Both workers who were previously underemployed and are now given work in these supplier activities, and the owners of capital with spare capacity, will have their incomes raised by the extra demand for these inputs. These additional incomes will be an external benefit from the original investment, and will be covered in an appraisal by the relatively low economic values placed on the cost of non-traded inputs supplied under these conditions. The shadow wage for underemployed workers will be below their market wage, and the difference between these two wages reflects their income gain. Similarly the extra profits generated in the input activities will be a gain to the owners of these firms, and will be shown in the analysis by valuing the non-traded items at their variable, rather than full costs of production. These external benefits will thus appear as lower costs, rather than as extra benefit items added to the value of output.

Direct or 'first-round' linkages of this type are captured fairly easily, whilst indirect linkages further back in the chain of production can be estimated if input-output analysis is employed. This means that gains to underemployed labour and capitalists with surplus capacity in a network of domestic supplier activities can be incorporated in the shadow price of non-traded inputs. However inducement to additional investment arising from a backward linkage to an input supplier, and the consequences of this investment, will not normally be covered unless the links between the project and its suppliers are very close, so that the latter's investment plans are known to the appraisers of the original project. Forward linkages to user industries, on the other hand, will not normally be picked up, since for industrial projects producing traded output it is conventional to assume that in the absence of the project equivalent goods would have been imported that would have created the same forward linkage as the project.[6]

Learning externalities, whereby others gain from the experience created by a project, are relatively easy to measure if it is labour training that is involved. Here one can estimate the workers leaving a project and the cost incurred previously in their training which is the external benefit for their new employer. However, less precise learning externalities, such as changes in attitudes or the spread of knowledge about particular innovations, are more difficult to quantify. Internal learning effects, for example in successful infant-industries, can be allowed for by projecting falling costs over time. The difficulty here is in making accurate projections, and in the absence of firm data qualitative judgement may have to be used.[7]

Cost-benefit appraisal techniques of either the CB or DRC variant discussed in Chapter 5 can have two important general contributions to industrial planning. First, they allow the incorporation of trade efficiency considerations and thus provide a measure of *ex-ante* comparative advantage in particular lines of production. For traded goods, if new activities do not appear economically competitive internationally after allowing for structural features of the economy, such as surplus labour, and additional benefits, such as positive externalities and learning effects, investment will not be justified. If relevant dynamic effects can be incorporated in the appraisal, so for example learning is estimated accurately, this will be a measure of dynamic not static comparative advantage.[8]

Second, the Structuralist arguments on the importance of linkages and externalities can be subject to detailed examination and at least in part incorporated quantitatively into the analysis of new investment. It was noted in Chapter 3 that the objective of building an integrated industrial structure by maximising domestic linkages need not be economically justified. Not all linkages are necessarily economically beneficial and cost-benefit criteria can be used to identify whether there is a case for setting up local production to either supply inputs to an existing activity or to process or use the output of that activity. The justification for setting up linkages can be examined on a case-by-case basis, however, it must also be acknowledged that there will be circumstances where a set of closely-linked new activities, which are major markets for each others products, should be appraised together as an industrial complex. This may give a different and more accurate picture of their economic effects than if each activity is judged in isolation. On the related question of externalities, it has been argued that these techniques allow quantification of at least the most direct and obvious external effects. None the less full coverage is not likely to be possible and there is a need in some cases to supplement quantitative estimates with qualitative judgements. What is important, however, is that such judgements should be exercised with caution and not used as a loose argument to justify schemes that make little sense on other grounds.

It is important to clarify that applying cost-benefit criteria in investment planning does not mean that all new investments need be internationally competitive, in the sense that their costs of production at market prices are comparable with those in major exporting economies. As we have seen, investments can be justified despite high initial costs, if they are infants with a potential for competitiveness, or if they are high cost in private, but not economic terms, due for example to their employment or external effects. Furthermore in economies where domestic needs and effective demand can be brought more closely into line, either through rising real wages and employment, or through major reforms of wealth and income distribution, there should be a significant expansion of the market for mass consumer goods. This is a market which imports may be ill-suited to serve, at least in some product lines, because of their high cost relative to domestic incomes, even without protection. In these products, there will be scope for simpler, re-designed local goods, that whilst less sophisticated than imports, are cheaper to produce and thus affordable by the majority of consumers. In economic appraisals such goods are best classed as non-traded and their economic value will be determined by reference to their value in domestic use, not by reference to the price of imports. In other words such goods are non-competing with imports, and production of this type is only import-substituting in a very general sense.

Cost-benefit criteria can be applied not only in assessing the viability of new investments, but also to measure the efficiency of existing production. This is particularly significant in the case of industries that need 'restructuring' due to their high costs relative to international competitors, since this form of appraisal can be used to judge whether such industries should continue to receive government support through either pro-tection or subsidy. Cost-benefit techniques are applicable most obviously to public sector investments. However they can be employed as part of an interventionist policy that attempts to direct private sector activity. For example, private firms wishing for government finance or tariff protection, or foreign investors wishing to enter the domestic market, can have their investment plans assessed by these criteria.

It is sometimes suggested that full market and trade liberalisation will remove the need for shadow pricing, so that cost-benefit calculations can be done at market prices, with an allowance for externalities where these are relevant. However an exact correspondence between shadow and market prices requires not just free-trade and full market liberalisation, but also the full employment of all resources domestically. This implies full employment of labour and no surplus capacity in domestic industry. This set of conditions is unlikely to be fulfilled for the majority of developing countries for a long time to come, so that even allowing for some future liberalisations it can be argued that for most countries shadow price estimates will remain important for assessing economic efficiency. Practical problems in their estimation should not be minimised, but in recent years applied work has demonstrated that fairly detailed shadow prices can be derived even for countries in which the basic data is relatively poor.[9]

IMPORT-SUBSTITUTION — REVISITED

In considering a broad outline of industrial policy few would now see 'old-style' import-substitution, often based on direct controls of the private sector, as a model to follow. Some of the discussion in the literature on industrial policy draws on the experiences of the industrially more successful developed economies, particularly Japan, where many argue that the role of the government was critically important in stimulating new industrial developments in the private sector post-1945.[10] The form of protection practiced in Japan, however, avoided most of the costs of import-substitution and allowed the establishment of internationally competitive industries that could break into export markets in a relatively brief time. There are many aspects of Japanese development post-1945 that distinguish Japan from most developing countries; particularly the accumulation of industrial experience pre-1945, the technical competence and nationalist commitment of the government bureaucracy, and the strength of the domestic capitalist class. None the less Japan provides an important example of a highly successful developmental capitalist state, where selective government intervention strengthened the private sector, and parallels have been drawn between Japan and the developmental states of South Korea and Taiwan.[11] Even allowing for the national peculiarities of the Japanese case there seems little doubt that given their geographical and economic proximity to Japan, policy-makers in these countries were influenced strongly by Japanese experience. The lessons for industrial policy of Japanese government interventions are discussed later in this chapter.

Chapter 2 has already noted reasons why distinctions between inward- and outward-looking policies can be too simplistic. The key issue is the degree to which governments should attempt to influence the pattern of industrialisation via interventions in trade, the branches or activities that should be subject to this intervention, and the incentives to earning foreign exchange through exporting as opposed to saving it through import-substitution. It is well established that in the absence of government intervention in the early stages of industrialisation there will be a tendency for production to be concentrated on relatively simple consumer goods, often involving labour-intensive technologies. In most industrialisation goods like textiles, clothing, leather, and footwear, for example, figure prominently in the early stages. Over time as experience grows, technology is imported or developed, and markets expand, backward linkages will be established with local suppliers and domestic production of intermediate and capital goods will commence. This implies that at different levels of industrial development different activities will grow at different rates, with the growth of intermediates and capital goods rising relative to that of consumer goods once a threshold level of industrialisation has been passed.[12]

As part of this process both import-substitution and export-substitution can take place 'naturally' as domestic production either captures markets previously supplied by imports, or breaks into export markets. The process is said to be natural if it is based on natural advantages such as lower transport costs, consumer preferences or simply growing competitiveness. This must be contrasted with policy-induced import- and export-substitution that endeavours to accelerate the process through government trade interventions. The real debate is on the wisdom of these interventions and on the pattern of industrial development that a government should attempt to establish. The Neoclassical view, as we have seen, is that government interventions should be relatively slight and limited to a few selected cases, so that in general the pattern of allocation arising from the decisions of private producers should not be altered. Given the appropriate incentives, in terms of exchange rate and related policies, private producers, it is argued, will be able to break into new export markets and thus diversify exports.

However, Structuralist and Radical analyses of industrialisation have concluded that both the level of industrial development and its composition should be something that governments should attempt to influence, both through price and non-price measures. Here the sequence with which new investments are undertaken becomes important as external effects, learning and productivity growth are likely to differ significantly between activities. Governments, in this view, should encourage investments where net economic benefits are greatest, and in particular should select and encourage new infant-industries that may be uncompetitive initially, but which have the potential for long-run international competitiveness. This policy necessitates protection from import competition for the industries concerned and a period of induced, as opposed to natural, import-substitution. Since some intermediate and capital goods activities are often seen as infants, with potentially large external benefits to the rest of the industrial sector, some discussions have given these particular prominence. This is an argument therefore for a pattern of industrialisation that prematurely gives greater emphasis to intermediate and capital goods activities; so-called secondary import-substitution.

If these are broadly the competing perspectives, what can be said about the debate on inward- versus outward-looking industrialisation in the light of the accumulated evidence both from NICs and other developing countries? The first qualification to make is that there is now widespread disillusionment with the actual practice of import-substitution, even amongst authors whose views can be said to have provided intellectual justification for many import-substitution programmes. This is not the place to repeat the arguments on the deficiencies of much of the industrialisation that has taken place behind protective barriers. However in broad terms old-style import-substitution has often created high cost uncompetitive industries, whilst failing to solve the problem of a scarcity of foreign exchange, which provided much of its original justification. As Radical authors have noted where industrial development occurs in a society with an initially unequal pattern of income distribution, and where its employment effects are weak, one can end up with a situation where at least initially much of the newly produced industrial goods serve the national elite. Simply setting up barriers to imports may do little more than ensure that luxury consumer goods, once imported, are now produced locally, and that the domestic capitalists who organise their production can earn monopoly profits in the protected domestic market. It has come to be recognised that the restrictiveness of import quotas and the height of import tariffs are in no sense a measure of commitment to socially progressive policies.[13]

The majority of developing countries have not pursued an inward-looking basic industry strategy of the type discussed in Chapter 4. To term this a Radical version of import-substitution would be misleading, since the aim is not to produce domestically goods that were previously imported, but to use domestic resources to produce the commodities required to meet basic domestic needs and demands. These needs may have little to do with goods available on the international market and produced in response to the needs of other societies. As we have seen, the basic industry strategy involves the concentration of resources on a range of basic industrial materials that can be used in a variety of activities; not only in manufactured mass consumer goods but also in agriculture and infrastructure. China and North Korea appear to have had success with policies that some have suggested are relatively close to this strategy, and it is likely to be important for economies experiencing a major redistribution of income and wealth. However two inherent problems can be noted. First, the difficulty of producing a wide range of basic materials, particularly in a small developing economy, without generating high unit costs due to the importance of economies of scale. A policy of maximising domestic linkages between basic material and user industries can lead to major long-run bottlenecks, if such linkages only generate economically high cost activities. Second, there is a danger of condemning industries to technological backwardness, if technology or equipment imports are not allowed periodically. The shift in policy in China in recent years can be interpreted as evidence that whilst an inward-looking basic industry strategy can generate sustained expansion in the relatively early stages of industrialisation there are limits to this process, and that beyond some point an infusion of foreign technology and imports will be required to strengthen and complement domestic resources.

Having noted the obvious limitations of much of the practice of import-substitution it none the less needs to be stressed that protection designed to either foster or shelter domestic industries can still be justified under two general headings. First, evidence from South East Asia and Latin America suggests that the infant-industry case for protection still has merit, although the number of potential infants will vary between economies, and several past errors in the implementation of this policy should not be repeated. Infant-industry protection appears likely to be more effective if it is selective and not general, so that only infants chosen on the basis of detailed assessment of their potential should be protected or promoted. Furthermore efforts should be made by government to encourage cost-reductions and technical change by infants, and the possibility of their exporting at a relatively early stage should not be neglected.

Second, there may be industries whose protection is justified on grounds of restructuring adjustment. As the term is used here these are industries currently uncompetitive internationally, but without the dynamic potential of infants. Their production would cease if they were exposed to world competition, even though they may be important generators of incomes and jobs. With a reasonable degree of resource mobility one can argue that if these activities closed down, resources could shift into alternative, more competitive lines of production, and that after a period of transition domestic incomes would be higher than initially. In most economies, however, transition periods tend to be long, and many governments including those of developed economies have employed protection or subsidies to maintain industries of this type. In developing countries, where it is likely that resource immobility is greater, there is undoubtedly a case for this type of restructuring protection. The policy issue is how many industries should be protected on these grounds, since blanket coverage of the whole industrial sector would simply maintain old inefficiencies. Furthermore this type of protection should be accompanied by positive measures to encourage new activities, with greater long-run potential that can absorb the resources presently committed to the industries that need restructuring.

As noted above an economic appraisal of operations can be used to identify industries whose protection can be justified on these grounds, since economic costs can differ significantly from private costs in a situation of resource immobility. For example if workers in these activities have no alternative employment opportunities their shadow wage will be zero, and if capital assets cannot be switched to other uses their economic cost will be no more than their scrap value. When these considerations are introduced industries that appear high cost in private or commercial terms, may be economically viable and thus justify protection.

EXPORT-ORIENTED INDUSTRIALISATION IN THE 1980s

If there is still a case for selective import-substitution, this does not mean that export opportunities should be neglected. There is ample evidence that many countries in the past have penalised their export sectors, including manufacturing, and as a consequence have kept the growth of their exports below its potential rate. The possible range of financial incentives to encourage exports will be considered below, but here it is important to stress that simply setting what is considered an appropriate exchange rate, and perhaps adding certain financial subsidies to exporting, are unlikely to be sufficient to sustain a major expansion of manufactured exports.

For example, in some industries, particularly those involving more complex technologies, a period of prior learning derived from experience in production for the home market is likely to be a prerequisite for later export success. This link between prior domestic production, generally in the form of import-substitution, and later export growth, is recognised as an important factor in explaining exports from South Korea and Taiwan, although the import-substitution pursued in these countries prior to the export boom is seen as both brief and avoiding many of the undesirable features noted in other countries. The link has been made also for Japan, and in Latin America, for Brazil and Argentina.[14]

In addition, it is clear that sustained export success will require efforts in areas like marketing, product design, quality control and the provision of financial schemes, such as export insurance. Evidence from South Korea, for example, shows the importance of establishing marketing networks that can service the needs of exporters. In the early stages of the export boom it appears that foreign buyers were relied upon for marketing, but gradually this responsibility was taken over successfully by domestic firms. The government helped exporters by establishing the national trade promotion corporation, and by promoting the development of private sector companies with a specialism in export and import trade.[15] Where transnationals are involved the marketing issue is likely to be less significant, since the parent corporations of such firms will have their own international marketing channels. However we have noted that transnational presence in export manufacturing varies substantially between countries and branches.

Furthermore sustained sales in foreign markets, even for relatively simple products like clothing, will require research into design and quality improvements. Access to intermediate and capital goods inputs of adequate quality and at a reasonably competitive price is also likely to be important.[16]

The question of export prospects for the manufactured exports of developing countries cannot be approached from the supply-side alone, however, since international demand conditions have to be considered. Both the future growth of incomes in the developed economies, to which around two-thirds of developing countries' exports still go and the barriers to entry to these markets that may restrain the expansion of developing country exports, will be relevant to any consideration of future industrial strategy. Chapter 2 has already commented on the 'fallacy of composition' argument which notes that simply because a small number of developing countries have been able to expand rapidly their manufactured exports of simple labour-intensive commodities, does not mean that this path of industrialisation is open to all developing countries because of the vast increase in imports to developed country markets that would be implied.

There is no doubt scope for further manufactured export growth from developing countries, particularly if the stages of comparative advantage view is valid so that the more industrialised developing countries 'make way' for the less industrialised by moving into more capital-intensive and technologically sophisticated products. However the important point is that the demand conditions of the 1960s and 1970s, which allowed the emergence of the major NIC manufacturing exporters, may not be repeated, particularly because of the evidence of emerging protectionist trends in developed economies.

Whilst demand projections are always uncertain, it is clear that export demand for manufactures is likely to be more responsive to changes in income in the developed economies than is the export demand for primary commodities. Estimates of the income elasticity of demand in developed economies for manufactured exports from developing countries vary, but are normally substantially in excess of 1.0, and in some studies are in excess of 2.0. In other words, every 1 per cent change in GDP in developed economies creates a change of more than 1 per cent in manufactured export volumes from developing economies.[17] World Bank (1986) sets out two alternative scenarios for the evolution of the world economy, which are described as 'high' and 'low' cases. Whilst these are not intended to be precise forecasts, they give an indication of the possible consequences for developing countries of a slower rate of growth in the world economy. Table 8.1 summarises some of the projections of significance for this discussion. It can be seen that in the high growth case with industrial countries expanding at over 4 per cent per year 1985–95, a rate significantly above the average for the period since 1973, developing countries manufactured exports are projected to increase at just under 10 per cent per year. This is above the average for the first half of the 1980s, but still below that for the longer period 1965–80. On the other hand, in the low growth case, with the industrial economies growing at 2.5 per cent per annum, which is a little above their actual average increase in GDP for the first half of the 1980s, the growth of exports of developing countries is projected to fall significantly. For manufactures, export growth is 5 per cent per annum 1985–95 which is less than half the rate of expansion achieved 1965–80. In other words, if the growth of the industrial economies 1985–95 is closer to that of the early 1980s, than to that of the 1960s and 1970s, whilst the expansion of manufactured exports from developing countries will continue, it seems unlikely that anything like the rapid rates of increase of the pre-1980 period will be achieved.[18]

Table 8.1: Alternative projections of economic performance (1985–95) annual growth (percentage)

Growth of	High case[a]		Low case[b]	
	Industrial countries	Developing countries	Industrial countries	Developing countries
GDP	4.3	5.9	2.5	4.0
GDP *per capita*	3.8	3.9	2.0	2.0
Total exports	n.a	7.1	n.a	3.2
Exports of manufactures	n.a	9.8	n.a	5.0
Exports of primary goods	n.a	4.3	n.a	1.5

[a] Assumes policy reforms introduced in both industrial and developing countries. For details of these reforms see the original source.
[b] Assumes policy reforms introduced only in developing countries.
n.a. = not available.
Source: World Bank (1986), tables 3.1, 3.2 and 3.3.

It is very difficult to incorporate the effects of shifts in trade policy in scenarios such as these. World Bank (1986) states that higher growth in the industrial countries should make it easier for reductions in the barriers to trade that restrain exports from developing countries and it appears that the high growth scenario assumes significant trade liberalisation. The converse of this, however, is that a continuation of the trend of historically relatively low rates of income growth in the industrial economies will increase pressure for import restrictions as a means of protecting jobs in activities where the industrial economies are becoming increasingly uncompetitive. Current trends in the mid-1980s appear to be towards greater selective protectionism rather than the reverse. A recent IMF survey of trade prospects, for example, commences with the following statement:

> The continued drift towards protectionism poses a threat to the balanced expansion of world trade in the medium term and to the prospects for sustaining economic recovery. In the past several years, most industrial countries have become more protectionist than before, despite the continued tariff cuts of the Tokyo Round and limited instances of liberalization of non-tariff barriers. Trade restrictions or trade distorting measures were intensified or imposed not only in the traditionally protected sectors, such as steel, textiles and clothing, and agriculture, but were also extended to new sectors such as electronics.[19]

The chief problem is not the tariffs imposed on the exports of developing countries, although for some product-lines these still remain relatively high; for example, whilst the average rate of import tariff on manufactured goods in OECD countries is now as low as 5 per cent, for certain commodities in which developing countries are generally viewed as either currently or potentially cost competitive, tariff reductions have been less dramatic. Tariffs on clothing imports into the main OECD markets currently average about 9 per cent, footwear and travel goods imports 13.5 per cent, and textile fabrics about 12.5 per cent.[20] Not all developing country exporters face these tariffs because of the extension of tariff preferences, whereby tariffs are waived on exports from countries eligible for preferential treatment. However certain sensitive products, such as textiles and clothing, are often excluded from the preferential scheme and there are often limits on the share of total imports of a product that can be imported at preferential tariff rates from a single supplier.

However it is generally non-tariff restrictions on trade that now receive the greatest attention in discussions of obstacles to trade expansion. Non-tariff barriers can take a variety of forms including direct import quota restrictions, regulations governing import licensing, total import prohibitions, additional price levies such as anti-dumping duties, government procurement policy, government quality control regulations, and voluntary export restraints.[21] It is estimated that around 20 per cent of all developing country exports to industrial economies were subject to some form of non-tariff restriction in 1984.[22] However, focusing specifically on manufactures, other estimates put the share of developing country exports that face such barriers significantly higher, in a range between 25 per cent to 40 per cent depending upon the developed economy market considered. Also it has been the more successful exporting countries which have faced the most significant restrictions; for example non-tariff barriers on exports of the 'Gang of Four' appear to have increased substantially during the first half of the 1980s.[23]

The incidence of non-tariff barriers tends to be distributed highly unevenly between manufacturing branches and as one would expect is generally high in activities where developing countries are threatening the market position of established producers. The most sensitive branches where barriers tend to be greatest are clothing and textiles, leather and footwear, and more recently iron and steel and some electrical products. The impact of existing non-tariff restrictions is difficult to assess. Estimates of the tariff equivalent of the combination of tariff and non-tariff protection — that is the full increase in price created by the protective system — show substantial variation both between branches and importing countries. Table 8.2 gives estimates of the tariff equivalents for the exports of developing countries in four product categories and four major developed country markets. Although only approximate these estimates give an indication of the relatively high incidence of non-tariff barriers, particularly in textiles and clothing where the market share of developing country exports in developed countries is highest.[24]

It is difficult to be precise about the degree to which exports from developing countries would expand should full trade liberalisation take place, since both export supply and import demand responses must be allowed for.[25] However major liberalisation, in the sense of substantially easier access to the markets of developed economies, does not appear a realistic

Table 8.2: Estimated tariff equivalent in developed country markets: developing country exports of manufactures[a] (percentage)

Category	Market			
	USA	EEC	JAPAN	CANADA
Textiles	68	59	13	39
Iron and steel	35	43	8	8
Clothing	79	59	18	39
Footwear	9	27	16	30

[a] For details of the calculations see the original source.
Source: Kirmani *et al.* (1984), table 4, p. 675.

prospect at least in the short-term. The key implication of this for the present discussion on trade strategies is that whilst the possibility of exporting should not be neglected, and attention should be given to ways of not only encouraging exporters, but also of overcoming various trade barriers, the scope for large numbers of developing countries relying heavily in their industrialisation programmes on export sales seems limited. An export-orientation must remain part of an industrial planning strategy, but one whose importance will vary between manufacturing branches and between countries.

AN OUTLINE OF INDUSTRIAL POLICY

Before turning to more specific questions of policy, it is necessary to stress the obvious point that industrial policy cannot be viewed in isolation from several broader issues. For example, the class basis of a government and its mechanisms for political control will limit the degree to which it is free to pursue policies in opposition to vested interests, even if in the abstract such policies appear economically rational. Similarly the degree of competence and honesty of a bureaucracy will limit the scope for detailed and complex forms of direct intervention and of sophisticated macro-economic management. Finally the macro-economic environment will influence the scope for industrial policy, since it is far easier to reallocate resources, and influence generally the private sector, when expectations are high in a buoyant economy. Bearing in mind the difficulty of generalising sensibly across countries the following discussion considers several important general areas; these are discussed under the headings:

- foreign trade and industrial policy;
- policy on industrial investment;
- structure and behaviour of industry;
- technology and industrial policy;
- treatment of foreign investors;
- picking winners.

It is assumed that the basic objective of industrial policy is to create a dynamic and diversified industrial sector that can contribute to the overall expansion of the economy.

Foreign trade and industrial policy

Although much of the discussion on industrial policy in developing countries has focused on foreign trade, this is only one aspect of industrial policy, and in this area more than most others macro-economic considerations limit the scope for policy changes. The vast majority of developing countries operate some system of trade controls and import tariffs; despite their important protective effect these measures were often introduced initially for balance of payments reasons to restrict the expenditure of foreign exchange. It follows therefore that in many countries full removal of these controls would imply a major shift in macro-economic strategy. If this shift is economically infeasible or politically unacceptable, the scope for import liberalisation as part of an industrial reform package will be limited. As an illustration of this one can note the reimposition of relatively high import tariffs in Chile in the early 1980s in response to the foreign exchange crisis. This is despite the explicit goal of industrial policy of opening the sector to foreign competition. However bearing in mind the limits imposed by balance of payments considerations, there are several ways in which trade reforms could be used to foster greater economic efficiency.

In economies where the rate of protection is both high and varied there is a case for both lowering absolute protection, in both nominal and effective terms, and for reducing its variance between branches and sectors. High industrial protection may

307

serve only to raise the profits of industrial producers at the expense of both consumers and non-industrial producers, and may give no incentive to reduce costs and break into export markets. The variation of effective protection between activities can be difficult to establish, particularly where import quota restrictions are in force, and often where it has been estimated appears to bear no relation to stated government priorities. Therefore highly protected activities to which resources will be attracted need not be among a government's set of priorities. Thus there is a case for simplifying protective systems and bringing them more closely in line with government priorities. This will involve reducing the number of quantitative import restrictions, and limiting these to commodities where there is a clear case for protection in this form rather than by tariffs. In addition nominal tariff rates will need to be both made more uniform, and lowered overall, provided this does not conflict with balance of payments management.

This type of reform could not be introduced too suddenly given the disruption that will be caused to import-competing producers, and the impact on import demand and the consequences of this for the balance of payments. However establishing a clear timetable for trade liberalisation is often seen as desirable because of its incentive effect on protected domestic producers. The argument is that if such producers are made aware, sufficiently far in advance, of the likelihood of having to face competition from imports, they will be forced to make efforts to lower costs and raise quality to face import competition when tariffs are finally lowered.[26]

None the less, as stressed earlier, there are still grounds for maintaining selective protection — either of the infant-industry or restructuring type; in other words there will be certain activities that justify special treatment, in the form of above-average protection. As far as possible a detailed assessment of the economic costs and benefits of these protected industries will be required. Once they have been identified selective protection can be administered in two ways, using either made-to-measure tariffs or a limited number of special nominal tariff rates for the selected industries. The former approach has the advantage that in theory it can avoid the creation of monopoly profits, so that tariff setting can be used as part of an anti-monopoly policy. However made-to-measure tariffs require considerable current information on costs, and need close monitoring. As a consequence they are time-consuming and more difficult to administer than the alternative of setting a relatively small number, perhaps three or four, special tariff rates for the industries that will receive selective treatment.

The introduction of selective protection will work against the objective of reducing the variation in rates of protection. However the argument is that this strategy will be based on an assessment of predicted costs and benefits from the protected activities, so that the variation arising from this type of system should be broadly in line with government priorities. Levels of selective tariffs have to be monitored to encourage improvements in efficiency, although as noted earlier there can be disagreement on what is an appropriate learning period for infants. This can vary not only between countries with similar industries, but between industries in the same country. As noted earlier at one extreme one can have an infant producer which never generated positive economic benefits on the basis of its own costs and revenues, but whose early establishment in an industry was necessary to allow other successful producers to follow at a later stage. The general point is that for infants, as for other producers, to stimulate greater efficiency, the aim should be to lower protection gradually over time, even if the process is slow and total tariff liberalisation is not appropriate.

Finally, one should note the Neoclassical emphasis on export possibilities. The earlier discussion pointed to the more limited scope for exports of manufactures from developing countries in the 1980s as compared with the 1960s and early 1970s. None the less this does not mean that export prospects should be ignored. One can argue that one of the main lessons of recent industrialisation experience has been that few countries can solve their foreign exchange crises by operating on the import side alone, and that measures to encourage exports are essential. This means giving broadly equal incentives to sales in the domestic and export markets for activities with export potential. One key incentive is the level of the exchange rate, but where there is import protection, domestic producers will be able to obtain prices above international levels for domestic sales. To offset this some form of export subsidy will be required. Export subsidies come in various guises; the most important are likely to include differential profits tax allowances for exporting, reduced interest charges or preferential access to credit for export-oriented production, tariff refunds on imported inputs used in export production, import tariff and indirect tax exemptions for domestic intermediate good producers who supply exporters, and preferential access to foreign exchange in proportion to export sales.[27] In addition, government support for the physical and financial infrastructure necessary to supply exporters is also likely to be necessary for a major export drive.

The case for selective protection can be applied to export as well as domestic sales. As we have seen there is evidence that when infants are encouraged to export at an early stage this can stimulate greater efficiency, and allow lower unit costs through larger output volumes. This implies that when priority activities receive higher rates of import protection, they should also receive above average rates of export subsidy to maintain an approximate balance between net incentives for sales at home and in the export market.[28] This is not to imply that all infants can break into export markets at an early stage, but simply that the incentive system should not make it commercially unattractive for them to attempt to do so.

Policy on industrial investment

Under this heading one can distinguish between policy in positive and negative senses, that involves both encouraging and holding back initiatives of individual firms. On the positive side various fiscal incentives can be granted either to investment in general or in particular activities. Common fiscal incentives include tax credits, which allow a proportion of investment to be offset against later tax liability, and tariff exemptions on imports of capital goods. The intention is to raise the profitability of investing, although the impact of such incentives is not always clear, and there is a view that the most effective way of stimulating private sector investment is not by such incentive schemes, but by raising the level of expectations about future economic growth, and by making finance available for investment. Credit allocation can have a key role on the positive side of investment policy, since if governments can influence the flow and cost of credit this provides a direct means of ensuring finance for priority investments perhaps at subsidised interest rates. This will be particularly important where priority activities appear high risk in commercial terms; for example small firms or those without a record of commercial success, and investments where returns are long rather than short-run.[29]

On the negative side of investment policy various forms of licensing controls can be used to ensure that government priorities are followed. Where licensing is used, for example to approve investment or foreign exchange allocations, the government can block what are judged to be undesirable activities. The difficulties often raised in relation to such a system include delays, so that even highly desirable investments may be held back, the possibilities of corruption, and the need for a technically competent administration that can apply consistent and appropriate criteria in the issuing of licenses. There is evidence of significant costs from the operation of such a system in several countries, however, it should also be noted that there are examples where licensing has been effective. A particular merit of the system, it can be argued, is the scope it gives for controlling the number of domestic producers in an industry.[30] There is no reason to believe that individual firms need assess the potential demand for a product accurately, and if they are over-optimistic, additional investment may lead to surplus capacity, either for the original investing firm or for its competitors. This argument for controls assumes that government planners are better able to carry out accurate demand studies than private firms; in some countries and industries this will be the case, but clearly this is not something one can generalise on. Another argument in favour of retaining some form of licensing is where government funds are to be committed to new investments. Detailed scrutiny of investment proposals at the licensing stage is a means of ensuring that they are economically viable and therefore a good use of government resources.

Structure and behaviour of industry

Industrial structure is a key area for industrial policy, since given that governments have a view on industrial priorities, they will wish the structure of industry to reflect these. Here industrial structure is considered in three aspects — the composition of output between different branches; the balance between large and small firms; and the scale of production.

In an economy where central planning is practiced governments can determine the composition of industrial output directly by a system of mandatory production targets. However in the more common situation in developing countries more indirect means are required to affect resource shifts. The selective use of tariffs, fiscal incentives, credit allocations, and licensing has been noted in this connection. It is also possible that there is a need not only to encourage some activities to expand, but also to encourage others to contract, due for example to a shift in world market conditions. As has been argued it is not necessarily the case that all restructuring industries need contract absolutely, since for some continued protection may be justified because of the low economic costs of the resources committed to them. However in other cases there will be a need to encourage a run-down of production, whilst easing the transition costs in terms of job losses and bankruptcies. There are undoubted difficulties in all countries in applying major restructuring measures of this type, although some developed countries, notably Japan, have achieved success in sharing relatively orderly contractions in output between producers in recession cartels.[31]

The balance between large and small firms is an issue on which many governments in developing countries have expressed concern, and in many countries there are specific small industry programmes. These include typically: provision for credit; industrial extension and advisory services; management and other forms of training; and various measures to develop infrastructure services and industrial estates for small firms. Some observers question how far this declared emphasis on small firms has been carried into practice in many countries, and part of the Neoclassical case for capital market reform is based on the argument that credit allocation by government results, in many countries, in a major bias against small producers.[32] It is necessary to point out, however, that where such biases exist it is not always obvious that allowing markets to allocate credit will significantly strengthen the position of small firms, many of which may appear high risk commercially, even if they are viable economically.

In devising a policy towards small industry the rationale for government support should be made clear; for example is it because of employment effects, since it is generally assumed that small firms are more labour-intensive than larger firms, or is it because of the natural economic advantages of small firms at certain stages of economic development? The economic advantages normally discussed include: a transport and distribution cost advantage in local markets, where poor transport and infrastructure facilities make it difficult for larger firms located outside these markets to compete; the specialism to developing sub-contracting links with larger firms to produce parts and components efficiently on a small-scale; and sufficient knowledge of local low-income markets to develop products differentiated from those of larger firms. Where there is an economic case for small industry it is important to establish the types of activities where these advantages hold, and the most effective means of supporting competitive small-scale production in these lines. On the other hand, the employment case for small-industry requires a broad policy to support small firms in general, rather than assistance devised to strengthen specific activities of small-industry.

A third aspect of industrial structure relates to scale of production. Here policy should be concerned with encouraging efficient plant scale, that as far as possible reflects attainable economies of scale. One measure is to control the entry of firms to an industry, so that additional producers are allowed entry only when there are good prospects that they can obtain this level of production. Others include the encouragement of rationalisation and specialisation, so that if several domestic firms produce the same mix of output there is a shift in each firm towards greater specialism in a limited number of products. The encouragement of formal mergers between existing producers is another way of raising production levels, where these originally are below the minimum efficient scale of production. Finally, as we have noted Neoclassical discussions stress the importance of breaking into export markets at an early stage, as a means of achieving long production-runs and economies of scale.

Where public ownership of industry is widespread governments should have relatively little difficulty in enforcing changes such as mergers and specialisation, and in controlling entry to industries. However where private firms have to be induced to change their existing patterns of behaviour, rationalisation of this type will be more difficult to implement. It will often be the case that where producers are operating at sub-optimal scales of production this can only be sustained because of protection from import competition. Changes in the form of mergers or specialisation will thus require a lowering of this protection, combined with financial and technical assistance to encourage firms to merge or rationalise.

On the question of the behaviour of established industrial producers a key aim of industrial policy must be to encourage a relatively competitive market environment. Reference has been made to the high cost nature of many infant-industries whose costs have failed to fall significantly over time. Industrial policy must be concerned with creating the environment in which firms feel under pressure to lower costs and experiment with new products and technologies. There is a serious contradiction here however. In relatively small economies in many industries the scale of production sufficient to capture economies of scale will allow only a small number of producers, and in some cases only a single producer. In this context the desirability of encouraging mergers and rationalisation has just been noted. None the less reductions in the number of producers, market-sharing by specialisation, and the creation of monopolies, are all likely to work against an internally competitive domestic market.

The Neoclassical response to this dilemma is that an open trade policy will resolve these difficulties. Economies of scale in production can be achieved by exporting, and domestic firms will be forced to compete with international producers if the domestic market is opened to imports. However we have argued that the feasibility and desirability of full trade liberalisation can be questioned on infant-industry, restructuring and balance of payments grounds. Lower protection should result in greater competition domestically, but if full liberalisation is ruled out, competition policy will have to be based on a combination of measures, that include some import liberalisation and measures to stimulate internal competition. None of the internal measures are likely to be wholly effective on their own, however. For example, where there are a small number of oligopolistic producers the government can attempt to stimulate more competitive behaviour by requiring competitive tendering for government contracts, and introducing legislation against cartels and looser market-sharing arrangements.[33] Also in these industries and in those where there is a monopoly, governments may try to use price controls to keep profits down to non-monopolistic rates. As noted earlier these controls can include made-to-measure tariffs. The implementation of a detailed system of price controls for this purpose is both complex and demanding in terms of the cost data and staff required. In all but a few countries one must doubt whether it could be introduced effectively for anything other than a limited number of industrial goods.[34] In addition it is likely to be necessary to utilise trade policy to stimulate greater efficiency by making it clear to protected domestic producers that their position will be reviewed periodically. For example, import tariffs, credit subsidies, or tax concessions, could be reduced gradually to a pre-announced schedule. This need not go as far as full import liberalisation, or the removal of all subsidies, but it could act as a spur to efficiency and induce a greater sense of competitiveness in the domestic market.

Technology and industrial policy

For technology, as with commodities, developing countries have a choice — to develop themselves or import from abroad. The technology aspect of industrial policy should be geared to both possibilities, although it appears likely that for most developing countries technology imports will continue to be the main source of industrial technical progress. As 'late-starter' industrialisers developing countries have the advantage of a wide range of existing technology on which to draw. There are many arguments as to the desirability and high costs of much of the technology that is on offer to developing countries, but in general these can be interpreted as a case for government scrutiny of the process of importing technology, rather than for a major domestic investment programme of basic research and development to develop local substitutes for imported technology. Several economies, particularly in South East Asia, have been highly successful in importing, and later adapting and modifying technology in the light of local market conditions. However there is also evidence that government intervention in this process, through the need for government approval of licences for technology import, altered the terms of technology purchases generally in the interests of the economy as a whole. Key issues for negotiation included royalty rates, scope for local dissemination and experimentation, and restrictions on the sale of products to be manufactured with the technology. Successful bargaining in

315

this area requires a competent and committed bureaucracy that is well informed of the possibilities offered by other technology suppliers.[35]

Much local technological development can take place on the basis of copying and modifying imported designs. However there is also a case that in countries with a scientific and engineering tradition, governments should support applied and basic research. This can be through either direct expenditure on research activity, through fiscal incentives for such expenditure by the private sector, or through protection of technology so that imports of technology are not allowed where there is scope for developing local technological substitutes. As noted earlier, the amount of best-practice industrial technology developed and applied originally in developing countries has been relatively small. However this does not mean that important initiatives cannot be taken where the aim is not a major new product or technology, but to improve and adapt known technologies through local research activity.[36]

Protection or promotion of domestic production of capital goods, such as machine tools, may be justified by the greater scope for modifying and adapting technologies when there is a domestic capability to produce the equipment in which the new technology will be embodied. The spread of knowledge between machine makers and users was an important externality in the historical experience of countries, such as the USA and the UK. Several authors have noted the key role of machine tool and other engineering equipment production due to their potential technological external effects, and as part of a policy to develop a domestic technological capability they are likely to be important candidates for infant-industry protection.[37]

A further aspect of policy in this area that should be commented on, relates to the pricing of factors of production. As we have seen, Neoclassical discussions of technology choice lay great stress on the significance of distortions in labour and capital markets, and the argument has been applied not only to choices between known technologies but also to the creation of new ones. To meet employment objectives more labour-using technologies will be required and employment subsidies have been mentioned as means of cheapening the relative cost of unskilled labour, and thus of encouraging the use or development of this type of technology. However employment subsidies are likely to have only a minor role in technology policy.

First, because the general application of such a scheme would create a major drain on government revenue, and secondly because the extent to which adaptations and modifications to technology would respond to the size of labour cost reduction that could be created by such a scheme is open to question. A broadly based labour subsidy programme that reduced unskilled labour costs by even 10 per cent would be very expensive in terms of lost revenue, and it is questionable how far a cost reduction of this magnitude would affect decisions on technology.

Other measures to change factor prices that have been mentioned are the removal of minimum wage legislation and the freeing of interest rates. Such changes can create a range of effects and some of the evidence on their impact has been noted in Chapter 7. It is likely, however, that shifts in factor prices will be only one of several influences on technology choice, and one can argue that even allowing for market distortions the market wages in developing countries should still be low enough to create pressures for the adoption of labour-using technologies. This implies that whilst factor pricing can have some impact on technology choice, it is unlikely to be a major concern of technology policy. This means that decisions on the level of interest and wage rates should be taken primarily on other grounds, for example, in terms of their effect on savings and investment, the distribution of income, or inflation, rather than for their likely impact on the factor-intensity of production.

Treatment of foreign investors

It has been argued in Chapter 4 that whilst foreign investment can be a progressive force raising the productive capacity of developing countries, there are also potential costs from collaboration with transnationals. An industrial policy should identify branches where foreign participation can be beneficial and the conditions under which such participation should be undertaken. This means that government should examine in detail proposals for foreign investment, assess their economic and social impact, and where possible negotiate to improve the terms on which transnationals invest in the economy.

Foreign investment normally comes as a package covering finance, technology, equipment and management services, and

317

one immediate question is whether it is appropriate to accept this package, or attempt to 'unbundle' it, so that transnationals are required to supply only individual elements such as technology or management services.[38] Where joint ventures involving foreign equity participation are decided upon there are generally a number of major issues for negotiation including: the tax incentives and protection offered to the transnational; the share of equity to be held by the national side; the extent to which linkages are established with local input suppliers; the restrictions imposed on the use of the technology that is transferred; and the role of foreign appointees in the management structure of the joint venture. Cost-benefit analysis can be used to assess the economic viability of alternative forms of involvement with transnational firms.[39] However since this type of calculation will be on a case-by-case basis it must be supplemented by a broader strategic view of the role assigned to foreign capital in economic development. This is likely to involve the identification of the sectors or branches that are open to foreign investment and guidelines on minimum requirements that foreign investors must meet.

Experience, particularly in Latin America, suggests the importance of using foreign investment to complement not weaken existing national firms. This implies the need to be selective in the industrial branches in which foreign investment is allowed, since where national producers are already established an open-door policy can lead to the denationalisation of an industry. Foreign investment can be encouraged where it provides resources — either of technology, foreign finance or management — that would otherwise be lacking or available at higher cost. However there is a need both to protect the interests of competing national firms, and to control the activities of transnationals, where it is felt that their interests and those of the economy in general imply different policies. It must be stressed however that where controls are imposed, for example, forcing foreign firms to export a proportion of their output, or utilising a certain proportion of local inputs, it is necessary to ensure that the objectives behind the controls are economically valid. If this is not the case, for example exports may be made at a high cost in domestic resources, and the locally purchased inputs may be of a low quality, thus reducing the competitiveness of the final product. It is clear that such dealings with foreign investors require a significant amount of information, particularly on alternative sources of supply to the foreign firm involved, and a technically competent and honest bureaucracy to implement policy in this area.

Picking winners

What is often described as picking winners is clearly an integral part of an infant-industry strategy. What is required is to identify dynamic industries, where local producers, currently uncompetitive, have the potential for productivity growth leading over time to cost reductions and international competitiveness. An assessment of industries using cost-benefit techniques will give guidelines on the efficiency of existing operations, however, picking winners involves projections of future costs and quality of output. General guidance can be given on some of the characteristics of dynamic industries, however, projections of productivity growth will have to be based in part on judgements regarding the potential of different activities.[40]

It is difficult to set out clear guidelines on selecting potential dynamic industries, however a few general comments can be made. Most developing countries will be picking winners not on, but well within the existing technology frontier. In other words, they will not be seeking to invest in activities that embody radically new technology, but in established industries with a past record of productivity gains. The performance of these industries in countries with similar production conditions provides one simple indication of their productivity potential. Naturally one cannot simply assume that success elsewhere will be reproduced in all countries, but it is generally argued that it is easier to pick winners within, rather than on, the international technology frontier.

Technological similarity between a new activity and existing industries can be important for a dynamic industry, since managers, workers, and researchers, are more likely to experiment, adapt and modify to create productivity growth, if they are already familiar with the basic technology involved. This is likely to be consistent with the emphasis on relatively mature industries just noted.

Another important feature is likely to be the potential to produce output that can be differentiated from goods produced

319

abroad, both in quality and product specifications. Where this occurs industries can secure a section of the domestic market that is non-competing with imports. Thus by modifying their output producers can rely for profitability on the advantages of proximity to and knowledge of local markets, rather than on import protection. In these circumstances rapid productivity growth abroad need not undermine local producers, who will be concentrating on essentially non-traded goods. This category of non-traded goods will be particularly significant, where there is a growing mass market for which locally designed or adapted products can be produced at a cost which makes them accessible to low-income consumers. These goods will often come from small-scale firms and a major aim of government small-industry policy should be to encourage this type of production.

Finally in identifying potential dynamic industries, the focus should not be simply on productivity and cost performance in individual firms, but should allow for their impact on productivity and costs in user or supplier activities. This means that firms or industries that in terms of their own performance never appear dynamic, may none the less stimulate important gains elsewhere, and thus be winners in economic not private terms. One needs to assess the likely external benefits of such activities, and to estimate whether they will be of sufficient magnitude to justify special protection for the industry concerned. The difficulty of quantifying externalities has been noted, but they are likely to be correlated with the number of linkages generated by an investment. Since not all linkages are necessarily economically beneficial, it is the number of economically viable linkages that are relevant for a consideration of positive external effects. These effects are likely to be particularly significant, where a new investment generates backward linkages with supplying activities previously working at below full capacity, due to a demand constraint. Here the economic cost of supply of additional inputs will be variable costs that do not include an element of capital charge, and extra wage and profit incomes will be generated in these supplying activities.

The Neoclassical view is that it is very difficult for governments to pick winners, since they lack the relevant data and expertise and that such decisions should be left to private sector initiatives, once price reforms have generated the appropriate market environment. This argument can be questioned however, in relation to the developing countries where there is difficulty in introducing major market reforms and thus removing the major divergences between private and economic costs, and where the private sector remains weak. A major part of industrial policy lies in taking a broad view of where the most important growth areas for industry will lie. These growth areas then become priorities to be stimulated and encouraged by the range of selective measures discussed here.

CONCLUSION

The chapter argues the case for active industrial interventions for those countries where governments have the political base and technical expertise to mount such a policy. The evidence surveyed in this study indicates that a substantial degree of industrialisation has occurred in many developing countries, often with heavy government involvement. However at times this involvement has generated economic costs. There are lessons to be learnt, and it is argued that reformulated policies can be instrumental in stimulating and guiding industrial growth.

On the familiar debate of inward- versus outward-looking industrialisation, what matters is that opportunities for efficient import-substitution and export promotion are both taken. Export growth has been neglected in a number of countries in the past, but the current international economic environment does not create optimism that rapid rates of export expansion can be maintained in the long-run for many developing countries.

Perhaps the most significant concluding point is that whilst necessary to development in a broad sense, industrialisation is by no means sufficient. Simply raising the share of industry in national income, or reaching self-sufficiency in certain industrial products, is likely to be insufficient to solve many pressing economic and social problems. In the past perhaps too much has been expected of industrialisation *per se*, which explains the disappointment when progress in the growth of industry is not necessarily accompanied by improvements in important economic and social indicators. The potential of industry to solve wider problems is limited in the economic sphere by government macro-policies and in the social by existing class and institutional structures. Industrialisation is one step on a long path to development in the broadest sense.

321

NOTES

1. This is not to deny that trade can be an important source of growth for certain economies, chiefly those with few domestic resources, a small domestic market, and an active trading community. See for example, Fong and Lim (1985) on Singapore, and Sung (1985) on Hong Kong.

2. See for example Guisinger (1980). Choksi (1979) surveys the price controls and investment licensing procedures in use in the 1970s.

3. See Balassa (1986).

4. See Joshi (1972) for a discussion of these arguments.

5. See Stewart and Streeten (1972) and the response by Little and Mirrlees (1972).

6. Forward linkages will be estimated however if it is assumed that the output of an industrial project is non-traded, so that imports are not an alternative source of supply. Powers (1981) explains the use of input-output analysis in cost-benefit appraisals.

7. See Weiss (1986b). One can also add a political economy argument to the objections noted in the text. This is that cost-benefit appraisals are in no sense 'social'; that is representing the interest of society, but are government appraisals representing government interests. In class societies it is argued governments represent class forces and are in no sense neutral agents; see Stewart (1975). One can note this argument, but still see cost-benefit analysis as part of the planning techniques of a developmental capitalist state, that can be used to raise material conditions.

8. The comparative advantage trade measures discussed in Chapter 6 are *ex-post*, and therefore of limited value for planning purposes.

9. Weiss (1987) surveys shadow price estimates for Nepal, Jamaica and Ethiopia.

10. For example Boltho (1985) and Weiss (1986a).

11. For example Blumenthal and Lee (1985).

12. Sutcliffe (1971), pp. 16–63, surveys evidence on patterns of industrial growth.

13. It is interesting that Francis Stewart once a firm critic of export-oriented strategies now concedes that in the absence of a radical commitment to reforms, import-substitution behind trade barriers can lead to worse outcomes in terms of employment and income distribution than would a more open trading policy: see Stewart and Ghani (1986).

14. For South Korea and Taiwan in this context see de Melo (1985) and Nishimizu and Robinson (1984); for Japan, see Weiss (1986a) and for Argentina and Brazil, see Teitel and Thoumi (1986).

15. See Rhee *et al.* (1984).

16. Morawetz (1981) gives a detailed case-study of clothing exports from Colombia. Their loss of market share in the USA is explained partly by a deterioration in financial incentives to export, but also by high costs, poor quality and delivery performance. High costs are put down in large part to the use of domestically produced and protected synthetic and cotton fabric inputs.

17. For example, Bond (1985) estimates the income elasticity of demand for total real exports of the group of developing countries classed as 'major exporters of manufactures' at 2.91; the corresponding income elasticity of 'all low-income countries, excluding India and China' is 1.28. Primary exports are clearly more important for the latter group than for the former. IMF (1986b), table 60, p. 166 summarises alternative estimates of income elasticities for the exports of developing countries.

18. The IMF also produces medium-term projections. IMF (1986a) considers the period 1987–91, and gives a number of alternatives, most of which are closer to the World Bank's low rather than high case. The IMF 'base-line' case, for example, projects a growth of GDP in the industrial countries of just over 3 per cent per year, a growth of GDP in capital importing developing countries of just under 5 per cent, and a similar growth in their total exports.

19. Anjaria *et al.* (1985), p. 3. The following paragraphs draw heavily on this survey.

20. Anjaria *et al.* (1985), p . 79.

21. Yeats (1979) gives details of non-tariff barriers affecting developing countries in the 1970s.

22. World Bank (1986), table 2.5, p. 23. These estimates are not comprehensive since they exclude the effect of monitoring measures anti-dumping and countervailing duties. They refer to total non-fuel exports. For further details see Nogues *et al.* (1986).

23. The estimates of restrictions in different developed countries come from Cline (1984) cited in Anjaria *et al.* (1985). The proportion of South Korea's major exports subject to non-tariff restrictions is estimated to have increased from 31 per cent in 1981 to 42 per cent in 1982; see Anjaria *et al.* (1985), p. 81.

24. Balassa (1984b), table 4, p. 17, demonstrates that it is only in clothing that imports from developing countries are a significant share of total consumption in developed country markets; that is 14 per cent in 1981. Even for textiles imports from developing countries are only 3 per cent of total consumption in 1981.

25. Kirmani *et al.* (1984) give some estimates of the export response to liberalisation for the products and markets they consider. The once-for-all increase in exports over all four markets varies between product categories, in the range of 90 per cent for clothing to 30 per cent for footwear. Ten developing countries are covered and on average the increase in their exports of the four products is 16 per cent. The results are particularly sensitive to the assumed elasticity of export supply, and the figures cited here assume an infinite elasticity.

26. Weiss (1986a) discusses the impact of a timetable for liberalisation in Japan in the 1960s.

27. For example Kwang (1985), p. 60, lists the export incentives employed at various times in South Korea. As we have noted, access to intermediates at world prices was a key aspect of export promotion in South Korea.

28. This recommendation would also apply to the restructuring industries provided they are genuinely competitive internationally once costs are calculated in economic terms.

29. Lim (1980) gives a general discussion of taxation policy in developing countries. Weiss (1984b) examines the incentive system used in Mexico in the late-1970s and early-1980s and concludes that it had only a limited impact on industrial structure and growth.

30. Ozawa (1980) gives a Japanese case-study of the government's control over the number of firms in an industry through its licensing powers for technology imports. Much of the evidence on the cost of direct controls comes from India; see particularly Bhagwati and Desai (1970).

31. See Roe (1984) for a survey of the issues in restructuring. Dore (1986) discusses examples of such policies in Japan.

32. Anderson (1982) surveys many of these issues.

33. Few developing countries appear to have been successful in legislating against restrictive business practices; see Kirkpatrick *et al*. (1984), pp. 206–7.

34. Whitworth (1982) discusses price control in Tanzania, and notes both the theoretical limitations of a cost-plus pricing system, and the small number of trained personnel available to administer the policy.

35. Ozawa (1974) examines Japanese government activity in this area in the 1950s and 1960s. Enos (1984) gives a case-study from South Korea.

36. India is the developing country where it is sometimes argued that protection of technology rather than production has been relatively successful. However, productivity growth in industry has been very low; see the data in Goldar (1986).

37. See Rosenberg (1976) for historical evidence. Little (1982) despite general scepticism about the importance of externalities acknowledges that mechanical engineering production of this type may merit infant-industry protection on these grounds.

38. Weiss (1986a) discusses Japanese policy in the 1950s and 1960s towards unbundling the foreign investment package. Restricting direct investment in Japan was used to induce foreign firms to transfer their technology, since technology licensing was the only means of exploiting this technology in the Japanese market.

39. See Weiss (1980). Lall and Streeten (1977) discuss the issue of bargaining with transnationals.

40. See Weiss (1986b) for a discussion of some of these issues.

Bibliography

Adelman, I. (1986) 'A Poverty Focussed Approach to Development Policy' in J. P. Lewis and V. Kallab (eds) *Development Strategies Reconsidered*, Transaction Books, Oxford

—— and Morris, C. (1973) *Economic Growth and Social Equity in Developing Countries*, Stanford University Press, Stanford, Calif.

Adhikari, R. (1986a) 'Industrial Projects and Economic Policies: Future Lessons from Past Projects (Nepal)' *Project Appraisal*, vol. 1, no. 3, pp. 177–87

—— (1986b) *Economic Efficiency of Manufacturing Industries in Nepal*, University of Bradford unpublished Ph. D. thesis

Agarwala, R. (1983) 'Price Distortions and Growth in Developing Countries', *World Bank Staff Working Paper*, no. 575, World Bank, Washington, D.C.

Ahluwalia, M. S. (1976) 'Inequality, Poverty and Development', *Journal of Development Economics*, vol. 3, no. 4. pp. 307–42

Amin, S. (1974a) *Accumulation on a World Scale*, Monthly Review Press, New York

—— (1974b) 'Accumulation and Development', *Review of African Political Economy*, vol. 1, no. 1. pp. 9–26

—— (1977) *Imperialism and Unequal Development*, Monthly Review Press, New York

—— (1980) *Class and Nation, Historically and in the Current Crisis*, Heinemann, London

Amsalem, M. A. (1983) *Technology Choice in Developing Countries: The Textile and Pulp and Paper Industries*, MIT Press, London

Amsden, A. H. (1977) 'The Division of Labour is limited by the Type of Market: The Case of the Taiwanese Machine Tool Industry', *World Development*, vol. 5, no. 3, pp. 217–33

—— (1984) 'Taiwan', *World Development*, vol. 12, no. 5/6, pp. 491–503

—— (1985) 'The Division of Labour is Limited by the Rate of Growth of the Market: The Taiwan Machine-tool Industry in the 1970s', *Cambridge Journal of Economics*, vol. 9, no. 3, pp. 271–84

Anderson, D. (1982) 'Small industry in developing countries: a discussion of issues', *World Development*, vol. 10, no. 11, pp. 913–48

Anjaria, S. J., Kirmani, N. and Petersen, A. B. (1985) 'Trade Policy: Issues and Developments', *IMF Occasional Paper*, no. 38, International Monetary Fund, Washington, D.C.

Arndt, H. W. (1985) 'The Origins of Structuralism', *World Development*, vol. 13, no. 2, pp. 151–9

Ayub, M. A. (1981) *Made in Jamaica: The Development of the Manufacturing Sector*, Johns Hopkins University Press, Baltimore, Md. (for the World Bank)

Bacha, E. L. (1978) 'An Interpretation of unequal exchange from Prebisch-Singer to Emmanuel', *Journal of Development Economics*, vol. 5, no. 4. pp. 319–30

Baer, W. (1971) 'The Economics of Prebisch and the ECLA' reprinted in I. Livingstone (ed.) *Economic Policy for Development*, Penguin, London, pp. 178–96

Bairoch, P. (1975) *The Economic Development of the Third World Since 1900*, Methuen, London

Balassa, B. (1971) *The Structure of Protection in Developing Countries*, Johns Hopkins University Press, Baltimore, Md.

—— (1974) 'Estimating the Shadow Price of Foreign Exchange in Project Appraisal', *Oxford Economic Papers*, vol. 26, no. 2, pp. 147–68

—— (1975) 'Trade, Protection and Domestic Production: A Comment', in P. Kenen (ed.), *International Trade and Finance*, Cambridge University Press, Cambridge, pp. 154–63

—— (1977) 'A stages approach to comparative advantage', *World Bank Staff Working Paper*, no. 256, World Bank, Washington, D.C.

—— (1978) 'Exports and Economic Growth: Further Evidence', *Journal of Development Economics*, vol. 5, no. 2, pp. 181–9

—— (1982) *Development Strategies in Semi-Industrial Economies*, Johns Hopkins University Press, Baltimore, Md. (for the World Bank)

—— (1984a) 'Adjustment Policies in Developing Countries: A Reassessment', *World Development*, vol. 12, no. 9, pp. 955–72

—— (1984b) 'Trends in International Trade in Manufactured Goods and Structural Change in the Industrial Countries', *World Bank Staff Working Paper*, no. 611, World Bank, Washington, D.C.

—— (1986) 'China's Economic Reforms in a Comparative Perspective', *World Bank Development Research Department Discussion Paper*, no. 177, World Bank, Washington, D.C.

Ballance, R., Ansari, J. A. and Singer, H. (1982) *The International Economy and Industrial Development: The Impact of Trade and Investment on the Third World*, Wheatsheaf, Brighton

Baran, P. (1957) *The Political Economy of Growth*, Monthly Review Press, New York

Baranson, J. (1967) *Manufacturing Problems in India*, Syracuse University Press, Syracuse, N.Y.

Barker, C. E., Bhagavan, M. R. and Wield, D. V. (1986) *African Industrialization: Technology and Change in Tanzania*, Gower, Farnborough

Bautista, R., Hughes, H., Lim, D. Morawetz, D. and Thoumi, F. E. (1981), *Capital Utilization in Manufacturing: Colombia, Israel, Malaysia and the Philippines*, Oxford University Press, New York (for the World Bank)

Behrman, J. (1976) *Foreign Trade Regimes and Economic Development: Chile*, Ballinger, Cambridge, Mass.

Bell, M., Scott-Kemis, D. and Satyarakwit, W. (1982) 'Limited Learning in Infant-Industry: A case-study' in F. Stewart and J.

James (eds) *The Economics of New Technology in Developing Countries*, Frances Pinter, London pp. 138–56

Bell, M. (1984) 'Learning and the Accumulation of Industrial Technological Capacity in Developing Countries' in M. Fransman and J. King *Technological Capability in the Third World*, Macmillan, London pp. 187–209

——, Ross-Larson, B. and Westphal, L. E. (1984) 'Assessing the Performance of Infant-Industries', *Journal of Development Economics*, vol. 16, no. 1/2, pp. 101–28

Bergsman, J. (1974) 'Commercial Policy, Allocative Efficiency and X-Efficiency', *Quarterly Journal of Economics*, vol. 88, no. 3, pp. 409–33

Berry, A. and Sabot, R. (1978) 'Labour Market Performance in Developing Countries', *World Development*, vol. 6, no. 11/12, pp. 1199–242

——, Bourguignon, F. and Morrison, C. (1983) 'Changes in World Distribution of Income between 1950 and 1977', *Economic Journal*, vol. 93, no. 370, pp. 331–50

Betancourt, R. P. (1981) 'The Utilisation of Industrial Capital and Employment Promotion in Developing countries' in N. Phan-Thuy, R. P. Betancourt, G. C. Winston and M. Kabaj *Industrial Capacity and Employment Promotion*, Gower, Farnborough (for the International Labour Organisation), pp. 26–91

—— and Clague, C. K. (1981) *Capital Utilization: A Theoretical and Empirical Analysis*, Cambridge University Press, Cambridge

Bettelheim, C. (1972) 'Theoretical Comments', Appendix 1, in A. Emmanuel, *Unequal Exchange: A Study in the Imperialism of Trade*, New Left Books, London, pp. 271–322

Beyer, J. C. (1975) 'Estimating the Shadow Price of Foreign Exchange: An Illustration from India', *Journal of Development Studies*, vol. 11, no. 4, pp. 302–15

Bhagwati, J. (1968) 'The Theory and Practice of Commercial Policy: Departures from Unified Exchange Rates', *Special Papers in International Economics*, no. 8, Princeton University Press, Princeton, N.J.

—— (1978) *Anatomy and Consequences of Exchange Control Regimes*, Ballinger, Cambridge, Mass.

—— (1984) 'Comment' in G. M. Meier and D. Seers (eds) *Pioneers in Development*, Oxford University Press, New York (for the World Bank), pp. 197–204

—— and Desai, P. (1970) *India: Planning for Industrialization*, Oxford University Press, London

—— and Srinivasan, T. N. (1975) *Foreign Trade Regimes and Economic Development: India*, Columbia University Press, New York

Bienefeld, M. (1981) 'Dependency and the Newly Industralising Countries (NICs): Towards a Re-appraisal' in D. Seers (ed.) *Dependency Theory: A Critical Reassessment*, Frances Pinter, London, pp. 79–96

Bigsten, A. (1983) *Income Distribution and Development: Theory, Evidence and Policy*, Heinemann, London

Bird, G. (1983) 'Should Developing Countries Use Currency Depreciation as a Tool of Balance of Payments Adjustment? A Review of the Theory and Evidence and a Guide for the Policy Maker', *Journal of Development Studies*, vol. 19, no. 4, pp. 461–84

Blomstrom, M. (1986) 'Multinationals and Market Structure in Mexico', *World Development*, vol. 14, no. 4, pp. 523–30

—— and Hettne, B. (1984) *Development Theory in Transition*, Zed Books, London

Blumenthal, T. and Lee C. H. (1985) 'Development Strategies of Japan and the Republic of Korea: A Comparative Study', *The Developing Economies*, vol. 23, no. 3, pp. 222–35

Boltho, A. (1985) 'Was Japan's Industrial Policy Successful?' *Cambridge Journal of Economics*, vol. 9, no. 2, pp. 185–201

Bond, M. (1985) 'Export Demand and Supply for Groups of Non-Oil Developing countries', *IMF Staff Papers*, vol. 32, no. 1, pp. 56–77

Booth, D. (1985) 'Marxism and Development Sociology: Interpreting the Impasse', *World Development*, vol. 13, no. 7, pp. 761–87

Bornschier, V. and Chase-Dunn, C. (1985) *Transnational Corporations and Underdevelopment*, Praeger, New York

Brailovsky, V. (1981) 'Industrialisation and Oil in Mexico: A Long Term perspective' in T. Barker and V. Brailovsky (eds) *Oil or Industry*, Academic Press, New York, pp. 71–134

Brewer, A. (1980) *Marxist Theories of Imperialism: A Critical Survey*, Routledge and Kegan Paul, London

Brodersohn, M. S. (1981) *Financing of Industrial Enterprises and Financial Repression in Latin America*, United Nations Industrial Development Organisation, Vienna

Browett, J. (1985) 'The Newly Industrializing Countries and Radical Theories of Development', *World Development*, vol. 13. no. 7, pp. 789–803

Bruno, M. (1985) 'The Reforms and Macroeconomic Adjustments: Introduction', *World Development*, vol. 13, no. 8, pp. 867–9

Byres, T. (1982) 'India: Capitalist Industrialization or Structural Stasis' in M. Bienefeld and M. Godfrey (eds) *The Struggle for Development: National Strategies in an International Context*, John Wiley, Chichester pp. 135–64

Carciofi, R. 1982) 'Cuba in the Seventies' in G. White, R. Murray and C. White (eds) *Revolutionary Socialist Development in the Third World*, Wheatsheaf, Brighton pp. 193–233

Cardoso, F. H. (1977) 'The Consumption of Dependency Theory in the United States', *Latin American Research Review*, vol. 12, no. 3, pp. 7–24

—— and Faletto, E. (1979) *Dependency and Development in Latin America*, University of California Press, Berkeley, Cal.

Chenery, H. (1979) *Structural Change and Development Policy*, Oxford University Press, New York (for the World Bank)

—— (1980) 'Poverty and Progress — Choices for the Developing World', *Finance and Development*, vol. 17, no. 2, pp. 12–16.

—— and Syrquin, M. (1975) *Patterns of Development 1950–70*, Oxford University Press, London

——, Ahluwalia, M. S. and Carter, N. G. (1979) 'Growth and Poverty in Developing Countries' in H. Chenery *Structural Change and Development Policy*, Oxford University Press, New York (for the World Bank), pp. 456–95

Choksi, A. M. (1979) 'State Intervention in the Industrialization of Developing Countries: Selected Issues', *World Bank Staff Working Paper*, no. 341, World Bank, Washington, D.C.

—— and Papageorgiu, D. (eds) (1985) *Economic Liberalization in Developing Countries*, Basil Blackwell, Oxford

Chudnovsky, D. (1979) 'The Challenge by Domestic Enterprises to Transnational Corporation's Domination: A Case-Study of the Argentine Pharmaceutical Industry', *World Development*, vol. 7, no. 1, pp. 45–58

——, Nagao, M. and Jacobsson, S. (1983) *Capital Goods Production in the Third World: An Economic Study of Technical Acquisition*, Frances Pinter, London

Cline, W. R. (1982) 'Can the East Asian Model of Development be generalized?' *World Development*, vol. 10, no. 2, pp. 81–90

—— (1984) *Exports of Manufactures from Developing Countries: Performance and Prospects for Market Access*, Brookings Institution, Washington, D.C

—— (1985) 'Reply', *World Development*, vol. 13, no. 4, pp. 547–8

Cody, H., Hughes, H. and Wall, D. (eds) (1980) *Policies for Industrial Progress in Developing Countries*, Oxford University Press, Oxford (for the World Bank)

Corbo, V. and de Melo, J. (1985) 'Overview and Summary', *World Development*, vol. 13, no. 8, pp. 863–6

——, de Melo, J. and Tybout, J. (1986) 'What Went Wrong with Recent Reforms in the Southern Cone?', *Economic Development and Cultural Change*, vol. 34, no. 3, pp. 607–40

Corden, W. M. (1971) *The Theory of Protection*, Clarendon Press, Oxford

—— (1974) *Trade Policy and Economic Welfare*, Clarendon Press, Oxford

—— (1975) 'The Costs and Consequences of Protection: A Survey of Empirical Work' in P. Kenen (ed.) *International Trade and Finance*, Cambridge University Press, Cambridge, pp. 51–91

—— (1980) 'Trade Policies' in J.Cody, H. Hughes and D. Wall (eds) *Policies for Industrial Progress in Developing Countries*, Oxford University Press, Oxford, (for the World Bank), pp. 39–92

Cornwall, J. (1977) *Modern Capitalism*, Martin Robertson, London

Cortes-Douglas, H. (1985) 'Opening Up and Liberalizing the Chilean Economy' in V. Corbo, A. E. Krueger and F. Ossa (eds) *Export Oriented Development Strategies: The Success of Five Newly Industrializing Countries*, Westview Press, Boulder, Col., pp. 155–86

Cripps, T. F. and Tarling, R. (1973) 'Growth in Advanced Capitalist Economies (1950–70)', *Occasional Paper* no. 40, Department of Applied Economics, Cambridge University, Cambridge

Dahlman, C. (1984) 'Foreign Technology and Indigenous Technological Capability in Brazil' in 'M. Fransman and K. King (eds)

Technological Capability in the Third World, Macmillan, London pp. 317–34

—— and Westphal, L. E. (1982) 'Technological Effort in Industrial Development: an Interpretive Survey of Recent Research' in F. Stewart and J. James (eds) *The Economics of New Technology in Developing Countries*, Frances Pinter, London, pp. 105–37

—— and Carter, M. (1984) 'Mexico', *World Development*, vol. 12, no. 5/6, pp. 601–20

—— and Sercovitch, F. (1984) 'Exports of Technology from Semi-Industrial Economies and Local Technological Development', *Journal of Development Economics*, vol. 16, no. 1/2, pp. 63–99

David, W. L. (1986) *Conflicting Paradigms in the Economics of Developing Nations*, Praeger, New York

Diaz-Alejandro, C. (1975) *Foreign Trade Regimes and Economic Development: Colombia*, Columbia University Press, New York

Domar, E. D. (1957) *Essays in the Theory of Economic Growth*, Oxford University Press, New York

Donges, J. B. (1976) 'A Comparative Survey of Industrialization Policies in Fifteen Semi-industrial Countries', *Weltwirtschaftliches Archiv*, vol. 112, no. 4, pp. 626–59

—— and Reidel, J. (1977) 'The Expansion of Manufactured Exports from Developing Countries: An Empirical Assessment of Demand and Supply Issues', *Weltwirtschaftliches Archiv*, vol. 113, no. 2, pp. 250–67

Dore, R. P. (1986) *Structural Adjustment in Japan 1970–82*, International Labour Office, Geneva

Dos Santos, T. (1981) 'The Structure of Dependence' reprinted in I. Livingstone (ed.) *Development Economics and Policy: Readings*, Allen and Unwin, London pp. 143–7

Dunning, J. H. (1981) *International Production and the Multinational Enterprise*, Allen and Unwin, London

Edwards, S. (1985) 'Stabilization with Liberalization: An Evaluation of Ten Year's of Chile's Experiment with Free-Market Policies 1973–1983', *Economic Development and Cultural Change*, vol. 33, no. 2, pp. 223–54

—— (1986) 'Monetarism in Chile 1973–1983: Some Economic Puzzles', *Economic Development and Cultural Change*, vol. 34, no. 3, pp. 535–59

Emmanuel, A. (1972) *Unequal Exchange: A Study of the Imperialism of Trade*, New Left Books, London

Enos, J. (1984) 'Government Intervention in the Transfer of Technology: The Case of South Korea', *Institute of Development Studies Bulletin*, vol. 15, no. 2, pp. 26–31

Evans, D. (1981a) 'Unequal Exchange and Economic Policies: Some Implications of the Neo-Ricardian Critique of the Theory of Comparative Advantage' reprinted in I. Livingstone (ed.) *Development Economics and Policy: Readings*. Allen and Unwin, London, pp. 117–28

—— (1981b) 'Trade Production and Self-Reliance' in D. Seers (ed.) *Dependency Theory: A Critical Reassessment*, Frances Pinter, London pp. 119–34

—— and Alizadeh, P. (1984) 'Trade Industrialization and the Visible Hand', *Journal of Development Studies*, vol. 21, no. 1, pp. 22–46

Evans, P. (1976) 'Foreign Investment and Industrial Transformation: A Brazilian Case-study', *Journal of Development Economics*, vol. 3, no. 2, pp. 119–39

—— (1977) 'Direct Investment and Industrial Concentration', *Journal of Development Studies*, vol. 13, no. 4, pp. 373–86

—— (1979) *Dependent Development: The Alliance of Multinational, State, and Local Capital in Brazil*, Princeton University Press, Princeton, N.J.

—— (1986) 'The State Capital and the Transformation of Dependence: The Brazilian Computer Case', *World Development*, vol. 14, no. 1, pp. 791–808

Fairchild, L. G. (1977) 'Performance and Technology of United States and National Firms in Mexico', *Journal of Development Studies*, vol. 14, no. 1, pp. 14–34

—— and Kosin, K. (1986) 'Evaluating Differences in Technological Activity between Transnational and Domestic Firms in Latin America', *Journal of Development Studies*, vol. 22, no. 4, pp. 697–708

Fajnzylber, F. and Martinez-Tarrago, T. (1975) *Las Empresas Transnacionales*, Fondo de Cultura, Mexico City

Farooq, G. M. and Winston, G. C. (1978) 'Shift Working, Employment and Economic Development: A Study of Industrial Workers in Pakistan', *Economic Development and Cultural Change*, vol. 26, no. 2, pp. 227–44

Fei, J. C. H., Ohkawa, K. and Ranis, G. (1985) 'Economic Development in Historical Perspective: Japan, Korea and Taiwan' in K. Ohkawa, G. Ranis and L. Meissner (eds) *Japan and the Developing Countries: A Comparative Analysis*, Blackwell, New York, pp. 35–64

Ffrench-Davis, R. (1983) 'The Monetarist Experiment in Chile: A Critical Survey', *World Development*, vol. 11, no. 11, pp. 905–26

Fishlow, A. (1984) 'Summary Comment on Adelman, Balassa and Streeten', *World Development*, vol. 12, no. 9, pp. 979–82

Fitzgerald, E. V. K. (1985) 'The Problem of Balance in the Peripheral Socialist Economy: A Conceptual Note', *World Development*, vol. 13, no. 1, pp. 5–14

Flemming, J. M. (1958) 'External Economies and the Doctrine of Balanced Growth', reprinted in A. A. Agarwala and S. P. Singh *The Economics of Underdevelopment*, Oxford University Press, London, pp. 272–94

Fong, P. E. and Lim, L. (1985) 'Rapid Growth and Relative Price Stability In A Small Open Economy: The Experience of Singapore' in V. Corbo, A. O. Krueger and F. Ossa (eds) *Export Oriented Development Strategies: The Success of Five Newly Industrializing Countries*, Westview Press, Boulder, Col., pp. 79–110

Forsyth, D. (1985) 'Government Policy, Market Structure and Choice of Technology in Egypt' in J. James and S. Watanabe (eds) *Technology, Institutions, and Government Policies*, Macmillan, London (for the International Labour Organisation)

Foster-Carter, A. (1976) 'From Rostow to Gunder Frank: Conflicting Paradigms in the Analysis of Underdevelopment', *World Development*, vol. 4, no. 3, pp. 167–80

—— (1978) 'The Modes of Production Controversy', *New Left Review*, no. 107, pp. 47–77

Foxley, A. (1983) *Latin American Experiments with Neoconservative Economics*, University of California Press, Berkley, Cal.

Frank, A. G. (1967) *Capitalism and Underdevelopment in Latin America*, Monthly Review Press, New York

—— (1969) *Latin America: Underdevelopment or Revolution*? Monthly Review Press, New York

Fransman, M. (1982) 'Learning and the Capital Goods Sector under Free Trade: The Case of Hong King', *World Development*, vol. 10, no. 11, pp. 991–1014

—— (1984) 'Exploring the Success of the Asian NICs: incentives and technology', *Institute of Development Studies Bulletin*, vol. 15, no. 2, pp. 50–6

—— (1985) 'Conceptualising Technical Change in the Third World in the 1980's: an Interpretive Survey', *Journal of Development Studies*, vol. 21, no. 4, pp. 572–652

Frobel, F., Heinrichs, J. and Kreye, O. (1981) *The New International Division of Labour: Structural Unemployment in Industrialised Countries and Industrialisation in Developing Countries*. Cambridge University Press, Cambridge

Fry, M. J. (1980) 'Saving, Investment, Growth and the Cost of Financial Repression', *World Development*, vol. 8, no. 4, pp. 317–27

—— (1985) 'Financial Structure, Monetary Policy and Economic Growth in Hong Kong, Singapore, Taiwan and South Korea 1960–83' in V. Corbo, A. O. Krueger and F. Ossa (eds) *Export-Oriented Development Strategies: The Success of Five Newly Industrializing Countries*, Westview Press, Boulder, Col. pp. 275–324

Galbis, V. (1979) 'Money, Investment and Growth in Latin America 1963–73', *Economic Development and Cultural Change*, vol. 27, no. 3, pp. 423–43

Gereffi, G. (1983) *The Pharmaceutical Industry and Dependency in the Third World*, Princeton University Press, Princeton, N.J.

Godfrey, M. (1982), 'Kenya: African Capitalism or Simple Dependency!' in M. Bienefeld and M. Godfrey (eds) *The Struggle for Development: National Strategies in an International Context*, John Wiley, Chichester, pp. 265–91

Goldar, B. (1986) 'Import Substitution, Industrial Concentration and Productivity Growth in Indian Manufacturing', *Oxford Bulletin of Economics and Statistics*, vol. 48, no. 2, pp. 143–64

Government of Mexico (1984) *Programa Nacional de Fomento Industrial Y Commercio Exterior 1984–1988*, Mexico City

Green, R. H. (1982) 'Industrialization in Tanzania' in M. Fransman (ed.) *Industry and Accumulation in Africa*, Heinemann, London, pp.80–104

Griffin, K. and Gurley, J. (1985) 'Radical Analysis of Imperialism, The Third World, and the Transition to Socialism: A Survey Article', *Journal of Economic Literature*, vol. 23, no. 3, pp. 1089–143

—— and James, J. (1981) *The Transition to Egalitarian Development: Economic Policies for Structural Change in the Third World*, Macmillan, London

Guisinger, S. E. (1980) 'Direct Controls on the Private Sector' in J. Cody, H. Hughes and D. Wall (eds) *Policies for Industrial Progress in Developing Countries*, Oxford University Press, Oxford, pp. 189–209 (for the World Bank).

Gurley, J. (1979) 'Economic Development: A Marxist View' in K. Jameson and C. K. Wilber (eds) *Directions in Economic Development*, University of Notre Dame Press, N.J., pp. 183–251

Hamilton, C. (1983) 'Capitalist Industrialization in the Four Little Tigers of East Asia' in P. Limqueco and B. MacFarlane (eds) *Neo-Marxist Theories of Development*, Croom Helm, London, pp. 137–80

Harberger, A. C. (1985) 'A Primer on the Chilean Economy 1973–1983' in A. M. Choksi and D. Papageorgiu (eds) *Economic Liberalization in Developing Countries*, Basil Blackwell, Oxford, pp. 233–40

Havrylyshyn, O. and Alikhani, I. (1982) 'Is there a case for export optimism? An inquiry into the existence of a second generation of successful exporters', *Weltwirtshaftliches Archiv*, vol. 118, no. 4, pp. 651–63

Herrick, B. and Kindleberger, C. (1983) *Economic Development*, McGraw-Hill, Tokyo

Hirschman, A. O. (1958) *The Strategy of Economic Development*, Yale University Press, New Haven, Conn.

—— (1968) 'The Political Economy of Import Substitution Industrialization', *Quarterly Journal of Economics*, vol. 82, no. 1, pp. 1–32

—— (1981) 'The Rise and Decline of Development Economics' in M. Gersovitz, C. Diaz-Alejandro, G. Ranis and M. R. Rosenzweig *The Theory and Experience of Economic Development*, Allen and Unwin, London, pp. 372–90

Hone, A. (1974) 'Multinational Corporations and Multinational Buying Groups: Their Impact on the Growth of Asias Exports of Manufactures — Myths and Realities', *World Development*, vol. 2, no. 2, pp. 145–9

Hsia, R. and Chau, L. (1978) *Industrialization, Employment and Income Distribution: a Case-Study of Hong Kong*, Croom Helm, London (for the International Labour Organisation)

Hufbauer, G. C. (1971) 'West Pakistan Exports: Effective Taxation, Policy Promotion and Sectoral Discrimination' reprinted in W. P. Falcon and G.F. Papanek (eds) *Development Policy II: The Pakistan Experience*, Harvard University Press, Cambridge, Mass., pp. 56–114.

Hughes, H. (1978) 'Industrialization and Development: A Stocktaking', *Industry and Development*, no. 2, pp. 1–27

—— (1980) 'Achievements and Objectives of Industrialization' in J. Cody, H. Hughes and D. Wall (eds) *Policies for Industrial Progress in Developing Countries*, Oxford University Press, Oxford (for the World Bank), pp. 11–37

ILO (1984) *Yearbook of Labour Statistics*, International Labour Office, Geneva

IMF (1985) 'Foreign Private Investment in Developing Countries',

Occasional Paper, No. 33, International Monetary Fund, Washington, D.C.

—— (1986a) *World Economic Outlook April 1986*, International Monetary Fund, Washington, D.C.

—— (1986b) *Staff Studies for the World Economic Outlook July 1986*, International Monetary Fund, Washington, D.C.

Irvin, G. (1978) *Modern Cost-Benefit Methods*, Macmillan, London

Islam, N. (1972) 'Comparative Costs, Factor Proportions, and Industrial Efficiency in Pakistan' reprinted in K. Griffin and A. R. Khan *Growth and Inequality in Pakistan*, Macmillan, London, pp. 149–68

Jacobsson, S. (1984) 'Industrial Policy for the Machine Tool Industries of South Korea and Taiwan', *Institute of Development Studies Bulletin*, vol. 15, no. 2, pp. 44–9

Jacobsson, A. (1985) 'Technical Change and Industrial Policy: The Case of Numerically Controlled Lathes in Argentina, Korea and Taiwan', *World Development*, vol. 13, no. 3, pp. 353–70

Jameson, K. (1981) 'Socialist Cuba and the Intermediate Regimes of Jamaica and Guyana', *World Development*, vol. 9, no. 9/10, pp. 871–88

—— (1986) 'Latin America Stucturalism: A Methodological Perspective', *World Development*, vol. 14, no. 2, pp. 223–32

—— and Wilber, C. (1981) 'Socialism and Development: Editor's Introduction', *World Development*, vol. 9, no. 9/10, pp. 803–11

Jenkins, R. (1977) *Dependent Industrialization in Latin America: The Automotive Industry in Argentina, Chile and Mexico*, Praeger, New York

—— (1984) *Transnational Corporations and Industrial Transformation in Latin America*, Macmillan, London

—— (1986) 'Third World Multinationals: Rhetoric or Reality?' *Journal of Development Studies*, vol. 22, no. 2, pp. 458–63

Jessop, B. (1977) 'Recent Theories of the Capitalist State', *Cambridge Journal of Economics*, vol. 1, no. 4, pp. 353–73

Jones, H. (1975) *An Introduction to Modern Theories of Economic Growth*, Van Nostrand Reinhold, Wokingham

Jones, L. P. (1976) 'The Measurement of Hirschmanian Linkages', *Quarterly Journal of Economics*, vol. 90, no. 2, pp. 323–33

Joshi, V. J. (1972) 'The Rationale and Relevance of the Little-Mirrlees Criterion', *Oxford Bulletin of Economics and Statistics*, vol. 34, no. 1, pp. 3–32

Kaldor, N. (1966) *Causes of the Slow Rate of Economic Growth of the United Kingdom*, Cambridge University Press, Cambridge

—— (1967) *Strategic Factors in Economic Development*, Cornell University Press, Ithaca, N.Y.

—— (1975) 'Economic Growth and the Verdoorn Law: A Comment on Mr Rowthorn's Article', *Economic Journal*, vol. 85, no. 340, pp. 891–6

Kalecki. M. (1976) 'Observations on Social and Economic Aspects of Intermediate Regimes', in M. Kalecki, *Essays on Developing Economies*, Harvester Press, Hassocks, pp. 30–9

Kaplinsky, R. (1982) 'Capitalist Accumulation in the Periphery:

Kenya' in M. Fransman (ed.) *Industry and Accumulation in Africa*, Heinemann, London, pp. 193–221

—— (1984a) 'The International Context for Industrialization in the Coming Decade', *Journal of Development Studies*, vol. 21, no. 1, pp. 75–96

—— (1984b) 'Indigenous Technical Change: What We Can Learn from Sugar Processing', *World Development*, vol. 12, no. 4, pp. 413–32

Katz, J. (1984a) 'Technological Innovation, Industrial Organization and Comparative Advantages of Latin American Metal Work Industries' in M. Fransman and K. King (eds) *Technological Capability in the Third World*, Macmillan, London, pp. 113–36

—— (1984b) 'Domestic Technological Innovations and Dynamic Comparative Advantage', *Journal of Development Economics*, vol. 16, no. 1/2, pp. 13–37

Kay, G. (1975) *Development and Underdevelopment: a Marxist Analysis*, Macmillan, London

Kennedy, C. (1971) *Productivity and Industrial Growth*, Clarendon Press, Oxford

Keesing, D. (1979) World Trade and Output of Manufactures: Structural Trends and Developing Countries' Exports, *World Bank Staff Working Paper*, no. 316, World Bank, Washington, D.C.

Kidron, M. (1965) *Foreign Investments in India*, Oxford University Press, London

Killick, T. (1978) *Development Economics in Action: A Study of Economic Policies in Ghana*, Heinemann, London

Kim, Y. C. and Kwon, J. K. (1977) 'The Utilization of Capital and the Growth of Output in a Developing Economy', *Journal of Development Economics*, vol. 4, no. 3, pp. 265–78

Kirim, A. S. (1986) 'Transnational Corporations and Local Capital: Comparative Conduct and Performance in the Turkish Pharmaceutical Industry', *World Development*, vol. 14, no. 4, pp. 503–21

Kirkpatrick, C. H., Lee, N., Nixson, F. I. (1984) *Industrial Structure and Policy in Less Developed Countries*, Allen and Unwin, London

Kirmani, N., Molajoni, I. and Mayer,T. (1984) 'Effects of Increased Market Access on Exports of Developing Countries', *IMF Staff Papers*, vol. 31, no. 4, pp. 661–84

Kitchen, R. and Weiss, J. (1987) 'Prices and Government Interventions in Developing Countries', *Industry and Development*, pp. 51–99

Koo, B. Y. (1985) 'The Role of Direct Foreign Investment in Korea's Recent Economic Growth' in W. Galenson (ed.) *Foreign Trade and Investment: Economic Development in the Newly Industrializing Asian Countries*, University of Wisconsin Press, Madison, Wis., pp. 176–216

Krause, L. B. (1985) 'Introduction' in W. Galenson (ed.) *Foreign trade and Investment: Economic Growth in the Newly Industrializing Asian Countries*, University of Wisconsin Press, Madison, Wis., pp. 3–41

Krueger, A. O. (1972) 'Evaluating Restrictionist Trade Regimes:

Theory and Measurement', *Journal of Political Economy*, vol. 80, no. 1, pp. 48–62

—— (1974) *Foreign Trade Regimes and Economic Development: Turkey*, Columbia University Press, New York

—— (1978) *Liberalization Attempts and Consequences*, Ballinger, Cambridge, Mass. (for the National Bureau of Economic Research)

—— (1984) 'Trade Policies in Developing Countries' in R. W. Jones and P. B. Kenen (eds) *Handbook of International Economics*, vol. I, Elsevier Science Publishers, Amsterdam, pp. 519–69

—— (1985) 'The Experience and Lessons of Asia's Super Exporters', in V. Corbo, A. O. Krueger and F. Ossa (eds) *Export-Oriented Development Strategies: The Success of the Five Newly Industrializing countries*, Westview Press, Boulder, Col. pp. 187–212

—— and Tuncer, B. (1982) 'An Empirical Test of the Infant Industry Argument', *American Economic Review*, vol. 72, no. 5, pp. 1142–52

Kuznets, S. (1955) 'Economic Growth and Income Inequality', *American Economic Review*, vol. 45, no. 1, pp. 1–28

Kwang, S. K. (1985) 'Lessons from South Korea's Experience with Industrialization' in V. Corbo, A. O. Krueger and F. Ossa (eds) *Export Oriented Development Strategies: The Success of Five Newly Industrializing Countries*, Westview Press, Boulder, Col., pp. 57–78

Lall, S. (1975) 'Is "Dependence" a Useful Concept in Analysing Underdevelopment?', *World Development*, vol. 3, no. 11/12 pp. 799–810

—— (1978) 'Transnationals, Domestic Enterprises and Industrial Structure in Host LDCs: A Survey', *Oxford Economic Papers*, vol. 30, no.2, pp. 217–48

—— (1981) 'Recent Trends in Exports of Manufactures by Newly Industrializing Countries' in S. Lall *Developing Countries in the International Economy*, Macmillan, London, pp. 173–227

—— (1982) 'The Emergence of Third World Multinationals: Indian Joint Ventures Overseas', *World Development*, vol. 10, no. 2, pp. 127–46

—— (1984a) 'Exports of Technology by Newly Industrializing Countries: An Overview', *World Development*, vol. 12, no. 5/6, pp. 471–80

—— (1984b) *The New Multinationals: The Spread of Third World Enterprises*, John Wiley, Chichester

—— (1984c) 'India: Technological Capacity' in M. Fransman and K. King (eds) *Technological Capability in the Third World*, Macmillan, London, pp. 225–43

—— (1984d) 'India', *World Development*, vol. 12, no. 5/6, pp. 535–65

—— (1985a) 'Transnationals and the Third World: Changing Perceptions' in S. Lall, *Multinationals, Technology and Exports: Selected Papers*, Macmillan, London, pp. 65–81

—— (1985b) 'Multinationals and Technology Development in Host Countries' in S. Lall *Multinationals, Technology and Exports*, Macmillan, London, pp. 114–28

—— and Streeten, P. (1977) *Foreign Investment, Transnationals and Developing Countries*, Macmillan, London

Langdon, S. W. (1979) *Multinational Corporations in the Political Economy of Kenya*, Macmillan, London

—— (1984) 'Indigenous Technological Capability in Africa: the Case of Textiles and Wood Products in Kenya' in M. Fransman and K. King (eds), *Technological Capability in the Third World*, Macmillan, London, pp. 355–74

Laumas, P. S. (1976) 'The Weighting Problem in Testing the Linkages Hypothesis', *Quarterly Journal of Economics*, vol. 90, no. 2, pp. 308–12

Lecraw, D. J. (1978) 'Determinants of Capacity Utilization by Firms in Less Developed Countries', *Journal of Development Economics*, vol. 5, no. 2, pp. 139–53

Leite, S. P. and Vaez-Zadah, R. (1986) 'Credit Allocation and Investment Decisions: The Case of the Manufacturing Sector in Korea', *World Development*, vol. 14, no. 1, pp. 115–26

Lewis, W. A. (1955) *Theory of Economic Growth*, Allen and Unwin, London

Leys, C. (1982) 'Accumulation Class Formulation and Dependency: Kenya' in M. Fransman (ed.) *Industry and Accumulation in Africa*, Heinemann, London, pp. 170–92

—— (1983) 'Underdevelopment and Dependency: Critical Notes' reprinted in P. Limqueco and B. McFarlane (eds) *Neo-Marxist Theories of Development*, Croom Helm, London, pp. 29–49

Lim, D. (1976) 'On the Measurement of Capital Utilization in Less Developed Countries', *Oxford Economic Papers*, vol. 28, no. 1, pp. 149–59

—— (1980) 'Taxation Policies' in J. Cody, H. Hughes and D. Wall (eds) *Policies for Industrial Progress in Developing Countries*, Oxford University Press, Oxford (for the World Bank), pp. 159–88

Lin, T. and Mok, V. (1985) 'Trade, Foreign Investment and Development in Hong Kong' in W. Galenson (ed.) *Foreign Trade and Investment: Economic Growth in the Newly Industrializing Asian Countries*. University of Wisconsin Press, Madison, Wis. pp. 219–56

Little, I. M. D. (1981) 'The Experience and Causes of Rapid Labour Intensive Development in Korea, Taiwan Province, Hong Kong, and Singapore and the Possibilities of Emulation' in E. Lee (ed.) *Export-led Industrialization and Development*, I.L.O, Geneva, pp. 23–45

—— (1982) *Economic Development: Theory, Policy and International Relations*, Basic Books, New York

—— and Mirrlees, J. A. (1968) *Manual for Industrial Project Analysis*, OECD, Paris

—— (1972) 'A Reply to Some Criticisms of the OECD Manual', *Oxford Bulletin of Economics and Statistics*, vol. 34, no. 1, pp. 153–68

—— (1974) *Project Appraisal and Planning for Developing Countries*, Heinemann, London

——, Scitovsky, T. and Scott, M. (1970) *Industry and Trade in Some Developing Countries*, Oxford University Press, London.

Marcussen, H. S. and Torp, J.E. (1982) *Internationalization of Capital: Prospects for the Third World*, Zed Books, London

Marx, K. (1967) *Capital*, vol. II, Lawrence and Wishart, London

Mellor, J. W. (1986) 'Agriculture on the Road to Industrialization' in J. P. Lewis and V. Kallab (eds) *Development Strategies Reconsidered*, Transaction Books, Oxford, pp. 67–89

de Melo, J. (1978) 'Estimating the Costs of Protection: A General Equilibrium Approach', *Quarterly Journal of Economics*, vol. 92, no. 2, pp. 209–26

—— (1985) 'Sources of Growth and Structural Change in the Republic of Korea and Taiwan: Some Comparisons' in V. Corbo, A. O. Krueger and F. Ossa (eds) *Export Oriented Development Strategies: The Success of Five Newly Industrializing Countries*, Westview Press, Boulder, Col., pp. 213–48

—— and Tybout, J. (1986) 'The Effects of Financial Liberalization on Savings and Investment in Uruguay', *Economic Development and Cultural Change*, vol. 34, no. 3, pp. 561–87

Merrett, S. (1972) 'The Growth of Indian Nitrogen Fertilizer Manufacture: Some Lessons for Industrial Planning', *Journal of Development Studies*, vol. 8, no. 4, pp. 395–410

Michaely, M. (1977) 'Exports and Growth: An Empirical Investigation', *Journal of Development Economics*, vol. 4, no. 1, pp. 49–53

Morawetz, D. (1977) *Twenty-five Years of Economic Development 1950 to 1975*, World Bank, Washington, D.C.

—— (1980) 'Economic Lessons from Some Small Socialist Developing Countries', *World Development*, vol. 8, no. 5/6, pp. 337–69

—— (1981) *Why the Emperor's New Clothes are not made in Columbia*, Oxford University Press, New York (for the World Bank)

Myrdal, G. (1957) *Economic Theory and Underdeveloped Regions*, Methuen, New York

Mytelka, L. K. (1985) 'Stimulating Effective Technology Transfer: The Case of Textiles in Africa' in N. Rosenberg and C. Frischtak (eds) *International Technology Transfer: Concepts, Measures and Comparisons*, Praeger, New York, pp. 77–126

Nayyar, D. (1978) 'Transnational Corporations and Manufactured Exports from Poor Countries', *Economic Journal*, vol. 88, no. 349, pp. 59–84

Nelson, R. R. (1981) 'Research on Productivity Growth and Productivity Differences: Dead Ends and New Departures', *Journal of Economic Literature*, vol. 19, no. 3, pp. 1029–64

Newfarmer, R. S. (1979a) 'Oligopolistic Tactics to Control Markets and the Growth of TNCs in Brazil's Electrical Industry', *Journal of Development Studies*, vol. 15, no. 3, pp. 108–40

—— (1979b) 'TNC Takeover in Brazil: The Uneven Distribution of Benefits in the Market for Firms', *World Development*, vol. 7, no. 1, pp. 25–43

Nishimizu, M. and Robinson, S. (1984) 'Trade Policies and Productivity Change in Semi-Industrialized Countries', *Journal of Development Economics*, vol. 16, no. 1/2, pp. 177–206

Nogues, J. J., Olechowski, A. and Winters, L. A. (1986) 'The Extent of Nontariff Barriers to Imports of Industrial Countries', *World Bank Staff Working Paper*, no. 789, World Bank, Washington, D.C.

Nurkse, R. (1958) 'Some International Aspects of the Problem of Economic Development' reprinted in A. A. Agarwala and S. P. Singh *The Economics of Underdevelopment*, Oxford University Press, London, pp. 256–71

O'Donnell, G. (1978) 'State and Alliances in Argentina 1956–1976', *Journal of Development Studies*, vol. 15, no. 1, pp. 3–33

O'Neill, H. (1984) 'HICs, MICs, NICs, and LICs: Some Elements in the Political Economy of Graduation and Differentiation', *World Development*, vol. 12, no. 7, pp. 693–712

Ozawa, T. (1974) *Japan's Technological Challenge to the West*, MIT Press, Cambridge, Mass.

—— (1979) *Multinationalism: Japanese Style*. Princeton University Press, Princeton, N.J.

—— (1980) 'Government Control and Technology Acquisition and Firms Entry into New Sectors: The Experience of Japan's Synthetic Fibre Industry', *Cambridge Journal of Economics*, vol. 4, no. 2, pp. 131–46

Pack, H. (1980) 'Macro-Economic Implications of Factor Substitution in Industrial Processes', *World Bank Staff Working Paper*, no. 377, World Bank, Washington, D.C.

—— (1981) 'Fostering the Capital Goods Sector in Developing Countries', *World Development*, vol. 9, no. 3, pp. 227–50

—— (1982) 'Productivity during Industrialization: Evidence from Latin America' in F. Stewart and J. James (eds) *The Economics of New Technology in Developing Countries*, Frances Pinter, London, pp. 83–104

Page, J. (1976) 'The Social Efficiency of the Timber Industries in Ghana' in I. M. D. Little and M. F. Scott *Using Shadow Prices*, Heinemann, London, pp. 88–126

Palma, G. (1981) 'Dependency and Development: A Critical Overview' in D. Seers (ed.) *Dependency Theory: A Critical Reassessment*, Frances Pinter, London, pp. 20–78

Petras, J. (1977) 'State Capitalism in the Third World', *Development and Change*, vol. 8, no. 1, pp. 1–17

Powers, T. A. (ed.) (1981) *Estimating Accounting Prices for Project Appraisal*, Inter-American Development Bank, Washington, D.C.

Prebisch, R. (1964) 'Commercial Policy in the Underdeveloped Countries' reprinted in G. Meier (ed.) *Leading Issues in Development Economics*, Oxford University Press, New York, pp. 286–9

—— (1971) 'Economic Development or Monetary Stability: The False Dilemma' reprinted in I. Livingstone (ed.) *Economic Policy for Development*, Penguin, London, pp. 345–84

—— (1984) 'Five Stages in My Thinking on Development' in G. M. Meier and D. Seers (eds) *Pioneers in Development*, Oxford University Press, New York, pp. 175–91

Raj, K. N. and Sen, A. K. (1961) 'Alternative Patterns of Growth under Conditions of Stagnant Export Earnings', *Oxford Economic Papers*, vol. 13, no. 1, pp. 43–52

Ram, R. (1985) 'Exports and Economic Growth: Some Additional Evidence', *Economic Development and Cultural Change*, vol. 33, no. 2, pp. 415–25

Ranis, G. (1985a) 'Can the East Asian Model of Development be Generalized?: A Comment', *World Development*, vol. 13, no. 4, pp. 543–5

—— (1985b) 'Employment, Income Distribution and Growth in the East Asian Context: A Comparative Analysis' in V. Corbo, A. Krueger and F. Ossa (eds) *Export Oriented Development Strategies: The Success of Five Newly Industrialising Countries*, Westview Press, Boulder, Col.

—— and Schive, C. (1985) 'Direct Foreign Investment in Taiwan's Development' in W. Galenson (ed.), *Foreign Trade and Investment: Economic Growth in the Newly Industrializing Asian Countries*, University of Wisconsin Press, Madison, Wis, pp. 85–137

Rhee, Y. W., Ross-Larson, B. and Pursell, G. (1984) *Korea's Competitive Edge: Managing Entry into World Markets*, Johns Hopkins University Press, Baltimore, Md. (for the World bank)

Riedel, J. (1976) 'A Balanced-Growth Version of the Linkage Hypothesis: A Comment', *Quarterly Journal of Economics*, vol. 90, no. 2, pp. 319–22

—— (1983) 'Trade as the Engine of Growth in Developing Countries: A Re-appraisal', *World Bank Staff Working Paper*, no. 555, World Bank, Washington, D.C.

Roe, A. R. (1982) 'High Interest Rates: A New Conventional Wisdom for Development Policy? Some Conclusions from Sri Lankan Experience', *World Development*, vol. 10, no. 3, pp. 211–22

—— (1984) 'Industrial Restructuring: Issues and Experiences in Selected Developed Economies', *World Bank Technical Paper*, no. 21, World Bank, Washington, D.C.

Roemer, M., Tidrick, G. M. and Williams, D. (1976) 'The Range of Strategic Choice in Tanzanian Industry', *Journal of Development Economics*, vol. 3, no. 3, pp. 257–75

Rosenberg, N. (1976) *Perspectives on Technology*, Cambridge University Press, Cambridge

Rosenstein-Rodan, P. N. (1943) 'Problems of Industrialization in Eastern and South Eastern Europe', *Economic Journal*, vol. 53, nos 2/3, pp. 202–11

—— (1984) 'Natura Facit Saltum: An Analysis of the Disequilibrium Growth Process' in G. Meier and D. Seers (eds) *Pioneers in Development*, Oxford University Press, New York (for the World Bank), pp. 207–21

Rowthorn, R. (1975) 'What Remains of Kaldor's Law?' *Economic Journal*, vol. 85, no. 337, pp. 10–19

Roxborough, I. (1979) *Theories of Underdevelopment*, Macmillan, London

Ruccio, D. F. and Simon, L. H. (1986) 'Methodological Aspects of a Marxian Approach to Development: An Analysis of the Modes of Production School', *World Development*, vol. 14, no. 2, pp. 211–22

Salter, W. E. G. (1966) *Productivity and Technical Change*, Cambridge University Press, Cambridge

Sandbrook, R. (1986) 'The State and Economic Stagnation in Tropical Africa', *World Development*, vol. 14, no. 3, pp. 319–32

Schdlowsky, D. (1984) 'A Policy-Maker's Guide to Comparative Advantage', *World Development*, vol. 12, no. 4, pp. 439–49

Schiffer, J. (1981) 'The Changing Pattern of Development: The Accumulated Wisdom of Samir Amin', *World Development*, vol. 9, no. 6, pp. 515–37

Scitovsky, T. (1958) 'Two Concepts of External Economies' reprinted in A. A. Agarwala and S. P. Singh *The Economics of Underdevelopment*, Oxford University Press, London, pp. 295–308

Sen, A. K. (1981) 'Public Action and the Quality of Life in Developing Countries', *Oxford Bulletin of Economics and Statistics*, vol. 43, no. 4, pp. 287–319

Singer, H. W. (1983) 'North-south Multipliers', *World Development*, vol. 11, no. 5, pp. 451–5

Singh, A. (1979) 'The "Basic Needs" Approach to Development vs the New International Economic Order: The Significance of Third World Industrialization', *World Development*, vol. 7, no. 6, pp. 585–606

—— (1982) 'Industrialization in Africa: A Structuralist View' in M. Fransman (ed.) *Industry and Accumulation in Africa*, Heinemann, London, pp. 24–37

Skocpol, T. (1979) *States and Social Revolution: A Comparative Analysis of France, Russia and China*, Cambridge University Press, Cambridge

Skouras, T. (1978) 'The Intermediate Regimes and Industrialization Prospects', *Development and Change*, vol. 9, no. 4, pp. 631–48

Smith, S. (1980) 'The Ideas of Samir Amin: Theory or Tautology?' *Journal of Development Studies*, vol. 17, no. 1, pp. 1–21

—— (1983) 'Class Analysis Versus World Systems: A Critique of Samir Amin's Typology of Underdevelopment' in P. Limqueco and B. McFarlane (eds) *Neo-Marxist Theories of Development*, Croom-Helm, London, pp. 73–86

Spraos, J. (1983) *Inequalising Trade? A Study of Traditional North-South Specialisation in the Context of Terms of Trade Concepts*, Clarendon Press, Oxford (with UNCTAD)

Squire, L. (1981) *Employment Policy in Developing Countries: A Survey of Issues and Evidence*, Oxford University Press, New York (for the World Bank)

—— and Van Der Tak, H. (1975) *Economic Analysis of Projects*, Johns Hopkins University Press, Baltimore, Md. (for the World Bank)

Staelin, C. P. (1974) 'The Cost and Composition of Indian Exports', *Journal of Development Economics*, vol. 1, no. 2, pp. 129–43

Steel, W. F. (1972) 'Import Substitution and Excess Capacity in Ghana', *Oxford Economic Papers*, vol. 24, no. 2, pp. 212–40

Stewart, F. (1975) 'A Note on Social Cost Benefit Analysis and Class Conflict in LDCs', *World Development*, vol. 3, no. 1, pp. 99–121

—— (1976) 'Capital Goods in Developing Countries' in A. Cairncross and M. Puri (eds) *Employment, Income Distribution and Development Strategy: Problems of the Developing Countries*, Macmillan, London, pp. 120–39

—— (1977) *Technology and Underdevelopment*, Macmillan, London

—— and Ghani, E. (1986) 'Trade Strategies for Development', *Economic and Political Weekly*, vol. 21, no. 34, pp. 1501–10

—— and Streeten, P. (1972) 'Little and Mirrlees' Methods and Project Appraisal', *Oxford Bulletin of Economics and Statistics*, vol. 34, no. 1, pp. 75–91

Sung, Y. W. (1985) 'Economic Growth and Structural Change in the Small Open Economy of Hong Kong' in V. Corbo, A. O. Krueger and F. Ossa (eds), *Export-Oriented Development Strategies: The Success of Five Newly Industrializing Countries*, Westview Press, Boulder, Col. pp. 111–54

Sunkel, O. (1973) 'Transnational Capitalism and National Disintegration in Latin America' *Social and Economic Studies*, vol. 22, no. 1, pp. 132–76

Sutcliffe, R. B. (1971) *Industry and Underdevelopment*, Addison Wesley, London

—— (1984) 'Industry and Underdevelopment Re-examined', *Journal of Development Studies*, vol. 21, no. 1, pp. 121–33

Taylor, J. G. (1979) *From Modernization to Modes of Production: A Critique of the Sociologies of Development and Underdevelopment*, Macmillan, London

Taylor, L., McCarthy, F. D. and Alikhani, I. (1984) 'Trade Patterns in Developing Countries 1970–81', *World Bank Staff Working Paper*, no. 642, World Bank, Washington, D.C.

Teitel, S. (1981) 'Productivity, Mechanization and Skills: A Test of the Hirshman Hypothesis for Latin American Industry', *World Development*, vol. 9, no. 4, pp. 335–71

—— (1984) 'Technology Creation in Semi-Industrial Economies', *Journal of Development Economics*, vol. 16, no. 1/2, pp. 39–61

—— and Thoumi, F. E. (1986) 'From Import-Substitution to Exports: The Manufacturing Exports Experience of Argentina and Brazil', *Economic Development and Cultural Change*, vol. 34, no. 3, pp, 453–90

Ten Kate, A., Bruce Wallace, R., Waarts, A. and Ramirez de Wallace, D. (1979) *La Politica de Proteccion en el Desarrollo Economico de Mexico*, Fondo de Cultura, Mexico City

Thirlwall, A. P. (1980) *Balance of Payments Theory*, Macmillan, London

—— and Bergevin, J. (1985) 'Trends, Cycles and Asymmetries in the Terms of Trade of Primary Commodities from Developed and Less Developed Countries', *World Development*, vol. 13, no. 7, pp. 805–17

Thomas, C. Y. (1974) *Dependence and Transformation*, Monthly Review Press, New York

Tuong, H. D. and Yeats, A. (1980) 'On Factor Proportions as a Guide to the Future Composition of Developing Country Exports', *Journal of Development Economics*, vol. 7, no. 4, pp. 521–39

Tyler, W. G. (1981) 'Growth and Export Expansion in Developing Countries', *Journal of Development Economics*, vol. 9, no. 1, pp. 121–30

UNCTC (1983) *Transnational Corporations in World Development Third Survey*, United Nations Centre for Transnational Corporations, New York

UNIDO (written by S. Marglin, A. K. Sen and P. Dasgupta)(1972) *Guidelines for Project Evaluation*, UN, New York

—— (written by J. Hansen) (1978) *Guide to Practical Project Appraisal*, UN, New York

—— (1979) *World Industry since 1960: Progress and Prospects*, UN, New York

—— (written by J. Weiss) (1980) *Practical Appraisal of Industrial Projects*, UN, New York

—— (1981) *Structural Changes in World Industry*, UN, New York

—— (1982) *Changing Patterns of Trade in World Industry*, UN, New York

—— (1983) *Industry in a Changing World*, UN, New York

—— (1984) *A Statistical Review of the World Industrial Situation 1983*, Division of Industrial Studies, mimeo.

—— (1985a) *Industry in the 1980s: Structural Change and Interdependence*, UN, New York

—— (1985b) *Handbook of Industrial Statistics 1984*, UN, New York

Vaitsos, C. V. (1974) *Intercountry Income Distribution and Transnational Enterprises*, Clarendon Press, Oxford

Vogel, R. C. and Buser, S. A. (1976) 'Inflation, Financial Repression and Capital Formation in Latin America' in R. I. McKinnon (ed.) *Money and Finance in Economic Development*, Marcel Dekker, New York, pp. 35–69

Wangwe, S. M. (1979) 'Excess Capacity in Industry' in K. S. Kim, R. B. Mabele and M. J. Schultheis (eds) *Papers on the Political Economy of Tanzania*, Heinemann, Nairobi, pp. 111–17

Warr, P. G. (1983) 'Domestic Resource Cost as an Investment Criterion', *Oxford Economic Papers*, vol. 35, no. 2, pp. 302–6

—— (1984) 'Exchange Rate Protection in Indonesia', *Bulletin of Indonesian Economic Studies*, vol. 20, no. 2, pp. 53–89

Warren, B. (1973) 'Imperialism and Capitalist Industrialization', *New Left Review*, no. 81, pp. 3–44

—— (1980) *Imperialism: Pioneer of Capitalism*, New Left Books, London

Weiss, J. (1975) *The Use of Project Appraisal Techniques in the Indian Public Sector*, University of Sussex unpublished D. Phil. thesis

—— (1980) 'Cost Benefit Analysis of Foreign Industrial Investments in Developing Countries', *Industry and Development*, no. 5, pp. 41–58

—— (1984a) 'Manufacturing as an Engine of Growth: Revisited', *Industry and Development*, no. 13, pp. 39–62

—— (1984b) 'Alliance for Production: Mexico's Incentives for Private Sector Industrial Development', *World Development*, vol. 12, no. 7, pp. 723–42

—— (1985) 'National Economic Parameters for Jamaica', *Project*

343

Planning Centre Occasional Paper, no. 7, Project Planning Centre, Bradford

—— (1986a) 'Japan's Post-War Protection Policy: Some Implications for Less Developed Countries', *Journal of Development Studies*, vol. 22, no. 2, pp. 385–406

—— (1986b) 'Industrial Projects and the Importance of Assumptions about Learning and Technical Change', *Project Appraisal*, vol. 1, no. 3, pp. 169–76

—— (1987) 'Approaches to Estimating National Economic Parameters: Jamaica, Nepal and Ethiopia', *Project Appraisal*, vol. 2, no. 1, pp. 21–30

Wells, L. T. Jr (1983) *Third World Multinationals: The Rise of Foreign Investment from Developing Countries*, MIT Press, Cambridge, Mass.

Westphal, L. E. (1981) 'Empirical Justification for Infant-Industry Protection', *World Bank Staff Working Paper*, no. 445, World Bank, Washington, D.C.

——, Rhee, Y. W. and Pursell, G. (1981) 'Korean Industrial Competence: Where it Came From', *World Bank Staff Working Paper*, no. 469, World Bank, Washington, D.C.

——, Rhee, Y. W., Kim, L. and Amsden, A. H. (1984) 'Republic of Korea', *World Development*, vol. 12, no. 5/6, pp. 505–33

——, Kim, L. and Dahlman, C. J. (1985) 'Reflections on the Republic of Korea's Acquisition of Technological Capability' in N. Rosenberg and C. Frischtak (eds) *International Technology Transfer: Concepts, Measures and Comparisons*, Praeger, New York, pp. 167–221

White, G. (1983) 'Revolutionary Socialist Development in the Third World: An Overview' in G. White, R. Murray and C. White (eds) *Revolutionary Socialist Development in the Third World*, Wheatsheaf, Brighton, pp. 1–34

—— (1984) 'Developmental States and Socialist Industrialization in the Third World', *Journal of Development Studies*, vol. 21, no. 1, pp. 97–120

—— Murray, R. and White, C. (eds) (1983) *Revolutionary Socialist Development in the Third World*, Wheatsheaf, Brighton

—— and Wade, R. (1984) 'Developmental States in East Asia: Editorial Introduction', *Institute of Development Studies Bulletin*, vol. 15, no. 2, pp. 1–4

White, L. J. (1978) 'The Evidence on Appropriate Factor Proportions for Manufacturing in Less Developed Countries', *Economic Development and Cultural Change*, vol. 27, no. 1, pp. 27–59

Whitworth, A. (1982) 'Price Control Techniques in Poor Countries: The Tanzanian Case', *World Development*, vol. 10, no. 6, pp. 475–88

van Wijnbergen, S. (1982) 'Interest Rate Management in Developing Countries: Theory and Simulation Results for Korea', *World Bank Staff Working Paper*, no. 593, World Bank, Washington, D.C.

Willmore, L. N. (1986) 'The Comparative Performance of Foreign and Domestic firms in Brazil', *World Development*, vol. 14, no. 4, pp. 489–502

Winston, G. C. (1971) 'Capital Utilisation in Economic Development', *Economic Journal*, vol. 81, no. 321, pp. 36–60

—— (1974) 'The Theory of Capital Utilization and Idleness', *Journal of Economic Literature*, vol. 12, no. 4, pp. 1301–20

—— (1981) 'Increasing Manufacturing Employment Through Fuller Utilisation of Capacity in Nigeria' in N. Phan-Thuy, R. P. Betancourt, G. C. Winston and M. Kabaj *Industrial Capacity and Employment Promotion*, Gower, Farnborough (for the International Labour Organisation) pp. 92–170

World Bank (1981) *World Development Report 1981*, Oxford University Press, New York (for the World Bank)

—— (1983) *World Development Report 1983*. Oxford University Press, New York (for the World Bank)

—— (1984) *World Development Report 1984*, Oxford University Press, New York (for the World Bank)

—— (1986) *World Development Report 1986*, Oxford University Press, New York, (for the World Bank)

Yagci, F. (1984) 'Protection and Incentives in Turkish Manufacturing', *World Bank Staff Working Paper*, no. 660, World Bank, Washington, D.C.

Yassin, M. M. (1984) *Evaluation of Industrial Projects in the Sudan*, University of Bradford unpublished Ph.D thesis

Yeats, A. J. (1979) *Trade Barriers Facing Developing Countries*, Macmillan, London

Yotopoulos, P. A. and Nugent, J. B. (1973) 'A Balanced Growth Version of the Linkage Hypothesis: A Test', *The Quarterly Journal of Economics*, vol. 87, no. 2, pp. 157–71

—— (1976) 'In Defense of a Test of the Linkage Hypothesis', *Quarterly Journal of Economics*, vol. 90, no. 2, pp. 334–43

Young, A. (1928) 'Increasing Returns and Economic Progress', *Economic Journal*, vol. 38, no. 152, pp. 527–42

Yue, C. S. (1985) 'The Role of Foreign Trade and Investment in the Development of Singapore' in W. Galenson (ed.) *Foreign Trade and Investment: Economic Growth in the Newly Industrializing Asian Countries*, University of Wisconsin Press, Madison, Wis., pp. 259–97

Index